BAR BRITISH SE

ARCHAEOL(

VOLUME 2

AIN

WORCESTER MAGISTRATES COURT

Excavation of Romano-British homes and industry at Castle Street

Andy Boucher

With contributions by
Lynne Bevan, O Craig, Kath Crooks, Brenda Dickinson, Jeremy Evans,
Peter Guest, Andy Hammond, Martin Henig, S Isaksson, David Jordan,
Paul Linford, Julie Lochrie, Jacqueline I McKinley, Phil Mills, Graham
C Morgan, P Nystrom, Paul Olver, Elizabeth Pearson, Alex Smith,
Peter Thomson, Callista Vink, Margaret Ward

Illustrations by
Julia Bastek-Michalska, Anna Sztromwasser and Brian Byron

BAR
PUBLISHING

Published in 2020 by
BAR Publishing, Oxford

BAR British Series 658

Archaeology of Roman Britain, Volume 2
Worcester Magistrates Court

ISBN 978 1 4073 5704 1 paperback
ISBN 978 1 4073 5705 8 e-format

DOI https://doi.org/10.30861/9781407357041

A catalogue record for this book is available from the British Library

BAR titles are available from:

BAR Publishing
122 Banbury Rd, Oxford, OX2 7BP, UK
EMAIL   info@barpublishing.com
PHONE   +44 (0)1865 310431
FAX   +44 (0)1865 316916
www.barpublishing.com

ARCHAEOLOGY OF ROMAN BRITAIN

Series Editors: Edward Biddulph (Oxford Archaeology) and
Martin Pitts (Exeter University)

Roman Britain presents a dynamic and exciting field of study, with an abundance of data amenable to multi-disciplinary approaches, 'big data' studies, the application of theoretical approaches, and a variety of visually stimulating artefacts and reconstructions that speak to our own age in a remarkably direct way. This series promotes research relating to the Roman province of Britannia, spanning a broad period from the late Iron Age to post-Roman Britain (roughly from the 1st century BC to the 5th century AD), as well as encompassing studies that examine the interaction between the British Isles, the nearby Continent, and other parts of the connected Roman empire.

If you are interested in publishing in the *Archaeology of Roman Britain* series, please contact editor@barpublishing.com.

Of Related Interest

Roman Nantwich: A Salt-Making Settlement
Excavations at Kingsley Fields 2002
Peter Arrowsmith and David Power

Oxford, BAR Publishing, 2012   BAR British Series **557**

Life and Industry in the Suburbs of Roman Worcester
Simon Butler and Richard Cuttler

Oxford, BAR Publishing, 2011   BAR British Series **533**

The Production, Use and Disposal of Romano-British Pewter Tableware
Richard Lee

Oxford, BAR Publishing, 2009   BAR British Series **478**

Roman Iron Production in Britain
Technological and socio-economic landscape development along the Jurassic Ridge
Irene Schrüfer-Kolb

Oxford, BAR Publishing, 2004   BAR British Series **380**

For more information, or to purchase these titles, please visit **www.barpublishing.com**

Dedication

The volume is dedicated to Darren Vyce, who directed the Magistrates Court excavations, but sadly passed away during the early stages of post-excavation work. Darren originally trained and worked as a plumber before changing direction and undertaking an archaeology degree at the University of Sheffield. He then became an integral part of Archaeological Investigations Ltd (now part of Headland Archaeology UK Ltd) from 1998-2002 and worked on a number of very important archaeological projects in Herefordshire, Worcestershire and further afield. These included the Left Bank Restaurant site, Hereford, which revealed a spectacular collection of medieval finds, and St Mary's Gate, Derby, which provided an important glimpse into earlier medieval industry in the city. Darren's direction of the excavations at Worcester Magistrates Court laid the groundwork for the insights and interpretations outlined in this volume.

Acknowledgements

The Magistrates Court excavations were directed by Darren Vyce with the post-excavation programme managed by Andy Boucher. Many thanks are due to James Dinn, the Archaeological Officer for Worcester City Council for his support throughout the long lifespan of this project. We would like to thank HBG Construction (now Bam) for funding the project and providing assistance with the site work and Mark Coppin from the client's side who worked with the author in developing the early stages of the project.

The staff who worked on the excavations are as follows:

John Raven, Liz Jones, Petra Adams, Simon Mayes, Ken Hoverd, Charlie Arthur, Carly Jones, Ian Howard, David Lockyer, Dale Rouse, Rachel Nowakowski, Bernice Persson, Thomas Rogers, Tom Ullathorne, Rodney Cottrell and Shaun Exelby.

Benedikte Ward was the finds and archive coordinator during the post-excavation phase and Samantha Porter digitised the pottery illustrations. Many thanks are due to Dr Jaco Weinstock, Associate Professor of Archaeology at the University of Southampton, who supervised the student undertaking work on the animal bone from the excavations. The volume was restructured and edited for publication by Julie Franklin and Alex Smith in 2019-20.

Contents

List of illustrations

List of tables

Abstract

In the summer of 2000 Archaeological Investigations Ltd, now part of Headland Archaeology UK Ltd, undertook archaeological excavation over 0.16 ha on the site for a new magistrates court in Worcester. The site lay within the area of the Roman nucleated settlement, which is known for its association with extensive iron production, particularly during the 2nd and 3rd centuries AD. For the most part the features excavated on the Magistrates Court site seemed to represent fairly low status domestic dwellings and light industrial activity on the periphery of the settlement, though hints of higher status occupation in the vicinity are glimpsed through objects such as the sandstone furniture fragment, a type more typically found carved in limestone within wealthy Cotswold villas.

The earliest activity on the site, dating to the early 2nd century, comprised a couple of small circular structures, one inside an enclosure, and another structure which may have been a small smithy. Occupation on the site appears to continue through the 2nd century AD with the establishment of at least five rectilinear timber-framed structures. A re-orientation of the buildings towards the end of the century may be associated with wider developments within the settlement. During this period the nature of occupation on site was predominantly 'low status' or 'rural' domestic with some limited smithing activity; it lay to the north of the main zones of iron production. Major changes during the 3rd century led to much of the site being levelled and a series of gravel and cobbled surfaces being laid out. A number of new structures were then built in this area, including a substantial post-built rectangular structure with an earth floor, later replaced on the same footprint by a building with a slag floor and slag post-pad construction. These structures defined a courtyard associated with a number of hearths, which may have been part of a substantial smithy complex. This complex adds to the growing evidence for smithing within Roman Worcester, a settlement more renowned for its association with iron smelting. It was perhaps associated with the production and maintenance of tools within the context of a settlement that was becoming increasingly focussed upon agriculture during the later Roman period. It may even have been part of a wider craftworking zone of the settlement, with evidence for pottery production and other metalworking in the vicinity. All industrial activity at Magistrates Court appears to have ceased before the middle of the 4th century AD and it seems likely that the area was abandoned – part of a general contraction of the settlement at this time.

Introduction

Andy Boucher

1.1. Background to the work

In the summer months of 2000, a team of archaeologists undertook a three-month excavation project on the site for a new magistrates court in Worcester. The site is bounded by Castle St and Britannia St with the new police station to its west and car parking to its north. The south-west corner of the site lay within the footprint of a Presbyterian Church. It is centred at NGR SO 8474 5544 (Illus 1.01).

Prior to the work taking place the excavation of a number of trenches as well as additional observations had been carried out on the site. It was clear from these that some level of Roman occupation had taken place within the area proposed for the new development. One trench in the north-east of the site had revealed a gravel surface associated with an unstated quantity of Roman pottery. Excavations to the west of the site had identified the remnants of what was interpreted as the north-west corner of a ditched enclosure. The trenches and observations between were recorded as containing no significant archaeological deposits or material (Illus 1.02).

An archaeological proposal was submitted to the archaeological advisor for the planning authority (James Dinn) in November 1998 and a final version of this was produced accommodating his comments in January 1999. The following is extracted from that final document and outlines the reasons for the work within the main area of excavation.

'The required foundation design for the building is a post-pad foundation. These will support the super structure. However, they will not support the basement slab which would need to rest on make up from the gravel surface up to the base of the basement slab. In this case it is necessary for the ground level to be reduced to sand and gravel which would destroy archaeological levels and their relationship to archaeological features. PPG16 would look to the preservation of deposits in situ and where this is not possible preservation by record (i.e. excavation). Taking into account the size of the proposed disturbances e.g. the foundation pads; and the nature of the likely archaeology, i.e. a single surface of Roman date, it is also important to note that the piecemeal excavation which would result from targeting pile caps or pads would not adequately tackle problems such as the subtlety of post Roman occupation on the site or the existence of temporary structures which would leave only very slight traces. In this case the preservation by record is likely to only be effective if the entire area of the

footprint of the building is recorded at once. However, having considered this it is important to note that there is also an engineering and logistical requirement to clear the entire footprint of the building.' (Boucher 1999)

Due to a lack of sufficient information about the volume of material to be expected on the site from previous investigations undertaken there, and the complexity of the stratigraphy encountered, the timescales for post-excavation work had to be reviewed. With approximately 30,000 sherds of Roman pottery requiring processing and assessment the whole programme was put on hold until spot dates could be obtained. In the interim all other material was processed and draft matrices produced for the site. Sadly, before all the spot dating information became available Darren Vyce, the site director, was diagnosed with cancer and passed away shortly afterwards. The task of assembling the report fell on the current volume editor and due to competing priorities over more than a decade it was beginning to look less and less likely that the large volume of research laid out in these pages would see the light of day. In 2009 Headland Archaeology UK Ltd acquired Archaeological Investigations Ltd and agreed to support the production of the final text and publication document based on the specialist reports that had already been produced for the site. Finally, in 2015, the company was in a position to make time and resources available to provide the final push that was needed to complete the report.

1.2. Geology, topography and drainage

The site lies on a late Devensian sand terrace of the River Severn (Morris 1974); beneath the site the outwash deposits are sands, but immediately to the west they become gravel (Jordan 1998). The depth of the drift deposit varies across the city and underlying these glacial outwash deposits is a solid geology of Triassic Keuper marl. These two materials have very different drainage characteristics so the local depth of the sand overlying the marl is likely to affect hydrology and therefore the formation and preservation of the site. The soils that develop locally upon these parent materials include typical brown sands and stagnogleyic brown earths. Such a deposit was identified in the excavations at Deansway where soil analysis indicated that a reddish-brown loamy-sand at the base of the archaeological sequence appeared to have been cultivated, with some suggestion it had been truncated by ploughing during the Iron Age (Dalwood and Edwards 2004, 39).

Topographically the site occupies the west side of a raised finger of land, the Severn to its west within a lower lying

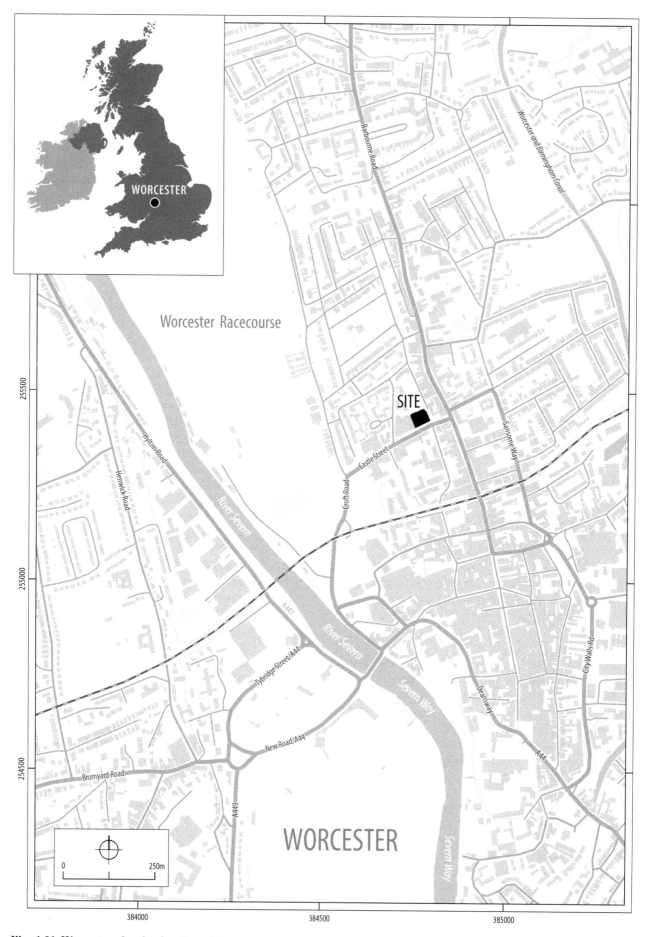

Illus 1.01. Worcester, showing location of site

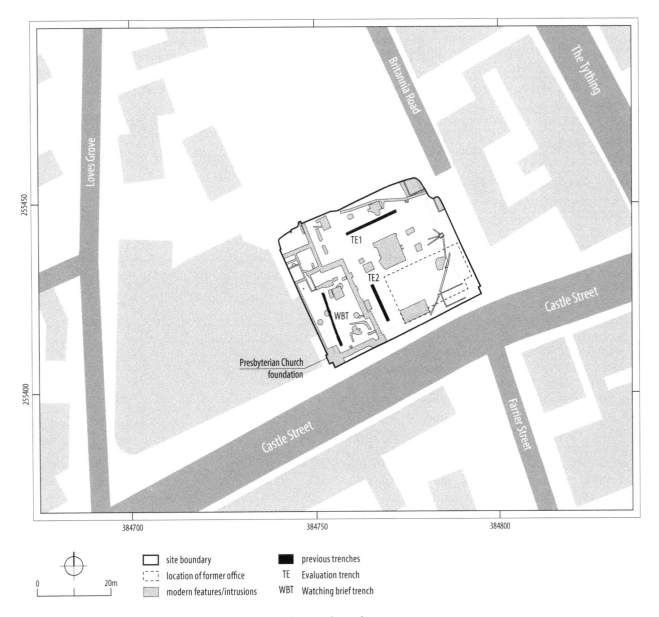

Illus 1.02. The site showing previous investigations and recent intrusions

flood plain, the historic core of Worcester to its south. Its location on this west facing slope some way outside the city has two significant consequences. Firstly, its distance from the medieval and post-medieval core of the settlement means that during these periods it was used as fields with the result that later intrusion and truncation from pits, footings or other occupation did not dramatically impact on buried Roman deposits. Secondly, and in addition to this, the site was sealed by up to 2m of soil dating from the medieval period and later with the consequence that even 19th and 20th century activity had a minimal impact on buried archaeological remains. As a result, stratified archaeological deposits of Roman date remained relatively intact across the entire area of the site, and given the natural slope of the ground these were thickest towards the south-west corner.

1.3. The nature of the archaeological record

The archaeological excavation undertaken here was carried out over the area of the whole footprint of the proposed new building and measured approximately 35m by 45m in extent (c 0.16ha). Archaeological deposits of Roman date lay deeply buried at around 1.5 – 2.0m below the present ground surface and were covered by bulk soil deposits of probable medieval and post-medieval date. These deposits were removed under careful archaeological supervision using a 360° tracked excavator and spoil removed from the site in lorries. A very large quantity of Roman pottery was identified in a mixed soil deposit at the base of the profile; this 0.15m thick deposit was excavated by hand and much of the pottery retained although it could not be assigned to context and was subsequently recorded as Phase 5 (see Table 1.01 for phases).

Resulting surfaces and deposits were then hand cleaned. Features were recorded using single context planning with profiles recorded of the fully excavated feature on the relevant record sheet for that feature. As the work was undertaken with considerable time pressure, and different areas of the excavation had varying densities of

Table 1.01. Principal phases of the site

Phase	Description	Date
Pre-phase 1	Plough marks?	Uncertain
1a-b	Early deposits and features	c AD 100–175
2	Establishment of rectilinear structures	c AD 125–225
3	Terracing of the site	c AD 250–320
4	Industry and occupation	c AD 250–320
5	Post-Roman mixed soil deposit	Post-Roman
6	Modern deposits	Modern

relationships and spot dates within them. It has resulted in the identification of clearly defined structures, something that would not have been possible should only the pad bases have been excavated. In fact, the site would have been entirely un-interpretable from key-hole investigation.

archaeology, then the area was divided into a 5m x 5m grid and each square worked at different rates to its neighbours depending on the amount of archaeology present. As a result very few structures were identified at the excavation stage from the 191 post and stake-holes present on the site. Even had this not been the case it is unlikely that many of the buildings would have been recognised due to the myriad of sub-phases in the two main occupation phases of the site (Phases 2 and 4). In practice most structures identified at this stage tended to not be supported by the stratigraphic relationships between features and other deposits. Therefore, all structures had to be re-determined following excavation in a meticulous and time-consuming manner. This was achieved by constructing the site stratigraphic matrix, plotting out all the stratigraphically early features, identifying obvious structures (like G88), removing these from the plot and checking other post-hole

Table 1.02. The make-up of the Roman archaeological record (by context) broken down by phase

Type	1	2	3	4	Total
Post-hole	36	100	0	39	**175**
Stake-hole	0	8	0	8	**16**
Pit	1	20	0	28	**49**
Ditch/gully cut	9	17	0	12	**38**
Ovens or hearths	7	13	0	4	**24**
Stone structure	0	0	0	1	**1**
Well	0	1	0	0	**1**
Layers/surfaces	2	10	39	48	**99**
Ditch/gully fills	15	9	0	17	**41**
Post-hole fills	40	112	0	50	**202**
Stake-hole fills	0	18	0	8	**26**
Pit fills	1	41	0	103	**145**
Oven or hearth fills	8	28	0	18	**54**
Well fills	0	9	0	0	**9**
Summary					
Total features/segments	53	159	0	92	**304**
Total fills	64	217	0	196	**477**
Total surfaces	2	10	39	48	**99**

Roman Worcester and its regional setting

Andy Boucher and Alex Smith

2.1. Regional overview

The Roman occupation of Britain involved a carefully planned combination of politics and force, and in that planning lay the key to decisions concerning factors such as the location of forts, settlements and roads. Archaeologists are fortunate in that with the Roman invasion came a partially documented account which included hints about the philosophical approaches to invasion, such as Tacitus' reference to how kings were made slave makers when referring to those tribal leaders such as Togidubnus (*Agricola* 14) that more peaceably accepted the Romans into their territories. Certainly, the varied socio-political landscape that the Romans first encountered may have had quite a defining influence on the initial nature of occupation, and a profound influence on the later prosperity and function of settlements so established (Illus 2.01).

At Worcester the key 'tribal' areas likely to influence the development of future settlement nucleation were the Dobunni (within which Worcester purportedly lies), their neighbours the Silures of southern Wales, Ordovices of central and northern Wales, Cornovii to the north and Corieltauvi to the north-east. The extents and boundaries of these various territories have not been determined with any accuracy, though some (notably in this instance the Dobunni) are hypothesised through various coin distributions; they are also generally believed to have evolved into the primary administrative units (*civitates*) of the Roman province (Rivet 1958; Cunliffe 2005, 144–77; Manning 1981, 19; Creighton 2006, 76; cf. Smith and Fulford 2016, 402–3). Manning, when determining the political situation surrounding the formation of the fort at Usk in South Wales, also considered hillforts (the larger of which cluster around the Wye, Lugg, Teme and upper Severn), as well as pottery, although in the latter case

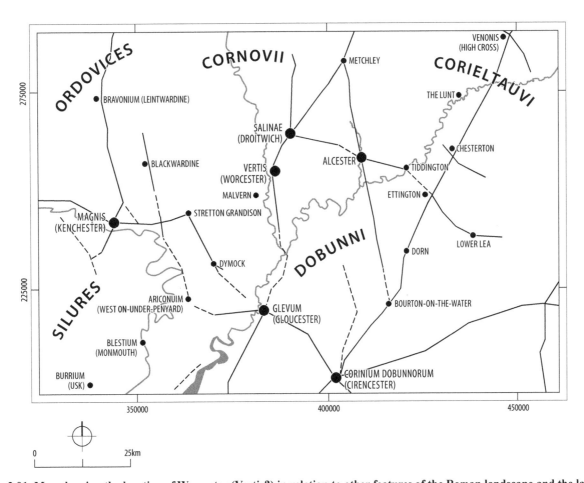

Illus 2.01. Map showing the location of Worcester (Vertis?) in relation to other features of the Roman landscape and the late Iron Age 'tribes'

Herefordshire (which is generally acknowledged by most authors to contain the western boundary of the Dobunni) is swamped by locally produced Malvernian wares, and Wales is pretty much aceramic (Manning 1981, 15–17). However, ceramic tradition is able to distinguish the northern and southern sections of the proposed Dobunnic territory from one another. Worcester lay within the northern half, retaining ceramics of Malvernic tradition with linear and stamped decoration beneath the rims on what were predominantly jars or saucepan type vessels. Manning (1981, 19–20) applied an additional degree of analysis to the distribution of late Iron Age coins. Although his concerns were mainly focused on the reasons for the establishment of the Roman legionary fort at Usk, the observation has equal validity with respect to Worcester. He observed that by only taking the distribution of silver and bronze coins then their geographic distribution ceased at the Severn (Ariconium apart), whereas the gold coins were spread as far as the Wye. Manning's proposal was that a part of the Silures' original territory lying between the Severn and Wye was tactically invaded and held by the Romans to prevent dissenting parties in the north joining forces with the rebellious Silures. In terms of the timing of these events there are a range of views, Manning (ibid., 24) placing the incursions by Ostorius Scapula into north-west Wales around AD 48–9 and noting that his successor, Aulus Didius Gallus, spent his five years as governor consolidating the current status, a period involving fort building.

This leads to consideration of the layout of military organisation in the wider area during the latter part of the 1st century AD. To the south, a fortress was established at Kingsholm, beside a former channel of the River Severn in what is now the northern part of the city of Gloucester, probably in AD 49 (Hurst 1999, 119). This military occupation was likely associated with Gallus' stabilisation of the region to the north and west of Gloucester, with the fortress seemingly sited on a native centre of some size and importance (Timby 1999, 38). The Kingsholm fortress was abandoned during the 60s, at around the same time as a new fortress was established on the site of the modern city centre (Hurst 1988, 50); this became a *colonia*, a settlement for retired soldiers, towards the end of the 1st century AD.

Military expansion further into Wales appears to have occurred during the occupation of the Kingsholm and Gloucester fortresses. The legionary fortress at Caerleon was established *c* AD 75, following the final defeat of the Silures by Frontinus, and continued for at least 300 years (Nash-Williams 1930, 12; Gardner and Guest 2009). Most other military detachments in forts across Wales and the Marches had a shorter lifespan, with many garrisons being given up particularly in the 2nd century AD, to be deployed further north.

In the Leintwardine area, *c* 50km to the west of Worcester, there is the largest known concentration of Roman forts and marching camps anywhere in the Welsh borderlands

(Ray 2002). Here, there was a sequence of military installations, with a supply-base within Brandon Camp between *c* AD 55 and 60, a timber fort at Jay Lane in the AD 60s, and a replacement fort at Buckton by the 80s, which was dismantled in the 140s. Earlier suggestions of a 'village fort' at Leintwardine from the AD 160s seem to be largely unjustified, with the nucleated roadside settlement having no obvious military associations (ibid.; Brown 1998).

Many of these early forts were placed in strategic positions to protect key military supply routes, such as the early Roman fort Dodderhill near the salt springs at Droitwich (Hurst 2006). At Alcester, *c* 25km east of Worcester, an early (Claudian?) fort was identified by cropmarks to the south of the River Arrow (Booth 1996, 28), while elements of another possible fort dating to the later 1st/early 2nd century AD have been revealed within the area of the later nucleated roadside settlement (Booth and Evans 2001; Craddock-Bennett 2008).

Further to the north-east of Worcester at Baginton, the 'Lunt' Roman fort was part of a line of defences along the Fosse Way, and appears to have been in use from *c* AD 60–64 to *c* AD 80, possibly established in the aftermath of the Boudican revolt (Hobley 1969, 24; Barrett 1997). To the north of Droitwich at Metchley, Birmingham, the fort had a complex and intense sequence of occupation from the latter half of the 1st century AD to its eventual abandonment at the end of the 2nd century (Jones 2011; 2012). Many other forts in the wider area also had an early foundation, and most were abandoned at some point in the 2nd century.

Overall, the impression from various archaeological investigations is that the region around Worcester was militarised to some extent between about AD 60 and AD 120. It might be expected that contrasts would therefore be apparent in the nature and form of occupation sites before and after the end of this period.

The development of nucleated centres in the region

The region around Worcester saw the development of many nucleated settlements during the Roman period, almost all lying on the main, and to a large extent newly established, road network. The extensive settlement at Droitwich, less than 10km to the north of Worcester, was an important centre of salt production from the late Iron Age to the later Roman period (Woodiwiss 1992; Hurst 2006), while to the west of Worcester the most significant Roman settlement was Kenchester in Herefordshire, a walled settlement which is often seen as the cantonal capital of the north Dobunni but is, in reality, very poorly understood (Ray 2002, 12).

The Roman nucleated settlement at Alcester in Warwickshire is located *c* 25km east of Worcester, seemingly originating as an early fort sited amongst dispersed Iron Age occupation (Hodgson 2012; Smith and

Fulford 2019). The main settlement developed in the later 1st and 2nd centuries AD around the east–west route of the Salt Way (from Droitwich to past Lower Lea), to the east of Ryknield Street, with an area just to the north of this being enclosed during the late Roman period, when parts of the settlement seem to have been in decline.

Further east along the Salt Way was the roadside settlement at Tiddington where occupation from the early 1st century AD was identified (Burnham and Wacher 1990, 310–13). The various excavations at Tiddington provide good evidence for settlement layout and methods of building construction in the Roman period. Roughly rectilinear buildings (including one that measured 15m by 6m and contained a bread oven and corn drying oven) were organised around roads dating from the 1st to 2nd centuries AD, alongside wells and clay-lined pits. Among the later buildings was a 3rd century structure measuring 9.5m by 6m in plan with stone post-bases and a stone-built oven.

Rural occupation in the region

Significant numbers of Roman rural settlements have been excavated in Worcestershire during recent years, with, for example, over 50% of the 67 sites from the county in the University of Reading's *Roman Rural Settlement Project* database being reported on after 2000, the year of the excavations at Worcester Magistrates Court (Allen et al 2015). The majority of these recent sites were classified as farmsteads, such as that at Bath Road on the southern edge of Worcester adjacent to the River Severn, where investigations revealed a settlement originating in the middle Iron Age and continuing into the Roman period with a peak in the 2nd century and significant decline thereafter. Excavated features comprised a number of enclosure and field ditches as well as a rectangular timber structure interpreted as possible forge, as it was associated with copious metalworking evidence consistent with smithing (Rogers 2014).

Very few rural settlements with architectural characteristics (masonry buildings, tiled roofs, tessellated floors, hypocausts etc.) that may classify them as villas have been found in the county, with the best example being the winged corridor building at Bays Meadow on the edge of the nucleated settlement at Droitwich, and probably connected with the salt production there (Hurst 2006). Nevertheless, there are a number of reasonably substantial 'complex' farmsteads, nearly all located in the Severn Valley, which are part of a more widespread distribution of such farms within the Central Belt (zone from Fen edge to Somerset Levels) (Smith et al 2016, 150). These farmsteads are generally associated with more intensive agricultural activity, with multiple enclosures, corn-drying ovens, storage structures and the like (ibid., 152; Allen et al 2017, 147). One such farmstead at Stonebridge Cross, Westwood, Worcestershire, was occupied from the middle Iron Age but with evidence of substantial reorganisation during the late 2nd century/3rd century

AD (Miller et al 2004). Three large, though apparently unadorned, stone buildings were constructed at this time, with geophysics revealing other such buildings arranged within a series of regular walled enclosures, along with a trackway and possible corn-drying oven. The changes here, and elsewhere in the wider region during the mid to late Roman period, may have been part of a consolidation into a smaller number of larger landholdings focused on maximising agricultural production, particularly the cultivation of spelt wheat, in what seems to have been the 'bread basket' of Roman Britain (Allen et al 2017, 174).

There are distinct chronological and morphological patterns within the Roman rural settlement of the wider Severn and Avon Vales landscape zone in which Worcester is situated (Smith et al 2016, 147–54). In particular is a steady rise in settlement numbers up to a peak at the end of the 2nd century AD, with a decline thereafter, this becoming more pronounced during the 4th century AD, very different from a neighbouring landscape zone in the Cotswolds where there is a much stronger late Roman signature (ibid., 148, fig 5.7). As just noted this may be partly down to an element of settlement consolidation, with the proportion of generally larger 'complex' farmsteads increasing significantly at the expense of smaller 'enclosed' farmsteads from the 2nd century AD. On the other hand, it could also signify a general decline in overall population during the later Roman period, especially as most of the nucleated centres in the region – Worcester included – also seem to peak during the 2nd and 3rd centuries AD.

Roman industry

The area around Worcester contains important evidence for three main types of industrial activity, ironworking, salt production and pottery manufacture. Worcester itself was a significant centre for ironworking (covered in more detail below) with other key sites of this date being Ariconium in Herefordshire and Dymock in Gloucestershire. Ariconium was a roadside settlement in the Wye Valley with an extensive iron production area, which reached its height in the 2nd and 3rd centuries AD (Jackson 2012). The main economic basis of the settlement was iron smelting, with many furnaces and huge quantities of slag, though bronzeworking was also attested, along with an agricultural capacity as suggested by the presence of a possible watermill. There was evidence for metalled streets and at least seven masonry buildings, some well-appointed with painted plaster, tessellated floors, window glass, tiled roofs and hypocausts, one a possible *mansio*. A number of small-scale excavations at Dymock in the Leadon Valley, Forest of Dean, revealed a roadside settlement with mostly timber buildings and evidence for extensive iron smelting as well as other metalworking. As with Ariconium, it seems to have flourished in the later 1st to 2nd/early 3rd century, with subsequent decline (Jurica et al 2008).

To the north of Worcester, Droitwich was one of the major inland salt production areas of Roman Britain (Woodiwiss

1992). Although production was evidenced from the late Iron Age to the late Roman period, it seems clear that the floruit of activity was in the 1st and 2nd centuries AD (ibid.; Smith 2017, 214).

At Malvern, to the south-west of Worcester, there have been a number of excavated sites with pottery kilns (part of the wider Severn Valley ware industry), including a 2nd century AD kiln at Newland Hopfields (Evans et al 2000) and mid- to late 2nd century AD pits and ditches containing evidence for nearby pottery manufacture at Great Buckmans Farm (Waters 1976). Later Roman pottery production is attested at Grit Farm (ibid.) and Yates Hay Road (Peacock 1968).

2.2. Roman Worcester

A considerable amount of archaeological investigation has occurred in Worcester since Burnham and Wacher's consideration of the Roman settlement in 1990, which revealed it as one of the most ill-understood Roman 'towns' in Britain (Burnham and Wacher 1990, 232). The most substantial pieces of work carried out within the city of Worcester since then include excavations at Deansway (Dalwood and Edwards 2004), the Butts (Butler and Cuttler 2011), City Campus (Sworn et al 2014) and the Hive (Bradley et al 2018), recently summarised by Smith and Fulford (2019) in the context of a discussion of defended *vici* in Roman Britain (Illus 2.02).

All of this more recent work, including that at the Magistrates Court, have taken place in what is usually described as the 'northern suburb', beyond the settlement 'core' defined by a substantial ditched enclosure adjoining the River Severn (Barker 1969). The nature of any occupation within the enclosed area is, however, uncertain, as is the status of the enclosure itself. Recent excavations at King's School confirmed earlier suggestions that the ditch originated in the early Iron Age, though at least parts of it seem to have been re-utilised during the Roman period (Napthan 2014). Until further excavation proves otherwise, it seems more likely that the northern 'suburb' is actually the main part of the settlement, defined at its height by fairly dispersed, though occasionally intensive, pockets of occupation, industrial activity, agricultural areas and metalled lanes covering a very wide area.

The origins of the settlement at Worcester remain uncertain. Although the ditched enclosure clearly signifies early Iron Age antecedents, the extent of any late Iron Age activity is more ambiguous. Some evidence for late Iron Age occupation has been discovered on excavations at Deansway, comprising six coins, Iron Age pottery, a possible roundhouse and a horse burial (Dalwood and Edwards 2004, 13 and 36), and scatters of Iron Age coins elsewhere could suggest a settlement of relatively high status (Worcester City Council 2007, 18). Early Roman military activity is attested by scatters of military finds mostly from excavations at Sidbury and Deansway, in the latter case supported by pre-Flavian samian, and mid-

1st-century weapons and other artefacts (Darlington and Evans 1992; Dalwood and Edwards 2004, 39). There is, however, no evidence for a fort at Worcester and the finds could just reflect the general high military presence in the area at this time, as noted above. A short-lived early Roman settlement lying just over 1km to the west of the River Severn at St John's was suggested as a trading post established by locals to exchange goods with the army (Wainwright 2014).

Whatever the precise origins, it is clear that by the end of the 1st century AD a thriving settlement was developing on the eastern bank of the River Severn, at the site of a probable ford across the river on the road from Gloucester (*Glevum*) to Droitwich (*Salinae*). It is generally understood that this settlement relates to that known as *Vertis* in the Ravenna Cosmography, a list of Roman place names compiled in the early 8th century. A reasonably wide variety of buildings and structures have been unearthed to date within the settlement, with at least some of these being of relatively high status (e.g. glazed, tiled, plastered and heated), such as those at Britannia Square to the north of Magistrates Court, and City Arcades further south (Dalwood and Edwards 2004; Griffin et al 2004; Napthan 2012). Quantities of high-status building material were also found in a late Roman well at the Butts (Napthan 2004; Butler and Cuttler 2011). Most other buildings would appear to be of timber construction, defined by post-holes and/or sill-beam slots, with evidence for rectangular 'strip' buildings at Sidbury and Hive. Excavations at the latter site revealed a series of timber strip-buildings, apparently part of a small-scale commercial district along a road leading to the riverside (Bradley et al 2018). This riverside area had evidence for extensive floodplain reclamation (possibly to aid with river trade and transport), which was also seen to the north at City Campus (Sworn et al 2014), to the south at Newport Street (Davenport 2015, 234), and even to the west of the river at Worcester Arena (Daffern 2016). In all of these cases the floodplain reclamation was done through massive dumps of ironworking slag, attesting to one of the primary economic drivers of the settlement.

There is little doubt that Worcester became a major centre for iron production during the Roman period, with smelting furnaces revealed at Broad Street (Barker 1969) and City Arcade (Griffin et al 2004), and possible furnaces within Deansway Area 4 (Dalwood and Edwards 2004, 43). All of these areas lie in the zone just to the north of the major enclosure ditch, though further areas of iron smelting are found as distant as the Worcester City Football club, almost 2km to the north (Bray 2016). The vast quantities of associated slag found in many excavations within the city attest to the overall scale of the operation; it was not just dumped in the reclaimed floodplain but also used as make up for road surfaces and yards across the settlement.

Most of the evidence suggests that iron production at Worcester reached its peak during the 2nd and 3rd centuries AD, similar to the situation at Ariconium and Dymock as noted above. The subsequent decline appears to have been

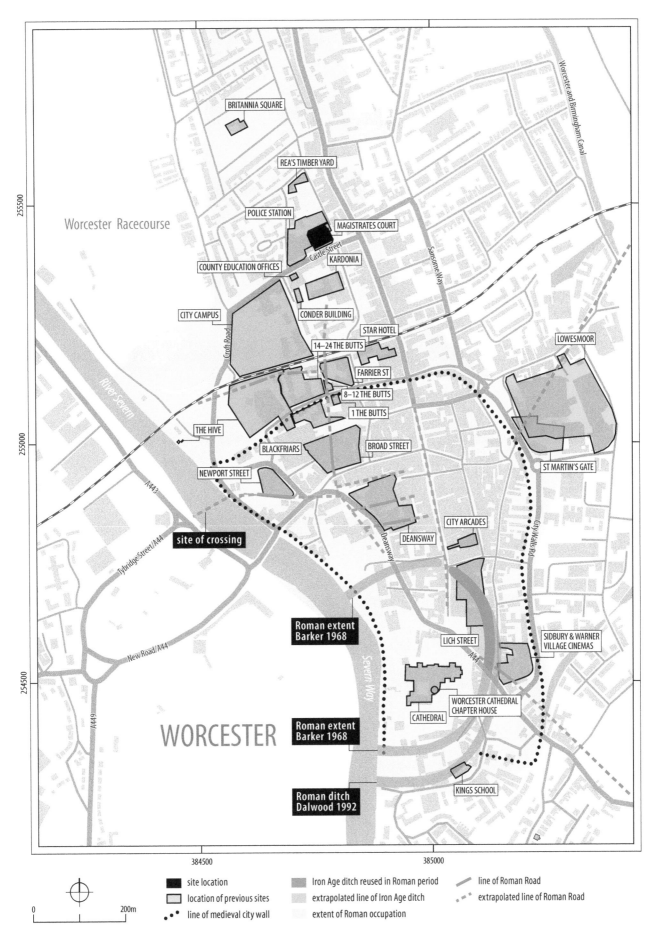

Illus 2.02. Worcester showing location of Magistrates Court excavations and other sites and the historic extents of the city

9

part of a wider re-alignment of the iron industry, perhaps in part linked to changes in military supply (Smith 2017, 183). There also appears to have been an economic re-alignment at Worcester, with stock enclosures, agricultural buildings and micromorphological studies indicating an increased emphasis on agriculture rather than iron smelting (Smith and Fulford 2019). It was partly in this context that the probable late Roman smithy revealed at the Magistrates Court must be set, perhaps used to produce and service agricultural tools for the surrounding community (see Chapter 10).

The 'end' of Roman Worcester is not easy to determine, though it is clear that the settlement was in particular decline after the early 4th century, with 4th century burials at Deansway, for example, cutting through the latest dark earth deposits (Macphail 2004, 77–78), implying that abandonment must have occurred sometime prior to this. This largely mirrors the situation in the surrounding countryside, at least in terms of numbers of settlements in use (see above). However, late Roman shelly wares from midden deposits do attest to some continued activity at least into the second half of the 4th century, with the late Roman aisled building at the Hive probably dating to this time (Bradley et al 2018, 390), perhaps associated with the maintenance of agricultural supply networks. How far any activity in Worcester extended into the 5th century is uncertain, though arguments have been made for some level of continuity to the 7th century and into the medieval period (Dalwood and Edwards 2004, 19–22).

3

Results of the excavations

Andy Boucher

This chapter presents the archaeological features and deposits that were investigated during the course of the excavation. With the exception of wells, all other features within the site were fully excavated. Six main phases of activity have been identified on the site. The phases are archaeological rather than historic in definition; that is, they are determined by evidence in the archaeological record, rather than any major changes in historic administration of the Roman town or phases of activity identified elsewhere within Worcester. The first of these relates to natural deposits that existed prior to the first occupation of the site. Phase 1 is the earliest Roman occupation of the site and is associated with an enclosure excavated to the west of the excavated area as well as possible industrial activity associated with hearths and ovens on its south side. Following the abandonment of the enclosure many more structures appear to have been built on the site and Phase 2 relates to their occupation and use. On the basis of analysis of the soil profiles across the site it would appear that after these structures had been occupied for a period of time a large proportion of the site was levelled and extensive gravel and slag surfaces laid. This episode has been grouped as Phase 3, and as such is much more short-lived than the other phases on the site, representing the boundary between Phases 2 and 4. Phase 4 is the later Roman occupation of the site. The latest phases relate to post-Roman deposits (Phase 5) and modern features (Phase 6).

The following section considers the archaeological evidence. The features are chiefly discussed as context groups (prefixed with a G), with individual context numbers (prefixed C) only included where relevant. Date ranges for each identified element have been provided and the basis used to arrive at them given where relevant. It is not intended that this section provides anything other than a structured description of the archaeology, allowing later interpretation of the evidence to amalgamate specialist reports and other background information.

3.1. Natural deposits and features

The area beneath the Magistrates Court excavations comprised predominantly glacial outwash sands beneath up to 2m of late Holocene soil deposits of combined anthropogenic and natural origin. These sands were investigated to a depth of 0.65m. For the most part they comprised well-sorted, rounded quartz grains the polished surfaces of which are typical of water-borne transport, and consistent with their deposition from late Devensian glacial outwash. Blocks of reddish sandy clay loam and sandy clay were observed towards the base of the sand and

probably represented the mixing of the base of the sands and the upper surface of the degraded underlying marl. Induration in some of the better-preserved marl blocks indicated that the upper surface of the marl had been subjected to periglacial conditions. There was evidence for casts of deep-living earthworms within the sand profile.

The upper surface of the sand deposits was sealed immediately beneath a layer of Roman cobbles/gravel across a large proportion of the site. Investigation of the sediments immediately underlying this surface exposed a 10–20mm humic layer, probably formed after the gravels were laid, and as a result of their presence. The deposits beneath this indicated that the gravel/cobble surfaces had been placed on a clean natural sub-soil surface indicating that a degree of truncation of the natural soil profile in Roman times had resulted in the removal of the humic horizon and upper part of the sandy natural subsoil. In the south-west part of the site there was some evidence to suggest that the lower portion of a topsoil survived beneath a yellowish silty clay deposit. This latter deposit appeared to have been deliberately laid on top of the partially truncated topsoil there. There was no evidence to indicate that the soil had been cultivated prior to the laying of the surface at this point (near to the Phase 1 enclosure). However, features interpreted as plough marks (G146) were recorded towards the centre of the site, and to the north of the Phase 1 enclosure. These demonstrated a roughly NW-SE orientation. The plough marks do not post-date any archaeological features and are therefore assumed to date from Phase 1 or earlier.

3.2. Phase 1 – early deposits and features (c AD 100–175)

Phase 1a – enclosure

Boundary/enclosure and associated features (G1, G3, G125, G148)

An enclosure was identified on the site excavated to the west for the new police station (Edwards et al 2002) and features continuing the line of its northern boundary survived on and off over a length of c 31m within the south-west corner of the current excavations. These were the earliest features excavated on the site (Illus 3.01). In summary they comprise sections of ditch of varying lengths, some of which appear to have been recut on a number of occasions as well as slots and post-holes which by their orientation, location and position within the stratigraphic matrix were almost certainly contemporary with this feature. As such Phase

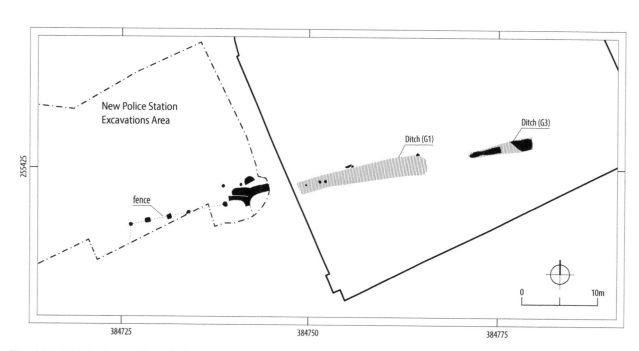

Illus 3.01. Distribution of Phase 1a features and location of Phase 1 enclosure ditches in relation to those within the adjacent New Police Station excavations

1a relates to the establishment and adaptation of part of a palisade enclosure. The extent of this appears to have been altered over time, clearly demonstrated by the presence of at least two butt ends visible from different sub-phases. There was evidence for nearby occupation or activity in the form of ovens or hearths and post-built structures.

During this earliest phase of the enclosure within the site two sections of the ditch were separated by a gap of about 6m (Illus 3.01). In and around that gap were a number of related features such as slots and post-holes. The westernmost of the ditch sections is referred to as Ditch G1 and had to be investigated in three sections as modern features had broken it up. The section of the feature that lay within the Presbyterian Church footprint measured *c* 1.2m in width and 1m in depth and was recorded in two segments. It had steep sloping sides with an irregular flat base, and within the westernmost 2.5m of the feature post-hole impressions were recorded in its base implying that the ditch was part of a post-in-trench construction for a palisade. The base fill within these sections was described as firm and much lighter than those above it and had indications of cobble packing against the north side of the ditch at its western end. This paler fill was not observed in the butt end of the feature to the east of the church wall. Nor was there any indication of post-holes in the base there. A likely explanation is that the lower fill was all that survived of packing material within the palisade trench the later recutting of the feature removing this from all but the base of its easternmost extremity. The cobbles observed on the north side of this fill could also be part of this packing material around the uprights.

To the east of the gap in the enclosure a much shallower ditch (G3) was recorded continuing for 5.4m before being cut by a late 2nd century well. Ditch G3 survived to a depth of 0.35m and width of 1.2m. The ditch had steep sloping sides with a flat base. This feature was originally recorded as post-dating or cutting the fill of the second phase ditch (G2; see Illus 3.09). There was very little overlap between the two features and no cut was observed continuing further into the fill of this later feature. Also, the base of Ditch G3 was not at the same level as in Ditch G2 which

Illus 3.03. West facing section showing the Phase 1b ditch cutting the earlier feature

was slightly deeper. Therefore, it is considered that Ditch G3 more likely formed the west terminus of a ditch running from the east as mentioned above. The original natural slope of the ground rose to the east, and, as will be discussed below, was terraced during the later Roman period. Therefore, although when viewed on a level the easternmost of the ditch sections appears to be shallower, at the time it was excavated the ground surface would have been much higher there than further to the west. As a result, the ditch is likely to have been reasonably uniform in depth along its length.

A group of post-holes (G125) and a slot appear to respect the entrance between the two stretches of ditch described above. Four post-holes match the alignment of the ditch very closely, effectively continuing the line of its outside, northern edge. To the south of these, and directly in line with the east end of ditch G1, a small slot (C2334; Illus 3.04) seems to replace a line of earlier post-holes of which only two survive. Though the post-holes vary in size they all have vertical sides and similar depths ranging from 0.15 to 0.21m. Pottery found within the backfilled features dates between the 1st and 2nd centuries.

A small group of post-holes (G148), similar in form to those identified as part of G125 above, all predate the construction of the Phase 2 rectangular structure G88 and therefore could also be contemporaneous with this phase of the enclosure. Two post-holes lie on the north side of the ditch and therefore continue the line of the four referred to in G125 above. To the south of the ditch a cluster of post-holes (some possibly replacing others) were identified, while at a distance of 4.7m from the south edge of G1 a further post-hole was recorded. The alignment between this and the cluster on the south side of the ditch forms a right angle and very closely matches the position and orientation of features described as part of G125.

These slots and post-holes appear to relate to a rectangular structure set against the south side of the palisade to the west of the entrance. Other post-holes on the north side appear to restrict the entrance, the central post-hole reduces

Illus 3.02. Phase 1a ditch following removal of the entrance, still visible on the left (north) side of the Phase 1b recut

Illus 3.04. Slot C2334 which replaced two post-holes that probably formed part of a temporary structure on the south side of the Phase 1 enclosure ditch

the gap to *c* 2.5m and could well represent evidence for a gateway within it (Illus 3.01 and 3.04).

The fills of the ditch during this sub-phase of activity are quite varied. On the west side of the church wall it contained a charcoal-rich secondary fill and large quantities of pottery (1325 sherds), something not observed in the fill of the feature to the east (102 sherds). It is quite possible that the more charcoal and pottery rich fill was a localised phenomenon within the ditch, a location where midden material was used as backfill rather than cleaner soil. However, regardless of the precise sequence of events the ceramic material within the primary fills of the feature suggests a start date for infilling on or after *c* AD 120.

Outside and respecting the rectangular structure defined by these post-holes was an oven (G8) and the remains of other associated features (G7).

Oven and associated features (G7, G8)

The four features in this group are clearly related by the presence of pink clay or flecks of pink clay, a rare inclusion across the site. Given this fact and their clear spatial association, they are likely to have been open at the same time (Illus 3.05).

Feature C1437 was an elongated cut feature with vertical or steeply sloping sides and a flat base becoming shallower and narrower to the east and measuring 2.18m by 1.04m with a depth of 0.35m. The feature is not recorded as having burnt sides, however, this could simply be a result of the total removal of any lining. If this were an oven then after the lining had been removed it must have been open whilst other features in the vicinity were in use as its lower fill was very charcoal rich. It was this quantity of charcoal that led the excavator to interpret the feature as having been burnt. An alternative is that the feature acted as a stoke hole or ash pit for G8. Its fills also contained early pottery which must have been deposited after AD 120. The base of the feature lay at 21.12m OD and was the deepest of the group of four features. It is the upper fill of this feature which contained white, yellow and pink flecks that places it within this group.

Situated to the south of this feature was C1502. It was oval in plan, measuring 0.8 by 0.66m, with steep sides and a rounded base. It survived to a depth of 0.28m and contained a number of fills. The most significant of these was a 30mm thick layer of pink and yellow/grey clay, which appeared to be the remnant of lining on the south-east side of the feature. Sealing this was a 0.17m thick dark black/brown sandy loam containing displaced chunks of the same material as the pit's lining culminating in the 80mm thick deposit which was a compact mid-pink clay spread across the centre and south-west part of the feature, although it was not in situ lining. The feature was finally filled with 0.11m of sandy silt loam containing a moderate number of pink flecks of clay. Feature C1502 lay at the east end of what was recorded as a linear feature of 'unknown purpose' (C1519). The base of C1502 was 0.11m deeper than that of C1519, the latter measuring 0.76m in width with a surviving depth of 0.19m and a U-shaped profile. The fill of this feature contained frequent yellow and pink flecks and occasional patches of pink clay; it was also notably stony and was interpreted as rubble and rubbish back-filling the feature.

A sub-oval feature (C1528), 0.76 by 0.58m in plan, with a U-shaped profile and base at a similar level to C1519, lay to the north of this feature and west of C1437. This

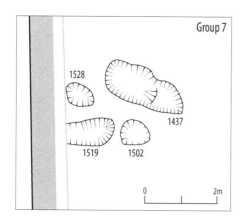

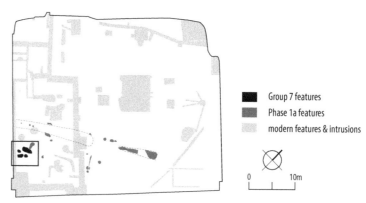

Illus 3.05. G7 features possibly associated with industrial activity

contained frequent pebbles and a moderate number of yellow and pink flecks in a dark fill. It was noted that the fill was most likely a deliberate single backfilling in this case.

The coarse pottery from the fills of these features provides a relatively early date in the late 1st or early 2nd century AD, although the presence of central Gaulish samian ware indicates a post-AD 120 date for the abandonment of the features. The only stratigraphic relationship is shared by all four features. Clearly the features are not contemporary with structure G31 as C1437 lies across its wall line; they are likely to predate it.

The group is defined through the presence of pink clay in the fills of its features. The features are not necessarily related in function and could simply have been open at the same time, although their proximity to one another would suggest the former. To understand the group, it is necessary to first consider the origin of the pink clay. This appears to derive from the lining of 1502. The lining was mostly removed from the sides of the feature, fragments being deposited with the feature's first true fill. Above this was an 80mm thick deposit of what was described as compact mid-pink clay. This was recorded as the original lining of the feature that had collapsed. However, its extent and position implies that the feature was relined, perhaps using the same material. The excavator did not state whether the clay had been fired or not, it could be that clay was being mixed in these features to form the superstructure for ovens in the area.

Oven G8 (C1381) was the most intact example of this sort of feature identified on the site (Illus 3.06–3.08). It had a distinctive tapering, elongated shape measuring 1.7m in length by 0.8m in width and 0.3m in depth. The narrow portion facing south-west was interpreted as the flue/stoke-hole. In this instance the stake-hole fills do not imply that the stakes were burnt in situ as they generally comprised mid-greyish-brown silty sand with occasional

charcoal flecks, compared to G63 below where the bases of the stakes appear to have carbonised in the hole. The stakes must have been removed prior to firing and perhaps were used as temporary props whilst constructing the superstructure, being subsequently removed when the structure was stable before firing. At the north end of the feature a small amount of fired clay lining survived against its edge as a mix of light yellow and mid-reddish-yellow clay with occasional pebble inclusions (Illus 3.08). Within the flue a charcoal rich deposit was uncovered and it is believed that this represented the last firing of the feature. It contained pottery of late 1st to early 2nd century date.

The subsequent demolition and disuse of G8 comprised a sequence of mid-greyish-brown silty sand deposits containing a moderate number of charcoal flecks. Most of these deposits contained pottery deposited after AD 120 with the exception of one which had 3rd to mid–4th-century pottery in it (it is possible that later features cut into these deposits and were not seen due to the dark nature of the fills). The whole feature was covered by a 50mm thick layer of mid-dark greyish-brown silty sand containing moderate charcoal flecks and occasional pebbles. It is likely that this was a deliberate levelling of the area, perhaps prior to laying the more substantial surface G41.

It is clear from the above that this is an oven that has been reconstructed on two occasions following its first use. It is possible that its first firing was a failure as the rods supporting the roof burnt in situ, the roof probably collapsing. It is interesting to note that in each case the oven structure was completely removed. One possible explanation could be that each was broken up to use as temper in the oven structures that superseded them. The function of the oven and associated features remains uncertain, though there is broader evidence for industrial activity in this part of the site in the form of metalworking residues (probably from smithing) in ditch G1 in the vicinity (see Chapter 5, Illus 5.09).

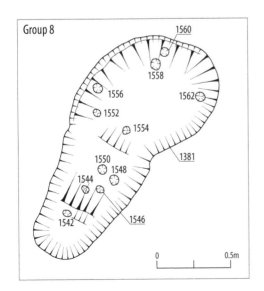

Group 8 features

Phase 1a features

modern features & intrusions

Illus 3.06. Oven G8

Illus 3.07. Oven G8 following total excavation

Illus 3.08. Oven G8 showing the positions of stake-holes used in its construction

Phase 1b – changes to the enclosure boundary

During this phase the boundary feature appears to have been adapted, in part to accommodate changes in the layout of adjacent structures (Illus 3.09).

Circular structure (G31)

From the spatial and stratigraphic relationships in this part of the site it appears that a circular structure, 5m in diameter (G31), was built adjacent to the western extent of the palisade within the excavated area (Illus 3.09 and 3.10). Eight post-holes were identified defining this (C1212, C1210, C1214, C1292, C1631, C1633, C1287 and C1285) each measuring between 0.2m and 0.3m in diameter and 0.15 to 0.47 in depth. The fills of these features were all a light to mid-greyish-brown silty sand with occasional pebbles and charcoal flecks. Pottery from the post-holes would indicate that they were filled sometime after AD 120. Stratigraphically it is known that the structure post-dates the fill of ditch G1, although further fills may have accumulated following its abandonment.

The second main recut of the boundary ditch, G2, appears to respect this structure both through a slight realignment northwards and by terminating before it reaches it. This would imply that the structure predates the digging out of this ditch. It could, however, be contemporaneous with a group of three burnt features interpreted as ovens (G63, G64 and G8).

The digging of ditch G2 recut the central part and eastern end of G1 and effectively removed the entrance gap between G1 and G3. As mentioned above this new feature did not extend as far as the western end of its predecessor as the primary and secondary fills from G1 remained intact here. In fact, the fills of all three parts of the recut are very similar, each *c* 5m section of this later ditch containing only around 100 sherds or less of pottery. The filling of the recut ditch appears to date to after AD 130.

A number of post-holes and other items of structural evidence were observed cutting into the last but one fill of the Phase 1b ditch, overlaid by the upper fill (G81). These include a beam slot (measuring 0.68m in length x 0.16m

☐ site boundary	G89 Group number
■ Phase 1b features	▨ modern features & intrusions

0   10m

Illus 3.09. Distribution of Phase 1b features

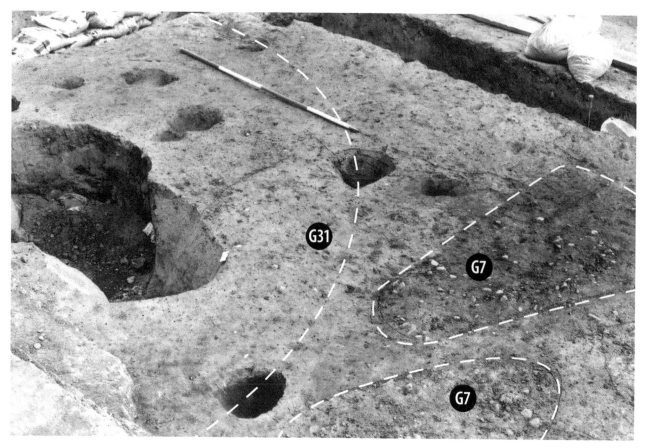

Illus 3.10. Circular structure G31

wide x 0.07m deep) which might be a soil mark left by a timber set in the ditch.

Burnt or industrial features (G85, G89, G109, G151, G156, G157)

Five features that may be hearths or oven bases were identified to the east of G31 in the south-west corner of the site. While some of these could be contemporaneous it is more likely that they represent a sequence of one operational feature being superseded by the next. These all appear to have spreads of charcoal associated with them as well as concentrations of hammerscale (see Chapter 5,

Illus 5.09), indicating likely smithing activity. They were sealed by a later deposit tentatively interpreted as a floor surface and possibly associated with levelling the area prior to the construction of a large rectangular post-built structure (G88) in Phase 2. A fragment from a bath flask of late 1st to early 3rd century date (SF159, No.78) was recovered from this 'floor' deposit.

One of the earliest features in this sequence was a hearth (G157; C1580). It was a shallow (0.1m deep) roughly circular feature with a diameter of 0.8m (Illus 3.11). Here a 0.12m thick layer of sand mixed with odd bits of charcoal had been deliberately laid in the base of the feature. This

Illus 3.11. Plan of industrial feature G157; no flue or rake-out pit survive

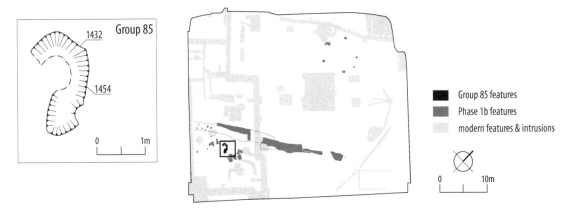

Illus 3.12. Hearth G85 which probably originally had a south facing flue

exhibited signs of having been substantially burnt and was overlaid by a very charcoal-rich deposit. No evidence remained for a flue or rake out pit.

Another feature (G85; Illus 3.12) of similar dimension (0.74m diameter) was originally recorded as a sub-circular hearth (C1454) whose charcoal-rich fill had later been cut by a shallow scoop (C1432). This latter feature, which extended over an area of *c* 2m by 1.2m and had a depth of 0.1m, does not appear to be associated with any other features. It very likely relates to the removal of an oven-type feature and has identical dimensions in plan to oven G89 to its south-east. The shape of the scoop and location of the hearth within it implies it probably had a south facing flue or stoke-hole; this latter aspect being observed in all the oven-type features in this part of the site and phase of activity.

A better preserved base of a key-hole oven (G109; Illus 3.13) had a 1m diameter 80mm deep circular cut at its north end (C1643) with a rectilinear cut to its south measuring 1m by 0.7m and 120mm in depth. The latter had a U-shaped, flat-bottomed profile with steep west and east sides and contained a very dark, grey-brown sandy silt with frequent charcoal flecks. The fire pit (C1643) contained a dark grey sandy silt with occasional red burnt

sand and frequent charcoal inclusions. A spread of material sealed the remains of the structure and probably relates to the demolition of oven G109. Another spread of charcoal may be associated with the original use and cleaning out of the oven, as it lay to one side of the feature rather than over it and was much more charcoal rich. There appears on stratigraphic grounds to be two post-holes (G156) associated with the oven on its south-west side. Both of these contained considerable quantities of charcoal within their fills underlining their association with the burnt features. The spread of charcoal indicates that the structure was levelled following its abandonment, the presence of charcoal in the post-holes possibly indicating that this took place during a very short time period, with posts being removed and the residual heaps of rakings being spread across and within the feature.

Another oven (G89, C1617; Illus 3.14) was recorded between ovens G109 and G157. It was originally suggested that this feature was a post-pad from the Phase 2 structure G88. However, there are no other post-pads in this structure and there is a much greater quantity of charcoal associated with this feature than in other post-holes from G88. Therefore, it is proposed that this was in fact the base of an oven and another feature to its south (C1579)

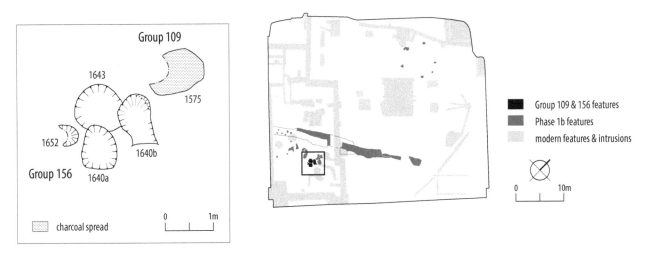

Illus 3.13. Hearth G109 and associated post-holes and charcoal spreads

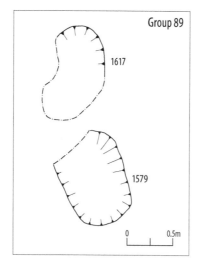
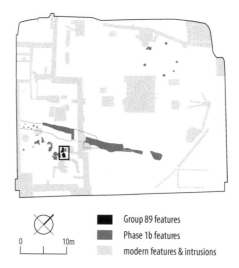

Illus 3.14. Industrial feature G89

may have been a rake out pit or flue associated with it. Both features were later sealed by a layer of charcoal. The pottery in this feature derives from the upper fills of both features and while these were only *c* 0.1m thick, the fact that they were sealed by a very rich charcoal deposit indicates a later date for the hearth and scoop than G109. Its fills contained pottery of AD 120–200 date.

The spatial relationship of this possible industrial activity to other features from this phase of occupation on the site is interesting. Firstly, all the industrial features and spreads of charcoal lie more than 1.5m to the south of the palisade trench or boundary ditch. Secondly, all the flues that were observed point away from that feature. Finally, they all lie between the small circular structure and the linear slot and post-holes associated with the butt end of the earliest ditch. It could be that at least some of the post-holes observed were for open-sided temporary shelters associated with the industrial activity here.

Ovens with stake-holes (G63, G64)

These were originally grouped with Phase 2 on the basis of a stratigraphic relationship between them and a post-

hole. However, the fact that they all fall on the south side of the enclosure ditch and cluster in an area where similar features are recorded, as well as the likely use of structure G88 until after AD 200 and the very early pottery in the fills of these features, means they are more likely to form part of this phase of activity. It would appear that the earliest burnt features from this phase were carefully constructed and left signs of stake-holes relating to their superstructure; the later ones contain less information about their method of construction.

The earliest of the three was G64 (C1627) (Illus 3.15), which was a feature with charcoal-rich stake-holes (practically carbonised in-situ implying it probably burnt down). Little remained of this feature, which was subsequently replaced by G63 (C1614/C1587). Three stake-holes were recorded in each of the two parts of the structure, which had otherwise been heavily truncated by later features and bisected by an archaeological monitoring trench dug in 1991. Both parts of the feature investigated did not demonstrate burning other than the contents of their fills. However, comparison with G8 shows that it is probable that the lining of the feature was removed.

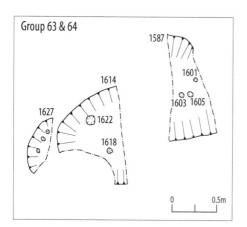

Illus 3.15. Plan showing the remains of ovens G64 and G63; both used stake-holes in their construction

Features to the north of the boundary ditch (G52)

Another circular structure, this time 7.3m in diameter, was recorded in the north-eastern part of the site. This comprised six post-holes (G52) organised in three opposing pairs (Illus 3.16; C2330 and C2087; C2071 and C2318; C2079 and C2304/C2313). They had bases varying from 21.65m OD on the east side of the structure to 21.45m OD on its west side (possibly reflecting the historical natural slope of the site). Post-holes C2087 and C2071 were the deepest recorded as part of the structure being 0.55m and 0.31m deep respectively, they also both had a distinctive 'funnel-shaped' profile with shallow sloping upper sides leading to a vertical sided central hollow. There were signs of post packing in the form of stones in the bases of C2330, C2087 and C2079, the presence of these possibly indicating the removal of the posts allowing the packing to fall into the base. Pottery from the fills of the post-holes forming G52 would indicate that the structure was abandoned sometime after AD 120.

Little other activity was observed during this phase to the north of the enclosure ditch.

3.3. Phase 2 – establishment of rectilinear structures within the site (c AD 125–225)

The Phase 1 ditch G2 appears to have been backfilled deliberately to level the area. Pottery recovered from the fills date this episode to between AD 125 and 175 (although the pottery dates could run as late as the end of the century). Sandwiched between the upper fills of the ditch are post-holes associated with rectilinear buildings on a different alignment to that displayed by the Phase 1 ditch. It is also apparent that following the abandonment of these early Phase 2 buildings the fills of the ditch must have subsided and further deposits needed to be laid in the upper portion of the ditch to level the ground again. These later levelling deposits contained pottery dating to AD 240 or later. On the basis of this evidence it would appear that structures from this phase of occupation of the site date from between AD 125 and 240.

Consideration of post-holes that are stratigraphically early in the site matrix, predominantly those sealed by the laying of Phase 3 gravel surfaces, identifies two areas within the site that the presence and orientation of structures can be confidently determined. These are in the south-west corner over the Phase 1 ditch, and in the north-east part of the excavation area.

Early east-west aligned structure in the south-west part of the site (G149)

Given the date of material in the features associated with structure G149 it is likely that this was a short-lived building that followed the filling of the Phase 1b ditch (Illus 3.18). It was made up from a line of large of post-holes on an east-west alignment and a beam slot at right angles to them and differs in its style of construction from the other buildings on the site. The northern edge of the structure is formed by large post-holes C1201, C1258, C1461 and C1503. The beam slot C1326 may form the western wall of the structure. Pottery from these features was mostly from the beginning of the 2nd century AD.

Rectangular structures (G10, G53, G54, G145) (early-mid-2nd century)

One of the earliest and most well-defined structures in the north-east part of the site was G10 (Illus 3.19 and 3.20). This was a three-bay timber building of earth-fast post-built construction measuring 5m in width by 9m in length based on the features recorded during excavation. Seven posts can be confidently associated with the building (C2237, C2306/C2322, C2239, C2147, C2233, C2209 and the unpaired C2153). The structure was in use long enough to have been repaired as post-hole 2322 appears to be a replacement for C2306. The date of pottery from the fills of the post-holes would place the structure in the first half of the 2nd century AD. A further post-hole (C2292) lies south-east of C2239 on the line of the south-west wall and may be part of this structure because of its close alignment with the south wall and contains pottery of similar date. However, no opposing post-hole was discovered to form

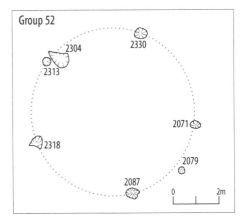

Illus 3.16. Plan of structure G52

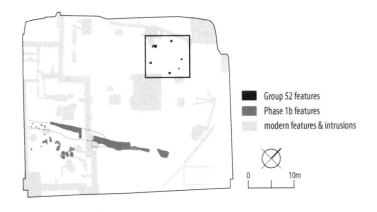

Group 52 features

Phase 1b features

modern features & intrusions

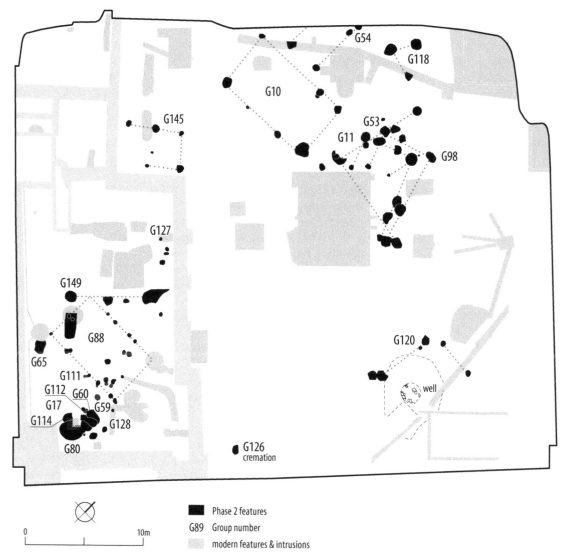

Illus 3.17. Distribution of Phase 2 features

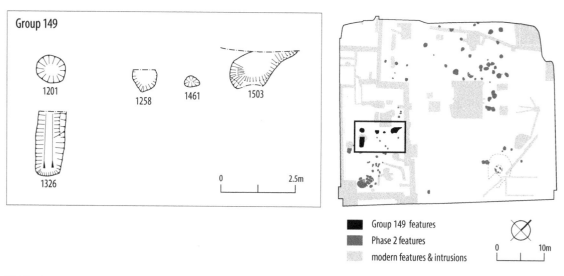

Illus 3.18. Early east-west aligned beam-slot and post-hole structure G149

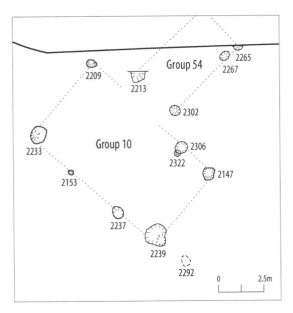 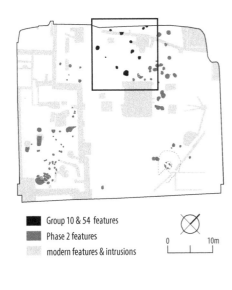

Illus 3.19. Earliest Phase 2 structures in the north-east corner of the site (G10 and G54)

a pair with this. The structure was abandoned sometime after AD 130. In terms of date there is little to distinguish this structure from the circular one that preceded it (G52) in Phase 1 (see above).

Illus 3.20. Post-holes making up part of rectilinear structure G10

A further four post-holes near the edge of the excavation (G54; C2213, C2302, C2265 and C2267) were not only closely aligned to G10, but occupy a location on its north-east edge directly centred on the gap opposite the unpaired post C2153. The most probable explanation is that this was part of the same building. As such it created a 2.7m wide projection from the north-east side of structure G10, perhaps a porch or entrance into the main part of the building. Pottery from its fills provides a date of abandonment after AD 140 pushing the whole structure towards the middle of the 2nd century in date.

Other structures of this date were less well preserved and therefore less easily defined. A possible small rectangular two-bay structure (Illus 3.21) measuring 4.7m by 3.2m (G145) lay to the west of structure G10. It may have been larger, but the foundations of the Presbyterian church would have removed any further evidence for it. It comprised six post-holes with a central divide indicated by C2181 and

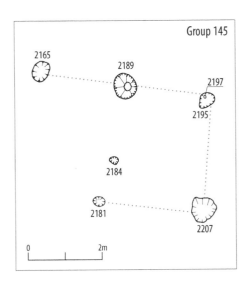 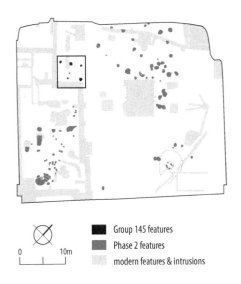

Illus 3.21. Remnant of a rectilinear structure (G145)

C2184. It is notable that the edges of the gravel surfaces in Phase 3 follow the outline of this structure, possibly indicating that the building continued into this phase. If so the posts must have remained in situ as the latest pottery within them dated to *c* AD 150, thus providing a date for its construction rather than its abandonment.

Other structures were even less complete although there was still sufficient evidence to identify them (Illus 3.17). A group of five post-holes defines G53 which lies to the south of G10 (although it is slightly skew to the alignment of that structure). The clearest evidence came from a line of three large post-holes all about 0.7m in diameter and 0.2m in depth (C2072, C2042 and C2077). Two smaller post-holes lay roughly parallel to the south of these. Material recovered from these implies construction of the structure after AD 160. Three post-holes on a similar alignment to these are worth noting, C2292, C2316 and C2061. These are predated by a truncated dog burial G802 (C2073).

Three post-holes in the north-east corner of the excavation (G118) form a right angle with a similar alignment to G10. However, dating evidence from the fills of two of these would place the structure in the last quarter of the 3rd century AD, a century later than other features in this area.

Rebuilt structure (G11, G98) (late 2nd century)

Of the structures that were built in the first half of the 2nd century it would appear that G53 was the shortest-lived. It was replaced by a structure measuring 4.5m in width and 7.4m or more in length (G11; Illus 3.22), rectangular in plan and orientated 45° to north. As its location and orientation respect the building to the north (G10) it is likely this was still in use at the time.

This structure (G11) is notable as it provides much more information than is usually available for methods of construction. There is compelling evidence to suggest that it was taken down and rebuilt (G98) with exactly the same footprint, but on a slightly different orientation. The distances between the post-holes (C2065 and C2059; C2065 and C2044; C2044 and C2160) in G11 closely match those between the corresponding post-holes (C2067 and C2075; C2067 and C2294; C2294 and C2167) in G98, and the dimensions of the post-holes are also roughly similar in each of these locations. The construction of the later building (G98) used large stones in the packing of the post-holes, and these were probably reused from the earlier post-holes as the fills from G11 are simply a sandy silt with occasional inclusions of gravel or some slag. Post-holes C2091 and C2050 probably identify the positions of intermediate timbers that were used to prop up parts of that phase of the building when the original posts started to decay.

The ability to replace a building with another of identical plan is strong evidence for the structure being timber framed. One possible reason for it being rebuilt was that the bottom ends of the posts had started to rot. If this were the case then it could suggest the building had more than one floor, because much of the original framing (G11) must have been reused to enable the post layout of the two structures to match so closely. It would have been easier to build a single storey structure from scratch. The use of fresh post-holes may be due to the structure being re-erected a frame at a time, to ensure a firmer fit for the new posts or simply to avoid transference of rot. The fact that the structure could be moved in this manner also indicates that there was sufficient space around it to manoeuvre the frames. Alternatively, the structure

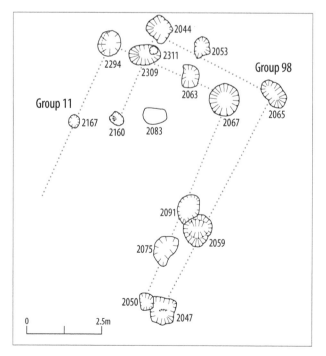

Illus 3.22. Post-holes making up structures G11 and G98

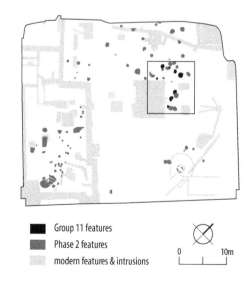

Group 11 features

Phase 2 features

modern features & intrusions

0   10m

may simply have been moved when the gravel surface was laid to its north as the new building appears to lie adjacent to the area of gravel.

The pottery from the post-holes provides an indication of the possible life span of the later structure. This is based on the assumption that the latest pottery arrived in the fills of the post-holes when each building was abandoned and the posts were removed. The abandonment of structure G11 occurs some time between AD 150 and 200 whilst structure G98 appears to have been abandoned sometime between AD 240 and 300 giving a life span for structure G98 of at least 40 years.

A small unusually-shaped cut feature (C2083) could have been an internal feature to G11. The excavator believed nails in it indicated the presence of a box. However, whatever the feature's original purpose it appears to have ended up collecting rubbish including what may have been a pair of hobnailed boots (SF167; not a box) alongside animal bone and fragments of pottery. The pottery was much the same date as that associated with the structure.

Structure and associated industry in the south-west part of the site (G88, G111, G112) (late 2nd century)

A clearly defined rectilinear building (G88) was observed in the south-west corner of the site over the reclaimed Phase 1 ditch (Illus 3.23 and 3.24). It measured at least 7.4m in length by 4.6m in width. It appears to have been built using eight opposing pairs of post-holes. Evidence for four of these pairs survives. In the case of the three central

pairs (C1445 and C1450; C1593 and C1451; C1470 and C1419) the posts were separated by *c* 0.6-0.8m, the pair at the southern corner of the building being more closely spaced (C1420 and C1423). Any opposing pair at the east corner of the structure would have been lost during the construction of a post-medieval well at this location. Similarly, a later beam slot or ditch would have removed the northernmost post-hole of the structure. There is some evidence to suggest that the building had a pair of central posts at each end; post-holes C1325 and C1329 may have housed one of these pairs, however, at the opposite end no evidence for another survives.

The majority of the post-holes described above contained grey-brown silty sand and occasional pebbles or stones in their fills. Two other post-holes may be associated with this group on the grounds of their alignment C1455 and C1446 and the fact that their size, fill and depth matches that of post-hole C1451 very well. The date of pottery within the fills of its post-holes spans from between AD 140 and 200 implying it must have been abandoned sometime after AD 140. A possible floor surface was associated with the structure with many of the post-holes cutting through it; this contained pottery spanning from AD 150 to 200 as well as a small find of late 1st to early 3rd century date (SF159, No.78). A number of other post-holes within the structure could relate to internal arrangements such as partitions or fixed ladders.

Post-dating structure G88, but on the same alignment, were two groups of post-holes (G111, G112), possibly used to support temporary structures such as a windbreak or fence

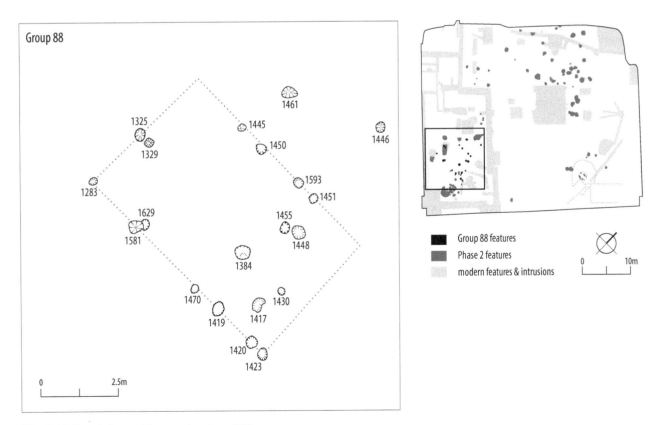

Illus 3.23. Post-holes making up structure G88

Illus 3.24. Location of G88 with respect to the Phase 1 ditch

(Illus 3.17). The date of pottery from these features spans from AD 120 to 200.

Associated industrial activity (G17, G30, G44, G59, G60, G80, G128) (mid-2nd century)

A sequence of burnt features (Illus 3.25) was located to the south of structure G88, and quantities of hammerscale found here and in adjacent features suggest that low-level smithing was certainly one activity taking place in this area of the site (see Chapter 5, Illus 5.10). The earliest of the features was a small oven base or hearth (G60) measuring more than 0.8m in length by 0.5m in width. The connection between the main bowl of the feature (C1492) and its flue (C1371) had been truncated.

The fire chamber survived to a depth of 0.3m with steep sides and a level base. Set in the bottom of the feature in its centre, and covering its base and lower sides, was a clay lining about 0.1m thick. On top of this was a 40mm

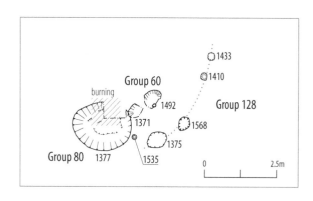

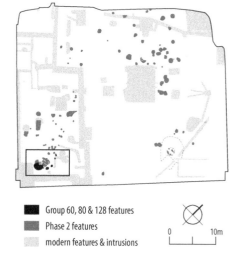

Group 60, 80 & 128 features
Phase 2 features
modern features & intrusions

Illus 3.25. Group of industrial features and associated wind break

thick deposit of charcoal believed to represent its final firing. There was no evidence to suggest that the lining had carried on up the sides of the feature either as lumps of burnt clay in the upper fill or on the base of the feature. Its flue (C1371) fed the feature from the south-west and measured 0.7m by 0.4m. The feature contained some of the earliest pottery identified on the site and most probably went out of use some time between AD 120 and 200.

This oven (G60) lay very near what was recorded as a much larger oven type structure. In this case the fire pit measured 1.98m by 1.72m and had a surviving depth of 0.65m. The base of the feature contained a 50mm thick, very ashy deposit over both red, compact sand, and lighter, loose natural sand. This had been (deliberately?) sealed by a flat 0.1m thick layer of natural sandy silt on top of which was a further 50mm of thick ashy deposit that showed signs of burning. Overlying this was a 65mm thick layer of 'heat affected' dark red sand. The upper part of the feature appears to have been filled with a natural silty sand following this last phase of use. The feature appears to lack a flue and therefore its interpretation as part of a structure used for firing is questionable. One alternative is that the feature functioned as an ash pit for the adjacent oven. After each firing the hot ash would be thrown into this pit. Such action would result in heat affected edges, but does not require a flue as there is no need to control temperatures within the feature. The layers of sand may have been used to 'quench' the hot ashes, the fact that a number of deposits survive in the base of the feature could suggest that it was not always efficiently cleaned out. The pottery from the lower fills of this feature dates from the 1st to 2nd centuries AD. Over the top of all the fills was an area of burnt clay measuring roughly 1m square and interpreted by the excavator as the squashed superstructure of an oven. It comprised a sequence of burnt deposits (G44). The bottom layer was a 30–70mm thick, heat-affected, red sand roughly 0.55m square. Directly in the middle of this was a 20mm thick layer of sand all of which was covered by a mixture of hard burnt red clay and softer yellow/red

clay. One interpretation was that this 0.16m thick clay deposit and sand beneath it were part of a structure that had subsequently been flattened; another less convincing one, that it was a post-pad. The nature of these deposits and features could reflect some kind of metalworking process such as annealing where the metal is cooled slowly to soften it and make it easier to work.

A group of post-holes (G128) to the east of oven G60 and associated pit G80 appear to be part of a fence/windbreak associated with the ovens. Post-hole C1433 must predate structure G88, implying that the whole group does (though believed to be in the same broad phase). This feature aligns closely with C1410 and C1568 and all three of these have bases at approximately the same level.

The cut (C1364) for the construction of another oven (G59) removed some of the upper fill of G60 indicating the feature had been fully levelled and filled before the construction of G59 (Illus 3.26). This latter feature measured 0.8m in diameter and was 0.2m deep, circular in plan with near vertical sides. Around its edges it had what was described as a clay lining, which survived on the east side and, more patchily, on the south side of the feature, and as recorded would appear to be more akin to the remnant of the base of some kind of superstructure for the feature. The presence of burnt clay lumps within the feature's fill were perhaps pieces of a demolished superstructure. The fill contained pottery of 2nd century or later date. Adjacent to and contemporaneous with this was a very shallow hollow (0.13m deep) measuring 0.52m by 0.44m in plan (G30). It contained pottery dating to between AD 200 and 350.

The final structure in the sequence was of another industrial feature (G17; Illus 3.27 and 3.28). It consisted of a stoke hole (C1274; 0.5 by 0.6m in plan and 0.26m deep), situated to the west of a wide flue into a fire chamber (C1308; 1.1m by 0.6m in plan and 0.3m deep). In the lower portion of the dark grey-brown silty clay filling the stoke hole were frequent clay lumps and charcoal flecks,

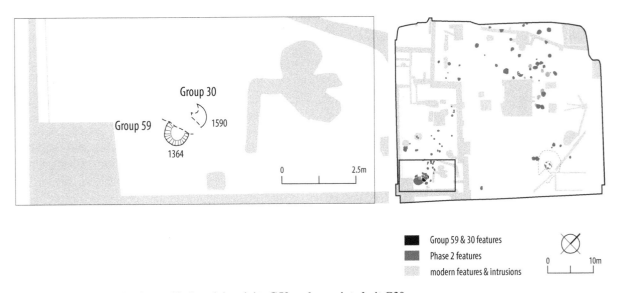

Illus 3.26. Subsequent sub-phase of industrial activity G59 and associated pit G30

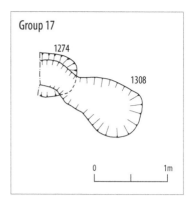
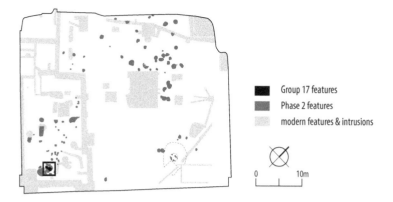

Illus 3.27. Oven G17

possibly part of the superstructure of the oven or its flue. The flue was lined with orange/red clay. The base of the oven comprised a yellowish-grey clay 50mm thick and the sides were similarly lined with clay which demonstrated variable degrees of firing. The main fill of the feature contained frequent large reddish-yellow clay lumps, possibly also part of the superstructure. Pottery from within this latest fill, which almost certainly represents the collapse and abandonment of the structure, dates from AD 200 or later. An archaeomagnetic date was taken from the flue and provided the following date of last firing, AD 170 to 210 (63%) / AD 130 to 220 (95%), which tallies quite

Illus 3.28. Fully excavated oven G17

closely with the pottery date. These features are similar to later Phase 4 features G13 and G15.

Well (G120)

The well was only investigated to a depth of 1m below the working surface as it was not affected by the development (Illus 3.29 and 3.30). It appeared to comprise a large cut feature (C2358) measuring 6.9 by 4.9m in plan and over 1m in depth. Within the section exposed during the project the feature had an irregularly stepped profile.

The first two fills were *c* 0.2m thick lenses of compact sand adhering to the side of the cut at a roughly 45° angle. Above this was a sequence of looser sandy-silt layers filling the cut to its top. A circular feature was visible in the last of these deposits, describing the outline of a well *c* 1.7m in diameter (C2363). The well appeared to have been stone-built the upper two courses being exposed during excavation (C2360). A black clayey sand filled the well at its uppermost exposed level; more pieces of masonry, possibly from the collapsed upper well wall, were recorded on top of this deposit. Two coins spanning the late 3rd to early 4th century were recovered from the upper fill of the well (SF141, No.6 and SF144, No.9).

There appeared to be a timber structure around the top of the feature, the remnants of which were indicated by post-holes C2386, C2382 and C2383. The widths of the three post-holes range from 1m to 0.6m with depths between 0.19m and 0.30m and would therefore have held a frame of substantial posts. At a later date C2386 appears to have been replaced by C2388 with similar proportions, possibly as a result of the original post-hole lying too close to the edge of the well construction cut. Two smaller post-holes C2367 and C2369 may have added support to the structure.

The pottery recovered from post-holes around the well dates from up to the beginning of the 3rd century AD, material found in the upper fill of the well being a century later than this. On the basis of the finds evidence it is likely that the well was constructed and in use by AD 200, but had silted up by AD 300.

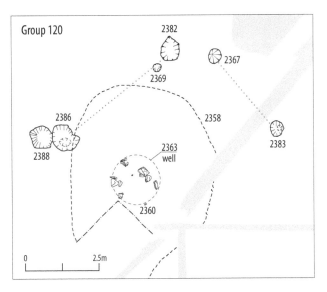

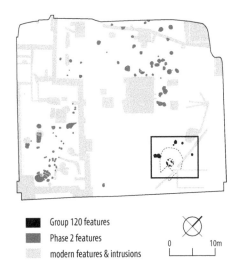

Group 120 features
Phase 2 features
modern features & intrusions

Illus 3.29. Upper part of the well showing associated structural features

The above section describes the main structures in use some time during the 2nd century AD and after the enclosure ditch was backfilled in the south-west corner of the site. Across the rest of the site were a number of isolated features which will be described below.

Cremation burial (G126)

A cremation urn (G126) was recovered (Illus 3.17 and 3.31) from within a cut measuring 0.76m by 0.52m and with a depth of 0.20m. The urn itself was stood in the north-west corner of the feature and was located just to the south of the Phase 1 structure G125 (Illus 3.01). It is interesting to note the similarity of the dimensions of the grave cut to those of the post-holes forming structure G125, and the possibility that C2253 could have actually been the south-east corner post-hole to the structure and the cremation urn deposited within the pre-dug hole once the post was removed should be considered.

Illus 3.30. Upper part of the well showing the stone wall lining

Illus 3.31. Top of the cremation urn following discovery

Pits and other cut features (G65, G114, G127)

A small group of features (G114) (Illus 3.32) were recorded predating the industrial features to the south of G88 described above. These include three pits C1406, C1572 and C1598 and some stake-holes which predate pit C1406.

A steep sided gully or pit G65 (C1067) with a flat base and whose upper fill contained large amounts of sandstone probably derived from the spread of sandstone that later sealed the feature 1028. Pottery from the fills of the feature dates from after AD 200.

To the north of structure G88, an arc of four similar sized post-holes was identified (G127). They all have bases at roughly the same level and are similar in size and construction, about 0.3-0.4m diameter and *c* 0.2m deep.

3.4. Phase 3 – terracing of the site (*c* AD 250–320)

Conceptually this is a complex phase division that needs some careful consideration. At its simplest Phase 3 comprises a spread, or in some cases a sequence, of horizontal layers and surfaces (Illus 3.33). Therefore, in the truest sense it is not easily defined as a phase in its own right. As an analytical tool for unlocking the chronology of the site it is, however, the key phase. Everything that it seals is classed within Phases 1 and 2, whilst features cutting it

are defined as Phases 4 or later. In this respect Phase 3 is the greatest assumption affecting the interpretation and chronology of the site.

Based on the results of the sedimentary assessment undertaken on the site, alongside the distribution of surviving features, it is proposed that the action defining Phase 3 is one of wholesale site clearance through the levelling of the site into a shallow terrace upon which a series of made surfaces were formed. The one difficulty that presents itself with this approach is that the laying of the surfaces could fall within Phase 4 (the latest and last phase of Roman occupation on the site) whilst early layers to the west of the site could be late Phase 2 surfaces. This has been carefully considered when interpreting various layers and features below (Illus 3.34).

Soil layers in the south-west corner of the site

An extensive area of soil was observed on the west side of the Presbyterian church foundation measuring 12m by 17m. While this was recorded as two different contexts (Illus 3.35) it is a post-depositional change that defines the difference between them. The larger area to the west (C1034) comprises more intrusions from later deposits, while on the other hand the small rectangular area measuring 9m by 6m (C1359 and C1475) in its south-east corner was much cleaner due to having been sealed by a later clay layer (C1137).

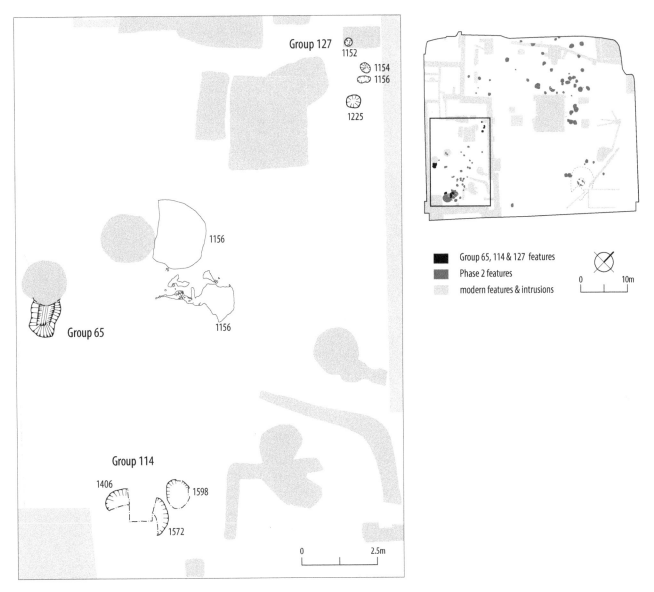

Illus 3.32. Other Phase 2 features

It was the excavator's view that the soil layers had developed over time here rather than representing a dump of material although it is worth noting that within C1034 a patch of burnt sand (C1239) was identified indicating that some human activity occurred during the build-up of the deposit. It is possible that the area beneath the later clay layer (C1137 which is indeed recorded as being 0.2m thick) was dug down and the clay laid within it, as the level of the top of the deposit in this part of the site is *c* 0.2m shallower than to the west.

Although slightly cleaner, it was considered whether C2260 was the continuation of this deposit on the east side of the church wall. The slightly cleaner appearance of this deposit is likely to be due to it being below the base of the top-soil horizon (i.e. cut into the top of less humic sub-soil), as the original ground level may have been slightly higher here before it was levelled off. C2260 is possibly the same as C2245, however, the base of the layers above it are recorded as lying between 21.45 and 21.65m OD which would mean there was a much greater

level of truncation here than on the other side of the church wall. The level of the upper surface of this deposit was *c* 21.8m OD.

Main surface and patching (G19)

This is the largest gravel surface identified on the site (G19). It appears to have some longevity on the basis that areas of slightly different gravel have been introduced at later dates for patching more worn parts of the original surface. The original surface survives as an extensive area of gravel and cobble across most of the north-east part of the site. It is characterised by the fact it contained very little slag (10%) and 70% of its make-up was of stones less than 10cm across with more than half of these measuring 5cm or less, The upper surface lay at 21.65m OD. The surface was very flat, rising by only 0.05m towards its north-west and 0.10m towards the north-east. Given that the natural slope of the ground is very much steeper than this then it is clear that the site must have been terraced prior to the laying of the gravels to form this surface.

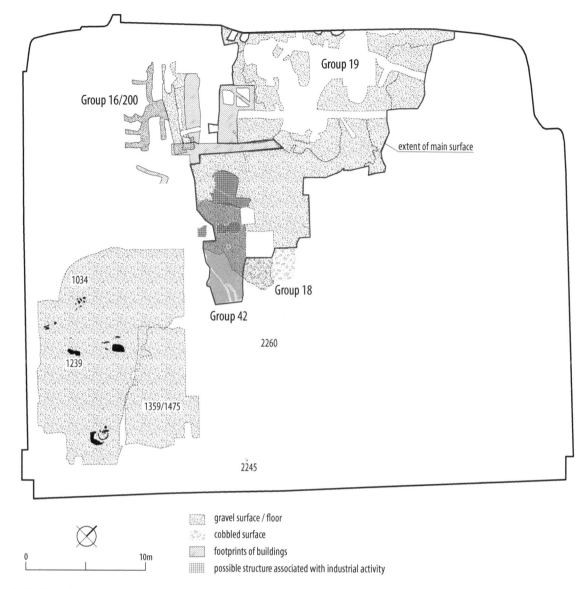

Illus 3.33. Phase 3 surfaces

So what defines the extent of this surface? At one point there is a continuous spread of deliberately laid gravels, while in other areas these are not present. In the first instance could they have been present and then lost to truncation? This seems unlikely as the site was buried beneath nearly 1m of soil that was medieval or earlier in date and another 1m of post-medieval build-up. Therefore, any wholesale truncation would have had to have taken place in the Roman period. It is unlikely that this was the case as a deposit rich in Roman pottery covered a large proportion of the site and would therefore have protected the surfaces. Also, there is evidence for structures outside of the area of gravels such as the rebuilt timber-framed building G11 and G98 (Illus 3.36 and 3.37). It is therefore likely that the extent of the surface was intentional. The clue to how it was defined lies in the layout of the Phase 2 structures. The gravel surfaces when plotted, despite having an irregular edge, appear to form a band of gravel running south-west to north-east and measuring between 10m and 15m in width

(partly dependant on areas of modern truncation), the larger measurement being closer to its original extent. The gravel spans from the east wall of the Presbyterian church and disappears under the north baulk. Gravel layers do not survive within the church footprint continuing this spread and it must be assumed that the construction of the church truncated gravel layers in its northern end. The reason for survival of archaeology at the south end of the church is due to the natural slope in ground level to this point, so deposits were more deeply buried and not affected by 19th century construction. Returning to the 2nd-century features it can now be observed that the position and orientation of the gravel spread is almost exactly centred on structures G88 and G10. Equally, the newly erected G98 lies entirely outside of the gravel spread (although notably its predecessor, G11, overlapped it). It would appear that the gravel spread and orientation of structures immediately preceding it provide evidence for property boundaries on the outskirts of the city.

Illus 3.34. Full extent of the Phase 3 gravel surface over the north-east part of the site

Group 19

extent of main surface

Group 42

1034

Group 18

1239

1359

2260

2245

■ Phase 3 features
modern features & intrusions
footprints of buildings

0   10m

Illus 3.35. Possible earth floor in south-west part of the site

33

Illus 3.36. Looking east showing extent of gravel surfaces and structure G98 outside their edge

Given the discussion above it is also interesting that the only patches of gravel described as showing wear, rather than simply being low density (C2135, C2114 and C2129), occur in and around the footprint of structure G10. It is also notable that the area within the footprint of that structure and its north-east annex is devoid of cobbles. This would imply that the structure was still standing when the gravels were laid and the site levelled or terraced.

Possible gravel base for a small rectangular structure

The putative Phase 3 structure (G42) measures about 4m in width by 10m in length and lies directly opposite a similar shaped gravel surface to its north (Illus 3.33 and 3.35). Given the ephemeral nature of the evidence it is difficult to provide a definitive interpretation as to why these gravel surfaces have been raised above the rest. They are too isolated to be trackways, and in any case they lie within a well-made gravel surface already. It is suggested that they may have formed a north-south orientated structure, perhaps with timber sleepers on raised gravel sills. Concentrations of hammerscale on the surfaces of this area indicate metalworking activity (see Chapter 5, Illus 5.11), though it is uncertain if this is connected to possible structure G42 or the more concentrated spread of micro-residues associated with the Phase 4 workshop in the south-west of the site.

Impressions in the gravel for rectilinear structures (G16, G200, G18)

The features discussed here were very clearly identifiable during the excavation. They cannot be explained through later truncation and are a real element of the site. Initially the various features were described as either being either pathways (G200) or stalls (G16). Given the prevalence of cob in the building material from the site it could be considered that these are the impression of building footings. However, the spread of pottery across these is more likely to imply that they were timber sills, as cob would have prevented pottery from reaching the surface.

Further to the analysis of the main gravel surface G19 above, it is clear that the possible structure defined by the westernmost bands of gravels (G16) does not lie within the expected extent of this surface. This means that the gravels here have been laid down for another purpose. In most cases the configuration of gravel patches does not easily resolve into a footprint for a building. One suggestion, based on the small rectangular structure at the end of C2156, is that timber beams were laid on gravel sills. In the case of G16 it could be that these formed stalls. However, it is also plausible that they provided a combination of sills for external framing and joists for raised timber floors. The wider areas of gravel C2113, C2116 and C2156 could well form paths connecting these to the end of building G10 where an area of trampled gravel was recorded.

A couple of areas of the cobble surface were higher than others recorded. They might again be the location of a timber structure for which no other evidence is available.

3.5. Phase 4 – industry and occupation (*c* AD 250–320)

Phase 4 represents the last major phase of Roman occupation on the site and is dated ceramically and through scientific dating to the mid-3rd to early 4th century AD (Illus 3.37). The most significant feature belonging to this phase is a substantial rectangular timber building interpreted as a smithy.

Cess pit (G141)

A large square pit (G141, C1073) measuring 2.1m in plan and 2.1m in depth occupied the south edge of the site. From its fills this appears to have been a cess pit. It contained 13 fills many of which had a greenish/blue tinge to them. The date of material filling it spans from the 2nd century into the late 3rd century AD (Illus 3.38 and 3.39).

Workshop in the south-west part of the site (G5, G15, G24, G25, G41, G43, G45, G129, G134, G137)

A rectangular building (G45) with a beaten earth floor was identified near the southern edge of the site (Illus 3.40), and is suggested as a workshop. This measured *c* 5.9m by 11m in plan. It was clearly an earth-fast timber structure which on the basis of the post-holes around it contained at least three bays within the excavated area. The post-holes making these up were C1306, C1386, C1356, C1208, C1093 and C1298. The post-holes were all roughly 0.25m deep and 0.4m diameter except for the central northern post C1298 which was nearly twice as deep and the north-west corner post C1208 which was slightly larger in diameter. A deposit of burnt daub (G5) recorded adjacent to the east side of the church wall near this structure is believed to be part of a collapsed wall from this building. Other features here include the remnant of wall footings and daub walls and a line of cobbles possibly supporting a sill on the same alignment. They were sealed by the later rebuilding of the structure.

The beaten floor of the building (G43) appears to have been laid directly on a remnant of natural soil, sealing

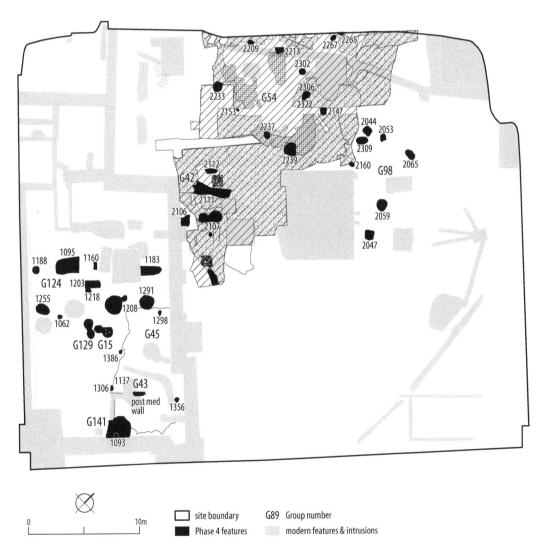

Illus 3.37. Plan of Phase 4 features in relation to the extent of the gravel surfaces

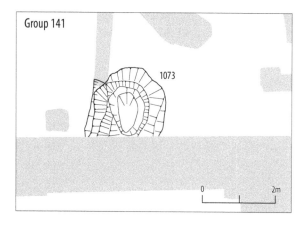

Illus 3.38. Cess pit G141

Illus 3.39. Fully excavated cess pit G141

part of it and leaving the other part to the west and north exposed (G41). It comprised a mid-greenish-yellow clay with occasional slag and stones. Pottery from the post-holes places the structure in the 3rd century AD although the layer (G41) sealed by floor G43 as well as the floor itself contained material dating from AD 250 or later placing the first phase of this structure in the latter half of that century.

There appear to be two ovens associated with the first phase of the building, although they probably weren't

contemporary with one another as their flues point in different directions. Oven G129 (C1340) measured 1.7m by 0.6m with a depth of 0.45m. It was figure-of-eight shaped in plan with steep sided U-shaped profile and slightly rounded base (Illus 3.41). It was lined with a heated yellowish-red clay (C1315; Illus 3.42) and contained residues from burning episodes that must have been tipped back into the feature after its last firing. It had stake-holes throughout its length indicating that a super-structure must have existed over the whole of the feature (Illus 3.43).

The second oven G15 (C1309) measured 1.7m by 0.9m with a depth of 0.4m (Illus 3.44 and 3.45). Four stake-holes were recorded, three in the main bowl of the oven, the other where the flue met it. An archaeomagnetic date for the last firing of this oven based on samples from its fired lining was AD 260 to 320 (95%).

From the backfilling of the ovens (G137) it is notable that the pottery within their fills was generally quite early in date (AD 150+) implying that it derives from pit digging nearby and that the features were deliberately backfilled with spoil arising from other excavations in the vicinity alongside waste from the use of the ovens. It would also appear that a clay-lined pit (G134) was created during this earlier phase of activity (Illus 3.46). It is likely this was some form of cistern. This large pit lay to the west of the workshop and just to the north of the ovens described above (Illus 3.40). It was a deep conical shaped feature with a soft red clay lining measuring 2.4 by 1.6m in plan and 2m in depth.

Structure G45 was rebuilt on the same footprint but in a slightly different way resulting in a building measuring 8m x 11.5m within the constraints of the site (Illus 3.47 and 3.48). Instead of using post-holes compact areas containing large quantities of iron slag were laid around the outside of the location of the floor (G24). They cover former post-holes and form post-pads (C1027, C1029, C1030, C1033, C1042, C1053, C1055, C1056, C1070, C1167, C1071 and

Illus 3.40. Workshop G45 that later became a smithy

C1104). Prior to these being laid down the whole area of the former clay floor appears to have been re-laid in slag (G25). It is likely that some form of framing combining sill beams and post-pads was used, which in turn supports such an argument for the structures located on raised areas of gravel further north in the site. The levels of this surface are around 21.75m. Pottery associated with the

construction of this phase of the structure dates to the late 3rd century AD.

To the north of the west side of building G45 there appear to have been a number of cobbles placed in the top of an already backfilled ditch. It is possible these relate to the later phase of this workshop which predominantly uses

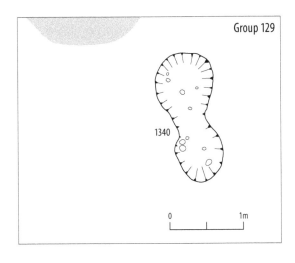

Illus 3.41. Oven G129

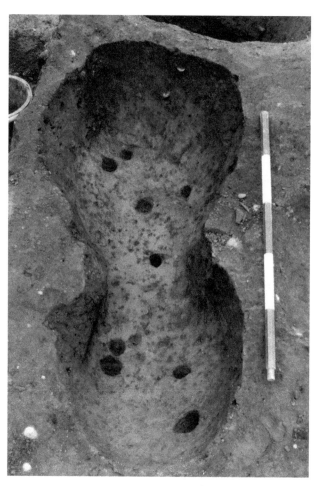

Illus 3.42. Oven G129 showing burnt lining (C1315) and rake out pit as well as fragment of quern stone used in its construction

Illus 3.43. Oven G129 showing stake-holes as part of original construction

pads rather than post-holes. The whole of the slag floor for the replacement workshop as well the clay-lined pit and other features in the vicinity produced considerable quantities of micro hammerscale, suggesting that smithing was the primary function of this complex (see Chapter 5, Illus 5.12).

Other industrial activity (G26, G123, G124, G142)

A sequence of consecutive slots of varying lengths, but all measuring about 1m in width, were observed to the north of workshop G45 (Illus 3.50). Given the two phases of use of the original building then it is not surprising that

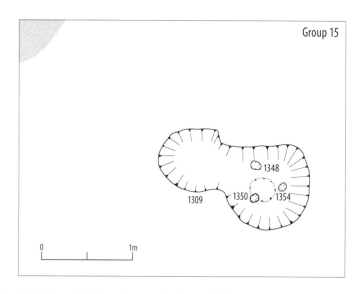

Illus 3.44. Oven G15 showing post-holes used in its construction

ancillary features also demonstrate multiple periods of use. There were several phases (G123) of linear features on an east-west alignment found within the south-west portion of the site. The northern feature was excavated in three sections (C1097, C1160 and C1204). Its average width was 1m and average depth 0.3 metres. Cut C1194 appeared to be an earlier incarnation of the eastern end of this feature. The southern linear (C1204) had a similar width though the depth was recorded as 0.71 metres. The features were filled with a dark brown sandy loam and both contained frequent slag inclusions. However, critical to their interpretation as open features rather than structural ones, is the presence of quantities of hammerscale within them. A further reason for the grouping of the two features together is that both appear to have been re-cut along the same alignments. Pottery within C1194 dates between the 1st and 4th centuries.

As mentioned above further similar features (G124) re-cut the earlier (G123) ones. They follow along the same alignments and are of similar dimensions to their earlier counterparts. Although the fills are similar, the pottery from within sections C1183 and C1095 dates to the 2nd to 3rd centuries. Whilst it is still a possibility that these features represent the positions of sill beams for a large structure which have been replaced on a number of occasions, it seems more likely that they were timber troughs sunk into the ground and serving a purpose related to smithing, perhaps for quenching. A third east-west slot (G26) was also

Illus 3.45. Oven G15 showing burnt lining and rake out pit

Illus 3.46. Clay-lined pit (G134) associated with industrial activity in the south-west part of the site

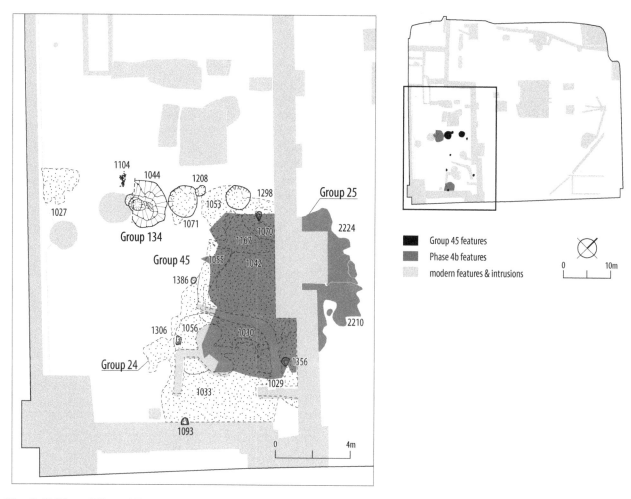

Illus 3.47. Plan of Phase 4 Roman workshop (G45)

Illus 3.48. view of workshop (G45) looking south

Illus 3.49. Workshop (G45) looking north, post-pads clearly showing in foreground

recorded which appears to replace the features within G123 and G124 indicating a continuity of activity in the area. These all measure about 1m across and *c* 0.7m in depth. There was no other evidence for sills being buried on the site as part of structures, and no evidence for opposing walls was recovered either, again adding weight to the argument these were troughs associated with industrial activity.

A number of groups of post-holes were associated with the troughs described above. Whilst it is not possible to define a specific structure based on these they could present a small structure to cover the features or act as a frame over them. The groups by necessity remain fairly loose, however, post-holes (G142) lying to the west of G123 possibly form part of an east-west aligned structure and are truncated by the secondary phase of ditches in G124 (Illus 3.50).

Sandstone footing (G131)

This phase of activity appears to coincide with the latest phase of the newly reconstructed workshop. The gravel post-pad C1037 appears to replace post-hole C1060 in G130 (a posthole group to the west of G45, which could be phase 2-4) and the surface C1028 covers post-hole C1020 (G130). Post-pad C1216 is stratigraphically later than oven G129 (Illus 3.41) which appears to have been backfilled rapidly to facilitate the positioning of pad C1216, and thus these features were clearly associated with the earlier phase of structures in this area.

An L-shaped foundation layer of crushed sandstone (G131, C1066) and gravel levelling deposits (C1105 and C1091) form a clearly defined right angle with post-hole C1047 lying parallel with its northern point. There are a number of other post-pads in the vicinity that could be part of this structure. Its extent appears to line up with the later workshop and could be the remains of a dwelling associated with this (Illus 3.51–3).

Associated industrial features (G138, G139, G140)

G138, G139 and G140 were all found within cut C1117 whose original function was structural. Cut C1117 (G138) held three successive rectangular structures, probably timber-lined tanks, on north-south and east-west alignments suggesting that these features related to a long standing structure that was replaced on at least two occasions (Illus 3.54). It is possible that G138 was related to the sandstone structure to its north (G131), though it is equally likely to be part of a building to the south, outside of the excavated area. The three stake-holes found within the base of the feature appear to have provided further structural support.

Following the disuse of G138 as a structural feature, an oven/hearth (G139) constructed of tightly packed sandstone and pink clay was laid within gravel surface C1150 (Illus 3.55). The final use of the feature (G140) appears to have been as a domestic hearth with large quantities of broken pottery found within its burnt fill. This feature would have sat within the courtyard adjacent to structure G45.

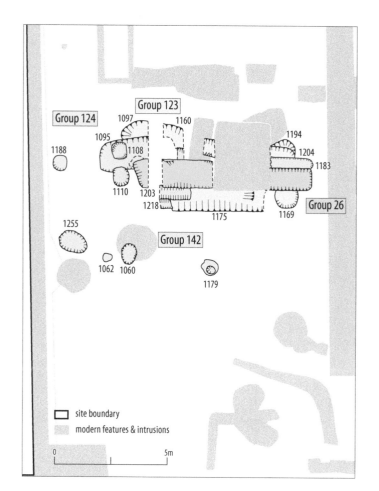

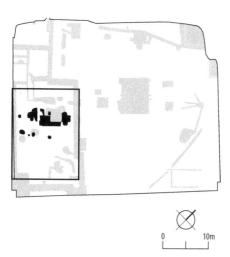

Illus 3.50. Possible sequence of timber troughs associated with industrial activity

Illus 3.51. Sandstone footing (G131) and its relationship to the clay-lined pit (G134)

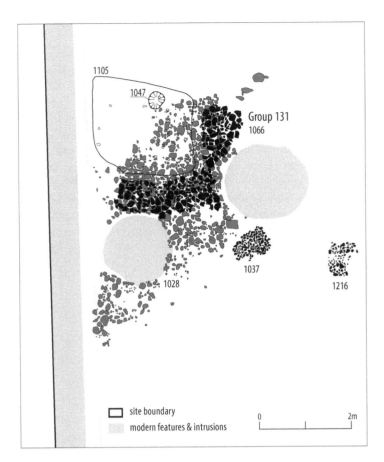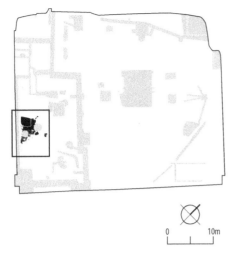

Illus 3.52. Sandstone footing (G131)

Illus 3.53. Detail of sandstone footing (G131)

Illus 3.54. Fully excavated rectangular feature that possibly once housed a timber tank

Wheel ruts on the main surface (G143, G161)

These indicate that carts were probably being used across the surface to bring material in and out of the site.

Other pits (G95, G121, G147)

A collection of pits/post-holes (G121) in the north-west corner of the site were largely similar, containing some slag pieces and material in their fills dating to the 3rd century (they could range from Phase 2 to Phase 4). This is very similar to a collection of pits observed in the north-east corner of the site (G95). All contained a mid-brown sandy clay loam with high proportions of slag and moderate amounts of hammerscale. The pottery within these pits also ranges up to the end of the 3rd century AD.

A large pit (G147) on the south side of the site measured 1.79 by 1.68 metres with an excavated depth of 1.2 metres. It is possible that this pit has some relation to structure G125 which lies just to the north, though, as very little domestic refuse was found within it, its interpretation remains unclear.

3.6. Post-Roman archaeology

A 'dark earth' deposit was observed in the east end of the south section of the site where the Presbyterian Church wall stood forward from the excavation baulk and also in the north section of the site. Close inspection was

Illus 3.55. Heap of material suggestive of a collapsed oven or hearth

undertaken of the southern exposure where the deposit was 0.25-0.3m thick and overlay sand deposits. It had an amorphous humic nature and showed signs of considerable worm action. There were also reasonable quantities of slag within the deposit meaning that magnetic susceptibility could not be used to analyse the deposit.

A possible plough soil of medieval date overlay the dark earth described above. Due to the presence of bands of gravels within the profile it is likely that cultivation of this soil had ceased for a considerable period before the soil layer was sealed by the post-medieval soil that provides almost 1m of cover across the site. Medieval finds were recovered from the site although none of these were in situ.

Most of the post-medieval archaeology relates to buildings that were previously known to occupy the site, the presence of their cellars and wall foundations clearly visible in the base of the excavation. In addition to this a number of post-medieval wells were uncovered although these were not investigated. As with the medieval period no finds were in situ.

4

The pottery

Jeremy Evans and Margaret Ward with contributions by Phil Mills and Brenda Dickinson (report submitted in 2003 with some updates in 2020)

4.1. Introduction and methods

Some 29,105 sherds have been recorded from the excavations, weighing 521.297kg, representing a minimum number of rims (MNR) count of 3,263 and with an RE total of 30,091%. The vast majority of these were found in stratified Roman contexts. These account for 27,383 sherds, 488.640kg and representing a minimum number of rims per context count of 3,013 and with an RE total of 27,667%. This represents all the stratified pottery from Phases 1, 2, 3 and 4.

The pottery has been recorded to fabric following the Warwickshire Museum Fabric Type Series, using the general ware class and specific fabric divisions devised by Booth (Booth 1991) and cross-references to the Worcester Fabric Type Series (http://www.worcestershireceramics.org/). Thus all the fabrics are divided into 11 major ware classes;

- A - amphorae
- B - black burnished wares
- C - calcareously tempered wares
- F - non-samian finewares
- G - gritted wares
- M - mortaria
- O - oxidised wares
- Q - white-slipped oxidised wares
- R - greywares
- S - samian wares
- W - whitewares

Individual fabric types are then defined as numbered fabrics within these classes, eg G44, Malvernian metamorphic tempered ware. A complete list of all fabrics, with descriptions and equivalents is given in Appendix 1, with quantification by phase given in Appendix 2.

In order to process the large volume of pottery in a reasonable time it was decided to fully record material from Phase 2 deposits, but to record non-diagnostic pottery from the extensive Phase 3–4 surfaces just to the ware class level. Thus all rim sherds are fully recorded by fabric and form, but body sherds from Phase 3–4 surfaces are just recorded to ware class.

Quantification was carried out by sherd count (Nosh), weight (Wt), minimum numbers of rims in each context (MNR; Evans 1991) and rim equivalent (RE; Orton 1975).

Tables and histograms have been provided to summarize the forms, fabrics and date-ranges of the collections.

The samian report is based on that written in 2003, employing Hartley and Dickinson's numbering system, using Roman numerals in lower case after the potter's name. However, names can now be found in their definitive series, *Names on Terra Sigillata* (*NoTS*) (Hartley and Dickinson 2008-2012). Where helpful, the numbering of decorative styles in Stanfield and Simpson (1958; 1990), is provided in upper case. Abbreviations **SG**, **CG** and **EG** indicate South, Central and East Gaulish products. For other terminology employed (eg Rogers for Rogers 1974, Oswald for Oswald 1936, etc), see Webster 1996. Date-ranges such as *c* AD 70–110 or *c* 120–200, given instead of epochs such as 'Flavian to Trajanic' or 'Hadrianic to Antonine,' should not be thought to be more precise than the use of epochs. They are employed to facilitate detailed analysis of the material. Maximum numbers of vessels were employed to quantify samian ware in 2003 (for rationale, see Ward 2011, 74–7; 2012, 22–3, 26).

The catalogue of pottery with illustration references is given in Appendix 3, while Appendix 4 notes the occurrence of each form by phase. Lastly, Appendix 5 notes where sherds from the same samian vessels were found across several contexts. The relatively distinctive ware may act as a tracer for disturbances and redepositions; other sherds from these contexts may be connected.

4.2. Taphonomy

There is relatively little pottery from Phase 1, however, the material present is relatively complete, with an average sherd weight of 33.9g and an average RE value of 14.8% (Table 4.01). These are high values and clearly reflect both the absence of residual earlier material, as might be expected, and fairly primary deposition of material which had not been subject to much more than its primary breakage. Phase 2 contains more pottery, some 12.7% (Nosh), however, given the date distribution plot (Illus 4.01) for the site as a whole, it appears to only contain a fraction of the pottery which dates to this period. Sherds from Phase 2 are also fairly large, at 23.3g and 11.8% (RE), although within Evans' range for northern urban and military sites (Evans 1985), unlike Phase 1, which exceeds this range. The slightly lower average sherd size in this period would seem to reflect both the presence of some residual material from Phase 1 (the two phases would

Table 4.01. Proportions of pottery by phase

Phase	% Nosh	% Wt	% MNR	% RE	Average sherd weight	Average RE %
1	7.1%	13.3%	8.4%	13.4%	33.9g	14.8%
2	12.7%	16.6%	16.4%	21.0%	23.3g	11.8%
3	64.0%	52.4%	55.2%	45.7%	14.7g	7.6%
4	10.3%	11.4%	12.3%	11.9%	19.9g	8.9%

anyway seem to overlap chronologically) and perhaps more intense activity resulting in the greater fragmentation of material and more re-deposition. This should not be over-stated however, as average sherd size is still at the higher end of the usual range.

There is a considerable change in Phase 3. Most of the pottery from the site was found in deposits dating to this phase, some 64.0% (Nosh). However, as Illus 4.06 shows, there is a major element of residual 2nd century material within this. The latter may be part of the explanation for the sudden fall in average sherds size to 14.7g. Also of significance is the nature of the Phase 3 deposits, many of which are gravel layers (Table 4.4) where the residual pottery may have been incorporated as hard core.

Relatively little pottery came from Phase 4 deposits, just 10.3% (Nosh). The proportion of residual 2nd-century material in this period may be a little lower than in Phase 3, but there is apparently considerable residual 3rd century material (Illus 4.08). Given that residual material is still found in considerable quantity it would seem to be the reduction in the numbers of gravel surfaces has led to this minor increase.

The deposit types containing most pottery here are road surfaces and gravel layers, at 60.8% (Nosh) of all sherds (Table 4.02), with layers as a whole containing 71.4% (Nosh). Ditches and gullies contained just 13.1% (Nosh) of all the pottery and pits 7.5% (Nosh), with 4.8% from post-holes and beamslots.

These figures form a stark contrast to datasets collected from rural sites. In comparison Table 4.03 shows similar data from the rural site at Haddon, Cambridgeshire (Evans 2003). Most of the pottery from Haddon came from ditch fills, which are by far the most common feature type on the site, certainly in terms of volume, the second largest in terms of quantity. Far lesser quantities came from other features: only 8% from pits; 6% from post-holes and beamslots. This seems to be a fairly typical pattern for a rural farmstead. Martin (2002; 2003) has produced similar data from three Essex sites (Ship Lane, Aveley; Great Holts Farm, Boreham; and Bulls Lodge Dairy, Boreham), with pot proportions from ditches etc of 65%, 68% and 68% respectively and 10%, 3% and 22% from pits. Similar figures were also recovered from Little Paxton, Cambridgeshire.

The average sherd weight and average percentage of rim (RE) figures in Table 4.03 highlight major variations in average sherd size at Haddon. The major deviations are the kiln and stokehole fills, from which much more complete vessels were recovered.

It is clear that the Worcester figures are very different from those on the basic level rural sites. The fundamental difference is in the large quantity of pottery deriving from horizontal stratigraphy. It is likely that this is a general distinction between urban and rural sites. Considerable levels of horizontal stratigraphy are a typical feature of the former, but rarely found in quantity on basic level rural sites.

When broken down by phase, the Worcester figures show that there are considerable changes in the amount of pottery from different feature types over time on the site (Table 4.04).

In Phase 1 the vast majority of the pottery comes from the ditch fills. In Phase 2 there is a marked drop in this, with a remarkable rise in pottery from post-holes, beamslots and pits. In both of these periods the taphonomic breakdown of the pottery is fairly comparable with that from basic level

Table 4.02. Proportions of pottery by feature type for all recorded pottery

Feature type	% Nosh	% Wt	Average sherd weight	% Min no rims	% RE	Average % rim per vessel
Layers	10.6	10.1	16.9g-	23.5	20.5	8.6-
Road/gravel layers	60.8	48.8	14.4g-	50.0	40.6	7.5-
Post-holes/beamslots	4.8	4.7	17.2g-	5.9	5.4	8.5-
Pits	7.5	9.0	21.5g+	9.6	10.8	10.4+
Ditches/ gullies	13.1	22.6	31.0g+	16.0	24.0	13.9+
Wells	0.2	0.2	20.1g-	0.2	0.2	6.5-
Graves	0.02	0.2	205.5g+	0.03	0.3	100+
Wall	0.02	0.04	28.1g+	0.03	0.04	13.0+
Hearth/oven	1.0	1.6	28.0g+	1.4	1.7	11.2+
Other	0.9	0.9	17.4g-	1.4	1.3	8.7-
N	29,105	521,297g	17.9g	3262	30,088%	9.2%

Table 4.03. Haddon, Cambs; proportions of pottery by feature type (chiefly phases 1–4)

Feature type	% Nosh	% Wt	Average sherd weight	% Min no rims	% RE	Average % rim per vessel
Layers	0.4	0.3	12.8g	0.3	0.5	49
Post-hole and beam slot	5.8	3.9	11.8g	4.3	5.0	23.0
Pit	8.3	9.1	19.3g	7.7	6.6	23.3
Ditch/gully	79.1	73.6	16.4g	79.3	71.6	24.4
Hearth	0.2	0.1	9.3g	0.8	0.3	12
Kiln and stokehole	2.7	9.4	57.3g	3.1	9.6	85.2
Grave	0.3	1.1	60.4g	0.3	0.1	8
Indeterminate	2.9	2.5	15.2g	2.8	6.3	60.5
N	3763	66,234g	17.6g	392	10608	27.1

Table 4.04. Proportions of pottery by feature type and phase

Feature type	% Nosh	% Wt	Average sherd weight	% Min no rims	% RE	Average % rim per vessel
Phase 1						
Layers	0.7%	0.5%	21.0g	0.4%	0.10%	5.0%
Post-holes/ beamslots	6.2%	3.0%	16.3g	4.0%	2.2%	8.0%
Ditches/ gullies	91.8%	95.4%	35.2g	93.4%	95.8%	15.2%
Hearth /oven	0.5%	0.8%	53.3g	1.5%	1.8%	18.5%
N	2,051	69,439g	33.9g	273	4,037%	14.8%
Phase 2						
Layers	9.4%	5.8%	13.1g	9.0%	6.7%	8.3%
Post-holes/beamslots	25.2%	18.8%	17.4g	24.8%	19.0%	9.0%
Pits	15.9%	13.9%	20.5g	14.6%	14.8%	12.0%
Ditches/gullies	45.1%	55.2%	28.5g	44.4%	49.4%	13.1%
Wells	1.7%	1.4%	20.1g	1.5%	0.8%	6.5%
Graves	0.2%	1.4%	205.5g	0.2%	1.6%	100%
Hearth/oven	2.1%	1.7%	18.5g	2.8%	3.8%	16.0%
Other	5.9%	4.8%	19.0g	6.7%	5.4%	9.4%
N	3,709	86,516g	23.3g	536	6311	11.8%
Phase 3						
Layers	12.5%	14.4%	17.0g	17.6%	19.3%	8.3%
Road/metalled layers	87.5%	85.6%	14.3g	82.4%	80.7%	7.5%
N	18,621	272,966g	14.7g	1,802	13,735%	7.6%
Phase 4						
Layers	18.0%	15.7%	17.3g	18.7%	17.5%	8.3%
Road/metalled layers	13.0%	7.9%	12.1g	7.2%	7.9%	9.7%
Post-holes/beamslots	10.0%	7.8%	15.6g	8.7%	7.4%	7.6%
Pits	43.7%	51.3%	23.3g	50.9%	53.9%	9.5%
Ditch/gully	8.2%	6.3%	15.3g	7.5%	7.3%	8.7%
Wall	0.3%	0.4%	28.1g	0.2%	0.4%	13.0%
Hearth/oven	6.9%	10.7%	30.6g	6.7%	5.7%	7.5%
N	3,000	59,660g	19.9g	401	3,581%	8.9%

rural sites, in stark contrast to the overall site breakdown (Table 4.02). The high level of pottery from post-holes and beamslots in Phase 2 presumably reflects the relatively intense use of the site for timber structures in this period.

Phase 3 provides a total contrast with the vast majority of sherds from gravel layers, and the remainder from other horizontal stratigraphy. This period represents the major remodelling of the site with truncation and terracing and must have taken place over a very limited time-span. As shown elsewhere (Table 4.01, Illus 4.06), while most of the site's pottery derives from this phase, there is a reasonably large element of residual 2nd-century material. Thus it would not be surprising if much of the 2nd-century pottery from this gravel was actually introduced onto the site in this period as hardcore, rather than being archaeologically residual on the site from the disturbance of earlier features, especially as there are no cut features in this phase except for the site truncation.

In Phase 4 a substantial percentage (31%) of the sherds derive from horizontal stratigraphy, including 13% from gravel layers, with only a small percentage from ditch fills. This is a distinctly urban distribution pattern. Pits are also strongly represented and combined with numbers of hearths/ovens perhaps suggest some emphasis on industrial activity.

4.3. Chronology

Considering the date distribution for dated vessels from the site (Illus 4.01), there is nothing which suggests pre-Flavian pottery deposition here and little to suggest much Flavian activity. The site samian list is very clear with no pre-Flavian forms present and no moulded bowls of form 29 (which went out of production *c* AD 85 in South Gaul). There were only four samian vessels which could be dated as early as *c* AD 70–90; three of these were fragments of moulded bowls. Most of the samian ware in this collection was dated loosely in the range *c* AD 70–110 and much of it will have been produced after *c* AD 80. A similar picture comes from the coarse pottery. There is only a single 'Belgic' style grog tempered ware sherd and Malvernian Paleozoic Limestone tempered ware, dating to before AD 70, was completely absent. It is certainly possible that the small quantities of pre-Flavian material present were brought onto the site later.

Only 3% of the samian collection is considered likely to have been produced at Les Martres-de-Veyre, representing perhaps 45 vessels. This is also a low level for predominantly Trajanic material and pottery deposition may not have started before this period.

Amongst the coarse pottery early material in the assemblage includes quite a quantity of rustic ware jars, of perhaps Trajanic to early Hadrianic date, and some 1st- to 2nd-century Severn Valley wares, as well as some early Malvernian forms (ie bucket/barrel jars). There are also, surprisingly, sherds from at least two Roman glazed ware vessels which are probably Trajanic. These latter are an unusual find, which like the quantity of rustic ware, might suggest some military link.

In contrast to the weak later 1st century and Trajanic samian lists, as much as 94.3% of the vessels were produced in Central Gaul in the Hadrianic to Antonine period. There is little doubt that there seems to have been intense occupation on the site from the Hadrianic period onwards.

The site samian list is very strongly dominated by Central Gaulish material (94.3%) with only 2.6% of East Gaulish material. This latter is lower than the low 5% recovered from the Worcester site of Deansway (Dickinson 2004), suggesting the vast majority was deposited in the 2nd century and most of this material is Antonine. Despite the low level of East Gaulish samian it is clear from the coarse pottery that Phases 3 and 4 contain quantities of later 3rd- to 4th-century material.

The date of the end of pottery deposition on the site is unclear, particularly in the absence of a strong site coin list. Oxfordshire wares, whilst present on the site, are generally in such small quantities as to be of little aid to dating. Stamp decorated Oxfordshire wares are absent from the stratified deposits, although this may well reflect the nature of the

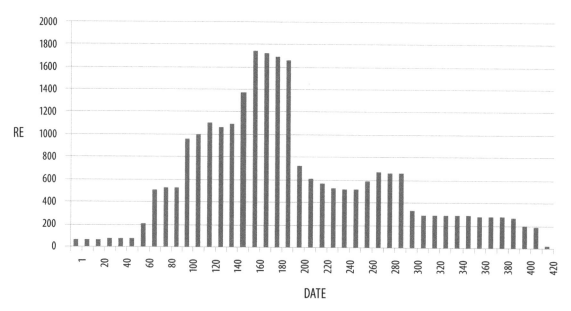

Illus 4.01. Date distribution of vessels with a span of less than 200 years by RE

site rather than chronological factors. As at Deansway, the latest material comprises later 3rd- to 4th-century Severn Valley ware types and BB1. Shell-tempered wares are absent, again similar to Deansway where only three sherds were recovered. The evidence from Alcester, Warwickshire (Evans 1996), Gloucester (Hassall and Rhodes 1975), Wroxeter, Shropshire and Segontium, Gwynedd (Casey et al 1993) suggests that by AD 390 urban pottery assemblages in the region might be expected to contain high proportions of shell-tempered ware (probably from Harrold, Bedfordshire), and thus their absence tends to suggest the site came to an end before *c* AD 390, or ceased using pottery by then.

Phase 1

The date distribution of vessels from Phase 1 deposits (Illus 4.02) indicates some possible Flavian activity, but certainly suggests strong pottery deposition from the beginning of the 2nd century, probably running on until the end of the 2nd century, although levels weaken a little in the later 2nd century.

When broken down by context group for the larger group assemblages (Illus 4.03) the results are much the same as for the period as a whole. The larger groups, G2 and

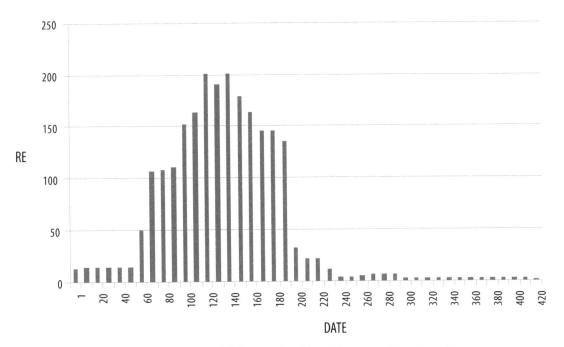

Illus 4.02. Phase 1 date distribution of pottery by RE for vessels with a date range of less than 200 years

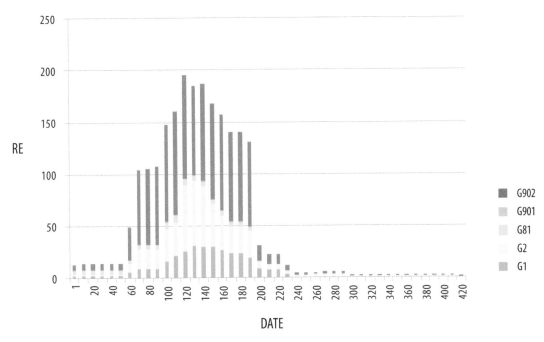

Illus 4.03. Phase 1 date distribution of pottery by RE for vessels with a date range of less than 200 years from context groups with more than 10 rim sherds for vessels

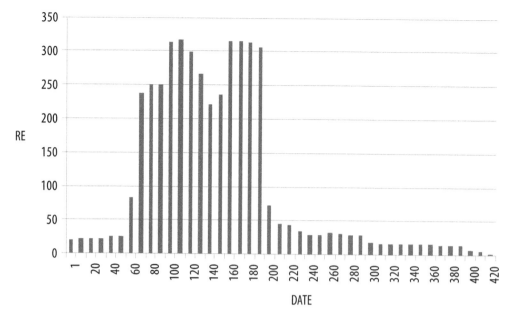

Illus 4.04. Phase 2 date distribution of rim sherds by RE with a date range of less than 200 years

G902, show the peak of pottery deposition ending around AD 200, although G81 seems to peak in the early-mid-2nd century. The latest material with a close date range from Phase 1 is a Central Gaulish Dr 33, dated AD 150–200, (C2270) indicating the phase could not end before AD 150/60. Intrusive material in this phase includes vessel types O27 B3.1 and O231 WMJ1.3 both from G2 and O55 WMJ1.1 from G902.

Phase 2

The date distribution profile of vessels from Phase 2 (Illus 4.04) is similar to that from Phase 1, with some Flavian material, but with most dating between AD 100 and AD 200. There is a peak in the Hadrianic period and a further peak in the late Antonine period. Although some Phase 2 features clearly post-date the Phase 1 ditch, it is difficult given this date distribution to envision this phase not being partly contemporary with Phase 1.

When this data is broken down for the larger groups (Illus 4.05), G901 seems to reflect the overall range of the period, but G2 (which dates to phase 1 but was clearly filling in phase 2) seems to be predominantly early and G121 has a noticeable late Antonine to early 3rd century range. Possible intrusive material in the forms of vessels

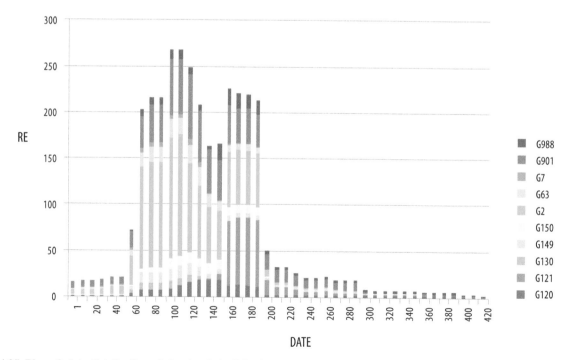

Illus 4.05. Phase 2 date distribution of rim sherds by RE with a date range of less than 200 years from context groups with more than 10 dateable rims

with a later 3rd century or later date range comes from G38, G72, G121, G149, G901, G988.

Phase 3

The pattern for Phase 3 is very different than for previous phases (Illus 4.06). Material from AD 200 onwards is reasonably represented, although at a lower level to residual 2nd century material. This is followed by a peak between *c* AD 270 and 300, followed by a plateau through most of the 4th century, with quantities falling off at the end of that century.

Given the earlier discussion about the origin of the 2nd-century residual material here (see Chapter 4.2), the date distribution might also suggest that the early-mid-3rd century material on the site was brought in with the truncation and levelling, and it could be that actual activity on the site in this period is absent, although this is far from certain.

When plotted by group (Illus 4.07) it is clear that residual and contemporary material is generally spread through most of the groups, although G41 is almost entirely 2nd century.

Phase 4

Phase 4 (Illus 4.08) is remarkably similar to Phase 3. There is a substantial element of residual 2nd-century material, some dating to the early-mid-3rd century, followed by a small late 3rd-century peak and a plateau through much of the 4th century, falling-off at the end of the century. The Phase 3 surfaces were largely contemporary with this period so this similarity is therefore to be expected.

The larger groups (Illus 4.09) such as G132 and G147 again reflect well the overall date distribution for the period. G130, however, is exclusively of residual 2nd-century material.

4.4. Fabrics

Class A, amphorae, 0.6% (Nosh) (Illus 4.10–4.11)

The quantity of amphorae was low at 163 sherds, 0.6% (Nosh) and 2.7% (Wt). This level is hugely below that found on military sites and below that found on most urban sites (Evans 2001, fig 11). Levels in small towns tend to be around 1% (Nosh), whereas basic level rural sites tend to have less than 0.5%, if the type is found there at all. In contrast quantities of amphorae on the Deansway site (Williams 2004) were larger at 2% (Nosh) and 8% (Wt). Deansway falls above the limited evidence for a small town range, but a 1st-century fort (Dalwood and Edwards 2004) has been proposed on the site which would account for this.

As usual on most Roman period sites in the province the assemblage is dominated by Dressel 20 oil vessels. However, the level of Gauloise wine amphora sherds seems particularly low at 3.7% (Nosh) (Table 4.05). At Deansway some 93% (Nosh) and 91% (Wt) of amphorae sherds were from Baetican, Dressel 20 oil vessels, the remainder mainly being Gauloise 4. Again, this allows for a poor representation of Gauloise sherds.

Dressel 20 oil amphorae, **A21** (Illus 4.10), first appear in Phase 1 but only at 0.2% (Nosh), a low level often found on rural sites. They rise to 1.6% (Nosh) in Phase 2, before

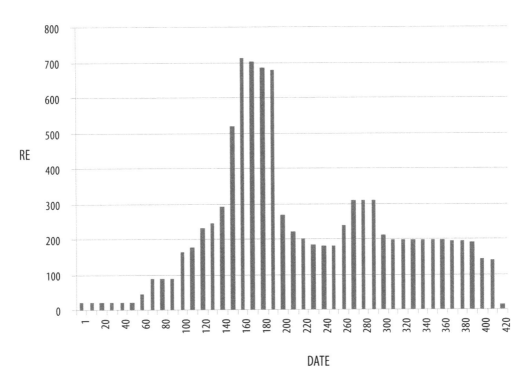

Illus 4.06. Phase 3 date distribution of rim sherds by RE with a date range of less than 200 years

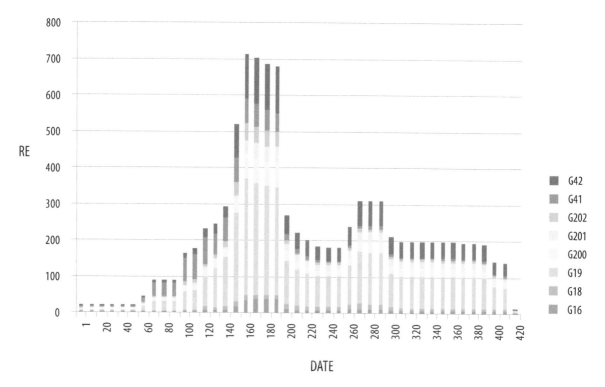

Illus 4.07. Phase 3 date distribution of rim sherds by RE with a date range of less than 200 years from context groups with more than 10 dateable rims

falling again in Phases 3 and 4. The Dressel 20 sherds are probably residual in Phases 3 and 4.

Gauloise sherds, **A22**, only occur in Phase 3, and at very low levels. Levels of Gauloise sherds from *civitas* capitals *colonia* and major towns seem to run usually in the range 10–20% (Holbrook and Bidwell 1991; Arthur 1986; Williams 1990). Similar levels are generally found on military sites

which were in supply zones which used Gauloise amphorae (Evans forthcoming), eg north-east England, so the proportion at Binchester fort in that region is 19.1% (Nosh) and 6.6% (Wt). However, these generalisations are made on relatively little evidence and also tell us nothing about supply to small towns so it may be worth looking here at the supply of Gallic wine amphorae to southern military and civilian sites in Britain in a little more detail.

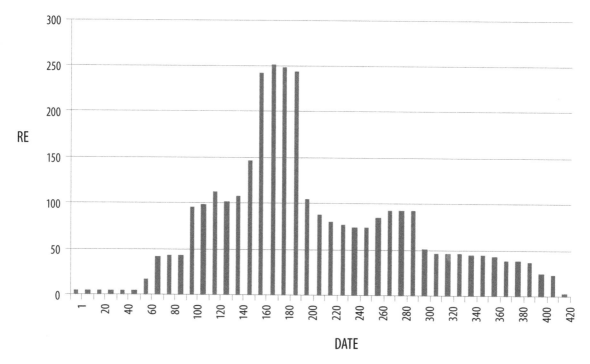

Illus 4.08. Phase 4 date distribution of rim sherds by RE with a date range of less than 200 years

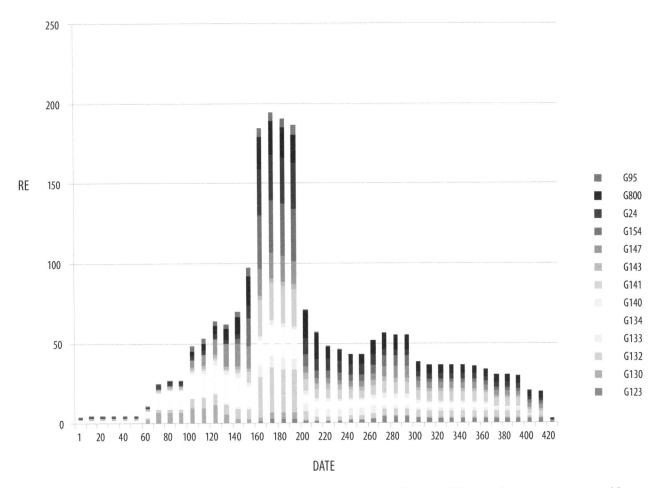

Illus 4.09. Phase 4 date distribution of rim sherds by RE with a date range of less than 200 years from context groups with more than 10 dateable rims

Illus 4.11 shows the proportionate occurrence of Gallic amphorae on military sites, civitas capitals and 'small towns' generally from lists which encompass the whole Romano-British period. Rural sites are not included as they will only confuse the picture, since Gallic wine amphorae rarely reach basic level rural sites, and since the overall quantities of amphorae on basic level rural sites are generally far too few to obtain an accurate determination of the proportions of different amphora types.

The map shows a number of interesting trends. Bidwell and Speak (1994) made an important demonstration that wine amphorae are generally very rare or absent from Hadrian's Wall. They argue persuasively that this reflects the supply of wine to the Wall in barrels from the Rhineland. This is clearly reflected in the absence of Gallic amphorae from Burgh-by-Sands (Masser and Evans 2005), Birdoswald (Evans 2009a), Wallsend (Croom 2003) and South Shields (Bidwell and Speak 1994).

Table 4.05. Relative occurrence of amphorae by fabrics type for all recorded amphorae

Fabric	% Nosh	% Wt
A21 Dressel 20 - oil	96.3%	98.2%
A22 Gauloise - wine	3.7%	1.8%

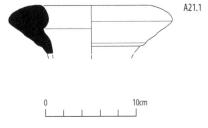

Illus 4.10. Fabric A21

The distribution also shows that Gallic amphorae were used in some quantity on military sites in north-east England, at levels comparable with other areas of the province. The numbers suggest that the primary port for the importation of Gallic amphorae for north-eastern supply was York, where a massive 31% of sherds were from this source (Williams 1997, table 175).

This would be logical. There is evidence for York operating as the secondary northern port for the importation of BB2 for example (Evans 1985; Bell and Evans 2002, fig 196). York was clearly being supplied by vessels on the east coast trade, as was South Shields, though Gallic amphorae were not being imported to the latter.

Similar evidence exists on the west coast trade. Gallic amphorae were well supplied to military sites in Wales,

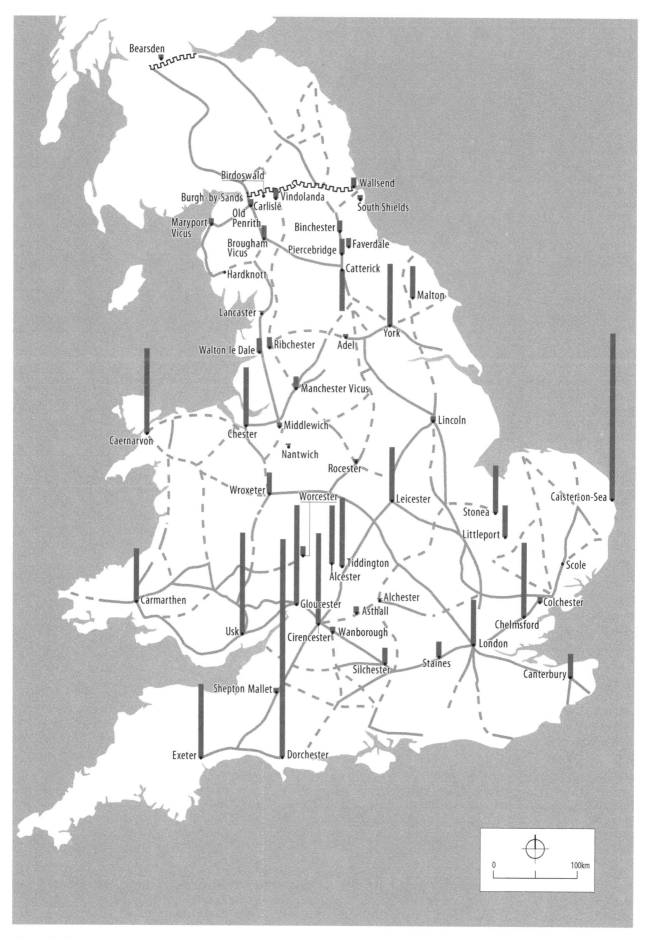

Illus 4.11. Quantitative distribution map of Gallic amphorae on military and urban sites in Britain

10% at Carmarthen (Brennan 2003), 15.8% at Segontium (Webster 1993, table 17.2), 11% at Chester (Mason 1980) and 16% at Wroxeter (Darling 2004, table 4.16). However, north of this, things are very different, with just 2.6% at Middlewich (Evans 2002), 2.5% at Nantwich (Mills 2012) and 0.4% at Rocester. This continues going north with >2% at Ribchester and 5.9% at Walton-le-Dale (all from one phase), 0.6% at Adel in the Pennines (Evans in prep), 0.9% at Mitchell's Brewery Lancaster (Evans and Rátkai forthcoming b) and 1.2% from Blackfriars Street, Carlisle (Taylor 1990), and none from Castle Street, Carlisle (Taylor 1991). Thus, while common south of Chester, in the north-west Gallic amphorae were rare or absent. The evidence from Bearsden (Fitzpatrick 2016, 173) indicates that the Antonine Wall, like Hadrian's Wall, lacked Gallic wine amphorae, with just 0.8% (Wt) and 1.2% (Nosh) of the fabric.

For these patterns to develop requires that from the Flavian period until the early 3rd century there was a stable supply arrangement to the sites just discussed. In other words, there seem to have been four or five supply zones covering; Wales; the north-west from Rocester to Carlisle along King Street and the Manchester Road (and including Adel in the Pennines); Hadrian's Wall; the Antonine Wall and the Scottish lowlands; and north-eastern England (north of the Humber). There is supporting evidence for the north-western grouping in the forms of consistent and unusual compositions to samian ware assemblages from sites in this region (Evans forthcoming).

In terms of the west coast trade the distribution also indicates a series of port sites which would seem to be part of this supply route: Dorchester (Seager-Smith and Davies 1993, tables 28 and 43); Exeter (Holbrook and Bidwell 1991); and Gloucester (Timby 1986). Indeed the remarkably high levels of Gallic amphorae (41.3%) at Dorchester (Seager-Smith and Davies 1993, tables 28 and 43) might well suggest the channel crossing from Gaul for this trade made landfall in the vicinity of this town, with Dorchester, like York, forming a redistribution point.

This leaves the south-east of England from the Humber to the Severn, which also shows some interesting patterns. The low levels at Worcester are not borne out by nearby towns and forts. Levels at Wroxeter, Leicester, Alcester, Tiddington and Gloucester all being 'normal'. However, if the Worcester site is at the heart of Romano-British cider country, as this author has suggested (Evans 1999) it may be simply that wine was not the drink of choice for much of the population.

Whilst in eastern England Gallic amphora levels seem to be 'normal' there is a large patch of low values on and south of the Thames in a triangle from Alchester to Shepton Mallet to Staines. Some of these sites are of high status like Silchester, with 1.2%, others are small towns such as Wanborough with 0.9% and Staines with 2.9%. Many, however, are in or near the central belt of limestone and chalk where modern British vineyards are located and

the area includes the Verulamium region potteries which produced amphora type forms often described as lagenae.

It is at least possible that this area of low amphora use, and also possibly Kent, to judge by the figures from Canterbury, is to be explained by local viticulture, rather than in some difficulty of supply, with the local products generally being distributed in barrels.

Class B, black burnished wares, 3.2% (Nosh) (Illus 4.12–4.13)

Overall Dorset Black Burnished 1 comprises some 3.2% (Nosh) and 2.4% (Wt) of the recorded pottery. This is quite closely comparable to levels from Deansway (Bryant and Evans 2004, fabric 22) of 3.0% (Nosh) and 2.0% (Wt). Jars comprise just under half of the vessels (Table 4.6), with the remainder being dishes and bowls. This is the type of functional composition, such as might be found on sites in the north (Williams 1977; Evans 1985), where cooking pots dominate the BB1 functional range. However, it is a little surprising here, where BB1 is in such low supply. In eastern England (Bedfordshire, Cambridgeshire, Northamptonshire; Evans et al 2017) where BB1 levels are similarly low, it is the tableware forms which are marketed but the jars are not, apparently being replaced by more local competition.

At Deansway the majority of BB1 vessels dated to the mid-2nd and 3rd centuries (Bryant and Evans 2004, 265). At Magistrates Court it is clear that the majority of BB1 vessels are Antonine (Illus 4.13), like most of the pottery from the site, with a much lower tail of 3rd-century material, and a further tailing off in the 4th century.

The ratio of acute lattice decorated sherds to obtuse lattice decorated ones is 137:97 sherds (or 58.5% acute to 41.5% obtuse). This indicates a slightly greater emphasis on the Hadrianic-Antonine period than the 3rd to mid-4th centuries, though this is the case for the site as a whole (Illus 4.01). There is no suggestion that BB1 was more common in the Hadrianic-Antonine period than later, indeed perhaps the reverse. In terms of occurrence by phase (Table 4.07) BB1 amounts rise from Phases 1 to 2, fall in Phase 3 and rise again in Phase 4.

Fulford and Allen (1996, fig 1) have produced quantified distribution maps for south-west England, Wales and the West Midlands. Their map highlights the land distribution along the Fosse Way from Dorset up the Cirencester road, as well as highlighting the high levels at Gloucester and the Severn estuary and along the south Welsh coastal plain, and thereafter on military sites close to the coast at Carmarthen, Caernarvon etc. Further up the Severn, the map appears to indicate levels of around 10% at Worcester, which is clearly an over-estimate. It is interesting to see that levels fall off rapidly up the Severn after Gloucester, and the obvious water transport corridor does not seem to have been pursued. Rather, north of Cirencester, BB1 seems to travel by road north towards Alcester and Wall.

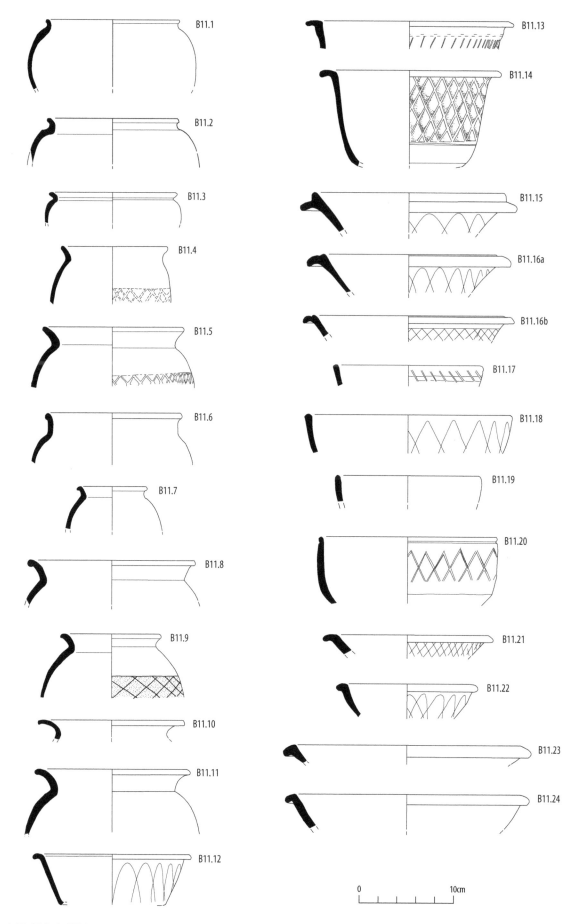

Illus 4.12. Fabric BB1

Table 4.06. Functional analysis of BB1 vessels from the recorded assemblage (MNR and RE)

Jars	Bowls	Dishes	N
49.1%	16.1%	34.8%	224 rims
59.5%	13.3%	24.8%	1881% of rim

Table 4.07. Occurrence of BB1 by phase

Phase	% MNR	% RE
Phase 1	5.1%	4.5%
Phase 2	9.9%	7.8%
Phase 3	4.7%	3.8%
Phase 4	12.2%	11.5%

At Alcester BB1 supply amounts to around 15% of the assemblage in the 2nd century, rising to 30% or more in the 3rd and earlier 4th centuries. East of Alcester levels fall-off, and at Tiddington they are around 10%, whilst west at Worcester they are around 3% and levels are similarly low at Droitwich and on other mid-Severn Valley sites.

The obvious explanation of this might be local competition with Malvernian wares (Hodder 1974, fig 5; Evans 2005, fig 9.7), though these generally provided less of their local assemblages (less than 7%) than BB1 did of assemblages on neighbouring sites. There are also few Malvernian tablewares, though these make up half of BB1 assemblages. It appears that BB1 was simply in much lower demand in this area.

Class C, shell-tempered ware, 0% (Nosh)

No shell-tempered ware sherds were recovered from the site. This is similar to Deansway where only three sherds were recovered (Bryant and Evans 2004). Given the presence of this fabric at sites in Wales in the late 4th century as far as Segontium, and its frequency in the latest deposits at Gloucester (Hassall and Rhodes 1975) its absence may betoken an absence of the latest 4th century activity on both these sites.

Class F, colour-coated wares, 0.4% (Nosh) (Illus 4.14–4.18)

Colour-coated wares are surprisingly rare at this site and this is equally true for Deansway (Bryant and Evans 2004). Interestingly Nene Valley colour-coated wares (F52) only ranked third, behind Oxfordshire wares (F51) and the dominant fineware is the early roughcast colour-coated ware (F42) (Table 4.8).

The earliest fineware from the site is Terra Nigra, **F91** (Illus 4.14), represented by a single rim sherd of a Cam 16 dish (G2, Phase 1-2). It is probably of Flavian date (Rigby 1977) and, like the glazed ware sherds and the rustic wares, is likely to be related to the early fort at the town.

One unusual feature of the finewares is the presence of glazed ware **F12** (Illus 4.15). F12 is in an oxidised fabric with an orange core and margins and green/brown glazed surfaces, with some fine sand. As might be expected it is only found in Phases 1 and 2, both at 0.1% (Nosh) and 0.03% (Wt). The source of the fabric is not clear; the Caerleon/Usk or Holt/Chester groups are both possible (Arthur 1978). Forms represented are two bowls, perhaps

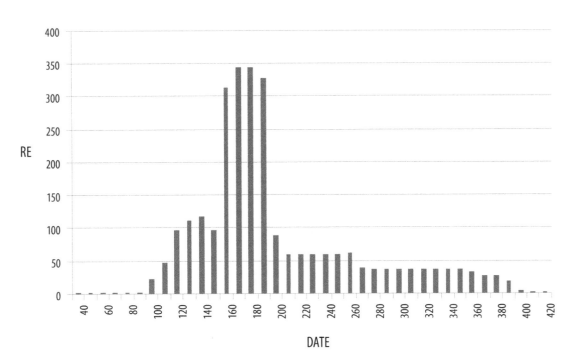

Illus 4.13. Date distribution of BB1 vessels by RE

Table 4.08. Relative frequency of colour-coated wares

Fabric Code	% Nosh	% Wt	% MNR	% RE
F12	8.00%	4.86%	9.09%	7.98%
F32	3.00%	0.82%	4.55%	7.36%
F42	44.00%	43.63%	36.36%	46.01%
F43	3.00%	7.06%	0.00%	0.00%
F51	20.00%	29.70%	31.82%	25.15%
F52	19.00%	11.09%	13.64%	9.20%
F53	2.00%	1.28%	0.00%	0.00%
F91	1.00%	1.56%	4.55%	4.29%

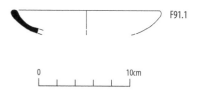

Illus 4.14. Fabric F91

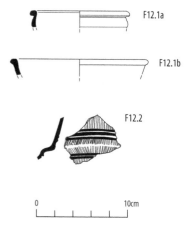

Illus 4.15. Fabric F12

Dr 37 copies and there are body sherds from a straight-walled carinated bowl.

There are two sherds of 'Central Gaulish 'Rhenish' ware' **F32** from the site, dating to the later 2nd century. The fabric occurs at 0.03% (Nosh) in Phase 2 and 0.01% (Nosh) and in Phase 3.

The most common fineware is an oxidised roughcast fabric **F42** (Illus 4.16), with orange-brown core, margins and surfaces, with some sand. It is probably fairly local and equivalent to Worcester fabrics 31 and possibly 45. Some 13 beakers, all variants of the roughcast cornice rimmed type were found. At Deansway (Bryant and Evans 2004) Fabrics 31 and 45 combined (both of which contain roughcast sherds) represent the same proportions of the overall assemblage. Forms represented there include the same cornice rimmed beakers and a hemispherical bowl

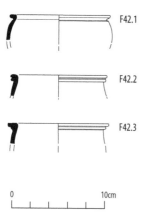

Illus 4.16. Fabric F42

(Bryant and Evans 2004, fig 165.7). A little to the north-east at Droitwich (Lentowicz 1997, fig 63) Worcester fabric 31 is found in the 3rd to 4th century representing around 3% of the assemblage.

At Alcester F42 is quite common, representing 39.4% of all finewares from the 3rd-century phase (Evans 1996). As well as the ubiquitous cornice rimmed roughcast beakers, there is a 'finely rouletted beaker in this fabric, copying a Central Gaulish or Trier form (Gillam 1970 types 47–8, AD 200–50)' and a 'necked beaker' (Evans 1996, F42.1–4). As at Magistrates Court, F42 at Alcester outnumbers Nene Valley colour-coated ware. Booth (pers comm, cited in Evans 1996) suggests that F42, being quite common at Chesterton and Tripontium, may originate to the east of Alcester.

The evidence of the forms from Alcester and the quantity in a 3rd-century phase at Droitwich (Lentowicz 1997, Phase 3) suggest the fabric was still contemporary in the early to mid-3rd century, and perhaps a later 1st to mid-3rd century range ought to be assigned to it. The fabric is absent from the large assemblage from Coleshill (Booth 2006) in northern Warwickshire, and similarly absent from sites on the Warwickshire Churchover to Newbold Pacey pipeline (Evans 2009b). F42 is at its most common at Magistrates Court in Phase 1 at 0.5% (Nosh). The fabric is probably residual after the end of Phase 2.

Also present were a few sherds of **F43**. This is a brown-slipped oxidised fabric with buff-grey core and orange-brown margins, with some sand. It is similar to F42, again probably equating with Worcester fabric 31, but lacks roughcast decoration. It occurs in Phases 2 and 4 but must be residual in Phase 4.

Nene Valley colour-coated ware, fabrics **F52/F53** (Illus 4.17), is poorly represented on the site, with only 19 sherds. Forms represented are a 'Castor box', a jar and a beaker, the latter of later 3rd- to 4th-century date. There are a few sherds in Phase 2, rising slightly over the next two phases to reach 0.2% (Nosh) and 0.04% (Wt) in Phase 4.

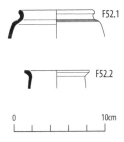

Illus 4.17. Fabric F52

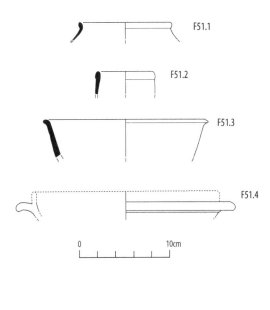

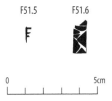

Illus 4.18. Fabric F51

A similar picture is seen at Deansway (Bryant and Evans 2004) where Nene Valley colour-coated ware is only represented by 18 sherds accounting for 0.1% (Nosh) of the assemblage. The paucity of Nene Valley wares here is slightly surprising; although they do fall off in western Britain as might be expected, they are not generally as rare as this.

Further north-west at the Welsh fort of Segontium (Webster 1993, table 17.2) Nene Valley wares do not appear until the later 3rd to early 4th century, but they amount to 3% of the overall site assemblage (MNR). They are almost as rare at Walton-le-Dale in Lancashire (Evans and Rátkai forthcoming a), appearing at 0.1-0.4% (Nosh), but that site was a production site for brown roughcast colour-coated ware in the Wilderspool tradition. Further north in Lancashire at Mitchells Brewery, Lancaster (Evans and Rátkai forthcoming b) Nene Valley products were much more common ranging from 1% to 5% (Nosh). Thus in the absence of local production of a competing fineware Nene Valley wares in western England generally seem to run at a higher level than that found at Worcester.

Oxfordshire colour-coated wares, **F51** (Illus 4.18), appear on the site in Phase 3. They are also rare, rising from 0.02% (Nosh) in Phase 3 to 0.4% (Nosh) in Phase 4. The levels at Magistrates Court are reflected at Deansway (Bryant and Evans 2004) where they represent the same overall percentage of the assemblage. Nonetheless Oxfordshire colour-coated ware is the third most common fineware at Magistrates Court and represents about a quarter of all the finewares. Forms represented are six bowls and two beakers, bowls being the usually dominant type in Oxfordshire colour-coated ware assemblages. Forms consist of Young (1977) C22.1 (AD 240–400+), C23–30 (AD 270–400+), C45 (four examples, AD 240–400+) and C51 (two examples, AD 240–400+). It is of note that C45 is the most common bowl type. At Alcester (Booth and Evans 2001, 289) type C51 tends to outnumber type C45 in groups dated after *c* AD 370, and this has been confirmed in groups from Cambridgeshire (Evans et al 2017) so the emphasis on C45 here tends to confirm that the Oxfordshire wares reached the site before the late 4th century.

Class G, gritted wares, 6.6% (Nosh) (Illus 4.19–4.21)

(NB G numbers in this section all refer to gritted ware fabrics not context groups)

The vast majority of the gritted wares are in Malvernian fabrics. These have been divided here into three principal fabrics: handmade Malvernian metamorphic tempered ware, G44, (Peacock 1965–7) Worcester fabric 3; wheel-made Malvernian Metamorphic tempered ware, G46, Worcester fabric 19; and G47, a variant on G44 with the same inclusions but a black core, orange-brown margins and grey-brown surfaces, used for storage jars and portable ovens, Worcester fabric 3. A number of other fabrics are probably minor variant sherds of G44, namely **G37** and **G71**.

A single sherd of fabric Milton Keynes Pink Grogged Ware (Booth and Green 1989), **G11** (Worcester fabric 17) was recovered from Phase 4. It is of later 3rd- to 4th-century date. The fabric is not recorded at Deansway (Bryant and Evans 2004) and is absent from Droitwich (Lentowicz 1997) to the north-east. It is more common however at Alcester to the east (Evans 1996) where it is fairly consistently present at Gas House Lane, though still at the low level of around 0.1% (Nosh).

Two other very minor grog tempered handmade fabrics are recorded from the site: **G15**, a reduced fabric with abundant angular grey grog *c* 0.1-0.7mm and occasional organic voids (up to 0.5mm in length); and **G16**, a handmade reduced fabric with common-abundant red-brown grog. These may relate to Worcester fabrics 16 and 16.2. No source for these is known.

The handmade standard Malvernian Metamorphic-Tempered Ware, **G44** (Illus 4.19), amounts to 2.0% (Nosh)

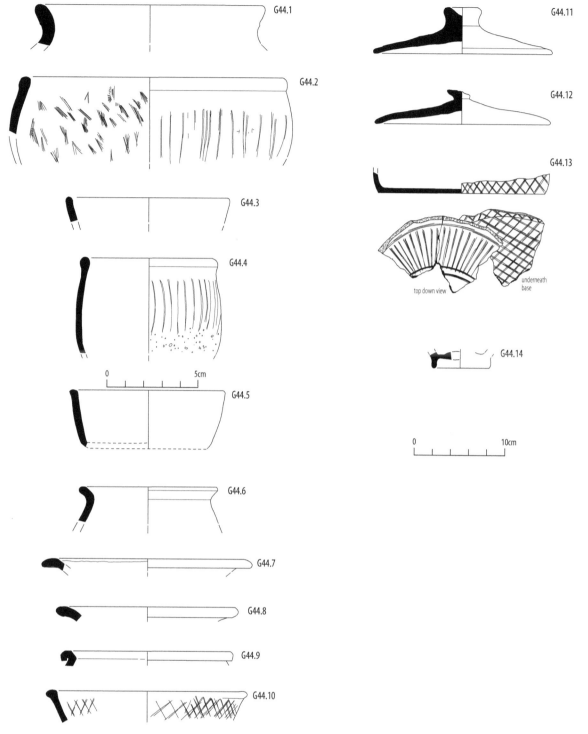

Illus 4.19. Fabric G44

and 2.3% (Wt) of the assemblage. It occurs from Phase 1 onwards 5.7% (Nosh), reducing slightly in Phase 2 and declining notably in Phases 3 and 4. It appears this group is largely residual from Phase 3 onwards.

At Deansway the fabric is slightly more common with an overall 3% (Nosh) and 5% (Wt) (Bryant and Evans 2004). The most common forms there are 'tubby cooking pots' and bead rimmed globular vessels with acute burnishing, whilst at Sidbury, Worcester, smaller cooking pots/jars also predominated (Darlington and Evans 1992, 48–50).

Elsewhere in the city sites such as Farrier Street (Buteaux 1994, 94) and at many rural sites in the county (Dalwood et al 1998, 18) the majority of the vessels in this fabric are very large heavy storage jars of a type first noted by Peacock (1965–7, fig 4, nos 80–82). The reason for this is not clear but seems, at present, to relate to date as well as function (Dalwood et al 1998, table 5).

At Magistrates Court the picture is similar in the G44 group with 40 globular jars (form G44.2) and 13 jars of form G44.4 which would seem to fall in Peacock's 'tubby cooking pot' group. These latter occurred from Phase 1 onwards. It has been suggested (Evans et al 2000) that they date back into the 1st century in contrast to Peacock's (1965–7) Hadrianic-Antonine dating. There are only three vessels in this group with everted rising rims (G44.6 and G44.8) and one with a hooked rim (G44.9).

The range of forms present (Table 4.09) is predominantly made up of jars. Bowls are absent but there are quite a few lids (forms G44.11 and G44.12) and a few slightly beaded dishes (G44.5) and a few flange rimmed dishes (G44.10) along with a few storage jars with everted rising rims (G44.1).

The handmade variant fabric with the grey-brown surfaces, **G47** (Illus 4.20) contrasts with G44 in terms of forms and dating. The excavation of a complete example at The Hive, Worcester (Jane Evans 2018) shows that most of the material listed here, except forms G47.1-G47.3, come from the Worcester form of portable oven. It is present at low levels from Phase 1 (1.0% Nosh), rising to 4.4% (Nosh) in Phase 2 and maintaining these levels through to Phase 4. Its most common jar form (G47.1) with 14 examples has a straight everted rising rim like the wheel-made forms in G46 (Table 4.10). Forms in phase 1 are restricted to lids, but fragments of the portable ovens occur from Phase 2 onwards.

A comparison of Tables 4.09 and 4.10 shows these contrasts in form between G44 and G47. Fabric G47 includes few ordinary jars, but an enormous number of storage jars. Dishes are few, and lids at a similar level to G44, but there are a very high proportion of portable oven fragments vessels. Peacock (1965–7, no 86–7) illustrates two sherds from Malvern Link of the portable ovens. Also in the 'other' category is one 'chappati disc' (*cf* Evans 2009b, 129–33). This type of object seems to be associated with the portable ovens at The Hive (Jane Evans 2018) but they seem to be an independent class of cooking instrument, not associated with ovens elsewhere (Evans forthcoming).

Table 4.09. Functional analysis of Malvernian ware vessels in fabric G44 (MNR and RE)

Storage jars	Jars	Bowls	Dishes	Other	Lids	N
6.1%	74.4%	0	11%	0	8.5%	82 rims
4.1%	84.3%	0	3.9%	0	7.7%	701% of rim

Table 4.10. Functional analysis of vessels in fabric G47 (MNR and RE)

Storage jars	Jars	Bowls	Dishes	Ovens	Lids	N
55.5%	15.8%	1.9%	2.0%	15.8%	8.9%	101 rims
57.1%	17.7%	1.7%	0.8%	10.9%	11.3%	751% of rim

The vast majority of the identifiable rim sherds in this fabric group came from Phases 2–4 (Table 4.11) and it would appear that although this fabric variant may occur from at least around the mid-2nd century it is only really common in the 3rd and 4th centuries.

Fabrics G44 and G47 account for 5.2% (Nosh) and 3.7% (Wt) of the total assemblage at Magistrates Court, a similar level to the 3% (Nosh) and 5% (Wt) from Deansway (Bryant and Evans 2004, Worcester fabric 3).

Fabric **G46** (Illus 4.21) is the wheel-made Malvernian Metamorphic tempered ware and is equivalent to Worcester fabric 19. Its overall level amongst the recorded pottery is 0.9% (Nosh) and 1.0% (Wt), which is a little below the 2.4% (Nosh) and 4.4% (Wt) from Deansway (Bryant and Evans 2004). At Deansway the fabric appears in small quantities *c* AD 100, but is much more common in the period AD 120–240, dropping thereafter.

At Magistrates Court it occurs at 0.1% (Nosh) in Phase 1, rising to 2.6% Nosh by Phase 4 (Table 4.11). Thus, the fabric would appear to originate in the early 2nd century, but only becomes relatively common in the 3rd and 4th centuries. The form range consists of everted rimmed jars, there being three types present: eight with straight, everted rising rims (G46.2); 20 with outcurving everted rising rims (G46.3) which could be BB copies; and three with everted rising rims which are fairly clearly 3rd century BB copies (G46.4). There are also four flange rimmed bowls (G46.6) and an incipient beaded and flanged bowl (G46.5), along with three simple rimmed lids (G46.7) and a storage jar with an everted, rising, thickened rim (G46.1).

Whilst many of the forms are of similar form to the earlier dishes/bowls, lids and storage jars, the jar forms have changed completely. The jars seem to be related, if a little distantly, to BB1 forms. This could relate to increasing competition with BB1. BB1 may have failed to penetrate the core markets of Malvernian ware much, but it was certainly taking increasing market share on sites which had been on the periphery of Malvernian markets to the east, such as Alcester (Evans 1996).

The forms present are essentially cooking pots, with a few bowls and lids and an occasional storage jar (Table 4.12). The form range is actually very similar to that for the earlier handmade range in fabric G44. The G46 and G47 vessels are largely contemporary, the majority of rim forms in both deriving from Phases 3 and 4. Thus the products in G47 provide a supplementary range of storage jars and portable ovens.

The distribution of Malvernian Metamorphic Tempered Wares was studied by Hodder (1974, fig 5) in his seminal paper on Romano-British marketing models. He argued from the distribution plotted at that time that it provided evidence of urban marketing of the fabrics from Worcester. However, a re-examination of this based on updated data

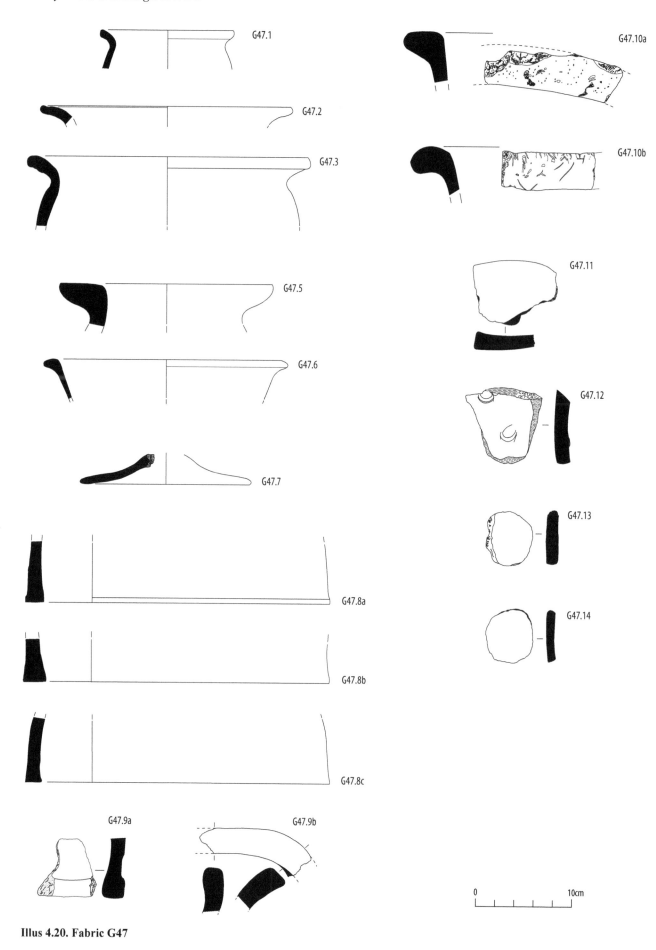

Illus 4.20. Fabric G47

Table 4.11. Occurrence of Malvernian Metamorphic tempered ware fabrics by phase

Fabric Code	Phase	% Nosh	% Wt	% MNR	% RE
G44	1	5.7%	5.1%	7.0%	5.2%
G44	2	4.6%	3.7%	5.4%	3.8%
G44	3	1.1%	1.2%	1.3%	1.2%
G44	4	1.4%	1.5%	1.5%	1.5%
G46	1	0.1%	0.02%	0.0%	0.0%
G46	2	0.6%	0.5%	0.4%	0.2%
G46	3	0.7%	0.7%	1.4%	1.5%
G46	4	2.6%	3.2%	2.7%	3.4%
G47	1	1.0%	1.3%	0.4%	0.3%
G47	2	4.4%	4.2%	1.3%	1.2%
G47	3	3.2%	5.5%	3.8%	3.5%
G47	4	4.5%	12.5%	2.5%	2.2%

Table 4.12. Functional analysis of vessels in fabric G46 (MNR and RE)

Storage jars	Jars	Bowls	Dishes	Ovens	Lids	N
2.3%	79.1%	11.6%	0	0	7.0%	43 rims
2.1%	79.1%	11.8%	0	0	7.0%	373% of rim

(Evans 2005, fig 9.7) suggested this was not the case. The present assemblage does not change this latter conclusion. Magistrates Court at 7.2% (Nosh) and 9.7% (Wt) leaves the town on a 7–9% range which is only equal to rural sites in the Avon Valley.

Class M, mortaria, 1.2% (Nosh) (Illus 4.22–4.27)

Mortaria are present in reasonable quantities although they seem to become more common in later Roman deposits. Overall they represent 1.2% (Nosh) and 2.7% (Wt). Quantities rise from 0.3% (Nosh) in Phase 1, to a peak of 1.1% (Nosh) in Phase 3. Surprisingly, they are rather more prolific at Magistrates Court than at Deansway with a 0.6% (Nosh) occurrence (Bryant and Evans 2004).

The earliest mortaria from the site are those of fabric M12, from Noyon, in north Gaul, M21 from Verulamium and M45 probably from the Severn Valley. The Gaulish **M12** (Illus 4.23) is represented by a single vessel (G902, Phase 1) of form Bushe-Fox type 26–30, dated *c* AD 80–150 (Bushe Fox 1932). **M21** from Verulamium is only slightly more common, represented by two identifiable rim sherds, both of type M21.1 (G151, Phase 1; G88, Phase 2). They probably date to the period AD 60–120.

The most common of the early mortaria fabrics is the Severn Valley **M45** (Illus 4.24) (Worcester fabric 37). This amounts to 7.7% (Nosh) of the total mortaria assemblage (Table 4.13). It is more common still at Deansway (Bryant and Evans 2004, 257) representing 21% of the mortaria there. At Deansway it appears in Phase 3, AD 50–120 and is regarded as residual by the mid-2nd century. At Magistrates Court, two forms are represented, M45.1 and M45.2, both of which would seem to date in the later 1st to early 2nd century bracket, with the identifiable rim sherds all coming from Phase 2 deposits.

The most common type of mortaria found in the assemblage are Mancetter-Hartshill products, **M22** (Illus 4.25), which make up 62.3% (Nosh) of the mortaria and start arriving on site from the beginning of the 2nd century. As many as 36 of the identifiable vessels date to the 2nd century compared to 21 dating to the 3rd and 4th centuries. Mancetter-Hartshill vessels are much more common at Magistrates Court than at Deansway, where they comprised only 26% (Nosh) and 18%. A number of 2nd-century mortarium stamps are represented, including Marcellinus and Iunius.

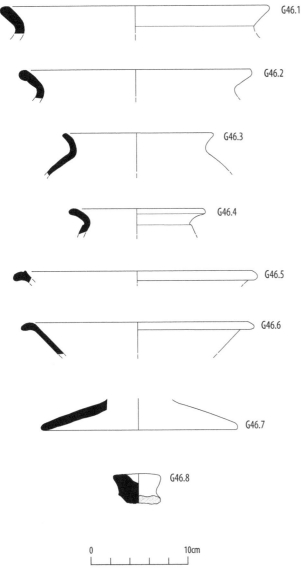

G46.1

G46.2

G46.3

G46.4

G46.5

G46.6

G46.7

G46.8

0   10cm

Illus 4.21. Fabric G46

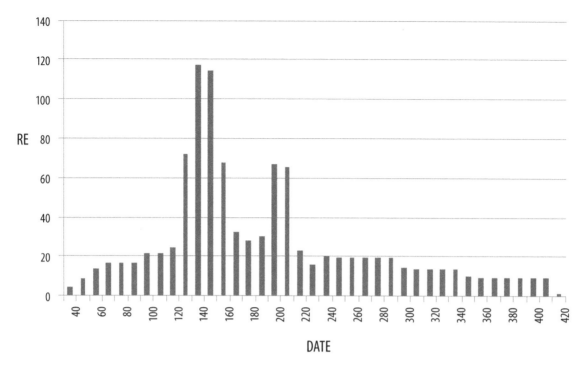

Illus 4.22. Date distribution of Mortaria by RE

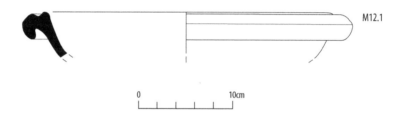

Illus 4.23. Fabric M12

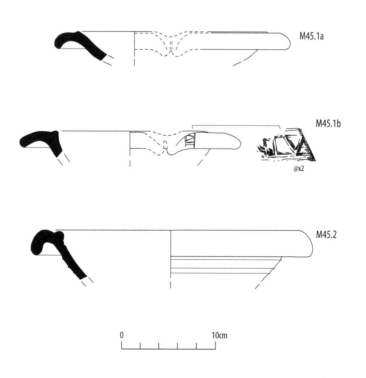

Illus 4.24. Fabric M45

Table 4.13. Relative occurrence of mortaria fabrics

Fabric Code	% Nosh	% Wt	% MNR	% RE
M12	0.30%	0.99%	0.80%	1.24%
M21	2.08%	3.37%	4.00%	5.26%
M22	62.31%	71.61%	66.40%	71.99%
M23	12.46%	7.37%	11.20%	10.90%
M37	10.39%	7.23%	8.80%	5.07%
M44	2.67%	3.02%	0.80%	0.57%
M45	7.72%	5.80%	7.20%	4.68%
M71	0.89%	0.32%	0.00%	0.00%

Fabric **M23** (Illus 4.26), Oxfordshire ware, the second most common mortaria fabric, may also occur on the site in the 2nd century as it represents 0.1% (Nosh) of the pottery from Phase 2. However this may be intrusive. No rim sherds were found at this early date and the fabric does not appear to be present in any quantity before the 3rd century. However, the presence of Oxfordshire ware in the 2nd century here is reasonably consistent with the evidence from Deansway where the earliest forms were Young's (1977) types M10 and M11 dated AD 180–240. Oxfordshire forms represented at Magistrates Court are four examples of Young (1977) type M17, dated AD 240–300, and two of Young type M23, dated AD 240–400+. Oxford colour-coated ware mortaria are represented by body sherds only.

Fabric **M37** (Illus 4.27) (Worcester fabric 34) would also seem to have had a role in site supply in the 2nd century. It is a whiteware with cream-buff margins and surfaces, with abundant angular translucent sand. Trituration grits are common white quartz and common brown ironstone. Overall it is the third most common type of mortaria fabric from the site (Table 4.13). A source near Wroxeter has been suggested for this (Bryant and Evans 2004, 263) and a date range of AD 100–150. At Deansway it represents 14.5% (Nosh) of all the mortaria and was first found in a phase dating to AD 120–240. At Magistrates Court, but for a single context in Phase 1 (G151) and a handful of Phase 2 contexts (G2, G88 and G121), most occurrences are in Phase 3.

The absence of Raetian type mortaria may be noted. There were a few sherds of this at Deansway but they amounted to less than 2% of all the mortaria sherds there.

The last 2nd century mortaria fabric from the site is **M44**. This is an oxidised white-slipped fabric with an orange core and margins, with common moderate sand temper. Trituration grits are of sub-rounded brown stone, some white quartz and some sub-angular grey stone. It amounts to 2.7% (Nosh) of the mortaria, although no fully identifiable rim sherds are represented. This fabric does not seem to be represented in the Worcester type series, unless it is regarded as part of the Worcester fabric 37 group, though that, unlike M44, is not sandy. The fabric

first appears in Phase 2 and is clearly residual in Phase 4. Booth (1994) suggests a 2nd-century date for the fabric. This fabric is quite common at Alcester, amounting to 4.2% (Nosh). Given that this quantity is equivalent to that at Worcester a source equidistant to these two sites might be sought.

When the proportions of the different mortaria fabrics are plotted by date using the dating of the vessel forms (Table 4.14), it gives approximate quantification to the above dating discussion. It shows Verulamium M21 and Severn Valley M45 as the only substantial pre-Flavian material present, although in very small quantities. Verulamium (M21) seems to have remained the principal mortarium fabric in the Flavian-Trajanic period, followed by Severn Valley Ware (M45), Mancetter (M22) products, whiteware mortaria from the Wroxeter area (M37) and then Noyon products (M12).

By the Hadrianic-Antonine period a major change in mortarium supply is taking place with Mancetter (M22) accounting for almost all the supply, and the Wroxeter area (M37) being a distant second. Later Roman supply at Magistrates Court site seems to have been entirely between the Mancetter-Hartshill (M22) and Oxfordshire (M23) industries. It shows Mancetter dominating supply in the early 3rd century, with Oxfordshire contributing around 10%, but with Oxfordshire rising to nearly half the market share in the later 3rd century, then falling back in the early 4th century as Mancetter reasserted its dominance. There are few vessels covering the later 4th-century part of the range, and figures for this period are probably misleading, since Mancetter supply is assumed to have come to an end in the later 4th century and the site may well have ended before or during this period.

Thus, Mancetter remained the dominant supplier at Worcester from the 2nd to the 4th centuries. This is an interesting contrast with the situation at Alcester. There it is clear that in the course of the 3rd century Oxford drove Mancetter out of the market even though the Oxfordshire kilns were a little more distant than those of Mancetter. However, at Worcester, Mancetter has a greater advantage of distance over Oxfordshire, and this seems to have preserved the Mancetter dominance there.

Class O, oxidised wares, 76.0% (Nosh) (Illus 4.28–4.48)

Oxidised wares overall provide 76.0% (Nosh) and 71.2% (Wt) of the assemblage, the vast majority of these being Severn Valley wares. Similarly, at Deansway (Bryant and Evans 2004) oxidised Severn Valley wares provided 54% (Nosh) and 53% (Wt) of the assemblage there, although quantities there were noticeably lower than at the Magistrates Court.

Plotting the major ware classes by phase (Illus 4.28) shows the overall dominance of Severn Valley wares throughout the sequence. They comprise 65.8% of the assemblage in Phase 1, falling a little in Phase 2, before

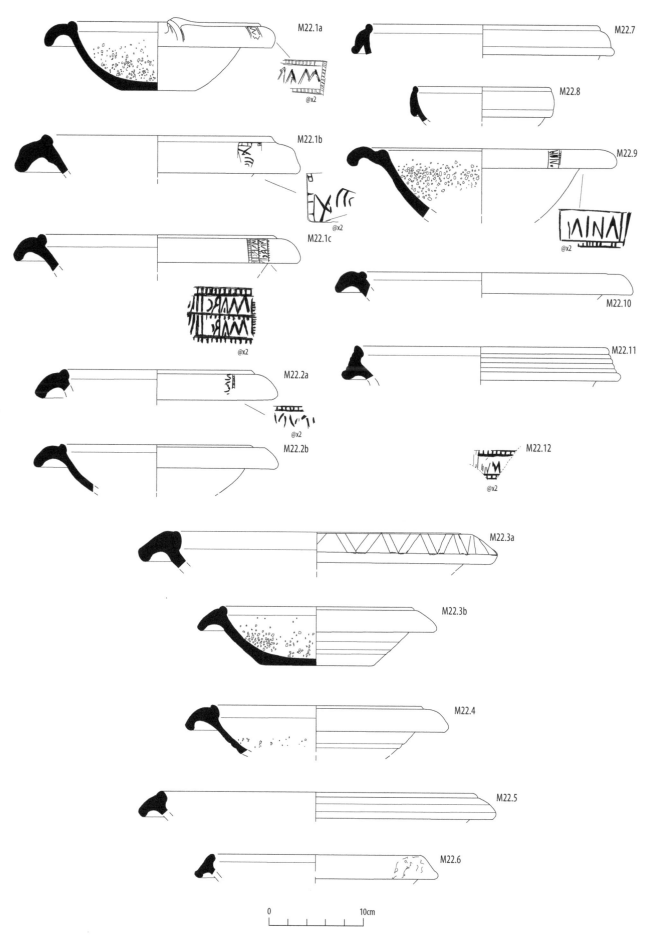

Illus 4.25. Fabric M22

peaking at 83.4% in Phase 3, and then falling back again in Phase 4. This basic profile is similar to the one seen on many Alcester sites, with Severn Valley wares particularly dominant in the 3rd century as early greyware production ceases and importation from North Warwickshire lessens. This is followed by a slight decline in the 4th century as Warwickshire Greywares again re-enter markets and the late BB1 peak is reached. However, at Worcester, Severn Valley wares are more important in the 1st and 2nd centuries compared to Alcester where greywares are more significant at that time.

The Severn Valley fabric **O21** (Illus 4.29) contains abundant organic temper voids and equates with part of Worcester fabric 12.2. Overall O21 represents 0.4% (MNR) of the oxidised wares. It is related to O36, which it probably shades into, but is more heavily organically tempered. Worcester fabric 12.2 would appear to cover both and it is likely that both have been classified together in earlier reports using the Warwickshire Museum type series. The fabric is most common in Phases 1 at 0.7% (MNR), falling to 0.3% (MNR) in Phase 4. All the forms represented seem to be of 1st- to early 3rd-century date. Forms are limited to a jar, three tankards and three wide-mouthed jars.

The related **O36** (Illus 4.30–4.32) (also Worcester fabric 12.2), has some common organic temper voids though less than O21, and sometimes some white possibly non-calcareous inclusions or possible siltstone/clay pellet inclusions. It is much more common representing 34.7% (MNR) of all the recorded oxidised wares, making it the most common single Severn Valley ware fabric. Again, it is most common in the earlier phases, representing 20.3–23.4% (MNR) in Phases 1 to 3, declining to 13.0% (RE) in Phase 4. Plotting the date distribution of the vessels shows a similar pattern (Illus 4.33), that it is a predominantly 1st- to 2nd-century group, which continues into the 3rd century, but probably not into the 4th century.

The date distribution of both O21 and O36 is consistent with their correlation with Worcester fabric 12.2 which has been dated to the 1st and 2nd centuries (Bryant and Evans 2004). Worcester fabric 12.2 is the largest single fabric at Deansway, at 57% (Nosh) of the Severn Valley wares there (Bryant and Evans 2004, 253).

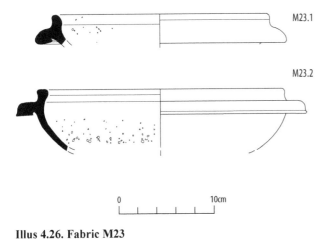

Illus 4.26. Fabric M23

Illus 4.27. Fabric M37

Table 4.14. Proportions of mortaria sources by fabric in half-centuries calculated from the date ranges of vessels in each fabric

Fabric Code	Preflav	Flav-Traj	Had-Ant	EC3	LC3	EC4	LC4
M00	1.2%	0.3%	0.1%	0.2%	0.4%	0.6%	2.1%
M12	0.0%	9.9%	0.0%	0.0%	0.0%	0.0%	0.0%
M21	54.3%	33.3%	0.2%	0.0%	0.0%	0.0%	0.0%
M22	0.0%	19.6%	87.7%	89.1%	51.3%	72.3%	3.7%
M23	0.0%	0.0%	1.1%	10.5%	48.3%	27.1%	94.2%
M37	3.0%	14.2%	6.8%	0.1%	0.0%	0.0%	0.0%
M44	0.0%	1.3%	1.5%	0.0%	0.0%	0.0%	0.0%
M45	41.5%	21.4%	2.7%	0.0%	0.0%	0.0%	0.0%
N	16.86	137.61	493.58	188.57	95.44	67.68	26.79

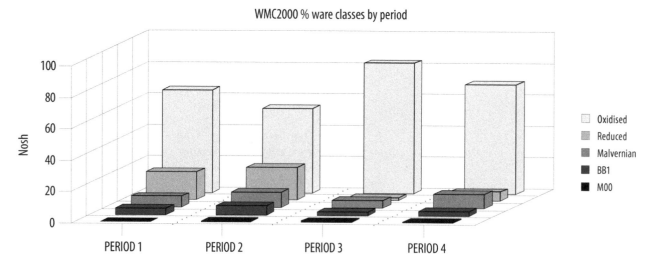

Illus 4.28. Proportions of major ware classes by period by Nosh

Table 4.15. Occurrence of Oxidised Wares fabrics amongst all recorded pottery rim sherds

Fabric	% MNR	% RE
O21	0.4%	0.4%
O36	34.7%	36.0%
O23	0.7%	0.5%
O231	30.9%	32.1%
O24	0.5%	0.4%
O27	28.9	26.9%
O29	1.2%	0.9%
O291	1.3%	1.0%
O35	0.2%	0.2%
O53	0.1%	0.6%
O55	1.2%	1.1%
O57	present	present
O81	0.1%	0.2%
O91	present	present

Illus 4.29. Fabric O21

Although jars are the largest single vessel type (Table 4.16) these are mainly wide-mouthed jars, with very few medium-mouthed jars, which in other regions would usually be the most common category in the most common ware type. This is however, typical of Severn Valley ware assemblages which contrast with typical Romano-British assemblages in this respect. Bowls appear to be the second most common category but dishes are very poorly represented, so that overall tableware elements in the assemblage are quite low. Tankards are the third most common vessel type and these are an all but unique type to this region. This author has made the case elsewhere (Evans 1999) that these are for cider consumption. There is also a small further contribution of drinking vessels in the form of beakers. Again, this is perfectly typical for a

Severn Valley ware assemblage but can be contrasted with assemblages from other regions.

The next Severn Valley Ware is fabric **O23** (Illus 4.34), with abundant very fine sand temper. It is visually similar to Cirencester fabric 108 and it presumably falls within the range of Worcester fabric 12. Fabric O23 provides just 0.7% (MNR) of the recorded oxidised wares. Surprisingly, compared to O231, the fabric seems most common in Phase 1 at 0.9% (MNR) falling to 0.2% (MNR) in Phase 4. The forms certainly suggest the fabric was contemporary until at least the later 3rd century. The dominant classes are bowls and tankards, followed by wide-mouthed jars (Table 4.16), though fine analysis of these figures is not worthwhile due to the low numbers of rims present.

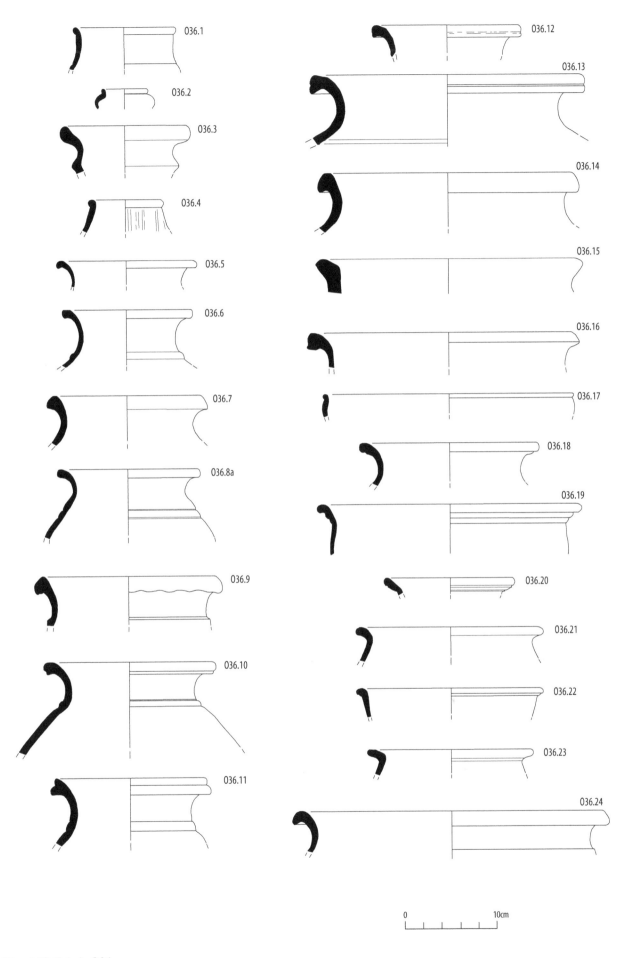

Illus 4.30. Fabric O36

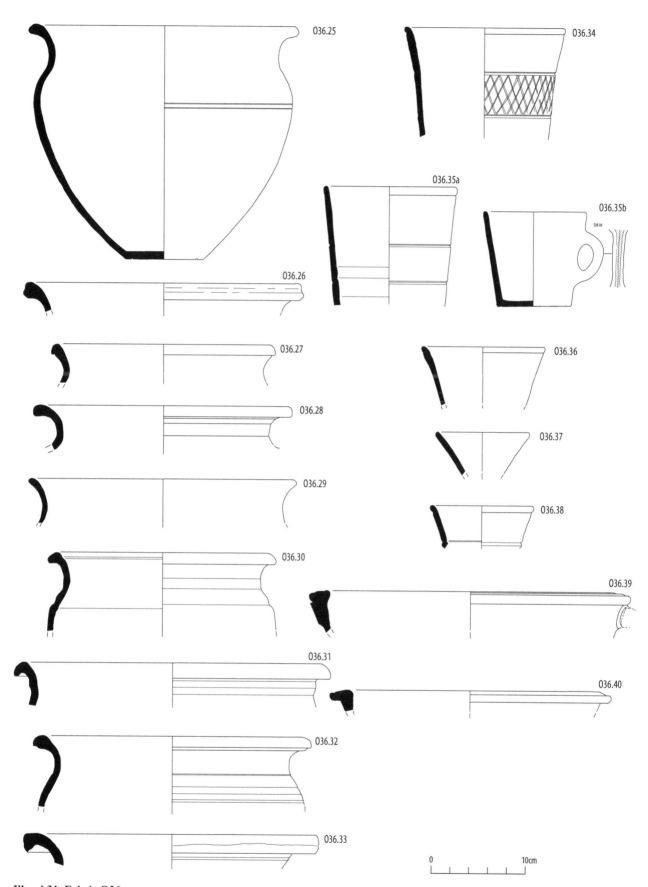

Illus 4.31. Fabric O36

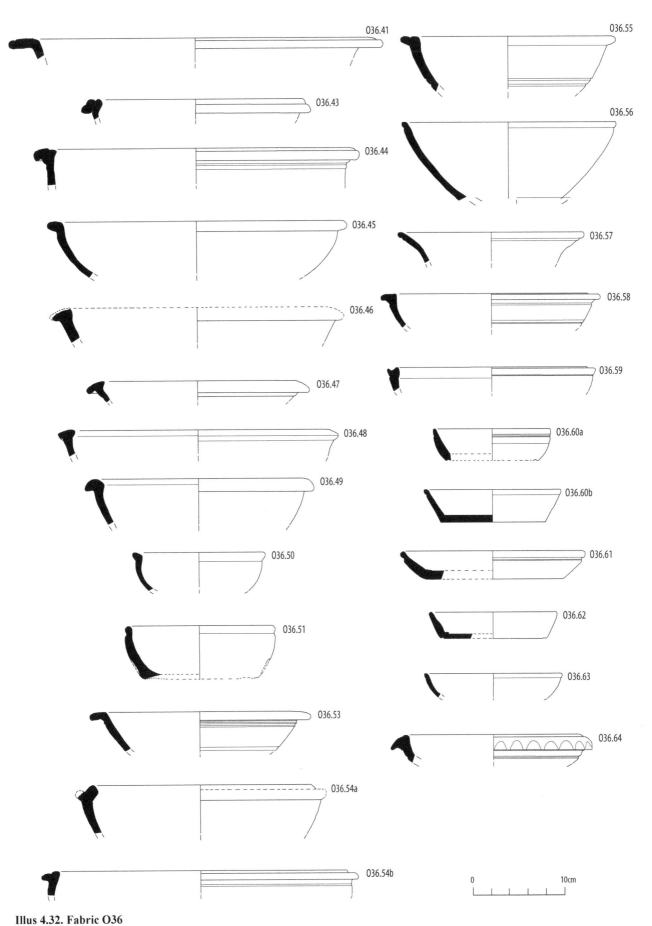

Illus 4.32. Fabric O36

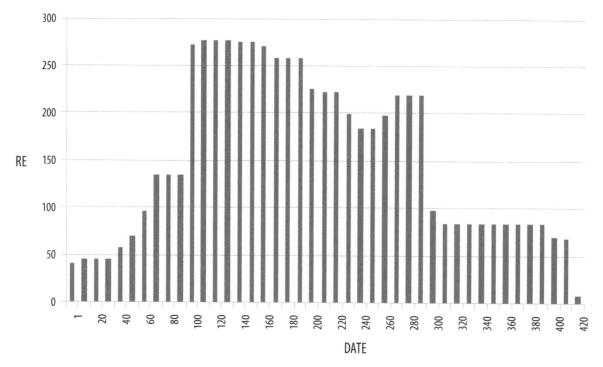

Illus 4.33. Date distribution of Fabric O36 vessels by RE

Fabric **O231** (Illus 4.35–4.37) is similar to O23 and will have been grouped with it in earlier reports using the Warwickshire Museum type series. It is generally pale yellow-orange in colour, sometimes with a pale grey core, with a 'soapy' texture, and with surfaces which have a finely micaceous appearance. There are occasional brown ironstone inclusions and sometimes some rounded siltstone. It presumably falls within the definition of Worcester fabric 12. This is the second most common Severn Valley Ware at Magistrates Court, representing 30.9% (MNR) of the oxidised wares.

The fabric appears from Phase 1 onwards at around 10% (MNR), but more than doubles in quantity between Phases 2 and 3 to 21.3% (MNR), maintaining this high level into Phase 4. The date distribution of forms (Illus 4.38) suggests the group originates in the 2nd century and rises to a peak in the later 3rd and levelling-off to a plateau through most of the 4th century.

The forms present are largely 2nd to 4th century. Again wide-mouthed jars are the largest category and bowls are the second largest (Table 4.17), although they are rather more common than amongst O36 (Table 4.16). Similarly tankards are also rather more common than in O36. The

next largest category are constricted-necked jars. Between the tankards, beakers, constricted-necked jars, jugs and flagons some 35.4% (MNR) of the entire assemblage in this fabric seems to be about handling liquids, presumably largely cider. It is also of note that a few lids are found in this group.

Fabric **O24** (Illus 4.39) is a Severn Valley Ware with some moderate sand temper and brown siltstone and some ironstone. It amounts to 0.5% (MNR) of the oxidised wares and there is little obvious chronological trend in the sherds from this assemblage. Forms in this fabric seem to be mainly 2nd- and 3rd-century. Forms appear to be broadly similar to other Severn Valley wares.

Fabric **O27** (Illus 4.40–4.41) is a Severn Valley ware which is visually very similar to products of the Great Buckman's Farm and Newlands kilns in the Malvern Link complex. It has common fairly fine white inclusions and is equivalent to Worcester fabric 12.6. It is the third most common fabric at Magistrates Court comprising 28.9% (MNR) of all the oxidised wares. The fabric appears in low levels, 7–9% (MNR) in Phases 1 and 2, rising threefold to a peak of 22.5% (MNR) in Phase 3, before falling back slightly in Phase 4. Analysis of the dating distribution of

Table 4.16. Functional analysis of vessels in fabric O36 (MNR and RE)

Flagon	Jug	Lagena	Constricted-necked jars	Storage jar	Wide-mouthed jar	Jar	Tankard	Beaker	Bowl	Dish	Other	N
0.6%	0.7%	0.6%	19.4%	3.3%	33.7%	4.1%	16.1%	0.1%	19.2%	1.9%	0.1%	676 rims
0.5%	1.2%	1.3%	28.4%	5.2%	25.4%	3.4%	15.9%	0.1%	13.0%	3.1%	0.1%	6,504% of rim

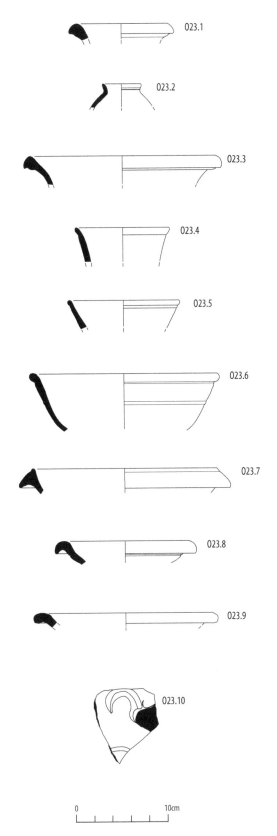

023.1

023.2

023.3

023.4

023.5

023.6

023.7

023.8

023.9

023.10

0   10cm

Illus 4.34. Fabric O23

the forms present (Illus 4.42) shows the same pattern, that the fabric is present through the 2nd century but is much more common in the 3rd and 4th centuries.

In terms of form (Table 4.18), as usual the most common class are wide-mouthed jars followed by bowls and

tankards. Again, as with O231, a large 37.8% (MNR) of these wares are liquid containers.

Fabric **O29** (Illus 4.43) is a minor Severn Valley Ware fabric with common-abundant moderate sand temper. It is probably equivalent to Worcester fabric 12.5. It comprised just 1.2% (MNR) of all the oxidised wares. Again the distribution by phase and date distribution of the vessels suggests a later Roman date. The vessels types present are dominated by 63.7% liquid containers, to an even greater degree than amongst vessels in fabric O231 (Table 4.19).

The other sandy Severn Valley Ware is **O291** (Illus 4.44), which has some moderate sand temper, but much less so than O29. The fabric would seem to equate with Worcester fabric 12.5. It is another minor fabric providing 1.3% (MNR) of all the recorded oxidised wares. It is present in small quantities in Phase 1, rising to 1.3% (MNR) by Phase 4. Forms present are most commonly wide-mouthed jars, followed by tankards and constricted-necked jars (Table 4.20). Bowls are very poorly represented and there are also a small quantity of lids. Again, liquid containers are far more common than tablewares.

Fabric **O35** (Illus 4.45) is a very minor Severn Valley ware with a fairly 'clean' break and a slightly 'soapy' texture, with occasional fine white inclusions up to 0.2mm, occasional sand, and common very fine silver and gold mica. It presumably falls within Worcester fabric 12. It represents 0.2% (MNR) of all the recorded oxidised wares. It occurs in Phases 1 to 3 and forms represented are four tankards of 2nd- to 3rd-century date.

Fabric **O53** (Illus 4.46) is another very minor Severn Valley ware which is hard, with common sand and some white stone inclusions. It represents only 0.1% (MNR) of all the recorded oxidised wares and only occurred residually in Phase 6.

Fabric **O55** (Illus 4.47) is a relatively minor Severn Valley ware with a grey core and orange-brown margins, soft and with a laminar texture, which has occasional brown ironstone and occasional limestone/chalk sand inclusions. Its surfaces appear micaceous. It represents 1.2% (MNR) of all the recorded oxidised wares. It is principally found in Phase 1 where it represents 4.4% (MNR) of pottery in that period, dwindling to 0.3% (MNR) by Phase 4. However, the forms represented include O55.2 which is a later 3rd to 4th century form so not all the material from later periods is residual. Wide-mouthed jars are the principal vessel type at 37.5% (MNR) followed by bowls and tankards. Dishes were relatively well-represented compared to other Severn Valley wares as were storage jars (Table 4.21).

Fabric **O91** is another very minor Severn Valley ware. It is handmade, with an orange-brown core, margins and surfaces, with common siltstone/clay pellet/grog angular inclusions and some organic temper voids. It was represented by a single body sherd.

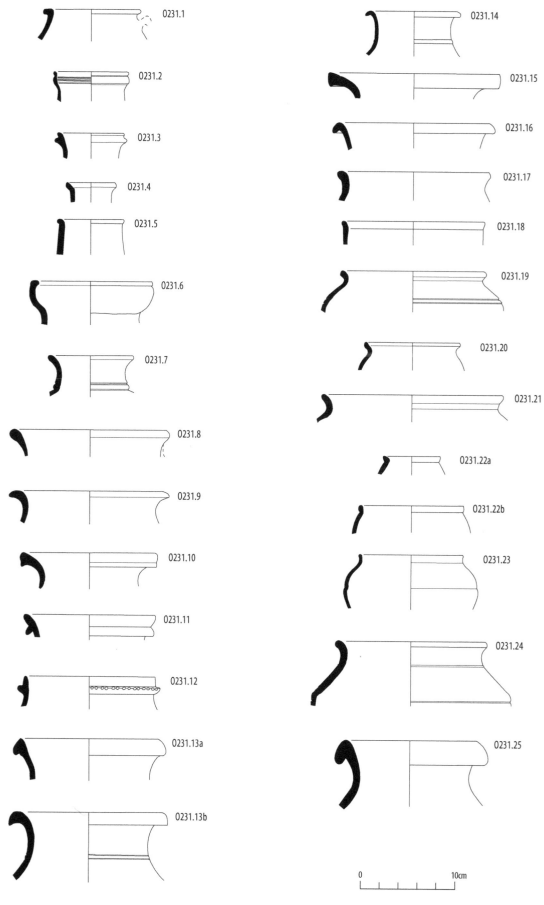

Illus 4.35. Fabric O231

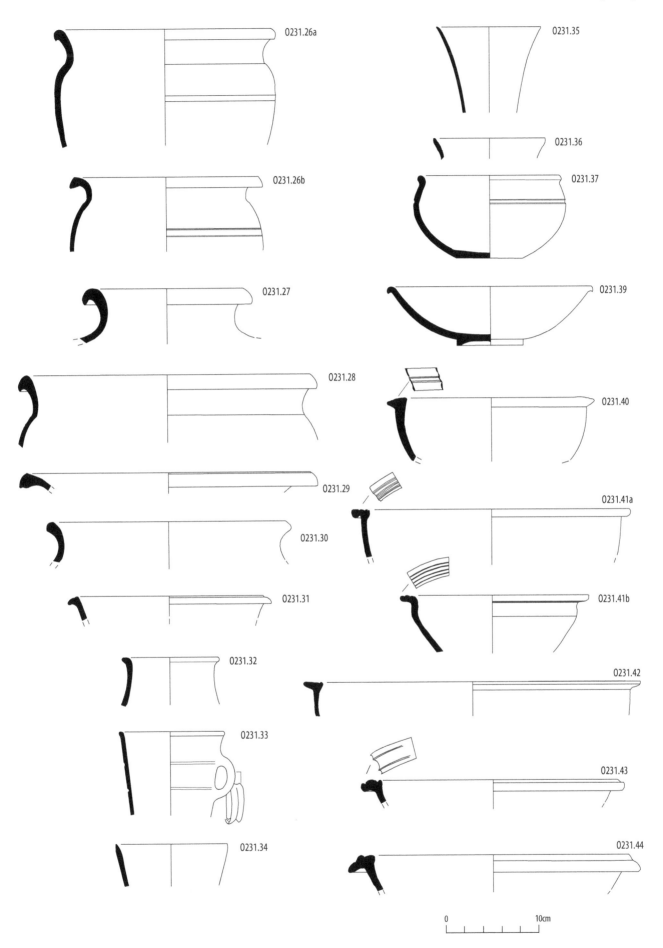

Illus 4.36. Fabric O231

0231.26a
0231.26b
0231.27
0231.28
0231.29
0231.30
0231.31
0231.32
0231.33
0231.34
0231.35
0231.36
0231.37
0231.39
0231.40
0231.41a
0231.41b
0231.42
0231.43
0231.44

0   10cm

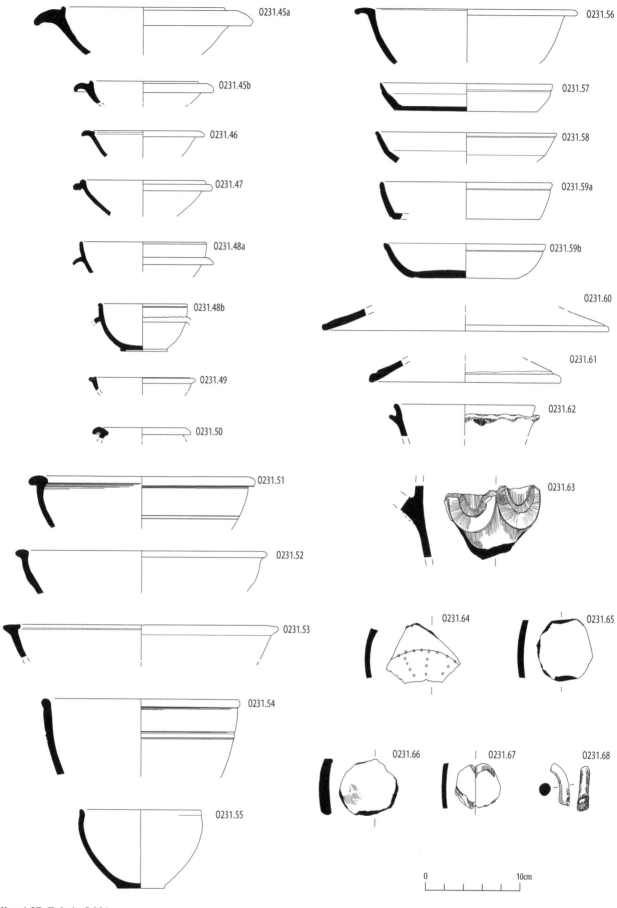

Illus 4.37. Fabric O231

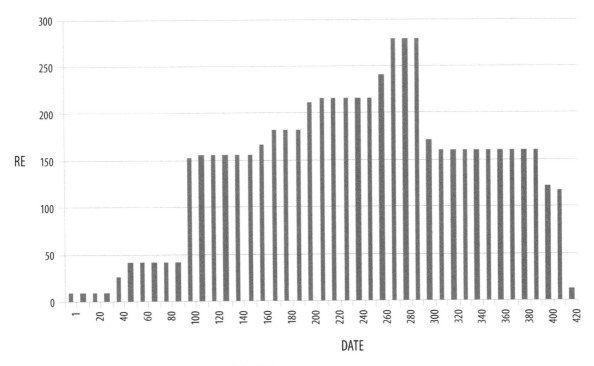

Illus 4.38. Date distribution of Fabric O231 vessels by RE

Table 4.17. Functional analysis of vessels in fabric O231 (MNR and RE)

Flagon	Jug	Lagena	Constricted-necked jars	Storage jar	Wide-mouthed jar	Jar	Tankard	Beaker	Bowl	Dish	Lid	Other	N
1.3%	0.8%	0	9.9%	1.2%	29.7%	6.2%	22.7%	0.7%	25.0%	1.5%	0.3%	0.5%	595 rims
2.6%	1.9%	0	15.0%	2.2%	21.7%	5.4%	21.4%	0.6%	23.9%	1.7%	0.2%	0.5%	5,662% of rim

Fabric **O57** is probably not a Severn Valley ware. It is a buff fabric with a buff core, margins and surfaces, with common angular black stone inclusions and occasional white inclusions. The only diagnostic sherd is a possible lamp top.

Fabric **O81** (Illus 4.48) is an oxidised ware, with common fine sand temper and some moderate red ironstone inclusions. It is probably from Whitehall Farm, Wiltshire (Cirencester fabric 96/98). It makes up just 0.1% (MNR) of all the oxidised wares. Though it occurs in Phases 3 and 4, it is probably residual there as the only form present, a flagon, is probably of later 1st- to early 2nd-century date.

When all the Severn Valley wares are analysed by function and phase (Table 4.22) there are few overall chronological trends. Flagons, jugs and lagenae are absent from Phase 1, but after that are generally present in small quantities. Constricted necked jars are consistently present in all periods. Storage jars are always a minor element of the assemblage but they do become consistently a little more common with time. Wide-mouthed jars consistently make up around a quarter of the assemblage. Other jars are weakly present reaching their high point in Phase 2.

Tankards are most common in Phase 1 making up over a third of the assemblage, thereafter declining to about a fifth. Beakers are a very minor element, which appear from Phase 3 onwards. Bowls provide around a fifth of the forms, there is a slight trend for these to increase in quantity in time. In contrast dishes are rare in Phases 1 and 2 and decline to less than 1% in Phase 3. Most of the Severn Valley ware dishes are Gallo-Belgic derived forms, and the increasing level of dishes with time seen on most Romano-British sites in greywares is not replicated amongst Severn Valley wares. Lids are rare and they only appear here in Phase 3, compared to greyware lids which tend to be early Roman. Vessels in the 'other' are all possible *tazze*, they appear rarely from Phase 2 onwards.

Comparison of Table 4.22 with figures from Alcester (Evans 1996, table 26) show some systematic differences in functional composition. Although the Alcester figures combine together storage jars and other jars, it is still quite clear that these principally medium-mouthed jars, are much more common at Alcester than at Worcester. Similarly tankards tend to be more common at Alcester, and in nearly all cases more common than wide-mouthed jars, whereas wide-mouthed jars are generally more common than tankards at Worcester, particularly in the later Roman period. These differences would seem to

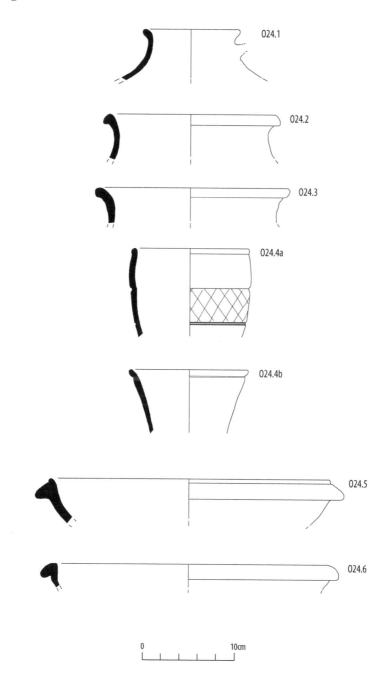

Illus 4.39. Fabric O24

reflect some contrast in the way these vessels were used at the core site of Worcester compared to the more marginal Alcester, near to the edge of the Severn Valley ware distribution.

Class Q, white-slipped oxidised wares, 0.4% (Nosh) (Illus 4.49–4.50)

Class Q wares, which are usually in the form of flagons, are found rarely in the assemblage. The class is slightly more common at Deansway, where it comprised 0.7% (Nosh) all of Worcester fabric 20, which is probably largely the equivalent to Q151.

Only two fabrics are worth mentioning, the first is **Q14** (Illus 4.49), South-Western White-Slipped Ware (Cirencester fabric 88). This is an oxidised fabric with common to abundant moderate to coarse sand and some moderate red ironstone. It is present only in Phases 1 and 2, and the only identifiable form represented was a single flagon of later 1st- to early 2nd-century date.

The second fabric, and the principal one in this class is **Q151** (Illus 4.50). It is a white-slipped oxidised fabric with a 'clean' fracture with occasional black ironstone inclusions and equates with Worcester fabric 20. Q151 amounted to 0.4% (Nosh) of the total recorded assemblage and represents 84% (Nosh) of all the white-slipped oxidised sherds from the site. The fabric has not been recorded in Warwickshire to date and it seems pretty certain it is a Severn Valley product. Forms represented are a tazza and five flagons.

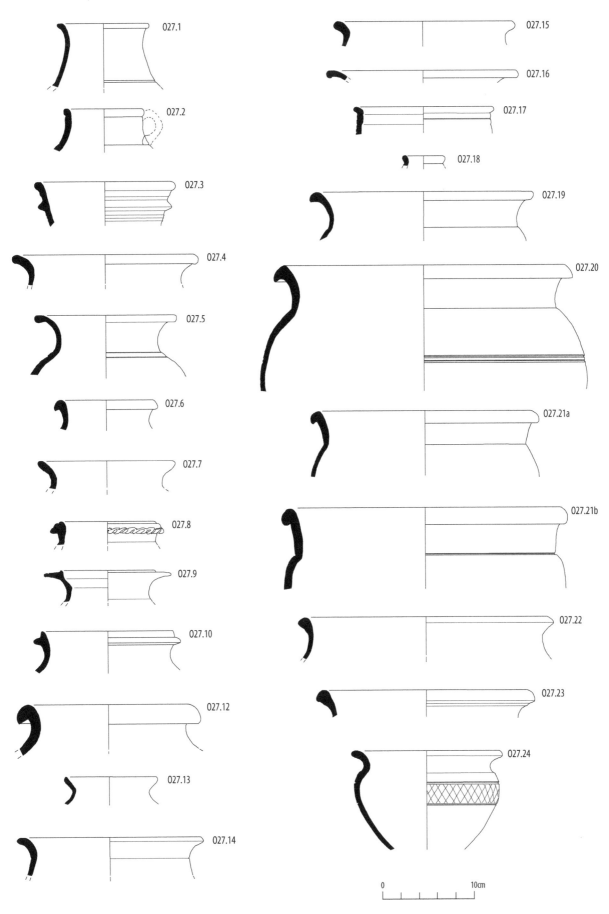

Illus 4.40. Fabric O27

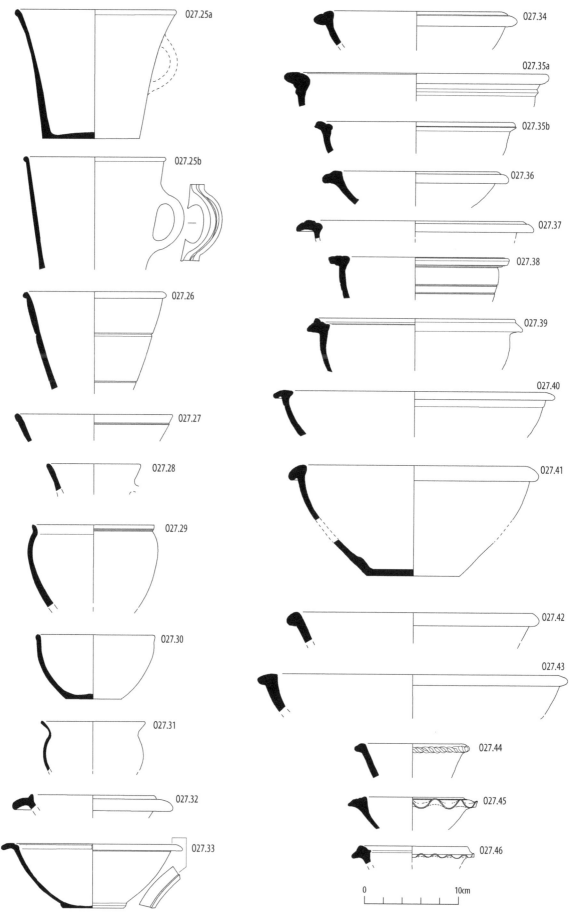

Illus 4.41. Fabric O27

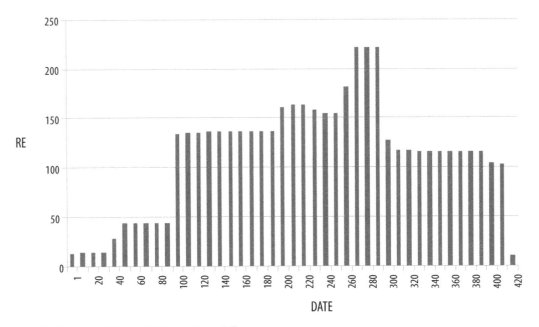

Illus 4.42. Date distribution of Fabric O27 vessels by RE

Table 4.18. Functional analysis of vessels in fabric O27 (MNR and RE)

Flagon	Jug	Lagena	Constricted-necked jars	Storage jar	Wide-mouthed jar	Jar	Tankard	Beaker	Bowl	Dish	Lid	Other	N
0	1.1%	0.2%	15.4%	3.5%	31.4%	4.4%	21.1%	0	21.6%	0.2%	0	1.1%	564 rims
0	1.7%	0.3%	21.5%	4.7%	25.7%	3.4%	20.0%	0	18.0%	0.0%	0	0.6%	4,872% of rim

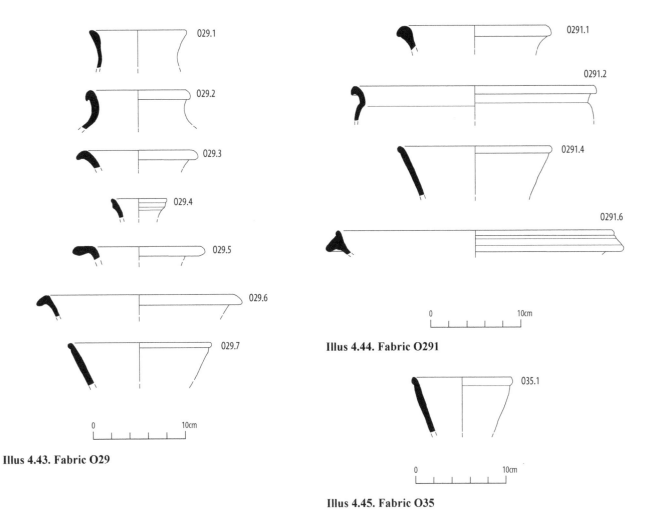

Illus 4.43. Fabric O29

Illus 4.44. Fabric O291

Illus 4.45. Fabric O35

Table 4.19. Functional analysis of vessels in fabric O29 (MNR and RE)

Flagon	Jug	Lagena	Constricted-necked jars	Storage jar	Wide-mouthed jar	Jar	Tankard	Beaker	Bowl	Dish	Lid	Other	N
0	0	0	45.5%	4.5%	18.2%	9.1%	18.2%	0	4.5%	0	0	0	22 rims
0	0	0	65.2%	2.5%	10.6%	5.0%	14.9%	0	1.9%	0	0	0	161% of rim

Table 4.20. Functional analysis of vessels in fabric O291 (MNR and RE)

Flagon	Jug	Lagena	Constricted-necked jars	Storage jar	Wide-mouthed jar	Jar	Tankard	Beaker	Bowl	Dish	Lid	Other	N
0	0	0	11.5%	0	42.3%	0	34.6%	0	7.7%	0	3.8%	0	26 rims
0	0	0	20.2%	0	38.8%	0	34.6%	0	3.7%	0	2.7%	0	188% of rim

Class R, reduced wares, 6.4% (Nosh) (Illus 4.51–4.57)

Reduced wares amount to 6.4% (Nosh) and 7.9% (Wt) of the total assemblage. Even for a site in the Severn Valley, this is a low level of reduced wares, and is substantially lower than levels at Deansway (Bryant and Evans 2004) where greywares total to 19.7% (Nosh) and 14.9% (Wt).

Analysis of phase distribution and typology of forms indicates that most of the greywares are of earlier 2nd-century date. There are quite a large number of rusticated jars and carinated bowls with everted rims. There are also a number of wastered sherds, and the fired clay included an object which would appear to be a kiln bar. Although there is no evidence that a greyware kiln existed on the site, it does seem likely that one was located in the vicinity, producing the common smooth greyware fabric, R813.

The coarse sandy greyware **R01/R11** (Illus 4.51), a reduced fabric with common fairly coarse sand temper, is a minor fabric representing 1.3% (MNR) of the greywares from the site. Two bowls and three jars occur in this group, probably of 2nd- to early 3rd-century date. The fabric is present from Phases 2 to 4. It is probably equivalent to Worcester fabric 15, which is present at similarly low levels at Deansway (Bryant and Evans 2004). The Deansway forms suggest a 1st to 2nd century date range (*ibid*, 259). The fabric is probably of North Warwickshire origin where production continues into the later 4th century although it ceases to reach Worcester earlier.

053.1

0   10cm

Illus 4.46. Fabric O53

Fabric **R18** (Illus 4.52) is a reduced fabric with occasional vegetable temper voids and some fine limestone/chalk sand. It represented 22.2% (MNR) of the greywares. The fabric is most common in Phase 1, falling off in Phase 2 and present in only small amounts in subsequent phases. All recorded forms in fabric R18 are of 1st- to 2nd-century date. The largest group are jars, closely followed by bowls (Table 4.24). Dishes and lids are very poorly represented. Storage jars are absent, as are liquid containers, with the exception of a few constricted-necked jars and cups/beakers. The fabric type sherd is from the north Warwickshire industry, but it is possible that some sherds of Severn Valley origin, which perhaps ought to be in R813 could have ended up in this group.

Fabric **R31** is represented by just seven sherds, none of which are rims. It is a hand-made reduced ware with common vegetable voids. It is found across the Severn Valley region from Ariconium to Alcester and seems to be largely 1st-century in date and predominantly pre-Flavian. In this assemblage it only appears residually in Phases 2 and 4.

Fabric **R32** (Illus 4.53) is a reduced fabric with common small vegetable voids equivalent to Worcester fabric 12.3. It represents 12.7% (MNR) of the greywares. It is found in all phases, peaking in Phase 2. Forms are of later 1st- to 2nd-century date, and it seems likely the fabric was residual on the site from Phase 3 onwards. The dating evidence from Deansway (Bryant and Evans 2004, 254–5) seems to be similar. As might be expected with a greyware the largest category are medium-mouthed jars, followed by bowls (Table 4.25). Also present are a few dishes and a few constricted-necked jars and jugs. Bryant and Evans (2004) suggest a local origin for this fabric group, and that will not be questioned here, but there is also an identical fabric to this with a North Warwickshire origin, found, for example, frequently at Princethorpe (Cutler and Evans 1998).

A minor reduced ware in this assemblage is **R341** (Illus 4.54), a reduced fabric with a mid-grey core and dark grey

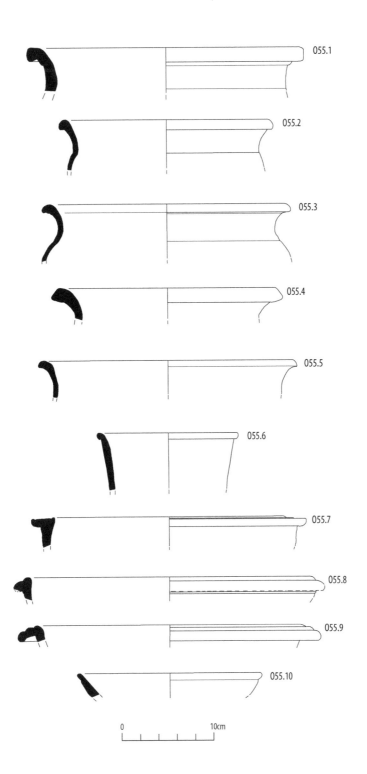

055.1

055.2

055.3

055.4

055.5

055.6

055.7

055.8

055.9

055.10

0   10cm

Illus 4.47. Fabric O55

surfaces, with abundant sand temper. This only amounted to 0.5% (MNR) of the greywares from the site. It may be related to the R01/R11 group. Forms represented are a bowl and a lid. The fabric occurs only in Phase 4 and the bowl, a developed and beaded flanged bowl, must be of later 3rd- to 4th-century date.

Another minor reduced ware is **R41** (Illus 4.55), with some moderate sand temper and occasional brown moderate ironstone. This provides 1.3% (MNR) of all the recorded greywares. The fabric occurs in Phases 2 to 4, but only in Phase 4 are rim sherds found. However, all the forms are Hadrianic-Antonine and the fabric is clearly residual

in Phases 3 and 4. Forms represented are a flange rimmed bowl and four jars.

Fabric **R813** (Illus 4.56–4.57) is the major reduced ware in the assemblage, making up 62.0% (MNR) of all the recorded greywares. It is a smooth greyware with abundant very fine sand temper and is probably equivalent to Worcester fabric 12.1. The fabric appears first in Phase 1 at 13.2% (MNR), peaking in Phase 2 at 19.0% (MNR) before falling off in subsequent phases. All the forms are of later 1st- to 2nd-century date and there is little doubt the fabric is residual after Phase 2. This contrasts with Deansway where Worcester fabric

Table 4.21. Functional analysis of vessels in fabric O55 (MNR and RE)

Flagon	Jug	Lagena	Constricted-necked jars	Storage jar	Wide-mouthed jar	Jar	Tankard	Beaker	Bowl	Dish	Lid	Other	N
0	0	0	0	8.3%	37.5%	0	12.5%	0	29.2%	12.5%	0	0	24 rims
0	0	0	0	10.6%	44.9%	0	15.0%	0	20.8%	8.7%	0	0	207% of rim

Table 4.22. Functional analysis of Severn Valley wares by phase (MNR and RE)

Period	Flagon	Jug	Lagena	Constricted-necked jars	Storage jar	Wide-mouthed jar	Jar	Tankard	Beaker	Bowl	Dish	Lid	Other	N
1	0	0	0	15.3%	1.5%	23.4%	2.9%	35.0%	0	18.3%	3.7%	0	0	137 rims
1	0	0	0	18.2%	1.0%	21.2%	3.2%	31.9%	0	14.3%	4.2%	0	0	2,160% of rim
2	0.9%	1.4	0.9%	22.9%	0.9%	22.9%	7.3%	23.4%	0	14.2%	4.6%	0	0.5%	218 rims
2	1.4%	2.1%	1.7%	33.0%	2.8%	19.0%	4.7%	20.3%	0	9.7%	4.9%	0	0.2%	2,713% of rim
3	0.6%	1.0%	0.2%	13.7%	3.2%	34.6%	4.6%	17.5%	0.2%	23.6%	0.6%	0.1%	0.2%	1,251 rims
3	1.2%	1.6%	0.4%	20.9%	5.3%	26.8%	3.8%	15.3%	0.3%	20.0%	0.7%	0.1%	0.1%	9,748% of rim
4	0.9%	0.9%	0	16.1%	2.8%	28.6%	3.7%	22.1%	0.5%	20.3%	1.4%	0	2.8%	217 rims
4	0.8%	3.0%	0	20.9%	3.7%	22.0%	3.5%	22.6%	5	405	17	0	39	2,090% of rim

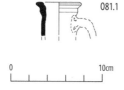

O81.1

0   10cm

Illus 4.48. Fabric O81

Q14.1

0   10cm

Illus 4.49. Fabric Q14

Table 4.23. Relative occurrence of Greyware fabrics amongst all greywares.

Fabric	% MNR	% RE
R01	1.3%	1.3%
R18	22.2%	25.0%
R31	Present	Present
R32	12.7%	11.9%
R341	0.5%	0.3%
R41	1.3%	1.0%
R46	Present	Present
R52	Present	Present
R55	Present	Present
R59	Present	Present
R65	Present	Present
R813	62.0%	60.5%
N	379 rims	4626%

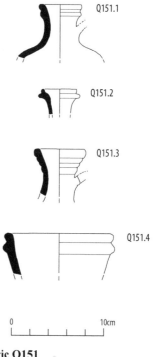

Q151.1

Q151.2

Q151.3

Q151.4

0   10cm

Illus 4.50. Fabric Q151

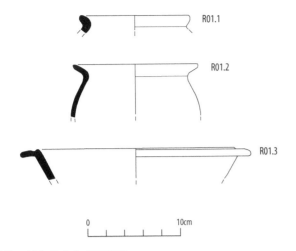

R01.1

R01.2

R01.3

0   10cm

Illus 4.51. Fabric R01/R11

12.1 comprises 31% (Nosh) of the greywares (Bryant and Evans 2004).

It should be noted that none of the numerous rustic ware jars in R813 are of the 'waisted' type (Evans 1994, fig 67A). This form is common in Warwickshire but is absent outside the West Midlands and seems to be a distinct regional form. The absence in fabric R813 tends to suggest this form was not produced in Worcester. However, waisted rustic ware jar forms were found in Worcester at Deansway (Bryant and Evans 2004, fig 162, no 2 in fabric 14, and fig 159, no 1 in fabric 12.3). Evans' (1994, fig 67A) map shows the form was made at Tiddington and Lapworth, and Worcester is on the south-west edge of the distribution. It seems likely that there are few examples both here and at Gloucester representing imports from northern Warwickshire.

Surprisingly the most common vessel type is the bowl, making up half the assemblage, followed by other jars (Table 4.26). Other forms, such as dishes, cups/beakers and flagons are rare. Greywares are usually predominantly jars and it is unusual for a tableware type to be the most common form. The most common bowl forms are: R813.23, a Dr 37 copy bowl, with 42 examples; and R813.31, a carinated bowl with an outcurving rim and groove on the girth, with 41 examples. R813.23 would appear to be 2nd-century and R813.31 later 1st to early 2nd century. Amongst the jars the most common forms are: R813.7 with a straight, everted rim, often with rusticated decoration, with 20 examples; and R813.8, a jar with a straight, everted rim with lid-seating groove, with 19 examples. Both are of later 1st to mid-2nd-century date.

Class S, samian wares, 4.8% (Nosh) (Illus 4.58–4.63)

Margaret Ward with contribution by Brenda Dickinson (report first submitted in 2003)

Forms, products and condition

There was a total of 1864 samian sherds, representing a maximum of 1481 vessels. The stamped and decorated vessels (catalogued in Appendix 3; illustrated in Illus 4.58-4.60) are treated separately here under their respective places of production. Most of the forms represented were the standard dish, cup and bowl forms. Discounting the indeterminate sherds, 52% of the assemblage consisted of dishes (both shallow and deep), 27% comprised moulded bowls and 12% were cups (Illus 4.61). Since data gathered by means of differing statistical methods is not always comparable (Ward 2012, 23-24), comparisons made below derive from the writer's database (Ward 2011).

Some forms were relatively unusual, such as one instance of the dish form 15/31, one or possibly two rouletted bowls of form 30R from Lezoux (see SD1) and a small bowl of late East Gaulish form Ludowici SMb/SMc from Trier, lacking its decoration en barbotine, but dated to the late 2nd or, probably, early 3rd century. In addition, there was an Antonine vessel found in G42 (Phase 3) whose pedestalled foot suggests a beaker of form 72. There was also at least one enclosed vessel of uncertain form but apparently a very large vessel, whether a jar, jug or flagon. With a footring of diameter 125mm, then (if a jar) it would have been much larger than the Cornhill vase which is itself an unusually large specimen of form 72 (footring diameter *c* 105mm; see Oswald and Pryce 1920, pl 81.1). The 50 sherds belonging to one vessel were scattered through eight contexts in Phases 3, 4, 5, 6 and 0 (see Appendix 5). It is uncertain whether a further three sherds from a high-necked vessel belonged to the same jar or a very large beaker; they were recovered from G2 (Phase 1) with further sherds in unphased context C2376. The vessel or, more likely, vessels represented by these 53 sherds were manufactured most probably in the second half of the 2nd century. That they were dispersed through so many contexts could suggest that numerous other sherds from rather less distinctive vessels belong to a far smaller number of vessels than is tabulated here.

Two other sherds found in Phase 3 are so rare a find that, recovered as they both were from G42, they may well represent the same vessel. Their ware is the so-called 'black samian' produced in a standard samian fabric

Table 4.24. Functional analysis of vessels in fabric R18 (MNR and RE)

8.465 mm	Jug	Lagena	Constricted-necked jars	Storage jar	Wide-mouthed jar	Jar	Tankard	Beaker/ cup	Bowl	Dish	Lid	Other	N
0	0	0	1.2%	0	0	47.0%	0	1.2%	44.6%	2.4%	3.6%	0	83 rims
0	0	0	5.6%	0	0	48.1%	0	1.0%	39.6%	1.0%	2.9%	0	1065% of rim

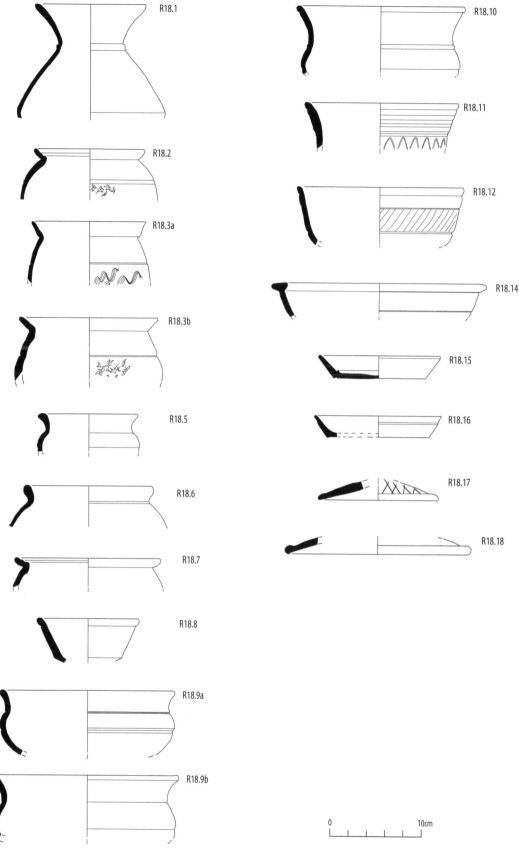

Illus 4.52. Fabric R18

with dark surfaces (see Simpson 1957 and 1973; Ward, forthcoming a), which came from the same kilns as Central Gaulish black-slipped ware (Hartley 1972a, 254; Greene 1978, 19). The decoration here included an *appliqué* mask.

The form was a small jar, probably the two-handled form Déchelette 74 (SD43, Illus 4.60). One example with a very similar mask was found at Chichester and other examples of this type have been found at such sites as Silchester,

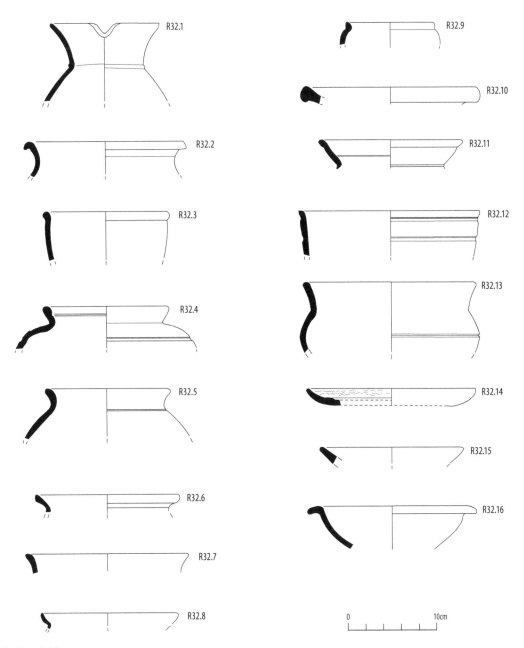

Illus 4.53. Fabric R32

Table 4.25. Functional analysis of vessels in fabric R32 (MNR and RE)

Flagon	Jug	Lagena	Constricted-necked jars	Storage jar	Wide-mouthed jar	Jar	Tankard	Beaker/cup	Bowl	Dish	Lid	Other	N
0	2.1%	0	2.1%	0	4.3%	55.3%	0	0	29.8%	6.4%	0	0	47 rims
0	8.4%	0	2.0%	0	1.7%	60.8%	0	0	19.7%	7.4%	0	0	538% of rim

Illus 4.54. Fabric R341

Illus 4.55. Fabric R41

89

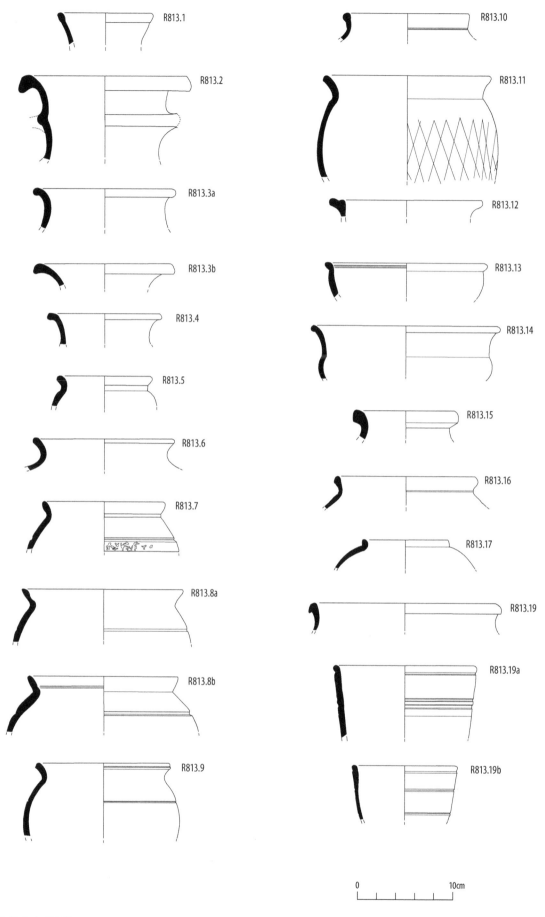

Illus 4.56. Fabric R813

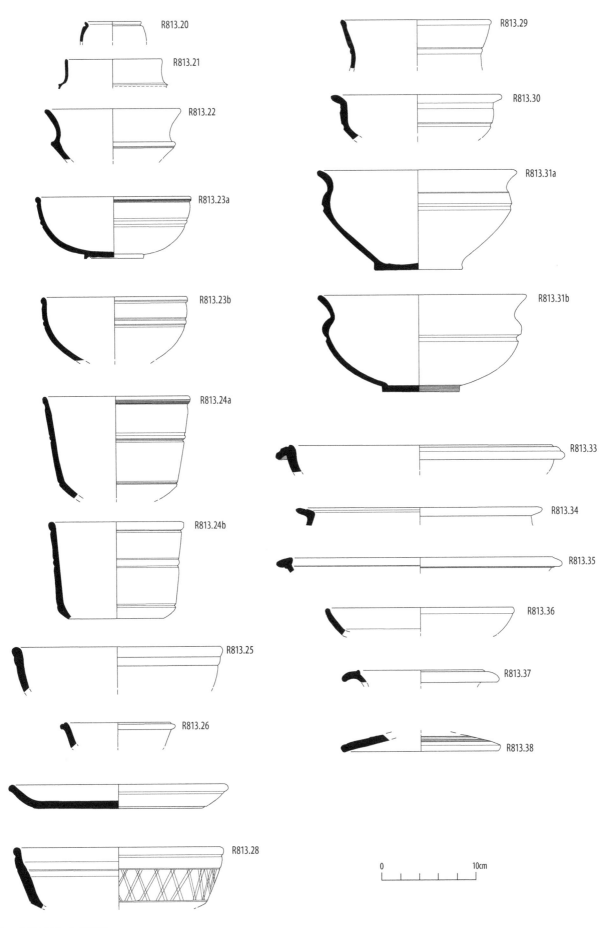

Illus 4.57. Fabric R813

Table 4.26. Functional analysis of vessels in fabric R813 (MNR and RE)

Flagon	Jug	Lagena	Constricted-necked jars	Storage jar	Wide-mouthed jar	Jar	Tankard	Beaker/cup	Bowl	Dish	Lid	Other	N
0	0.4%	0.4%	1.7%	0	0.4%	38.3%	0.9%	2.1%	51.5%	3.0%	1.3%	0	235 rims
0	0.4%	3.6%	2.3%	0	0.2%	40.7%	1.0%	2.3%	38.1%	1.3%	1.1%	0	2,799% of rim

Alchester, York, Caerleon and Verulamium. Black samian was produced by a limited range of Central Gaulish potters including Libertus (who was active in the Trajanic-Hadrianic period), Butrio (active from the Trajanic to the early Antonine period), and Paternus iii and Paternus v (working largely in the earlier and mid-Antonine periods, respectively). The Worcester sherds were produced at Lezoux at some point in the Antonine period, perhaps in the range AD 150-185, when Paternus v was active; alternatively, it could have been made by one of his successors. A single sherd from a Central Gaulish 'black samian' beaker, of 2nd-century date, was recorded at the neighbouring Police Station excavation (Edwards et al 2002, 126). It may represent the same vessel, but was not available for direct comparison. It may seem strange that such unusual pottery as this 'black samian' ware should be found in an assemblage which was not of the highest quality. However, black samian products are rarely found in specifically military contexts (Ward, forthcoming a).

More than 26% of the total consisted of sherds whose form was indeterminate. Many more could be assigned only to a general class of vessel (dish, bowl, etc). Although many of the sherds were battered and abraded, their fabrics survived in a relatively good state of preservation. Only 15 vessels showed signs of staining and there was little evidence of chemical attack from the soil. Only one piece, in G1001 (Phase 6), was badly eroded. Around 6% of the assemblage was burnt, a small proportion which comprised vessels ranging across all dates of samian production.

Two vessels survived in complete profile: SS9; and another vessel from G42 (Phase 3). The remains of seven other vessels (including SS27) presented almost complete profiles; these were spread across all phases. All nine of these vessels had been worn in use and one may display an unsuccessful attempt at repair-work (SR42).

South Gaulish wares

Only 3.1% of the samian collection, comprising 46 vessels, were produced in the factories of South Gaul (Table 4.27 and Illus 4.62). The South Gaulish samian ware, both decorated and plain, was little more than a collection of scraps. There were no pre-Flavian forms present and no moulded bowls of form 29 (which went out of production in the late 80s in South Gaul). There were no instances of form 15/17. There were only four vessels which could be dated as early as *c* AD 70–90; three of these were fragments of moulded bowls. Most of the samian ware in this collection was dated loosely in the range *c* AD 70–110

and much of it will have been produced after *c* AD 80. The sole stamp by a South Gaulish potter was on form 18 by L. Ter- Secundus, dated *c* AD 75–100 (SS20). This large piece, the worn and burnt footring of the dish, was recovered from a Phase 2 ditch fill.

In general, the South Gaulish assemblage on this site may be considered to represent rubbish deposition. At least two vessels represented 2nd-century production in South Gaul, probably originating at Montans in the period *c* AD 110–145/150. One was a tiny fragment found in a G120 (Phase 2) post-hole fill. The other, found in G1002 (Phase 6), represented a moulded bowl from Montans bearing a characteristic split-tongued ovolo in the style of Chresimus and Malcio (SD37, Illus 4.59). Second century Montans ware has been recorded at various sites, including Alcester where a bowl in Malcio i's style was found in a pit fill dated *c* AD 145–155 (Hartley et al 1994, 106, no 262), and at northern sites, including Chester, Wilderspool, Ribchester, Walton-le-dale, as well as in Scotland (Hartley 1972b, appendix 1; Ward 2015, 139–44). In contrast, no contemporary products of Banassac were noted in the Magistrates Court assemblage, although recorded at Alcester (Hartley et al 1994, 93); these are, however, always more rarely found in Britain (Ward 2015, 144–8).

Central Gaulish ware

As much as 94.3% of the samian assemblage (1396 vessels) were produced in Central Gaul, at both Les Martres-de-Veyre and Lezoux (Table 4.27 and Illus 4.62). All phases on this site included vessels produced in the 2nd century in Central Gaul. Only 3% of the collection were considered likely to have been produced at Les Martres-de-Veyre, representing perhaps 45 vessels. Around 30 of these were moulded bowls of form 37, of which 22 bore recognisable fragments of decoration. Very few were attributable to specific potters, but best represented were the styles of Drusus i (Potter X-3) (eg SD3, Illus 4.58) and X-9 (eg SD13, Illus 4.58). While most potters at Les Martres-de-Veyre, like Drusus i, were active in the period *c* AD 100–120/125, some worked later. One (Potter X-9) may have continued into the later Hadrianic period and indeed at Lezoux also. This style appears to have been represented by three or four bowls in this Worcester collection (eg SD8 and SD 13, Illus 4.58); all were found in Phase 2 contexts. One or two (fragments only and not catalogued here) could have been Lezoux products. The British distribution of X-9's products may prove revealing. Bowls in X-9 style and particularly those of Lezoux appearance have been

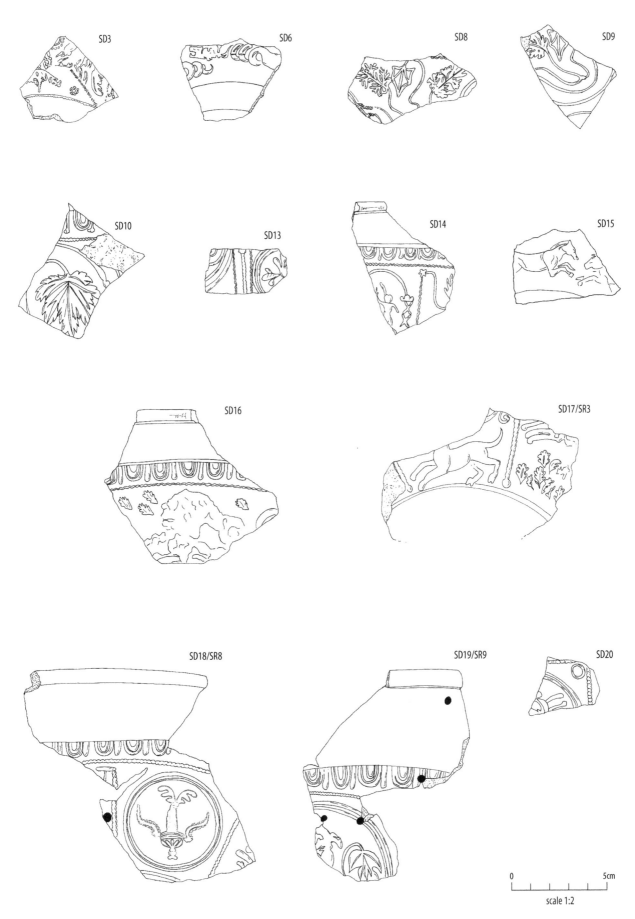

Illus 4.58. Samian ware

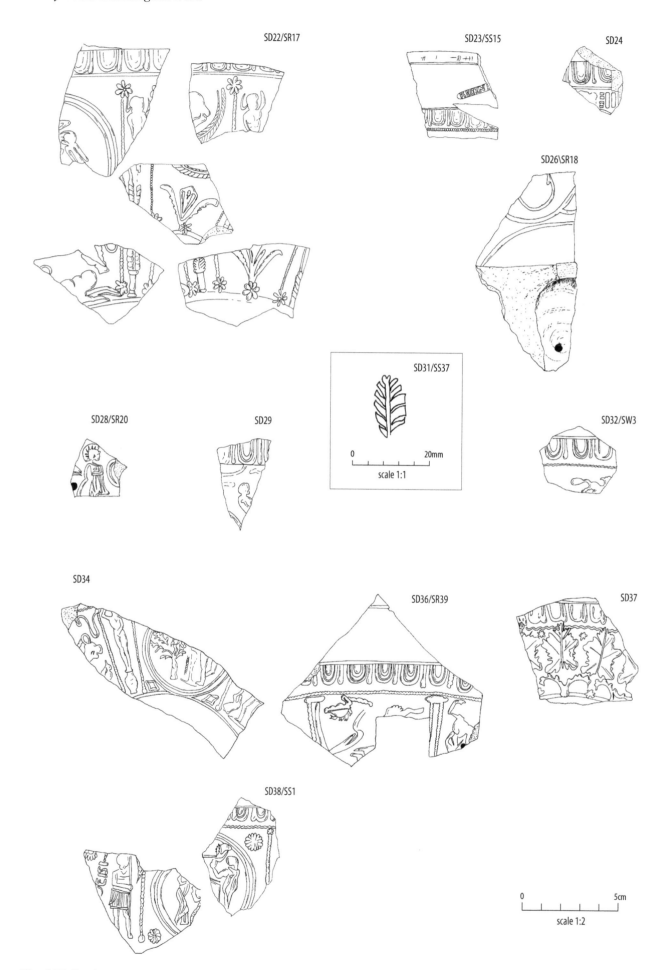

Illus 4.59. Samian ware

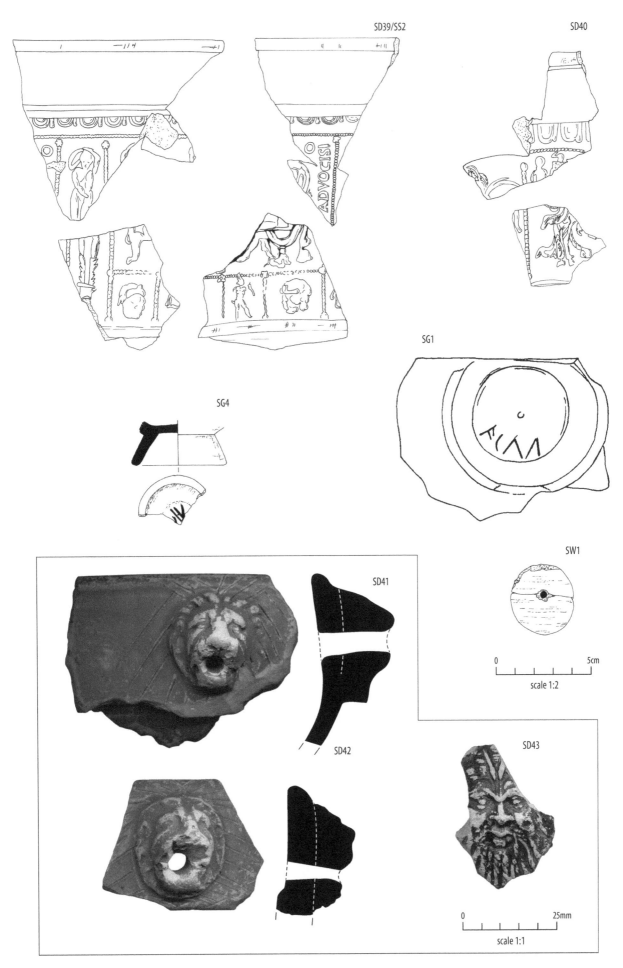

Illus 4.60. Samian ware

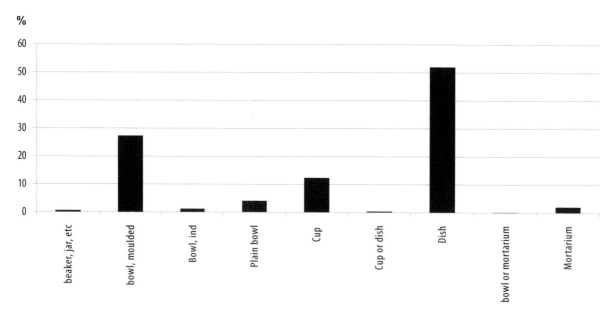

Illus 4.61. Samian types by max vessel count, excluding indeterminate sherds

Table 4.27. Samian forms and fabrics by max vessel count

Form	SG	CG	EG	Total
15/31		1		1
18	4			4
18 or 18/31	1			1
18/31	2	24		26
18/31 or 18/31R		9		9
18/31 or 31		31		31
18/31R	1	36		37
18/31R or 31R		100		100
18R	4			4
27	3	6		9
30	1	28		29
30 or 37		6		6
30R		2		2
31		103		103
31 or 31R		44		44
31R		115		115
31R group			16	16
32		4	3	7
33		101		101
33a		1		1
35		3		3
35 or 36		3		3
36		13		13
37	14	245		259
37 or 30		2		2
38		32		32

Form	SG	CG	EG	Total
38 or 44		1		1
40		2		2
43		7		7
43 or Curle 21		1		1
44		3		3
45		16		16
46		3		3
72		1		1
74		2		2
79		21	1	22
79 or 79R		1		1
79 or 80		1		1
79R		10		10
80		3		3
81		6		6
bowl		12		12
cup		4		4
Curle 15		6		6
Curle 21		2		2
dish		19	4	23
enclosed		2		2
indeterminate	16	359	13	388
jar, etc		2		2
O and P 1920, pl 55.13		2		2
SMb/SMc			1	1
Tb			1	1
Tg		1		1
Total	46	1396	39	1481

recorded in northern England at industrial or industrially related military locations and/or at sites with bath-houses (Ward, forthcoming a). One Worcester bowl (SD28, Illus 4.59) may represent Cettus, who worked late at Les Martres-de-Veyre (*c* AD 130–160 and perhaps 135–155). Amongst the stamped samian, there were two or three vessels which were, or could have been, produced at Les Martres-de-Veyre. One of these was by the Trajanic potter Nicephor i (SS11) and one was a late-Hadrianic or early-Antonine product of Suobnus (SS19). Thirdly, a repaired bowl could have been a Les Martres product of Secundinus ii (SS37, Illus 4.59), but as with other of his products, it is unclear from the fabric alone whether it was produced at Les Martres-de-Veyre or at Lezoux; at any rate, it will have been produced at some point in the range *c* AD 110–145. Also represented amongst the stamped plainware was Gnatus ii, active AD 125–155, who began work at Les Martres-de-Veyre. The Worcester stamp (SS9) represents his die 1a, used typically at Les Martres and found in Scotland (at Castledykes, Camelon and Newstead). The Worcester dish does not resemble Les Martres products, but was made in a highly micaceous buff fabric with poor, yellowish-orange surfaces, similar to some 'pre-export' products of Lezoux. This potter's Lezoux phase is thought to have started by AD 140 or very soon after (Hartley and Dickinson 2009, 214) and the Worcester dish may be amongst those products which Hartley (pers comm, 1978) identified as characteristic of the kilns in Lezoux's Chantier Audouart (Ward forthcoming a).

Of the 32 stamped vessels catalogued in Appendix 3, the 30 Central Gaulish products included one mould-signature, almost certainly by Criciro v (SS35), and a graffito X under the base of another bowl of form 37 which had been inscribed in the mould, possibly after firing (SS36). In all, 22 vessels could be attributed to specific potters. Another 14 stamps were not attributable (SS21-34) and one moulded bowl was stamped under its base with a leaf, which was partially impressed, but otherwise appears similarly on a Verulamium bowl in the style of Secundinus ii (SS37, Illus 4.59). Nineteen of the stamps were on dish forms (including one South Gaulish and one East Gaulish), eight were on cups and one was perhaps a plain bowl of form 38. The quantity of moulded bowls bearing potters' names was remarkably large: apart from SS35-37, five or six moulded bowls were stamped. Amongst the intra-decorative items, one fragment (SS33) may represent a decorative motif rather than a stamp. Two form 37s had been stamped on the rim by their bowl-makers: the first (Flo-Albinus, active AD 150–180) is known to have stamped bowls produced from moulds in the style of Laxtucissa and Paternus v (SS8). The second, Reginus iv, was active in much the same date-range, but stamping bowls produced from moulds in the styles of such potters as Advocisus and Clemens iii (SS15, SD23, Illus 4.59). Brenda Dickinson notes that one such stamped bowl (in the style of Clemens iii) has been recorded previously at Worcester. At the Magistrates Court site, two bowls of form 30 and one of form 37 were stamped intra-decoratively by Advocisus (SS1, Illus 4.59,

SS2, Illus 4.60) and Paternus v (SS12) respectively. Thus, five of the (six?) stamped bowls were made by, or had connections with, the factories of Paternus v (AD 150–185) and Advocisus (AD 160–200).

Of the samian assemblage excluding unidentified forms, 27% comprised moulded bowls (Tables 4.27–28). This may be contrasted with smaller proportions of those vessels by identified form, found at rural sites (20%) or smaller civil centres (17%) recorded by Willis (2005, tables 35 and 42): 16% was recorded by the present writer at Alcester (Ward 1996, 75). The proportion of 27% in this Worcester collection may be contrasted with the military and extramural data recorded by Willis (30% and 35%, respectively). The proportion at Worcester should also be compared with assemblages from industrial sites in the military north (Ward 2011, 84–7; 2016, 91–3). While some such excavations remain unpublished, figures range from 23% at Prestatyn, to 39–56% at various Middlewich sites (cf Ward 2008b, 138; and 2016, 91). Further statistical analysis of samian assemblages from Roman industrial sites further south is advocated. The poor quality of many products amongst this Worcester assemblage might be thought to indicate low status for this site; it seems likely that the inferior samian vessels (some, shoddy products) may not have been in the public eye. Significant in this respect may be six small bowls of form 37, perhaps the work of apprentices learning their craft in the larger factories (cf Ward 2018, 232); four may represent Cinnamus or an associate. Found in Phase 2, one small bowl displays the variation of ovolo B231 which is known on small bowls of Cinnamus with scroll compositions, as here (SD10, Illus 4.58). Another (SD16, Illus 4.58) was decorated in the (early) Cerialis ii-Cinnamus ii style. Further sherds, found in G42 (Phase 3), may represent another small bowl in this style. Another bowl (SD18, Illus 4.58) may be the work of an apprentice of Cinnamus using his standard ovolo, Rogers B143; it was recovered, repaired, from contexts in Phases 3 and 4. Two fragments from small bowls dated *c* AD 120–150, found in G41 (Phase 3-4) and G19 (Phase 3), were unidentifiable. Further north, small bowls of Hadrianic to early Antonine date which were substantially complete were found in Carlisle and in the Lancaster *vicus* (Brenda Dickinson, pers comm). At Walton-le-dale in Lancashire, Felicity Wild (pers comm) recorded as many as ten small bowls of form 37 from Central Gaul. Such items, especially if apprentice work, may have been available on the market at a lower price. This is, however, mere speculation. In unusual contexts, small bowls may have served unusual purposes: ten small bowls were found in Chester's amphitheatre (Ward 2018, 231–2).

On the evidence of both decoration and potters' stamps, there was considerable representation of Lezoux potters working in the Hadrianic to early Antonine period (Table 4.28 and Illus 4.63). Bowls of this period included several from the Sacer-Attianus group and Pugnus (early style). A similar picture is painted by the Lezoux stamps, of which five were produced in the Hadrianic to early Antonine

Table 4.28. Potters represented by moulded decoration

Period	Pottery	Vessels
Trajanic	Drusus i (X–3)	1
	Drusus i (X–3) or Igocatus	1
	X–13	1
Trajanic–Hadrianic	X–13	1
	Secundinus ii	1
	X–9	3
Hadrianic to early Antonine	X–9 or Attianus ii	1
	Sacer i/Attianus ii group	3
	Drusus ii?	1
	Pugnus (early style)	4
	Docilis i?	2
	Cettus?	1
	Criciro v	1
	Cerialis ii/Cinnamus ii group	5
Early to mid-Antonine	P–15	1
	Cinnamus ii (early or standard style)	3
	Cinnamus ii (standard styles)	6
	Pugnus-Secundus v	1
	Divixtus ii	2
	Divixtus ii or Advocisus	3
Mid to late Antonine	Advocisus	2
	Laxtucissa or Paternus v...	1
	Iullinus or Mercator iv	1
	Mercator iv	1
	Paternus v	2
	Doeccus i (Doveccus)	2
	Belsa (Arvernicus)?	1
Total		51

Of the 22 vessels stamped by identifiable potters, 14 were of Antonine origin. Eleven were produced after *c* AD 150, six of them after *c* AD 160. Indeed, up to 300 vessels (around 20% of the entire samian assemblage) were produced after *c* AD 160 (see Illus 4.62). A total of 27% of the potters' stamps and 20–25% of the decorated bowls attributable to specific potters were produced in this period (see Illus 4.63). In addition, amongst the plain ware, the numerous examples of the deep dish form 31R are typical of sites under steady occupation. Other late 2nd-century vessels included one dish stamped by Sextus v (SS17). Work by the prolific potter Casurius ii was not evident, but there were multiple bowls stamped by or in the style of his contemporaries such as Paternus v (3–4 bowls), Advocisus (2–5 bowls, including two stamped form 30s, SS1, Illus 4.59 and SS2, Illus 4.60), Mercator iv (1–2 bowls), Doeccus i (two bowls, including that in Phase 3, Illus 4.60) and, probably, Belsa (SD17, Illus 4.58). The activity of Doeccus and Belsa is currently dated no earlier than AD 170–200. It is suspected that Doeccus moulds were used up to *c* 240 (Richard Delage pers comm; Ward forthcoming c). Of the 33 vessels datable firmly after AD 170, there were 23 mortaria (2.1% of identifiable forms), all of them Central Gaulish and at least 16 representing form 45: at Lezoux, mortaria became popular after *c* AD 170 at the very earliest. Two of this form's *appliqué* lion-headed spouts (SD41, SD42, Illus 4.60), both poorly stratified, were produced no earlier than *c* AD 170–200 and perhaps some years later than this conventional British dating. Such specimens could have been produced in the late 2nd or early 3rd century (see Bird 1986, 178–81: Ward 2008a, 172, 178, 189; Ward, forthcoming c).

East Gaulish ware

Only 2.6% of the samian wares (39 vessels) originated in East Gaul (Table 4.27 and Illus 4.62), their distribution being concentrated in Phase 3. Given the greatly divergent numbers of vessels overall in each phase, the proportion of East Gaulish vessels remains fairly constant. None of the East Gaulish sherds appeared to belong to moulded forms; the great majority of the identifiable forms were dishes. There was only one potter's stamp (SS25), a dish which probably belonged to the 31R-related group of forms and which is likely to have been produced at Rheinzabern in the later 2nd or 3rd century. The evidence of the samian ware suggests that occupation continued, perhaps on a diminished scale, after *c* AD 170 and into the 3rd century. However, the very small amount of samian emanating from late East Gaulish workshops probably reflects trading patterns in the late 2nd and 3rd centuries as well as chronological factors on this site. The East Gaulish vessels consisted very largely of Rheinzabern ware (at least 30 vessels), with at least one vessel of form Ludowici SMb/SMc representing Trier ware, and three or more products from the Argonne in the Hadrianic-Antonine period. No products from earlier workshops in East Gaul were recognized.

period. Four stamps were probably early Antonine products and contemporary decorated bowls included between five and eight vessels which represented the early partnership of Cinnamus ii and Cerialis ii. These bowls compose as much as 10–15% of potters identified by name.

Antonine products were predominant in this collection. Amongst the decorated ware, although many were represented by mere fragments, there were many products from firms flourishing in the mid-Antonine period, such as Pugnus-Secundus (1 bowl), Divixtus (2–5 bowls) and Cinnamus (6–9 moulded bowls in his standard style). Both the early and the standard styles of Cinnamus were well represented by bowls on this site. This predilection for his firm's and his associates' goods (14 vessels) may well reflect their widespread availability on the market, rather than any specific chronological factor on this site.

The evidence of the samian ware suggests that occupation continued, perhaps on a diminished scale, after *c* AD 170

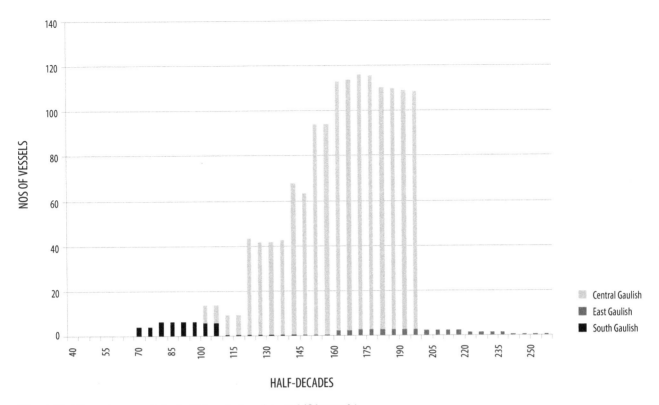

Illus 4.62. All samian vessels by half-decade (maximum 1481 vessels)

and into the 3rd century. However, the very small amount of samian emanating from late East Gaulish workshops probably reflects trading patterns in the late 2nd and 3rd centuries as much as a chronological factor on this site. East Gaulish ware is generally considered scarce in the west (Ward 2011, 91). At most excavations at Alcester, for instance, the East Gaulish products composed only

around 2% of the total (Ward 1996, 75–6; 2001, *passim*), the exception being Baromix 1972 where the proportion reached 9% (Ward 2001, 46). The sample from Worcester's Magistrates Court at 2.6% suggests that samian continued in use in the 3rd century, but without moulded bowls. The latest vessels comprised a rim probably of form Ludowici SMb/SMc noted above as produced at Trier in the the very

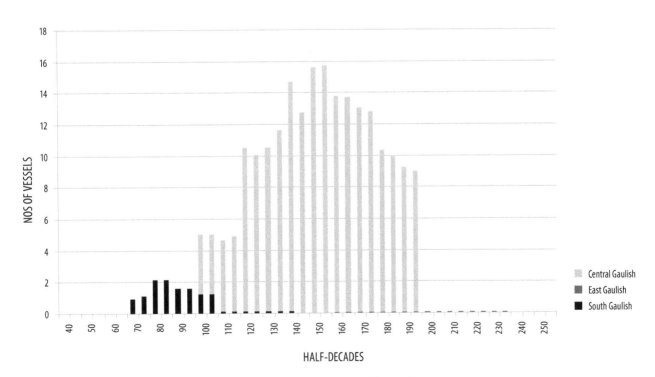

Illus 4.63. Stamps and/or decorated vessels by half-decade (maximum 223 vessels)

late 2nd or (probably) 3rd century; the other in a form related to 31R, was possibly a late product of Rheinzabern in a form related to 31R. The Rheinzabern piece was recovered from G16 (Phase 3), the Trier piece was unstratified.

Graffiti

There were six vessels with a graffito or probable marks of ownership. One dish (SG1), stamped in the period c AD 125–150 and deposited in Phase 1, bore a graffito which Roger Tomlin (2001, 395) read as FLM and which was presumed to represent Fl(avius) M…. Five other vessels (eg SG2–4) displayed intentional incisions, four of them on the standing surface of the footring. All five were produced in the Antonine period and four were found in Phase 3 contexts. Two vessels were inscribed X (SG5-6), one incised on the standing surface of the footring. It is generally considered that X represents a mark of ownership, rather than the Roman numeral (cf Evans 1987, 201). The same purpose may have been served by the nicks commonly found, as here, incised on the standing surface of footrings.

Wear and repair

Around 11% of the samian vessels on the site were noted as showing signs of wear from primary use. In addition, there was an unusually large proportion of repaired, re-worked and re-used samian. In total 41 vessels, forming as much as 2.8% of the assemblage, may have seen repair work. This proportion of repaired samian may be compared with that in collections from Alcester (c 1%). The proportion at other sites rarely exceeds 1% (eg Marsh 1981, 227). At sites where metalworking is known in the vicinity and where samian repairing was suspected, the proportion noted was at Prestatyn less than 1% and, at Piercebridge 1.4% overall (Ward 1989, 154; 2008a, 191). However, at the industrial site in Middlewich, the proportion reached 3% (Ward 2008b, 144). At the Magistrates Court site, the proportion of repaired vessels was particularly great in Phases 2 and 4 (c 4%).

The success of the repair-work is not always clear. Unsuccessful attempts at repair-work were observed or suspected in at least six cases. Certainly, one attempt at drilling (SR27) had been left incomplete. Many of the examples had broken at the repair-hole and such breakages could have occurred during or after the process of repair. Only three vessels retained lead rivets. However, slight traces of lead in repair-holes were observed or suspected on up to 12 of the vessels. Sherds from one decorated bowl (SR8, Illus 4.58) were found, repaired and scattered though five different groups in three different phases. Many of the repaired vessels found on this site were recovered in groups from specific contexts, mostly surviving as mere fragments: these included two vessels from G121, Phase 2-4 (SR4–5), three from G41, Phase 3-4 (SR7–9) and four from G42, Phase 3 (SR11–14).

In all, there were 24 repairs of the round, drilled variety and 14 were cut but no cleat-type/dove-tailed metalwork survived. In contrast, at Gas House Lane, Alcester, all nine repairs of samian ware were of the dove-tailed variety (Ward 1996, 76). At Magistrates Court, one bowl of Hadrianic-Antonine origin (SR12) may have seen repair-work of both drilled and cut varieties. In some cases, holes had been worked, presumably with difficulty, through the base (eg SR4).

The very large proportion of repair-work on plainware (79%) rather than decorated vessels (21%) suggests that samian ware of all types was highly valued in Worcester. The contents of a Bedfordshire pit representative of samian repair and recycling comprised only plainware (Wild 2013). This may be contrasted with comparable data from the northern zone, in Cumbria for instance. At Walton-le-dale, only c 12% of the repairs were of plainware (J Evans, pers comm, report unpublished). At Brougham cemetery, all the repaired samian vessels were plainware (Evans 2004, 360), but the funerary context does not reflect finds from the contemporary civil settlement, where bowls were also found repaired (Ward, forthcoming c). Most of the repaired sherds at the Magistrates Court showed signs that the vessels were worn in use, whether before or after their repair. Two repairs (SR28, SR42) were on vessels whose near-complete profiles had survived, both vessels having seen wear in use before deposition, the former in Phase 4. The earliest of the repaired vessels (SR1, SR24) were produced in South Gaul in the ranges c AD 70/80–110, repaired and finally deposited in contexts of Phases 2 and 4, the latter with traces of lead from the (presumably successful) riveting which suggests that it might conceivably have had a very long use life. It is significant for the chronology of repair types that of the 13 repairs on vessels made after c 160, four were of the round, drilled variety. Of these later vessels, one deep dish of form 31R (SR15), produced in the range c AD 160–200 and recovered from a Phase 3 deposit, displayed not only a repair-hole, but also a worn patch, a worn footring and nicks incised on its footring. Another was a bowl found in Phase 2, probably in the style of Belsa, c AD 170–200 (SR3, Illus 4.58); there are indications that this piece may have broken at an early stage of attempting to cut a repair-hole. A worn mortarium (SR4) produced at some point after c AD 170 may also have broken during attempted repair-work before its deposition in Phase 2.

Re-working and re-use

Further evidence of the extension of life of samian ware in terms of secondary use was observed in the collection. At least one sherd had been re-worked to form a rough disc of diameter 35–40mm (SW3, Illus 4.59). It was decorated in the style of Paternus v (II), c AD 150–185. Some specialists have considered c 30mm too large for use as discs with diameters, while others have included as counters those up to 50mm (Marsh 1981, 229). Whatever their size, groups of gaming counters and larger discs fashioned from samian ware occur at various sites in the west and north, including Alcester (seven at one site and two to three at another; Ward 1996, 77; 2001, 47), Chester amphitheatre (six; Ward 2018, 241, 338), Old Penrith (24 or more; Dickinson 1991, 135), Piercebridge (over 25; Ward 2008a, 192) and Brougham (52, at one extramural site; Ward, forthcoming c). At the Magistrates Court, another disc of diameter 35mm was found in Phase 1: fashioned from a late 1st- or early 2nd-century product, it was drilled through the middle (SW1, Illus 4.60). The small diameter of the hole, c 3mm, confirms that this was not a spindle whorl, but a large, perforated counter or disc. Another item, SR29, was not repair-work: this very worn base from a cup of form 33, had an angular hole cut through the centre, its purpose uncertain.

Five other vessels, all of indeterminate Central Gaulish form, appear to have been sawn or filed: one, a triangular piece found in C2155, Phase 4, was cut down for some unknown purpose, perhaps as a rubber or scraper. Another piece, belonging to a Central Gaulish dish of Antonine origin (G118, Phase 2) (SW2) shows considerable evidence of wear in use below the base inside the footring. This could indicate re-use of the piece upside-down, possibly as a mixing-palette, following breakage. Re-use of bases as mixing-palettes has been suggested at various sites such as Alcester, Piercebridge, Lancaster and Brougham *vici* (Ward 2008a, 192; forthcoming b and c).

It is likely that vessel repairs and re-working of pottery in Roman times would have been carried out locally, perhaps by craftsmen. In recent years, a samian repair and recycling workshop has been identified from the contents of a pit at Kempston Church End, outside Bedford, comprising 19 reworked vessels (Wild 2013), It seems likely that repairs and perhaps reworking were performed by craftsmen at work in the vicinity of this Worcester site. Re-used or repaired samian ware was found here in each site phase. Reworking has been found on other sites not simply in earlier Roman levels, but also in late contexts (see Ward 2008a, 191; Ward, forthcoming c).

Further discussion of samian ware

Jeremy Evans

The overall proportion of samian ware in the assemblage is 4.8% (Nosh) and 3.1% (Wt) in the recorded assemblage. These figures are similar to those from Deansway (Bryant and Evans 2004) at 5.2% (Nosh) and 1.7% (Wt). These levels are consistent with those from other small towns and are above levels found on basic level rural sites, which are generally less than 3%.

As Ward notes above, there is very little South Gaulish samian ware with no pre-Flavian forms and therefore there is little evidence for much activity here before AD 90, and none for pre-Flavian activity. This contrasts markedly with Deansway where 'It is noticeable about one third of the 1st-century samian is pre-Flavian' (Dickinson 2004, 275) and 'the pre-Flavian samian points to a foundation date between AD 45 and AD 60, probably not later than the early 50s.' Dickinson (2004) also notes that 'It is normal for British sites with

intensive 1st- and 2nd-century occupations to produce more samian of Flavian (AD 70–110) and Antonine (AD 140–195) date than of any other period. Deansway is no exception, but here, unusually, the balance is in favour of the 1st century. It is also noticeable than whilst the later Antonine forms (AD 160–200), such as 31R, 45, 79 and 80 are represented, the quantities are relatively low' (Dickinson 2004, 276). This contrasts markedly with the Magistrates Court site where the chronological emphasis is most definitely Antonine, and reflects the presence of a possible early fort or least early military activity at Deansway.

The overall proportion of decorated ware from the site, around 27%, is a reasonably normal urban level. However, poor quality noted amongst the assemblage as a whole, could serve to indicate lower status for this site. Ward (pers comm) helpfully suggests 'this may not indicate a basic level rural site, so much as a collection from an industrially oriented site where the samian was not perhaps on such public display as usual.'

Significant in this regard may be at least six small bowls which were noted: These small, moulded bowls of form 37 are thought likely (by Ward) to be the work of apprentices learning their craft in the larger factories, who suggests 'it is, however, speculation to suggest that these bowls may have been less expensive than those of the master-potters'.

Table 4.29 shows the occurrence of burnt samian ware on the site by phase. This exhibits an interesting pattern. The material from Phase 1 and Phase 2 runs at around 10%, but this changes markedly in Phase 3, falling to 3.5% (MNR) and 4.2% (RE), and remaining at the low levels of 4.6% (MNR) and 2.0% (RE) in Phase 4. This again hints at the possibility that the samian ware from Phases 3 and 4 comes from a different pool of material to that in Phases 1 and 2, ie that the levelling deposits of Phase 3 have brought in quantities of pottery to the site which is residual material not derived from earlier deposits on this site.

Class W, whitewares, 0.4% (Nosh) (Illus 4.64–4.68)

Whitewares form a very minor element of the assemblage. They are most common in Phases 1 and 2 but still present in the later phases. This is part of the usual Romano-British pattern and apart from late parchment wares none of the sherds are likely to be contemporary after

Table 4.29. Occurrence of burnt samian ware (by phase %)

Phase	NOSH%	Wt%	NOSH	Wt
1	9.38%	5.79%	32	1002
2	10.67%	9.28%	150	2811
3	3.46%	4.24%	1013	10134
4	4.57%	1.97%	175	1827

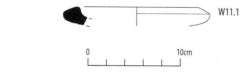

Illus 4.64. Fabric W11

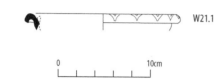

Illus 4.65. Fabric W21

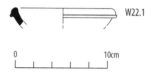

Illus 4.66. Fabric W22

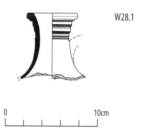

Illus 4.67. Fabric W28

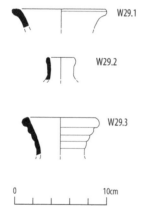

Illus 4.68. Fabric W29

the early 3rd century. There are a few sherds from the Verulamium region, **W11** (Illus 4.64), and some which may be attributed to Mancetter, **W21** (Illus 4.65), but for the most part these sherds are unsourced but probably not very local.

4.5. Functional and fineware analysis

Fineware levels are very low at Magistrates Court, the overall proportion of samian ware being around 4.8%, and the overall level of finewares being 5.2%. These data are very low for an 'urban' site, and almost low enough to fit into the rural range, which generally falls below 3%. Levels of decorated samian ware have been shown to be a useful indicator of site type (Willis 1998). These comprise 17.8% of all samian sherds, again a distinctly low level which could almost come from a rural site compared to the 25% which might be expected from urban sites. Table 4.30 shows a functional analysis of the pottery from Roman phases.

Overall, the indicators discussed above strongly suggest a low-status, urban fringe site, which has a number of rural or semi-rural characteristics. There are, however, some slight indications that early in the life of the site, its status may have been slightly different. It is of note that at least two Roman glazed ware vessels were present on the site probably in the pre-Hadrianic period. Also, the level of decorated ware amongst the South Gaulish samian from the site is 24.5%, a rather higher level than the site average, and much more like the level that might be expected from an urban site. It may be, however, that both these elements represent material from a rather higher status, and possibly military associated, assemblage imported on to the site with levelling material from elsewhere in the settlement.

Table 4.30 shows an overall functional analysis of all recorded vessels from the site, and Table 4.31 shows a functional analysis for the groups from each period. The overall assemblage shows the site to have quite a low jar total, 37.5% (MNR) and 36.2% (RE). Tableware levels (dishes and bowls) are reasonably high at 31.6% (MNR) and 25.8% (RE), but not notably so. Overall, the jar to tableware ratio would group the site with other nucleated settlements in the Midlands and south (cf Evans 2001, fig 5; Evans et al 2017). Drinking vessels are quite well-represented at 14.5% (MNR) and 14.3% (RE). These fit in an urban range, but so do rural sites on this measure in the Severn Valley region (Evans 1996) because of the large numbers of tankards on all sites in this region regardless of site type.

As usual for the region wide-mouthed jars are the commonest jar type, the only region in Roman Britain where this is the case, and this may say something about regional cuisine. It is of note that this phenomenon is not seen at Alcester (Evans 1996) on the edge of the Severn Valley ware distribution. Liquid storage vessels (flagons, jugs, lagenae and constricted-necked jars) are quite strongly represented at 10.6% (MNR) and 18.2% (RE) and if these are added to the drinking vessels 25.1% (MNR) and 32.5% (RE) of the vessels from the site are concerned with drinking. As has been argued elsewhere (Evans 1996) this is probably connected with local cider consumption, something which dates back to at least the 5th century AD, as evidenced by its preponderance in the continental areas of Severn Valley diaspora in Brittany and Galicia.

Dishes are poorly represented at the site, and seem to be more generally in the core Severn Valley area, although again this is not seen at Alcester (Evans 1996) on the edge of the area. Poor dish representation is also seen at Ariconium (Willis 2012) as is a strong representation of drinking vessels, particularly in the earliest phase.

Table 4.31 shows the functional analyses of the Phases 1–4 by MNR and RE. There are some long-term trends, although the data are fairly stable through time. Other jars start off in Phase 1 at 22.1% (MNR) and 22.6% (RE), rising slightly to 29.3% (MNR) and 29.7% (RE) in Phase 2, before falling strongly to 8.7% (MNR) and 8.7% (RE) in Phase 3, and then rising slightly to 12.9% (MNR) and 17.1% (RE) in Phase 4. Overall, the trend is for a fall in this group with time, after they rise to a peak in Phase 2. Wide-mouthed jars in contrast start at 12.5% (MNR) and 12.3% (RE) in Phase 1, continue similarly at 13.3% (MNR) and 10.3% (RE) in Phase 2, before peaking at 21.8% (MNR) and 18.3% (RE) in Phase 3 and then falling back to the usual level at 14.1% (MNR) and 12.6% (RE) in Phase 4. Storage jars start off at the low levels of 0.8% (MNR) and 0.6% (RE) in Phase 1, rising slightly to 1.4% (MNR) and 2.1% (RE), but in Phase 3 they rise to 4.5% (MNR) and 5.9% (RE) and remain at the relatively high levels of 3.3% (MNR) and 4.6% (RE) in Phase 4.

Putting all the jars together the sequence starts at 35.4% (MNR) and 35.5% (RE) in Phase 1, rising sharply to 41.7% (MNR) and 42.1% (RE) in Phase 2, before falling back to 35.0% (MNR) and 32.9% (RE) in Phase 3 and falling again to a low of 30.3% (MNR) and 34.3% (RE) in Phase 4. The usually expected trend for sites in southern Britain (Evans 1993; Evans 2005) is for jar levels to fall with time. Overall, this sequence conforms with that, although jar levels are quite low in Phase 1, reflecting the site's 'urban' status and, perhaps the presence of an early fort. The rise in Phase 2 would seem to be due to site specific factors, and given a level that falls on the margin between urban and rural sites it would seem to suggest that activity on the site here was peripheral and low status and only semi-urban.

Turning to the tablewares, bowls seem to provide around 20–25% of the assemblage throughout the sequence, with little obvious chronological pattern. Dishes, in contrast, are present from Phase 1, but in fairly low quantities, 7.6% (MNR) and 7.1% (RE), and remain at similar levels until Phase 4 when they increase to 13.4% (MNR) and 10.5% (RE). Dish levels, in Phases 2 and 3 at least, are low by the standards of other Romano-British 'small towns' (cf Evans 1996, Tables 28–30), and dish levels usually rise gradually with time rather than leaping up in the 4th century as they do here.

The overall level of tablewares (dishes and bowls) reflects the pattern of the incidence of dishes, starting at 34.1% (MNR) and 28.3% (RE) in Phase 1, falling slightly to 30.4% (MNR) and 24.2% (RE) in Phase 2, then rising slightly to 33.7% (MNR) and 26.8% (RE) in Phase 3, before rising strongly to 41.2% (MNR) and 32.9% (RE) in Phase 4. As noted above a rise with time on southern

sites is to be expected, but usually it is a more gradual affair. There are no obvious trends amongst the liquid containers, except that jugs and lagenae do not appear before Phase 2, and lagenae are absent after Phase 3. Constricted-necked jars remain at a fairly high level of 8–15% throughout the sequence. Drinking vessels do show some chronological patterning. In Phase 1 tankards appear at 16.9% (MNR) and 17.3% (RE), in Phase 2 they fall to 8.6% (MNR) and 9.0% (RE) and remain in the 11–12% range from Phase 3 onwards. In a reverse of this cups and beakers are only present at 1.2% (MNR) and 0.7% (RE) in Phase 1, after which they maintain a level of 2.2–2.8%. Outside the Severn Valley tankards are absent or very rare, and on urban sites cups and beakers would be expected to provide 10–20% of the assemblage. Lids also show a chronological pattern, although this is the usual one of a decline with time. Lids start off in Phase 1 at 1.6% (MNR) and 1.2% (RE) and decline to 0.2% (MNR) and 0.3% (RE) in Phase 4.

The final groups are 'Other' vessels; these are absent from Phase 1, and first appear in Phase 2 at 0.2% (MNR) and 0.2% (RE). These rise to 0.7% (MNR) and 0.7% (RE) in Phase 3, and peak at 2.6% (MNR) and 1.3% (RE). Overall the site follows the general southern trend of a move away from jars and a rise of tablewares with time, but mainly it reflects the regional trends in vessels function associated with the dominance of Severn Valley wares in the assemblage, with strong drinking vessels levels, frequent liquid storage vessels, and high levels of wide-mouthed jars.

4.6. Repaired vessels

About 51 sherds from stratified Roman deposits show evidence of riveting. Seven are on coarseware whilst 44 are on stratified samian ware. Thus, it is quite clear that samian ware is disproportionately selected for riveting. Amongst the coarsewares, two riveted sherds are mortaria, and all the rest are Severn Valley wares. Only one of the rivets appears to have been in iron. The overall riveting rate is 0.18% of all stratified Roman period sherds.

This is a relatively high figure compared to the 0.083-0.087% at Binchester fort, Co. Durham or the 0.08 per cent from the rural site at Chepstow (Evans 1996). The Worcester figure is comparable with the 0.12% at Shiptonthorpe (Evans 2006), 0.16% at the urban site of Bainesse Farm, Catterick (Bell and Evans 2002) and 0.1 per cent at the rural site of Worberry Gate, Somerset. All of these levels are well below those found on rural sites in the 'highland zone' (Longley et al 1998).

4.7. Burnt and sooted vessels

Burnt/sooted vessels occur throughout the sequence at a level of around 10% (Table 4.32). This level seems to be similar to that on many sites in Cambridgeshire (Evans et al 2017) and may be typical for lowland zone Romano-British sites. Few vessels (0.2–0.4%) show evidence of

Table 4.30. Overall functional analysis of all recorded vessels (MNR and RE)

Flagon	Jug	Lagena	Constricted-necked jars	Amphora	Storage jar	Wide-mouthed jar	Jar	Tankard	Beaker/cup	Bowl	Dish	Mortaria	Lid	Other	N
0.7%	0.6%	0.2%	9.1%	0.1%	3.5%	19.0%	15.0	12.1%	2.4%	24.9%	6.7%	4.0%	0.9%	0.9%	3263 rims
2.4%	1.2%	0.7%	13.9%	0.6%	4.1%	15.1%	17.0%	12.0%	2.3%	20.7%	5.1%	3.5%	0.9%	0.6%	29,088% of rim

Table 4.31. Functional analysis of period groups by MNR and RE

Period	Flagon	Jug	Lagena	Constricted-necked jars	Amphora	Storage jar	Wide-mouthed jar	Jar	Tankard	Beaker/cup	Bowl	Dish	Mortaria	Lid	Other	N
1	0.8%	0	0	8.4%	0	0.8%	12.5%	22.1%	16.9%	1.2%	26.5%	7.6%	1.2%	1.6%	0	249 rims
1	3.2%	0	0	12.0%	0	0.6%	12.3%	22.6%	17.3%	0.7%	21.2%	7.1%	1.5%	1.2%	0	3,699% of rim
2	0.8%	0.9%	0.5%	9.5%	0	1.4%	13.3%	29.3%	8.6%	2.4%	21.6%	8.8%	2.0%	1.1%	0.2%	663 rims
2	1.3%	1.8%	2.1%	15.1%	0	2.1%	10.3%	29.7%	9.0%	2.2%	17.8%	6.4%	1.4%	0.8%	0.2%	7,040% of rim
3	0.8%	0.6%	0.2%	9.5%	0.2%	4.5%	21.8%	8.7%	12.0%	2.3%	27.3%	6.4%	4.2%	0.8%	0.7%	1929 rims
3	2.6%	1.1%	0.4%	15.7%	1.0%	5.9%	18.3%	8.7%	11.4%	2.5%	22.6%	4.2%	4.2%	0.8%	0.7%	14,277% of rim
4	0.5%	0.5%	0	8.2%	0	3.3%	14.1%	12.9%	11.3%	2.8%	27.8%	13.4%	2.4%	0.2%	2.6%	425 rims
4	3.0%	1.8%	0	10.6%	0	4.6%	12.6%	17.1%	11.9%	2.4%	22.4%	10.5%	1.6%	0.3%	1.3%	3,536% of rim

Table 4.32. Deposits on vessels by phase

Phase	Deposit type	% MNR	% RE
1	Burnt/sooted	13.2%	13.9%
2	Burnt/sooted	8.0%	7.9%
3	Burnt/sooted	5.4%	5.5%
4	Burnt/sooted	10.2%	11.6%
1	Food residue	0.4%	0.3%
2	Food residue	0	0
3	Food residue	0.2%	0.2%
4	Food residue	0.3%	0.1%
1	Limescale	0.7%	0.9%
2	Limescale	0.4%	0.4%
3	Limescale	0.0%	0.1%
4	Limescale	0.5%	0.7%

Table 4.33. The origin of fabrics reaching the site by phase, by Nosh

Phase	Local	Regional	Interprovincial / Interdiocesan
1	83.4%	14.1%	2.5%
2	79.1%	15.8%	5.1%
3	91.2%	3.2%	5.6%
4	84.9%	8.9%	6.2%

burnt food residues, as is usual on Romano-British sites (Evans 1995). Vessels with limescale are also fairly rare, with a peak of 0.7% (MNR) in Phase 1. This material occurs so rarely as to suggest vessels with limescale have been brought to the site having acquired a limescale deposit from use elsewhere.

4.8. Discussion of pottery

Supply

The supply of pottery to the site was predominantly from local sources (Table 4.33). Over three-quarters of the assemblage consisted of oxidised wares, the vast majority of which are likely to have come from the local Malvernian kilns. Only three oxidised fabrics (O24, O29 and O291) may have had a different origin, and they are not common here. Similarly, amongst the gritted wares (class G) virtually all the vessels are from the local Malvernian kilns, whilst R813, the most common greyware, seems likely to have been made in Worcester. Q151, the most common white-slipped ware, also seems to have a Severn Valley origin.

Fabrics coming from other regions include BB1, which is surprisingly poorly represented, but most common in Phase 2. The low quantities of BB1 at Worcester, compared to the much higher quantities from Alcester (Evans 1996), would suggest the fabric was travelling north from Cirencester by road on the route from Bourton to Penkridge, and that despite the large quantities at the port at Gloucester it was not travelling up the Severn.

The most common fineware at the site, F42, which is generally roughcast, is also common at Alcester, and is probably of later 1st to mid-3rd century date. This seems to have a relatively local origin, perhaps somewhere between Alcester and Worcester. Regionally distributed finewares are present in very small quantities in terms of Nene Valley colour-coated ware (F52–F53) and later Oxfordshire colour-coated ware (F51).

The mortaria are largely from regional scale suppliers. The principal source was Mancetter-Hartshill from its inception at the turn of the 2nd century, but also Verulamium in the later 1st to early 2nd century, and Oxfordshire from the 2nd century onwards. There are small elements from the local area (M44 and M45), but these are of much smaller significance that the regional scale suppliers. The white-slipped wares are probably from regional scale suppliers, but the most common here, Q151, is fairly certain to be a local Severn Valley ware product.

The most common greyware, R813, representing 62% of the greywares, was probably made at Worcester. However, many of the remaining fabrics, and particularly R01, R18, and R41, fall within the range of fabrics produced in the northern Warwickshire industries, eg Bubenhall (Evans 2012).

Fabrics originating outside the province/diocese of Britannia are rare, and are largely restricted to South, Central and East Gaulish samian ware, and a few amphorae. Samian ware increases in frequency throughout the sequence, although it must have been residual, in terms of production, from Phase 3 onwards. The incidence of amphora sherds peak in Phase 2 and decline thereafter, reflecting the absence of contemporary amphora in Phases 3 and 4. The only other sherds of imported material are a few of Central Gaulish 'Rhenish ware', F32, and Noyon mortaria, M12.

In Phase 1 there is a very considerable local element to supply, but still around 14% of the assemblage comes from regional sources, with a mere 3% of imports. In Phase 2 local sources decline a little, to be substituted with more material from other regions and equally more imported material. There appears to be a marked change in Phase 3 with a distinct rise in local sourcing and a very marked decline in regional sources. Imports, however, seem to hold up at a similar level to Phase 2, albeit that the types found suggest they are in fact residual. There may be in part a methodological problem here for the oxidised sherds not fully defined to fabric have been allocated a local source however, this alone should not have so large an effect, and the trend does appear to be real.

In Phase 4 local sources decline somewhat, to a level a little above those in Phase 1, and regional sources increase, but still remain below those in Phases 1 and 2. In contrast imports appear to continue at a similar level to those in

Phase 3, although all of these would seem to be residual, at least in terms of their production date.

Status

The pottery delivers a fairly consistent message about the status of the site. It is very poorly supplied with finewares, at around 5% (Nosh), such that it is barely distinguished from a basic level rural site. This was even lower than 6.5% (Nosh) found at Deansway in its Phase 3 (Bryant and Evans 2004, table 47).

The functional analysis by phase from the site has been examined above. It indicates the site does fall within the 'urban' range, with an overall jar level of 37.5% (MNR) and an overall tableware level of 31.6% (MNR). Overall the jar to tableware ratio would group the site with other 'small towns' in the Midlands and south (cf Evans 2001, fig 5; Evans et al 2017). Put together these indicators would seem to suggest an 'urban' site, but a peripheral one where some indicators appear to have more of a rural aspect. It might be noted that where there is comparable evidence from Deansway that site looks more 'urban'.

The site phasing comes in two major blocks, Phases 1 and 2 and Phases 3 and 4. The taphonomic evidence suggests a major levelling of the site in Phase 3, and quantities of residual 2nd century pottery from a similar peripheral site seem likely to have been imported onto the site in this phase as levelling material. The overall evidence from micro-slags and features such as ovens/hearths and clay-lined pits suggest a concentration of industrial activity on the site in Phase 4, which may help explain the sudden rise in 'other' function vessels as these are chiefly Malvernian ware portable ovens.

5

The finds

Lynne Bevan, Andy Boucher, Kath Crooks, Peter Guest,
Martin Henig, Julie Lochrie, Paul Olver, Peter Thomso
(reports submitted 2002-3 except where stated)

5.1. Introduction and Summary

This finds report is based on the original finds assessment by Hilary Cool (Cool 2002). The finds assemblage included a number of identifiably Roman items. Some post-Roman finds were also present but are not included in this report. In contrast to the good standard of preservation observed among the copper alloy objects, many of which were identifiably Roman, iron objects tended to be corroded, fragmentary and less chronologically-diagnostic. Other items of lead, worked bone, ceramic and glass were well-preserved, although the Roman glass mainly comprised small body fragments from blue-green bottles.

The best of the finds dating evidence was provided by the coins. The earliest of these was a single coin (No.1, Table 5.01) dated to the early 2nd century AD. The bulk of the coins however dated to the second half of the 3rd and early 4th century. The lack of mid to late 4th-century coins implies a general lack of activity during that period, or at least lack of surviving deposits belonging to it.

Although many other items were diagnostically Roman, few were closely datable beyond a generally 1st- to 3rd-century date. Of interest was a lower torso from a ceramic figurine, probably Venus (No.55, Illus 5.05), part of the typical religious 'backdrop' often found in assemblages from Roman nucleated settlements, undoubtedly used in personal worship (Smith et al 2018, 180). Other items such as copper alloy brooches (No.14–25, Illus 5.01) and other jewellery (No.13, Illus 5.01, No.28–29), a clothing fitting (No.27, Illus 5.01), toiletry implements (No.30–31, Illus 5.02) and a fragment from a mirror (No.36) indicate a fairly high level of material culture and personal property, as well as an interest in grooming. A fragment from a bath flask of late 1st- to early 3rd-century date (No.79) is also suggestive of an interest in cleanliness (Cool 2002, 8). A total of *c* 570 hobnails was identified, most of which were found in six groups which are thought to represent the remains of complete, or partial, shoes.

Other items included a bell, probably from an animal halter (No.34, Illus 5.03), attesting to agricultural or possibly religious activity. Domestic activity is represented by a spoon handle (No.35), while textile crafts are represented by a needle (No.37) with the elongated eye typical of 3rd to 4th-century needles (Crummy 1995, illus 70: 1983, 66–7) and two fired clay spindle whorls made from modified pot sherds (No.56–7, Illus 5.05). Evidence for writing or record-keeping comes in the form of four fragments from styli, one of which was of copper alloy (No.38) and the other three of iron (No.45–7). Other iron objects included a spearhead (No.44) with a broad socket and a very damaged blade, which is probably similar to some 1st century types discussed by Manning (1985, Plates 76–8, 163–5). Various tools and fittings were also present in the iron assemblage, including a pickaxe head (No.48), part of a possible set (No.49), and a loop-headed spike (No.50). Other items included a fragment from an 'L'-shaped lift key (No.51), a bucket handle mount (No.52), and a conical ferrule (No.53).

The assemblage includes possible evidence for metal-working. Hilary Cool (2002, 7) has described an amorphous object listed in the Archive Catalogue (SF216) as a 'billet' and interpreted the presence of this object and two bar-shaped items (SF208, SF211, C1033, G24, Phase 4) as evidence for on-site iron-working. She also proposed that an amorphous item of copper alloy listed in the Archive Catalogue (SF77, C1134, G2, Phase 1-2) might be a fragment of casting waste.

A small collection of lithics attested to prehistoric activity in the area during the Neolithic or early Bronze Age though all was residual in Roman or later contexts. The assemblage was not of sufficient size or quality to characterise or accurately date this activity and this material has not been included in the report. The post-Roman finds, typically post-medieval, have also not been reported here. These include a copper alloy finger ring, a number of copper alloy wire pins, a bone spoon and button, a piece of silver wire, some iron finds and a pipeclay hair curler. Three undiagnostic lead finds have also been excluded. Details of all these finds are available in the archive.

Finds are referred to wherever possible by report catalogue number. Where no report catalogue entry exists, site small finds (SF) number is used instead. Catalogue entries give SF number, followed by context number (C), group number (G) and then phase number.

5.2. Coins

Peter Guest

The twelve coins from the Magistrates Court excavations represent an interesting, if small, assemblage from a

Table 5.01. Catalogue of coins

Catalogue	Denomin.	Obverse	Reverse	Date	SF	Context	Group	Phase
1	AEI	Hadrian	illegible	117–38	45	1063	133	4
2	radiate	Claudius II	illegible	268–70	105	1034	41	3
3	radiate	Tetricus I?	illegible	270–74	46	-	-	-
4	radiate	illegible	illegible	260–90	47	1068	65	4
5	barb. rad.	as Tetricus I	illegible	270–90	82	1184	124	4
6	radiate	Carausius	Pax Aug	287–93	141	2361	120	2
7	AE2	Constantine I	Soli Invicto Comiti	310–13	2	1002	1001	6
8	AE2	Constantine I	Soli Invicto Comiti	310–18	113	2245	19	3
9	AE2	Constantine I	Soli Invicto Comiti	313–18	144	2361	120	2
10	AE3	illegible	illegible	260–380	89	2111	42	3
11	AE3	illegible	illegible	260–380	90	2111	42	3
12	AE4 min	illegible	illegible	260–400	3	1002	1001	6

numismatically little known area. It should be noted that the latest coins are from the *Soli Invicto Comiti* issues produced during the second decade of the 4th century. The study has not identified a single coin from the middle and later 4th century, a period that produces a significant proportion of coins on most Romano-British sites. The coin list is sufficient for the purpose of dating the length of occupation of the site.

5.3. Copper alloy

Lynne Bevan

Copper alloy objects were the most numerous among the small finds and these tended to be fairly well-preserved, although some items had sustained damage and others were in a worn or degraded condition. For purposes of discussion, the large assemblage of Roman Objects was subdivided into Jewellery and Personal Items, Toiletry Instruments and Other Items.

Jewellery and personal items

Roman jewellery included an earring of simple form with tapered ends (No.13, Illus 5.01), and five brooches. The brooches included a 2nd-century trumpet-headed brooch with traces of blue inlay (No.14, Illus 5.01), a Colchester derivative type (No.15, Illus 5.01) and a penannular brooch (No.16, Illus 5.01), both of the latter two dating to the 1st century AD. A second fragmentary penannular brooch (No.17) was not closely datable beyond a 1st- to 3rd-century date, while a very corroded brooch was probably a Dolphin type brooch of 1st-century date (No.18). A brooch pin with attached spring was from a Colchester derivative type brooch of 1st-century date (No.19). Brooch pin and spring fragments came from two brooches of 1st- to 2nd-century date (No.20–21,not illustrated) and there were also some other less diagnostic brooch spring (No.22–23) and pin (No.24–25) fragments.

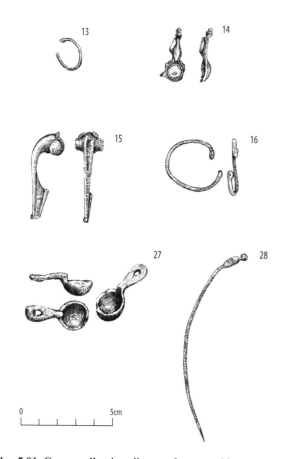

Illus 5.01. Copper alloy jewellery and personal items

Other objects comprised a ring fragment, though probably not from a finger ring (No.26), a dress fastener (No.27, Illus 5.01) of a type believed to be contemporary with the 'boss-style ornament' popular in north Britain in the 2nd century AD (Wild 1970, illus 1:IV, 139–140), a hairpin (No.28, Illus 5.01), and the head of a second hairpin (No.29). Both hairpins were of Cool's Type 3B (Cool 1990, 154), a long-lived type generally datable to the 1st–3rd century AD.

13. Earring with tapered ends, similar to an example from Colchester (Crummy 1983, illus 53, 50). Length *c* 40mm, width 1–1.5mm, thickness 1mm. SF40, C2034, G154, Phase 4. Illus 5.01.

14. Brooch, trumpet-headed type of 2nd century date (Hattatt 2000, illus 188: 87, 450–453, 970–971, 188), broken at both ends, and retaining traces of blue enamel inlay. Surviving length 30mm, width 11mm, thickness 7mm. SF76, C2107, G42, Phase 3. Illus 5.01.

15. Brooch, complete, Colchester derivative type of 1st century date (Hattatt 2000, Figs. 155–156, 296–297). Length 47mm, width at bow 16mm, thickness 12mm. SF122, C1034, G41, Phase 3-4. Illus 5.01.

16. Brooch, penannular, of 1st century date (Hattatt 2000, illus 199:650, 340). Diameter *c* 25mm, thickness 2mm. SF136, C2270, G2, Phase 1. Illus 5.01.

17. Penannular brooch fragment, comprising half of the brooch, and a fragment from the brooch pin, both now very degraded. Although not closely datable beyond a 1st–3rd century date, the design is most similar to Hattatt's Type A3 (Hattatt 2000, illus 198:647, 339). Original diameter *c* 36mm, diameter of terminal 6mm. SF161, C1531, G1004, Phase 0. Not illustrated.

18. Brooch, heavily encrusted with soil and attached to a stone by corrosion products, probably a Dolphin type brooch of 1st century date (eg Hattatt 2000, Figs. 157–158 and 160, 298–299 and 301). Length 62mm, width at shoulder 22mm. SF143, C2352, G2, Phase 1. Not illustrated.

19. Brooch pin with spring from a Colchester derivative type brooch of 1st century date (Hattatt 2000, Figs. 155–156, 296–297). Length 42mm, width at spring 18mm. SF57, C2193, G41, Phase 3-4. Not illustrated.

20. Brooch pin and spring from very small brooch, of 1st–2nd century date. Length 28mm, width at spring 7mm, thickness 3mm. SF139, C2333, G81, Phase 1. Not illustrated.

21. Brooch pin and spring fragments, Roman, of 1st – 2nd century date. Length of pin 15mm, length of spring fragments 10mm and 12mm. SF52, C2193, G41, Phase 3-4. Not illustrated.

22. Brooch spring fragment, heavily worn. Length 10mm, thickness 3mm. SF56, C1082, G141, Phase 4. Not illustrated.

23. Brooch spring fragment, heavily worn. Length 10mm, width 6mm. SF283, C1510, G148, Phase 1. Not illustrated.

24. Brooch pin. Length 40mm, thickness 1mm. SF4, C1002, G1001, Phase 6. Not illustrated.

25. Brooch pin fragment. Length 29mm, thickness 1.5mm. SF153, C1488, G902, Phase 1. Not illustrated.

26. Ring fragment, segmented, probably not from a finger ring. Length 32mm, diameter of globular segments 5mm–6mm. SF138, C2270, G2, Phase 1. Not illustrated.

27. Dress fastener, complete, Wild Type IV, with a hollow boss and a shank attached to the rim, a type believed to be contemporary with the 'boss-style ornament' popular in North Britain in the 2nd century AD (Wild 1970, illus 1:IV, 139–140). Length 36mm, diameter 16mm, thickness 2–3mm. SF115, C2245, G19, Phase 3. Illus 5.01.

28. Hairpin, complete, 1st–3rd century AD, Cool Type 3B (Cool 1990, illus 2, 153–154). Length 112mm, diameter of head 2mm, thickness 2mm. SF121, C2133, G19, Phase 3. Illus 5.01.

29. Hairpin terminal, very worn, with transverse grooving beneath a conical head, 1st–3rd century AD, Cool Type 3B (Cool 1990, 154). Length 28mm, diameter of head 4mm. SF160, C1526, Un-phased Not illustrated.

Toilet instruments

Toilet instruments comprised a pair of tweezers (No.30, Illus 5.02), two toilet spoons (No.31, Illus 5.02, No.32) and a nail cleaner (No.33). It was not possible to relate the fragment of nail cleaner to Crummy's recent typology (Crummy 2001) since it lacked a diagnostic terminal. However, the nail cleaner and toilet spoons might be of later Roman date, since they were similar in form to examples from late Roman deposits at Colchester (Crummy 1995, illus 64: 1897, 59–60 and illus 67: 1945, 62).

30. Tweezers (Crummy 1983, 58–59, illus 63). Length 47mm, width 4mm, thickness 0.5mm. SF29, C1002, G1001, Phase 6. Illus 5.02.

31. Toilet spoon, complete, with a coiled end for suspension as part of a toilet set (Crummy 1995, illus 67: 1945, 62). The spoon resembles a spoon from Late Roman deposits at Colchester (Crummy 1995, illus 64: 1897, 59–60). Its form is also similar to No. 20, below. Length 98mm, width of bowl 5mm, thickness 1.5mm. SF106, C2109, G18, Phase 3. Illus 5.02.

32. Toilet spoon, the bowl and end of which are both damaged, and is similar to No.19, above, and a to spoon from Late Roman deposits at Colchester (Crummy 1995, illus 64: 1897, 59–60). Length 84mm, width of bowl *c* 5mm, thickness 1.5mm. SF118, C2110, G19, Phase 3. Not illustrated.

33. Nail cleaner, broken across shaft and at flared blade, of simple form, like an example from Colchester of probable 3rd–4th-century date (Crummy 1995, illus

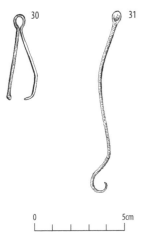

Illus 5.02. Copper alloy toilet instruments

67: 1945, 62). Length 42mm, width 1.5mm–2.5mm, thickness 1mm. SF154, C1003, G1002, Phase 0. Not illustrated.

Other items

Other Roman items included a damaged bell, probably from an animal halter (No.34, Illus 5.03), a fragment from a spoon handle (No.35) of a type which appears to have been in production by the first half of the 2nd century AD (Waugh and Goodburn 1972, 124), a corner fragment from a mirror (No.36), a needle (No.37) with the elongated eye typical of 3rd- to 4th-century needles (Crummy 1995, illus 70: 1993, 66–67), and a stylus fragment (No.38).

There were also fragments from two studs (No.39–40), some loosely-twisted chainlinks, possibly from a necklace (No.41), a fragment from the rim of a small vessel (No.42) and a small nail, possibly from upholstery (No.43).

34. Bell, of heavily-leaded copper alloy, now very distorted and damaged, the large size of which suggests it was attached to an animal halter (Crummy 1995, illus 143: 4165, 127). Original diameter *c* 60mm, height 44mm, thickness 3mm. SF75, C2107, G42, Phase 3. Illus 5.03.

35. Spoon handle fragment from intersection of bowl and stem, probably from a Type 2 spoon characterised by a pear-shaped bowl (Crummy 1983, 69–70, illus 73: 2014), a type which appears to have been in production by the first half of the 2nd century AD (Waugh and Goodburn 1972, 124). There are traces of decoration on the square-sectioned shaft. Length 51mm, width 3–9mm, thickness 1–3mm. SF1, C1002, G1001, Phase 6. Not illustrated.

36. Corner fragment from a mirror. Dimensions 10mm x 9mm x 1mm. SF73, C2137, G800, Phase 4. Not illustrated.

37. Needle with the elongated eye typical of 3rd to 4th-century needles from Colchester (Crummy 1995, illus 70: 1993, 66–67). Length 93mm, width 2mm, thickness 1.5mm. SF85, C2107, G42, Phase 3. Not illustrated.

38. Stylus fragment, comprising a spatulate end, broken across a circular-sectioned shank. Length 33mm, width at end 5.5mm, thickness 1mm–2mm. SF396, C1254, G130, Phase 4. Not illustrated.

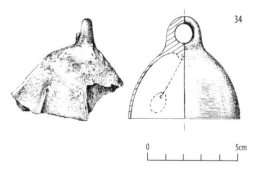

34

0   5cm

Illus 5.03. Copper alloy bell

39. Stud with a broken head. Length 11mm, thickness of shank 1–3mm. SF23, C1002, G1001, Phase 6. Not illustrated.

40. Half of the head of a stud. Original diameter 17mm, thickness 2mm. SF107, C1002, G1001, Phase 6. Not illustrated.

41. Chainlinks, loosely-twisted, possibly from a necklace. Length 58mm, average width of chain 1mm, thickness 0.5mm. SF74, C2179, G800, Phase 4. Not illustrated.

42. Fragment from the rim of a small vessel, the upper edge of which is thickened and defined by a groove. This is a plainer version of the illustrated vessel fragments from Colchester (Crummy 1995, illus 76: 2029–2034. 71–72), although this small fragment does not preclude the possibility of decoration on the vessel body. Length 44mm, height 17mm, thickness 1mm–3mm. SF86, C1003, G1002, Phase 0. Not illustrated.

43. Small nail, possibly from upholstery. Length 10mm, diameter of head 3mm. SF94, C1238, G45, Phase 4. Not illustrated.

5.4. Iron

Lynne Bevan

Iron objects

Iron objects were in a very corroded condition, precluding identification in some instances and illustration. Apart from hobnails (discussed separately below) and other nails (listed in Archive Catalogue), all iron objects have been catalogued and discussed together and, where possible, all diagnostically or potentially Roman items have been related to Manning's catalogue of Romano-British ironwork in the British Museum (Manning 1985). Of most interest in the collection was a spearhead (No.44) with a broad socket and a very damaged blade, which is probably similar to some 1st-century types discussed by Manning (1985, plates 76–8, 163–5). Evidence for writing came in the form of eraser ends from three styli (No.45–7), which, despite their corroded condition, appeared to conform to Manning's Type 4 styli (Manning 1985, Plate 36: N27, 85–7).

Various tools and fittings were present in the assemblage, including a pickaxe head (No.48), part of a possible set (No.49), and a loop-headed spike (No.50). Other items included a fragment from an 'L'-shaped lift key (No.51), a bucket handle mount (No.52), and a conical ferrule (No.53) and a sheet fragment with rivet at one end (No.54).

Unidentified objects included a small corroded object with fluted end (SF210, C1033, G24, Phase 4), a bar-shaped object obscured by corrosion products (SF208, C1033, G24, Phase 4), and four bar-shaped objects, possibly tools (SF201, C2041, G53, Phase 2; SF211, C1033, G24, Phase 4; No.49; SF253, C2107, G42, Phase 3). Two of these items (SF208, SF211, C1033, G24, Phase 4) have been interpreted as evidence for iron-working. There was also a possible billet (SF216,

1053, G24, Phase 4) which, again, is indicative of iron-working (Cool 2002, 7).

44. Spearhead, with a broad socket and a very damaged blade, the original dimensions of which are beyond reconstruction. It is probably similar to some 1st-century types discussed by Manning (1985, Plates 76–78, 163–165). Length 80mm, diameter of socket 14mm, width of blade 25mm. SF222, C2112, G42, Phase 3. Not illustrated.

45. Eraser end of stylus, very corroded and fragmentary, similar to Manning's Type 4 styli (Manning 1985, Plate 36: N27, 85–87). Length 50mm, width of eraser end 6mm. SF213, C1083, G124, Phase 4. Not illustrated.

46. Eraser end of stylus, very corroded and fragmentary, similar to Manning's Type 4 styli (Manning 1985, Plate 36: N27, 85–87). Length 60mm, width of eraser end 6mm, diameter of stem 5mm. SF200, C2018, G95, Phase 4. Not illustrated.

47. Eraser end of stylus, very corroded and fragmentary, similar to Manning's Type 4 styli (Manning 1985, Plate 36: N27, 85–87). Length 60mm, width of eraser end 8mm, diameter of stem 5mm. SF327, C2119, G200, Phase 3. Not illustrated.

48. Pickaxe head, very corroded. Length 225mm, width at centre 40mm, thickness 24mm. SF484, C1007, G1001, Phase 6. Not illustrated.

49. Possible set (a blacksmithing tool meant to be struck by a hammer). Fragment from the middle of the tool. Length 95mm, width 32mm, thickness 20mm. SF235, 2137, G800, Phase 4. Not illustrated.

50. Loop-headed spike (Manning 1985, Plate 59: RR27-R33, 130). Length 66mm, width 14mm. SF466, C2107, G42, Phase 3. Not illustrated.

51. 'L'-shaped lift key, comprising only the bit with the remains of three teeth, obscured by corrosion products and only visible on X-ray (Manning 1985, Plate 40, O26-O38, 90–92). Length of broken stem 65mm, length of bit 42mm. SF202, C2084, Unstrat. Not illustrated.

52. Bucket handle mount (Manning 1985, Plate 47: P11, 102). Length 117mm, width 33mm, thickness 13mm. SF457, C1034, G41, Phase 3-4. Not illustrated.

53. Conical ferrule, very corroded (Manning 1985, Plate 66: S57-83, 140–141). Length 30mm, diameter 13mm. SF178, C1198, G1, Phase 1. Not illustrated.

54. Sheet fragment with rivet at one end. Length 31mm, length 27mm, thickness 4mm. SF172, C1316, G138, Phase 4. Not illustrated.

Hobnails and nails

There were *c* 570 hobnails present in the collection, divided into five groups which are thought to represent the remains of complete, or partial, shoes. The largest comprised *c* 190 corroded hobnails, some of which were fused together in small groups of up to eight hobnails (SF100, C2204, G245, Phase 1, Illus 5.04). This collection probably represents the remains of more than one Roman sandal or shoe and the

Illus 5.04. Hob nails fused together, SF100

grouped hobnails are suggestive of the deliberate grouping of hobnails beneath the ball of the foot and under the heel as shown in an illustrated example of Roman footwear from London (Manning 1985, 136–7, plate 63: R104). Fragments of leather around many of the nails appear to have been preserved by corrosion products. The average length of the hobnails was 11mm and the head diameters were 10mm. The poor standard of preservation and high incidence of corrosion observed among the hobnails made it impossible to ascertain the extent of wear on shoe soles prior to discard. There were also another four smaller groups of hobnails (Table 5.02). In addition, a total of 17 ordinary nails used for timber or masonry was recovered, a full listing of which is provided in the Archive Catalogue.

5.5. Ceramic

Lynne Bevan

Part of a Roman figurine (No.55, Illus 5.05) was found made of a fine white ceramic. The piece comprised the lower back, buttocks and the upper thighs of the figure

Table 5.02. Groups of hobnails

Find	Context	Group	Phase	Notes
SF100	2204	245	1	190 finds, fused together in small groups of up to 8
SF58	2092	2083	2	95 finds, fused together in groups of up to 20
SF167	2093	2083	2	120 finds, approximately one third of which are fused together in rows
SF214	1127	140	4	116 finds, mostly separate
SF270	1422	134	4	49 finds, some of which are fused together

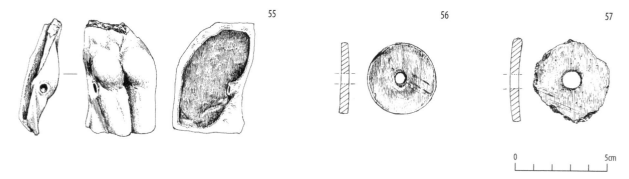

Illus 5.05. Ceramic finds

of Venus. Such figurines, also called 'pseudo Venus' figurines (Jenkins 1959, 60–76), were manufactured in Central Gaul and Cologne in the 1st and 2nd centuries AD (Green 1976, 20).

Two fired clay spindle whorls were identified, both of which are of Roman date and made from modified pot sherds (No.56–7, Illus 5.05), one of which (No.56) was more carefully-finished than the other (No.57).

55. Figurine fragment, comprising the lower back, buttocks and the upper thighs of a female figure, probably Venus. There is a small perforation on the upper, left hand thigh. This fragment appears to show the reverse of similar figurine fragments found in Colchester (Crummy 1983, illus 167: 4262 and 4263, 141). Length 66mm, width 37mm, thickness 5–7mm. SF111, C2126, G19, Phase 3. Illus 5.05.

56. Spindle whorl, circular, made from a greyware pot sherd with an oxidised surface. Roman. Diameter 38mm thickness 6mm. SF21, C2123, G16, Phase 3. Illus 5.05.

57. Spindle whorl, semi-circular, made from a greyware pot sherd with an oxidised surface. The central perforation has been carefully made but the outer edges have been left in a chipped and broken condition. Roman. Dimensions 40mm x 36mm x 7mm. SF331, C2385, G120, Phase 2. Illus 5.05.

5.6. Vessel and window glass

Lynne Bevan

Due to the fragmentary condition of the Roman glass, which consisted of mainly small, undiagnostic body fragments, only one item has been illustrated. The glass comprised a total of 32 fragments from vessels, a fragment of cast window glass, of 1st- to 3rd-century date (No.85) and a small melted fragment (SF127, C2131, G19, Phase 3). The vessel glass consisted mainly of 22 fragments of blue-green bottles, including a rim, neck and handle fragment (No.58, Illus 5.06), a shoulder fragment (No.59), fragments from a massive double-ribbed handle (No.60) and two reeded handles (No.61–2), and three base fragments, two from square bottles (No.63–4) and one from a prismatic bottle (No.67). The remainder of bottle glass consisted of undiagnostic body fragments, mainly from prismatic bottles of late 1st- to early 3rd-century date (Nos 66–78).

Other blue-green vessels comprised a loop handle fragment from a bath flask of late 1st- to early 3rd-century date (No.79), a cylindrical fragment from a jar (No.80) and fragments from a ribbed jug handle (No.81). Fragments from pale green vessels comprised a small fragment from the rolled rim of a jar, of late 1st- to early 3rd-century date (No.82), and a fragment from a jug or

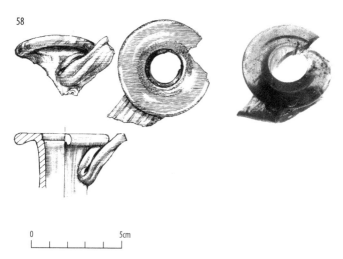

Illus 5.06. Glass bottle, SF58

112

flask (No.83). A body fragment from a colourless vessel of 2nd- to 3rd-century date (No.84) was also present in the assemblage.

Blue-green glass bottles

58. Rim, neck and handle fragment from a glass bottle of a late 1st- early 3rd century date. Diameter of bottle 50mm, surviving height 30mm, thickness 4–5.5mm. SF27, C1002, G1001, Phase 6. Illus 5.06

59. Massive double-ribbed handle, later 1st - early 3rd century in date. Length 60mm, width 50mm, thickness 8–13mm. SF37, C2034, G154, Phase 4. Not illustrated.

60. Reeded handle fragment, late 1st- early 3rd century in date. Dimensions 15mm x 19mm x 3mm. SF125, C2110, G19, Phase 3. Not illustrated.

61. Two joining reeded handle fragments, late 1st- early 3rd century in date. Width 48mm, length 32mm, thickness 3–12mm. SF268, C2132, G19, Phase 3. Not illustrated.

62. Fragment from square base, late 1st- early 2nd century in date. Length 50mm, width 38mm, thickness 9mm. SF277, C2110, G19, Phase 3. Not illustrated.

63. Lower body/base fragment from a square bottle of later 1st- early 3rd century in date. Dimensions 28mm x 10mm x 2–5mm. SF387, C1076, G141, Phase 4. Not illustrated.

64. Lower body/base fragment from a prismatic bottle of later 1st- early 3rd century in date. Length 57mm, height 25mm, thickness 6–7mm. SF71, C2107, G42, Phase 3. Not illustrated.

65. Triangular body fragment from a prismatic bottle of later 1st- early 3rd century in date. Dimensions 24mm x 15mm x 4mm. SF24, C1002, G1001, Phase 6. Not illustrated.

66. Body fragment from a prismatic bottle of later 1st- early 3rd century in date. Dimensions 50mm x 44mm x 5mm. SF59, C1123, G152, Phase 4. Not illustrated.

67. Body fragment from a prismatic bottle of later 1st - early 3rd century in date. Dimensions 34mm x 32mm x 3mm. SF325, C1034, G41, Phase 3-4. Not illustrated.

68. Body fragment from a prismatic bottle of later 1st- early 3rd century in date. Dimensions 15mm x 7mm x 6mm. SF385, C1033, G24, Phase 4. Not illustrated.

69. Body fragment from a prismatic bottle of later 1st - early 3rd century in date. Dimensions 51mm x 24mm x 1.5mm. SF32, C2034, G154, Phase 4. Not illustrated.

70. Body fragment from a prismatic bottle of later 1st- early 3rd century in date. Dimensions 19mm x 14mm x 5mm. SF494, C1002, G1001, Phase 6. Not illustrated.

71. Body fragment from a prismatic bottle of later 1st- early 3rd century in date. Dimensions 26mm x 18mm x 4mm. SF492, C1002, G1001, Phase 6. Not illustrated.

72. Body fragment from a prismatic bottle of later 1st- early 3rd century in date. Dimensions 22mm x 20mm x 3mm. SF123, C2121, G143, Phase 4. Not illustrated.

73. Body fragment from a prismatic bottle of later 1st- early 3rd century in date. Dimensions 24mm x 9mm x 3mm. SF116, C1137, G43, Phase 4. Not illustrated.

74. Body fragment from a prismatic bottle of later 1st- early 3rd century in date. Dimensions 40mm x 13mm x 3mm. SF130, C2140, G121, Phase 2-4. Not illustrated.

75. Triangular body fragment, 1st- 3rd century in date. Dimensions 16mm x 7mm x 1mm. SF35, C1033, G24, Phase 4. Not illustrated.

76. Body fragment, 1st- 3rd century in date. Dimensions 34mm x 17mm x 2mm. SF101, C1034, G41, Phase 3-4. Not illustrated.

77. Body fragment, 1st- 3rd century in date. Dimensions 36mm x 10mm x 2mm. SF242, C2048, G98, Phase 2. Not illustrated.

Other blue-green vessels

78. Narrow loop handle fragment from a bath flask of late 1st - early 3rd century in date. Length 30mm, width 15mm, thickness 10mm. SF159, C1482, G88, Phase 2. Not illustrated.

79. Cylindrical fragment from the lower body/base edge of a jar. Dimensions 35mm x 36mm x 1.5–3mm. SF120, C2110, G19, Phase 3. Not illustrated.

80. Fragments from a handle with a central rib from a blue-green glass jug, all five of which are small and abraded. The largest measures 28mm x 16mm x 5mm. SF63, C2157, G1000, Phase 6. Not illustrated.

Pale green vessels

81. Small fragment from the rolled rim of a jar, late 1st- early 3rd century in date. Length 28mm, width 7mm, thickness 3mm. SF95, C1034, G41, Phase 3-4. Not illustrated.

82. Straight-sided fragment from a jug or flask. Dimensions 36mm x 14mm x 1mm. SF33, C1055, G24, Phase 4. Not illustrated.

Colourless vessel

83. Body fragment, 2nd–3rd century in date. Dimensions 18mm x 10mm x 1mm. SF488, C1139, G140, Phase 4. Not illustrated.

Window glass

84. Cast fragment, 1st–3rd century in date. Dimensions 50mm x 40mm x 6mm. SF500, C1002, G1001, Phase 6. Not illustrated.

5.7. Stone

Julie Lochrie, Peter Thomson with contribution by Martin Henig and Paul Olver

The stone finds comprise ten fragmentary querns, a whetstone and a fragment of decoratively carved furniture.

Querns

The querns are all rotary including six upper stone and four lower stone fragments. All are made of sandstone, mostly coarse, with two coarse breccia examples (Nos.91 and 93) and one fine sandstone (No.88), though all are essentially from the same source material which is probably of local origin, or at least from the east side of the Malverns.

Rotary querns are composed of a lower and an upper stone, the latter affixed with a handle. The upper stone has a central perforation called a hopper and the lower stone has a central perforation within which a spindle would be set to hold the two stones together. Grain would be poured in the hopper and the upper stone could be moved by rotation or oscillation to grind the grain. Rotary querns were already in use in Britain before the arrival of the Romans and continued in use after. The native British querns were typically smaller, tall and heavy; termed beehive querns for their shape (Curwen 1937; 1941). They rise to prominence around the 2nd or 3rd centuries BC and continue as late as the 4th century AD (Wright 2002, 267). The Roman occupation brought with it a trend for flat and disc querns, often with a raised, projecting hopper (Buckley and Major 1983, fig 78, 74; Curwen 1937, 144) but there was a significant overlap in the use of Romano-British and native British varieties. The querns from Magistrates Court all appear to be flatter, disc varieties although No.93 may be from a beehive quern.

As so many of the querns are broken only a partial view of their shape and features is possible. Overall shapes reveal two types of upper stone and three types of lower stone. The upper stones are either thin and flat (Nos.85, 88–90) (No.88, Illus 5.07) or flat with a markedly concave grinding side (No.86, Illus 5.07). The lower stones are either flat (No.91), bun shaped with a convex base (No.93) or thin with a concave base and raised area around the spindle hole (No.92, Illus 5.07, No.94). The hopper is present on four upper examples and in all cases are either straight sided or hourglass shaped. In two cases the stones retained traces of handle holes (Nos.88, Illus 5.07, No.89) and in both cases they occur at the break. The handle holes are for radial slot handles which are open at the top. Interestingly both are inset at an angle but in the case of No.89 the handle is angled upwards towards the hopper and in the case of No.88 it is angled upwards away from the hopper. Radial handle holes are common on the flatter disc querns. A similar example from Iver, Buckinghamshire had been dated to the 1st century AD (Curwen 1937, Plate II, 134). All lower stones retained part of their spindle hole. They are fairly unremarkable but only one instance shows a spindle hole which did not perforate the entirety of the stone (No.91).

Some more unusual features can be seen on Nos.85–87. No.86 is the only quern with a raised border at the rim, the function of which would have been to hold the grain in the shallow well at the top (No.86, Illus 5.07). This is a feature more often seen on lava querns. In the case of No.85 the stepped hopper could have functioned in a similar way, creating a wider 'well' for the grain to be held. No.87 meanwhile has an indented ledge on the interior of the hopper which may have been to hold an iron rynd (a ring around the spindle) (No.87, Illus 5.07). Only one stone shows any sign of decoration, No.86 with linear grooves around its outside edge. This 'decoration' is irregular and worn in parts and may also relate to the shaping of the stone.

The querns were found in deposits dating to Phases 2, 3 and 4 which encompasses a period from the late 2nd to early 4th centuries AD. Querns are often difficult to date as some styles can remain in use for long periods of time as can the querns themsleves. Additionally the stones can often be reused for other activities or incorporated into buildings, hearths and other structures (Wright 2002, 267). Four of the Magistrates Court fragments were found incorporated into ovens and hearths, while a further four were found in surfaces or cobbles.

The Magistrates Court assemblage is too small to track any chronological trends. Most of the querns were found in Phase 4 deposits which might suggest that the same querns were in use for a long time until towards the end of the Roman period activity at the site. The earliest stratified quern, No.91, is very thick, to the extent that the spindle hole does not perforate the whole thickness of the stone. It may in fact be an Iron Age style beehive quern, though deposited a century or more into the Roman period.

Upper stones

85. Rotary quern fragment. Coarse sandstone. Radial sector with hopper. The hopper is stepped beginning at 150mm in diameter then narrowing to 90mm by way of a steep concavity. The remaining feeder pipe is convex. Peck-marks visible on rim and upper surface. 18% remaining. Diam 450mm, perforation diam 150–90mm, rim thickness 78mm; centre thickness 64mm. SF146, C2376, unphased, Not illustrated.

86. Rotary quern fragment. Coarse sandstone. Fragment with small amount of rim, very worn with some surface loss. Flat upper surface and very smooth, concave lower surface. The upper surface of the quern has a small part of the original edge remaining and this shows the remains of a raised rim 37mm wide. The upper surface is covered in small peck-marks and irregular vertical grooves can be seen on the remaining edge. These marks are the result of shaping but would also have had a decorative effect. Diam 520+mm, rim thickness 98mm, centre thickness 67mm. SF163, C1436, G7, Phase 1. Illus 5.07.

87. Rotary quern fragment. Coarse sandstone. Radial sector with rim and central perforation. Very little remains of the perforation, it widens towards the feed pipe but curves back towards the centre after 28mm with the remaining 8mm a broken edge. This may be a small ledge for an iron rynd or, despite its fairly central location it may suggest a handle hole rather than the hopper. Peck marks are visible to the

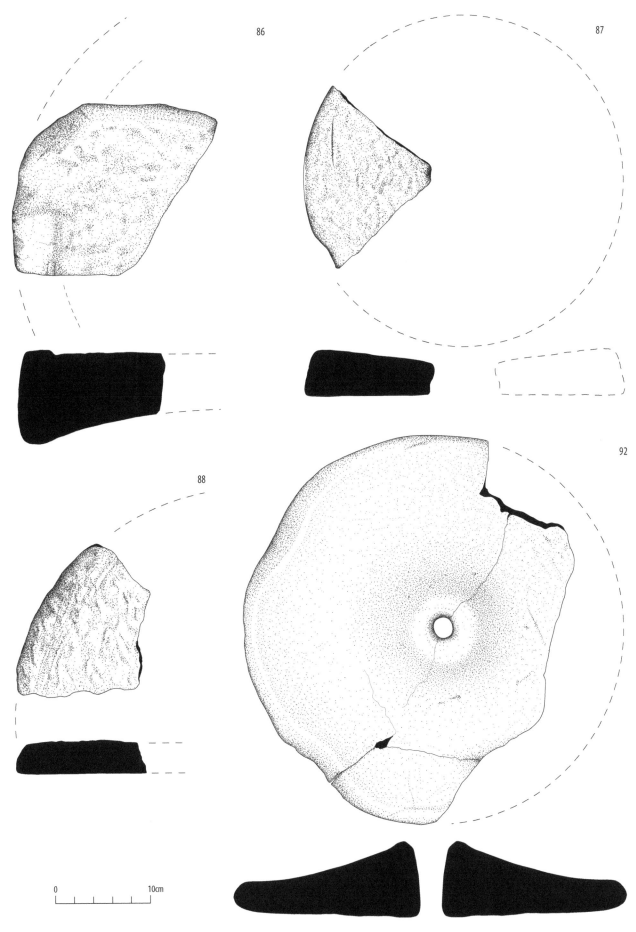

Illus 5.07. Stone querns

top and rim but the grinding surface is smooth with no traces of shaping. 20% remaining. Diam 350mm, rim thickness 36mm, centre thickness 48mm. SF98, C2110, G19, Phase 3. Illus 5.07.

88. Rotary quern fragment. Fine sandstone. Broken radial sector with remains of handle hole and rim but no hopper. There handle hole is a radial slot (open to the upper surface) whose depth increases towards the centre, beginning at the rim 13mm from the grinding surface and perforating the entirety at the hopper. Peck marks cover the top, rim and grinding surface. Very thin and probably worn down, possibly being redressed at some point. 7% remaining. Diam 490mm, rim thickness 32mm, centre thickness 32mm. SF60, C1125, G140, Phase 4. Illus 5.07.

89. Rotary quern fragment. Sandstone. Fragment with remains of slot handle and hopper at breaks, no original rim surface. Hopper is likely to have been conical. The handle hole is open to the upper surface at a depth of 20–27mm and is angled upwards towards the feeder pipe. Some peck-marks from shaping visible to the upper surface. Length 160mm, width 100mm, rim thickness 50mm, centre thickness 40mm. SF103, C1028, G131, Phase 4. Not illustrated.

90. Rotary quern fragment. Sandstone. Probable upper stone. The upper surface and perforation have surface loss. Peck-marks visible in hopper and rim. The grinding surface has been grooved with concentric circles roughly 10mm apart. 16% remaining. Diam 585mm, perforation diam 190mm, rim thickness 75mm, centre thickness 57mm. SF131, C2288, G147, Phase 4. Not illustrated.

Lower stones

91. Rotary quern fragment. Coarse sandstone breccia. Large section with spindle hole which is conical in shape with a concave base, does not perforate the stone and is 24mm deep. Only one side remains as there is an irregular break to the other side. The base is gently convex and unevenly pecked to shape. The grinding surface is smooth with some concentric lines visible near the spindle hole. The grinding surface is overall convex however towards the rim it becomes gently concave. 30% remaining. Diam 440mm, perforation diam 25mm, rim thickness 44mm, centre thickness 103mm. SF156, C1478, G908, Phase 2. Not illustrated.

92. Rotary quern fragment. Coarse sandstone. Large portion of the lower stone, only loss of rim to one half. The spindle hole is hourglass shaped and perforates through the entirety in a slightly diagonal placement the base is roughly pecked and concave while the grinding surface is smooth with to traces of manufacture. The grinding surface is gently concave but rises significantly towards the spindle hole. 80% remaining; Diam 390mm, perforation diam 22–40mm, rim thickness 30mm, centre thickness 85mm. SF112, C1339, G129, Phase 4. Illus 5.07.

93. Rotary quern fragment. Coarse sandstone breccia. Loss of grinding surface although the spindle hole can be seen at the break and perforates the entirety of the stone. The base of the stone is flat and very roughly shaped through pecking; this side remains uneven and rough. The rim is pecked and dressed more carefully. The grinding surface is convex and smooth. 25% remaining. Diam 410mm, perforation diam 40mm, rim thickness 55mm, centre thickness 85+mm. SF53, C1028, G131, Phase 4. Not illustrated.

94. Rotary quern fragment. Coarse sandstone. Almost half the stone survives but is broken through the spindle hole which is very slightly hourglass shaped and perforates the entirety. The base of the stone is concave and roughly dressed with peck-marks visible. The grinding surface is smooth with no trace of manufacture. The grinding surface is angled upwards towards the centre and fairly straight although ever so slightly kicks upwards towards the rim. 45% remaining. Diam 465mm, perforation diam 90mm, rim thickness 55mm, centre thickness 50mm. SF48, C1075, G160 (G45), Phase 4. Not illustrated.

Whetstone

95. Whetstone fragment. Fine grained waterlain Buff Sandstone: Silurian/Devonian. Sub-rectangular in section. Slightly rounded chamfer to corners along length, tapering away from surviving end. Wear indicates use as a whetstone. 70mm (broken) x 34mm x 18–12mm. SF539, C1182, G2, Phase 1-2. Not illustrated.

Furniture fragment

Martin Henig and Paul Olver (geology) (report submitted 2020)

This is the corner of a side table (Illus 5.08) of a familiar type from west-country villas, mostly therefore, carved in oolitic limestone. It has a recessed top with a raised edge to prevent whatever was placed on the table from slipping off and is embellished on the side with an excellently carved eight-petalled flower or rosette set within a raised ring.

There are a number of parallels to the rosette, one of the closest being from Bays Meadow villa, Droitwich (Barfield and Roe 2006, 185–8, figs 125–6, no.1), with a four-petalled rosette carved in similar style. However, a similar rosette is depicted on the side of a table from Winchester, Hampshire (Cunliffe and Fulford 1982, 48 and pl.42 no.176). The corner of a table from Gatcombe, Somerset, is also embellished with a rosette but not so well executed (ibid, 49 and pl.42 no.181). Likewise, nor is the rather star like flower on a fragment from Chedworth (T F C Blagg in Henig 1993, 76 and pl.58 no.243).

These side tables have, for the most part, been recorded from villas in Gloucestershire, Hampshire and Somerset and this example together with that from Droitwich are the most northerly known. The other side tables are all of

Illus 5.08. Furniture fragment

oolitic limestone and this is the only example known to date in dune sandstone.

96. Decorative stone furniture fragment. Bridgnorth Sandstone also known as Dune Sandstone (windblown). Permian. Fragment from the upper right corner of an item of furniture. The top is recessed with a raised border. The face and side of the stone has a deeply incised horizontal line which enhances the raised border on top. Directly below this, on the face of the stone, is a circular motif segmented by seven radial lines and a small central convex circle (a 'rosette-type' decoration). This motif is surrounded by a ring, created by deep incisions around the border of the face. Length 240mm, width 150mm, breadth 132mm. SF140, C2343, G125, Phase 1. Illus 5.08.

5.8. Ceramic building materials

Phil Mills and Graham C Morgan (report submitted 2001)

A total of 3274 fragments of ceramic building material, weighing 185.4kg, were recovered from the site. Of this, 2828 fragments (159.5kg) could be identified as of Roman date, based either on typology or stratigraphy though, given the fragmentary state of the material and the similarity of some of the medieval and Roman fabrics, clear separation was not always possible. Medieval and modern finds have been excluded from this report as far as possible. The fragments were examined under a x20 hand lens. Descriptions were made based on the systems outlined in Orton et al (1993), Peacock (1977b) and Tomber and Dore (1998). The report on the fired clay was prepared from an original report by Grahame Morgan, adapted in the light of later stratigraphic information.

The pieces were generally relatively small in size, suggesting that they were in fact rubble brought in as part of a manuring process or as hard core for ground stabilizing or levelling. They do not seem to be associated with any Roman structures in the immediate vicinity. The large proportion of tegula to imbrex fragments is also consistent with this idea and suggests that pieces may have been selected for being flat.

The fabrics were divided into 12 categories (WMC01-WMC12) though WMC06 was only represented by medieval tiles and has not been listed (see Table 5.03). Most of the fabrics would seem to be variants of WMC01. This implies that, though the rubble was made up from material from different sources, there was one major supplier in the area. The similarity between fabrics WMC01 and WMC03 suggests that both were produced locally and from the same sources of raw materials.

Brick and tile

No complete bricks were seen in the assemblage. One brick with a thickness of 65mm in fabric WMC07 was recorded.

Tegula flanges had thicknesses varying from 18mm to 60mm. They were formed on sanded moulds with flanges formed in equal numbers either by hand shaping or the use of a knife/wire. A few examples showed that trimming of the leather hard product prior to firing had occurred, probably as part of the same process that made the cutaways. The cutaways were typical of Romano-British bricks (Brodbribb 1987,16, fig 7 no 1 and 5). Fragments of signatures were observed on most of the tegula fragments, but not enough survived to attempt a reconstruction. There were also four animal prints, all on tegula and all in fabric WMC01 from G2, Phase 1-2 (C1134), G19, Phase 3 (C2178) and from modern makeup deposits C1002 and C1125. The amount of animal prints on the different tiles suggests possible agricultural practices in the vicinity as well as seasonal tile production. There were also some finger marks on a tegula fragment in fabric WMC01 from G800, Phase 4 (C2178).

The imbrex were of the standard horseshoe shape. Thickness varied between 10mm and 15mm. They were formed on sanded moulds. One imbrex had a cut lattice decoration similar to that seen on flue tiles (see below).

Lynne Bevan, Andy Boucher, Kath Crooks, Peter Guest, Martin Henig, Julie Lochrie, Paul Olver, Peter Thomso

Table 5.03. Ceramic building material fabrics

Fabric code	Description	Notes	Brick	Tegula	Imbrex	Flue	Fired Clay
WMC01	This is a light red (Munsell: 10R6/8) fabric with a hard sandy feel and a fine fracture, with inclusions of abundant moderately-sorted fine sub rounded mica, sparse well-sorted medium sub angular black iron stone, and sparse moderately-sorted medium sub rounded quartz.	It would appear to be similar to SVW OX2 (Tomber and Dore 1998,149). Possibly produced at Upper Sandlin Farm, Leigh Sinton SO 7551 (McWhirr 1979,139), 2nd to 3rd century AD.		X	X	X	
WMC02	A weak red (Munsell: 10R4/4) very hard sandy feel and a fine fracture, with inclusions of abundant poorly-sorted coarse angular black iron stone, abundant well-sorted fine rounded mica (silver), moderate poorly-sorted coarse sub angular calcite(?), and sparse moderately-sorted medium rounded quartz.	This is a variant of WMC01, but with more inclusions and also possibly falls in the range of SVW OX2.		X	X	X	
WMC03	A red with light reddish-brown surface (Munsell: 3.5YR5/8 Core: 5YR6/4) hard very sandy feel and irregular fracture, with inclusions of abundant well-sorted fine rounded mica, abundant poorly-sorted coarse sub rounded quartz, moderate poorly-sorted medium sub angular black iron stone, moderate moderately-sorted medium sub angular limestone (?), and moderately-sorted medium sub rounded quartzite.	This fabric is very similar to WMC01, suggesting the use of common raw materials. Inclusions tend to be less well sorted, coarser and have a greater range.	X				
WMC04	A pale red external surface with red internal surface (Munsell: 10R4/2, core: 2.5YR6/2) soft very sandy feel and hackly fracture, with inclusions of sparse poorly-sorted medium sub angular flint (?), sparse well-sorted medium sub angular green stone, sparse well-sorted fine rounded mica and sparse poorly-sorted coarse angular quartzite	A very under fired sample.		X	X	X	
WMC05	A light reddish-brown surface with dark reddish-brown (Munsell: 5yr3/3 5yr6/4) hard very sandy feel and irregular fracture, with inclusions of abundant well-sorted fine rounded mica, abundant moderately-sorted medium sub rounded quartz abundant moderately-sorted medium sub rounded quartzite and sparse moderately-sorted medium sub angular limestone.		X				
WMC07	A red with dusky grey core (Munsell: 2.5yr3/2 2.5yr4/8) very hard granular feel and irregular fracture, with inclusions of abundant well-sorted fine rounded mica, sparse moderately sorted medium rounded quartz and abundant poorly-sorted medium rounded voids.	A very high fired fabric. Possible variant of WMC03.	X				
WMC08	A reddish-yellow (Munsell: 5yr6/6) hard sandy feel and fine fracture, with inclusions of sparse well-sorted medium rounded limestone, abundant well-sorted medium sub rounded quartz and moderate well-sorted medium sub angular stone.		X				
WMC09	Sparse inclusions of charcoal and silver mica.						X
WMC10	Greyer, more reduced fired clay than WMC09						X
WMC11	A variant of WMC01. Hard and has a reduced core.			X	X	X	
WMC12	This is a buff variant of WMC01 with a red core and red paint/slip on surface.			X		X	

Table 5.04. Ceramic building material forms

Type	Fragments	Weight (kg)
Brick	51	3.2
Tegula	1218	88.0
Imbrex	110	10.8
Flue	102	7.9
Fired clay	1347	49.6
Total	2828	159.5

The flue tiles had been manufactured by forming slabs on a sanded surface that were then stuck together prior to drying and firing. Three distinct patterns were observed: combed; cut lattice; and wavy. Combing was created with a fine-toothed comb and was most common in Phase 2, but was present in later phases in small amounts. It was observed in fabrics WMC01, WMC02 and WMC12. Cut lattice was created by cutting a lattice pattern into the dried, but unfired surface. It was present from Phase 2, but was most common in Phase 4 and was found in fabrics WMC01 and WMC02. Wavy patterns were made using a broad toothed comb. They were present from Phase 3, but again, most common in Phase 4. This pattern was only observed in fabric WMC01. The range of different patterns on the box flue tiles found suggests different batches, possibly from the same source, but made by different tilers.

There is a Roman kiln located *c* 16km away at Upper Sandlin Farm, Leigh Sinton (McWhirr 1979,139), which produced the full range of products seen here. It is thought to have operated from the 2nd to 3rd century AD, though it does not necessarily follow that it is the source for the material found here as there may have been nearer sources as yet undiscovered.

Fired clay

A total of 50.2kg of fired clay was recovered, of which 49.6kg was found in Roman contexts (Phases 1–4). The finds were bulk weighed and examined microscopically. The pieces were all burnt to a greater or lesser extent, acquiring a reddish colour, although some became grey or remained brown. The colour resulting from burning depends on the temperature reached, the iron content and the nature of the fire (oxidising or reducing). Clay containing iron will become red if burnt in air to a temperature in excess of 500°C. Under reducing conditions it may be blackened or if there is little iron it may only become pink or grey. All of these conditions are seen in this material. Commonly chopped grass or straw was added to the mix to strengthen the clay. Some wattle impressions were noted in the form of twig-like impressions up to *c* 10mm in diameter, typically running parallel to each other. Some pieces show a great many small holes, which at about 0.5mm in diameter, may be grass impressions but could also be caused by the fermentation of the mud, grass and or dung mixture whilst awaiting application. Such fermentation processes

are actually encouraged in the production of mud brick in the near east.

The fired clay was particularly associated with Phase 4 industrial features (Tables 5.05–5.06). The largest concentration was associated with the workshop in the south-west part of the site from which 20.6kg of fired clay was collected. The majority of this was associated with the backfilling of the ovens (G137, 16.7kg) with further material from a clay-lined pit (G134, 2.4kg) and probably derives from these features. The only other large concentration was in another industrial feature, again deriving from an oven (G139, 16.7kg). Earlier smaller concentrations include a Phase 2-4 pit containing slag (G121, 0.9kg), and therefore likely to be related to ironworking activity, and more enigmatically, the Phase 1 boundary ditch (G1, 1.4kg) and Phase 3 gravel surface (G19, 1.0kg). Material in these latter features may be residual or may relate to wattle and daub or cob structures. The presence of twig impressions in pieces related to ovens suggest these structures were formed of clay over a wattle and daub superstructure.

5.9. Ironworking residues

Andy Boucher and Kath Crooks

The ironworking evidence took two different forms. Firstly, a large quantity of slag and secondly micro-residues recovered from sample retents. The former was judged to

Table 5.05. Fired clay by phase

Phase	Wgt (g)
1	2309
2	2737
3	1198
4	43310
Total	49554

Table 5.06. Groups containing over 0.5kg of fired clay

Phase	Group	Description	Wgt (g)
1	902	Ditch	900
1	1	Boundary/enclosure ditch	1409
2	121	Pit	900
3	19	Gravel surface	1026
4	24	Workshop in SW of site, floor	546
4	25	Workshop in SW of site, floor	640
4	134	Workshop in SW of site, clay-lined pit	2350
4	137	Workshop in SW of site, oven backfill	16713
4	139	Associated industrial features, oven	21540
Total			46024

be largely imported to the site and given the extent of this practice, it was impossible to be sure that any slag found associated with ironworking features actually derived from those features. The micro-residues were deemed a much better guide to on-site industry.

Slag

A very large quantity of slag was recovered from the site. It had been incorporated in surfaces and layers predominantly from Phases 3 and 4. This was assessed by the author (Andy Boucher) with Dr Gerry McDonnell and was viewed to be a tertiary deposit of slag, in effect material brought to the site from Roman slag heaps elsewhere to make surfaces. The recovered slag was bagged and sampled and the contents of every sack inspected to identify the nature of material present and assess its potential to assist in interpreting features within the site or contribute further to the analysis of iron working in Roman Worcester. The initial assessment established that all the slag was either tap or smelting slag and there was no indication of the presence of smithing hearths within the assemblage. Further to the work on the slag at Deansway all the sampled material was searched to see if any slag tubing was present as this was deemed to be a significant element of the Worcester ironworking assemblages (McDonnell and Swiss 2004). No slag tubing could be found and the remaining material was not deemed worthy of retention for further study.

Magnetic micro-residues

Further to the recommendations of the environmental specialist all the retent samples from the sieving of environmental samples were investigated for the presence of ironworking micro residues. These were separated out using a magnet (as all such residues tend to be highly magnetic and unfortunately non-magnetic micro-slags would not have been recovered) and inspected under a x10 to x30 lens to enable the nature of the residue to be characterised. For the purposes of the exercise a scale of abundance was used based on the weight of residues in grams against the volume of the sample they derived from in litres. Within each sample the types of residue present

were also recorded as this provides an indication of the nature of the process being undertaken. Three categories were recorded: flake; spheroid; lustre (the shininess of the material).

The presence of either flake or spheroid residues has been considered at some length by researchers and summarised by Dungworth and Wilks (2007). In practice flake hammerscale is well understood and produced through the heating of the iron in the hearth causing partial oxidation of the surface. When hit with the hammer the hot and temporarily 'soft' metal deforms whilst the brittle layer of iron oxide on the surface flakes off. The generally accepted model for spheroids is that they are formed by droplets of molten iron which have cooled rapidly (ibid., 4). Experimental forging and welding produced the following percentages of residues. In forging 93% to 1.7% flake to spheroid whilst in welding it was 79% to 5.8% respectively.

There is also the issue of temperature. When heated to below 570°C two layers form, the outer being haematite (Fe_2O_3) the inner magnetite (Fe_3O_4); above that temperature a thick layer of wustite (FeO) forms below these. The thickness of the flake hammerscale increases with an increase in temperature although many factors also affect this such as the length of time spent heating, the purity of the iron, and any impurities introduced through the process. Dungworth and Wilks suggest that for hot working iron (or forging) temperatures in excess of 910°C would be required, whilst welding could require temperatures up to 1100°C. From the above it is clear that where spheroid hammerscale is found then so to should flake. There is one occurrence where this might not be the case, where the metal is heated to the point of combustion, here just spheroid hammerscale is emitted, but this requires much higher temperatures and greater lengths of heating to achieve.

Several things are apparent from the Worcester assemblage. Firstly, the number of contexts containing hammerscale suggest that the majority of iron working takes place during Phases 3 and 4 (Phase 3 contains surfaces that were exposed during Phase 4 and thus residues here can

Table 5.07. Presence and nature of magnetic residues

Phase	No. contexts % of phase	Just flake	Lustre	Just Spheroid	Spheroid and flake	Lustre with spheroid	Average abundance g/l
1	10	6	5	0	2	2	0.19
	15%	60%	50%	0%	20%	20%	
2	17	10	7	0	6	3	0.34
	7%	59%	41%	0%	35%	18%	
3	3	1	1	0	2	0	0.36
	8%	33%	33%	0%	67%	0%	
4	61	28	20	2	30	11	0.96
	27%	46%	33%	3%	49%	18%	

be contemporary). A small amount of iron working also appears to be taking place in Phase 1, whilst the low level and broad distribution of hammerscale in Phase 2 might imply this was intrusive from later more intense activity in Phase 4. Considering the occurrence of spheroid and flake, and following the above discussion, it would appear that higher temperature processes were being undertaken in the later phases of the site compared to the earlier ones, as there is a much-increased prevalence of spheroids. It is also interesting (although not discussed in the literature) that the presence of shiny flakes seems to be more associated with the lower temperature process as there are higher percentages of the occurrence of this in the earlier phases, and notable that the percentage occurrence of samples containing shiny flakes and spheroids remains constant throughout.

Consideration of the distribution of hammerscale by phase across the site produces an interesting pattern. During Phase 1 (Illus 5.09) a hearth in the south-west of the site with associated spreads of debris and other shallow features occupies an area adjacent to a ditch with some metalworking residue getting into the ditch. This is clearly

clustered and not directly underlying the intensive areas of Phase 4 activity. It is, however, quite small amounts of material suggesting low levels of metal working (maybe tool repair). During Phase 2 (Illus 5.10) the majority of iron working residues again appear in the south-west corner of the site but the abundance is quite low and with no real clusters of material.

Phases 3 and 4 need to be considered together; here there is a clear correlation between hearths containing scale and features and surfaces to their north also collecting considerable quantities of the material (Illus 5.11–5.12). The whole of the slag floor for the replacement workshop in Phase 4 (G24) as well as the clay-lined pit (G134) and other features to the north produced evidence for this. It is notable that the Phase 3 surfaces that are immediately adjacent also contain hammerscale whilst those much further to the north are clean. Another interesting feature of this phase relates to what originally appeared to be relatively sparse pits in the north-west corner of the site. These also show evidence for iron working suggesting that there is either another centre of activity just outside the north edge of the excavation or that these were being

Illus 5.09. Distribution of industrial micro-residues in Phase 1

Illus 5.10. Distribution of industrial micro-residues in Phase 2

used for rubbish disposal associated with the activity in the south-west part of the site.

To conclude it would appear that during Phase 1, small-scale smithing was occurring in the south-west corner of the site. By the later phases of the occupation of this area it is likely that a larger-scale smithing complex grew up possibly working with greater efficiency and higher levels of heat as well as providing a much wider range of products based on the larger range of features that appear to have been in use at the time hammerscale was being deposited. This is supported through the associated small finds assemblage with two iron bars and a possible iron billet (SF208, SF211, SF216, C1033, C1053, G24, Phase 4), although the lack of vitrified hearth lining or macroscopic smithing slags does necessitate some caution with this interpretation. A lack of hearth lining is not necessarily that unusual, however, as smithing hearths were typically raised structures (and are certainly likely to have been housed in a relatively substantial structure such as this). It is also very rare for smithing hearths to survive (David Starley pers comm), and more often than not little or no evidence for them is found.

Discussion of ironworking residues

Worcester is known for the range of iron-working that took place there during the Roman period. A thorough consideration of slag and smelting products was produced following work at the Butts, about 200m south of the Magistrates Court site in 2011 (Blakelock 2011). This indicated considerable uniformity amongst slags analysed to date within the city and implied that the ores forming them derived from the Forest of Dean (ibid., 81). In terms of the location of processes with respect to the Roman settlement, waste products dated to the 2nd and 3rd centuries were found at Deansway with 3rd–4th century industrial activity identified around Farrier Street. At the Butts this comprised mainly furnace lining, tap and smelting slags spanning the 2nd to 4th centuries (ibid., 76). However, at none of these sites was there any evidence for this activity having taken place on site. Smelting furnaces were located to the south of the site at Broad Street (Barker 1969) and City Arcade (Griffin et al 2004). The current site also contained evidence of smelting in the form of slags but by contrast it also provided a good degree of evidence in the form of micro-slags that forging or high temperature

Illus 5.11. Distribution of industrial micro-residues in Phase 3

smithing were taking place on site. This evidence not only defines the extent, organisation and make up of the working area but includes the bases of features used in the process. The use of smelting slag in surfaces associated with these structures is coincidental and not related to the process. The latter assertion is based on the absence of micro slag beneath the slag surfaces. If the slag had derived as a result of the processes being undertaken on the site then these micro slags would be expected beneath the surface in the soil layers there too, these being known to be the upper level of the ground surface prior to laying of the slag layers.

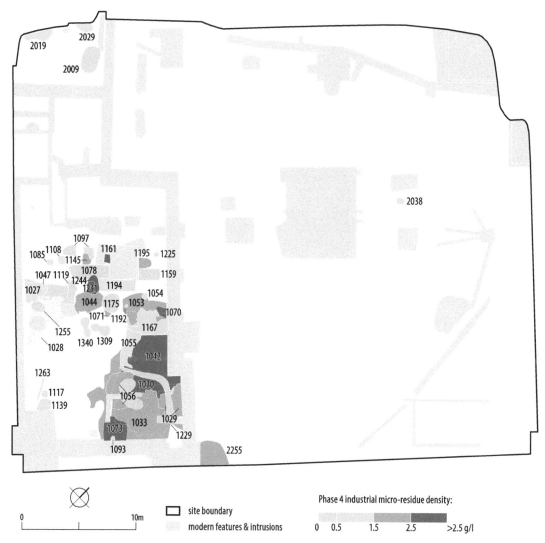

Illus 5.12. Distribution of industrial micro-residues in Phase 4

Environmental evidence

Callista Vink, Andy Hammond, Elizabeth Pearson,
David Jordan and Andy Boucher

6.1. Faunal remains

Callista Vink and Andy Hammond

The following text has been edited from a report produced by Callista Vink of Southampton University (Vink 2008) and an assessment of the animal bone undertaken by Andy Hammond prior to this. The assessment concluded that despite the fairly poor preservation of the material the assemblage had potential (mainly through species composition and mortality curves) to advance our understanding of husbandry practices and use of animal products in Roman Worcester.

The aims of the analysis focused on a number of questions some integral to the site others with respect to other sites and the Roman period as a whole. The nature and subsequent use of the Phase 3 surfaces was a key question as was the origin and type of material present, i.e. did it represent on-site consumption, on-site preparation or simply town waste brought to the site after its abandonment? The work also undertook to assess the types of butchery represented on the site and the wider question as to how this compared with other urban Roman settlements.

The material forming the assemblage was recovered using both hand collection and sieving through an 8mm mesh. Samples were generally 60 litres. It was viewed at assessment (Hammond 2001) that as a result recovery bias was unlikely to exist.

Methodology

It was decided to use the anatomical zone system established by Serjeantson (1996) as the basis for the identification of elements and species. Butchery adopted Lauwerier's (1988) recording system with new categories being introduced when required (Appendix 6). Both epiphyseal fusion (Reitz and Wing 2007; Noddle 1974; Purdue 1983; Schmid 1972; Silver 1970) and tooth wear (Halstead 1985; Greenfield and Arnold 2008; O'Connor 1988) were used to age elements of the assemblage. Out of the taxa present on the site skeletal elements required for sexing were only present in the case of pigs (canines after Schmid 1972) and cattle (metacarpals after Maltby 1990, 41 and Table 85).

Biometric measurement followed the system established by Driesh (1976) with sufficient measurements being taken with a view to further understanding the faunal composition of the assemblage such as whether animals were being brought in from a variety of places exhibited through wide variations in the size and shape of bones (O'Connor 2003). Due to the small amount of the assemblage that was available for biometric study this has not been reproduced here. Quantification used a combination of NISP (Number of Identified Specimens) and MNI (Minimum number of individuals) to establish relative frequencies of taxa in the assemblage (Reitz and Wing 2007).

Preservation

The preservation of bone surfaces (cortical integrity) demonstrated reasonable uniformity throughout the assemblage. The majority of the bone ranged from poorly preserved to moderately well preserved. This material was characterised by varying degrees of exfoliation and abrasion to their original surfaces. Damage, which would appear to be chemical rather than mechanical, was caused by the acidic nature of the sandy gravel soil matrix. A small amount of material was well preserved, having suffered little of the attrition affecting the majority of the assemblage, most notably from pit or post-hole fills.

The chemical attrition to the material may have introduced a bias into the assemblage. For instance, despite the extensive sampling regime, no small mammal or fish bone, and very little bird bone, was recovered from the excavation. If such a bias exists it may not be overly limiting, as urban Roman assemblages are normally dominated by the larger domesticated mammals anyway.

The assemblage comprised mainly the more robust ends of long bones (femur, humerous etc) or mandibles and teeth (the latter accounting for 28% of the total identified bones). Four types of damage were observed:

- Damage during or after excavation (unavoidable breaks due to poor levels of preservation)
- Damage prior to deposition (cuts or smooth breaks)
- Burning (either before or after deposition) – seen in 4% of the assemblage
- Gnawing (damage immediately following deposition) – seen in 9% of the assemblage

Residuality and contamination

Estimating the residuality of animal bone is notoriously difficult. Various methods have been employed, such as indices based on bone colour and surface abrasion. However, all have their own methodological problems (for example see Dobney et al 1995). One of the most common methods used to infer animal bone residuality is to use levels of pottery residuality as a baseline, although there may be no direct correlation between the two.

Initial results from this site indicate considerable quantities of residual material in many contexts and particularly on the surfaces. However, despite the problematic use of bone colour and abrasion indices it was noted that the material demonstrated considerable homogeneity within individual deposits (especially fills), which suggests rapid accumulation and a lack of re-working. The cobbled surfaces were more affected by problems of re-working, due to their length of exposure.

Fragmentation

Fragmentation throughout the assemblage was fairly extensive. A reasonably large proportion of the 'countable' (Albarella and Davis 1994; Davis 1992) fragments were comprised of isolated maxillary and mandibular teeth. This is also a reflection of the acidic burial environment, and it was apparent when the assemblage was scanned that it must have been impossible to lift many skull and mandible fragments during the excavation without them disintegrating. Taking this into account it was noted that fragmentation was generally consistent with the material being derived from normal butchery and kitchen waste.

Comparison of fragmentation against the percentage of large mammals (cows and horses) represented in each phase and against different deposits revealed an interesting picture. There appeared to be a distinction between the earliest two phases and those that followed them. In Phases 1 and 2 as the relative number of larger mammal bones in the assemblage decreased so did the completeness of bones within that part of the assemblage (measured as a factor of the total number of bones over the total number of fragments). The result would be expected in the case of normal accidental damage over a short period of time where the slighter bones of smaller mammals are more susceptible to damage. This could also mean that sheep and goats may be under-represented in the earliest two phases of the site. In Phases 3 and 4 the levels of fragmentation increase alongside an increase in the relative number of larger mammals present. The simplest explanation is that during these phases the whole assemblage is more evenly fragmented with many more of the undiagnosed fragments coming from the larger mammals. Plotting fragmentation against number of large mammals also demonstrates a distinction between Phases 3 and 4 with Phase 3 having the most fragmented assemblage and the largest proportion of large mammals. This latter situation would be expected as all the bone from Phase 3 came from surfaces and is not protected inside negative features.

Results of analysis

A total of 1509 bones were identified from the several thousand fragments recovered. These are broken down by taxon, phase and feature type in Table 6.01.

The minimum number of individuals was also estimated for each of the main taxa (Table 6.02).

Cattle

The age of cattle represented was identified based on tooth eruption and wear (Grant 1982) in 65 individual cattle mandibles. However due to the small number of ageable mandibles in the early phases (seven in Phases 1–2) no real comparison can be made between these. A similar situation arose with the assemblage from Deansway with poor preservation in the Roman and Saxon periods resulting in a paucity of information making comparison difficult again (Nicholson and Scott 2004). The overall conclusion is that most cattle were being kept into adulthood and as such were equally valued for traction and milk as they were for meat and hides.

In terms of the sex of cattle this could only be determined using the metacarpals (no intact horn cores were recovered) and as none survived intact the method proposed by Maltby (1990, 41 table 85) was used whereby metacarpals with a distal breadth of less than 56mm were classed as cows (as opposed to bulls). As a result five out of six specimens were classed as cows. It appears from the Deansway analysis (Nicholson and Scott 2004, 526–7) that little success was gained even with more complete bones being present and similarly this result should be treated tentatively as there are a wide range of factors other than the sex of the animal that might influence the outcome, and so few individuals could be analysed.

In comparison to the Roman material from Deansway (Nicholson and Scott 2004, 530–1) the material from this site demonstrated a considerable amount of butchery. One or more butchery marks were present on 21% of the cattle bones from the site (Table 6.03).

It is important to consider that much of the surface of the bone was not well enough preserved to enable slighter knife marks to be determined. In terms of patterns of butchery little distinction was observed between phases and these have been considered overall. The elements exhibiting the most signs of butchery and frequency of different types of butchery are shown in Table 6.04.

There were 18 different categories of butchery marks on the mandible (Appendix 6) (Lauwerier 1988). These included chop and cut marks to remove the mandible from the skull as well and knife marks to remove cheek meat (Johnstone and Albarella 2002). The use of the knife in this latter manner is something that has been noted to have an affinity with rural sites (Maltby 1989), urban centres tending to use heavier implements. The method

Table 6.01. Distribution of faunal remains within the assemblage by bone count (NISP) and percentage of total

Phase	Feature type	Cattle	Horse	Pig	Sheep/ goat	Bird	Dog	Deer	Total
1	Ditches	25 (53%)	14 (30%)	2 (4%)	6 (13%)	0 (0%)	0 (0%)	0 (0%)	47 (100%)
	Post-holes	4 (57%)	0 (0%)	1 (14%)	1 (14%)	0 (0%)	0 (0%)	1 (14%)	7 (100%)
	TOTAL	**29 (54%)**	**14 (26%)**	**3 (6%)**	**7 (13%)**	**0 (0%)**	**0 (0%)**	**1 (2%)**	**54 (100%)**
2	Ditches	30 (53%)	7 (12%)	0 (0%)	19 (33%)	1 (2%)	0 (0%)	0 (0%)	57 (100%)
	Pits	53 (38%)	5 (4%)	16 (12%)	61 (44%)	2 (1%)	1 (1%)	1 (1%)	139 (100%)
	Post-holes	46 (61%)	4 (5%)	4 (5%)	15 (20%)	0 (0%)	2 (3%)	4 (5%)	75 (100%)
	TOTAL	**129 (48%)**	**16 (6%)**	**20 (7%)**	**95 (35%)**	**3 (1%)**	**3 (1%)**	**5 (2%)**	**271 (100%)**
3	**Layers and surfaces**	**494 (84%)**	**35 (6%)**	**5 (1%)**	**53 (9%)**	**0 (0%)**	**0 (0%)**	**1 (0%)**	**588 (100%)**
4	Ditches	21 (66%)	2 (6%)	3 (9%)	6 (19%)	0 (0%)	0 (0%)	0 (0%)	32 (100%)
	Layers and surfaces	277 (81%)	6 (2%)	11 (3%)	44 (13%)	1 (0%)	1 (0%)	1 (0%)	341 (100%)
	Pits	79 (45%)	25 (14%)	14 (8%)	49 (28%)	0 (0%)	3 (2%)	5 (3%)	175 (100%)
	Post-holes	28 (58%)	6 (13%)	1 (2%)	13 (27%)	0 (0%)	0 (0%)	0 (0%)	48 (100%)
	TOTAL	**405 (68%)**	**39 (7%)**	**29 (5%)**	**112 (19%)**	**1 (0%)**	**4 (1%)**	**6 (1%)**	**596 (100%)**
All	Ditches	76 (56%)	23 (17%)	5 (4%)	31 (23%)	1 (1%)	0 (0%)	0 (0%)	136 (100%)
	Layers and surfaces	771 (83%)	41 (4%)	16 (2%)	97 (10%)	1 (0%)	1 (0%)	2 (0%)	929 (100%)
	Pits	132 (42%)	30 (10%)	30 (10%)	110 (35%)	2 (1%)	4 (1%)	6 (2%)	314 (100%)
	Post-holes	78 (60%)	10 (8%)	6 (5%)	29 (22%)	0 (0%)	2 (2%)	5 (4%)	130 (100%)
	TOTAL	**1057 (70%)**	**104 (7%)**	**57 (4%)**	**267 (18%)**	**4 (0%)**	**7 (0%)**	**13 (1%)**	**1509 (100%)**

Table 6.02. Minimum number of individuals

Phase	Cattle	Sheep/Goat	Pig	Horse
1	2	1	1	1
2	10	11	1	1
3	64	12	6	2
4	11	11	3	2

Table 6.03. Occurrence of cattle butchery marks

Phase	Number of cattle bones	Percentage showing butchery marks
1	29	38%
2	129	32%
3	494	16%
4	405	23%
Total	1057	21%

of butchery observed on the scapula was also akin to a more rural method where most of the knife marks relate to filleting the meat from the bone. Butchery of the humerus exhibited chop marks more like those seen at the urban site of Winchester (Maltby 1989) although there were still some knife cuts to the distal end of bones and on some shafts which are associated with rural traditions. The radius was predominantly split, probably more to disarticulate the bone rather than extract marrow (fragmentation was too great for it to be marrow extraction), and this had been done using a heavy blade, again in a more urban fashion. The range of butchery marks seen on the pelvis in part relate to the intended outcome. In some cases this was to split the pelvis, in others to separate the lower part of the torso from the upper or remove long bones. In most of these cases the result was chop marks on the bone very much in line with the butchers marks observed at Staple Gardens, Winchester (Maltby 1989). A similar patten emerges in the case of astragalus, metatarsal and metacarpal which all exhibit the more urban tradition of chopping the bones rather than cutting with a knife, although metatarsals exhibited both types of butchery. Overall the assemblage exhibited a mixture of rural and urban styles of butchery with the upper parts of the torso being cut in a more rural fashion.

Sheep/goat

As with the cattle tooth wear and eruption were initially considered to establish the age at death of these elements of the assemblage. This was possible for 12 individuals. Tooth wear again conformed to Grant's (1982) system of looking at the wear stages of the three molars. The wider eruption stages based on Grant's MWS outcomes have been used following Hambleton (1999, table 27). Due to the small sample size only general remarks could be made based on wear and eruption. For all phases of the site it can be said that the individuals present cluster around the sub-adult to adult, young adult and adult age categories. Animals that belonged to these age classes when they died would have been used for breeding and/or their wool.

Epiphysial fusion provides a slightly clearer picture of the age at which sheep/goat were being slaughtered. It appears that during Phase 1 many animals only survived to the early fusion stage and would have been between 3 and 10 months old. The Phase 2 assemblage demonstrated that some animals reached the intermediate fusion stage placing these animals in the 16–38 month bracket. In comparison, in Phases 3 and 4 animals were reaching the late fusion stage placing them between 30 and 42 months at death.

Comparison with the assemblage at Lincoln most closely matches the data from Worcester. There tooth eruption indicated that in the 1st–3rd century juvenile and young adults predominated alongside a few older individuals. By the 4th century most individuals were adults implying that animals were being kept for secondary products rather than meat in the later Roman period on these sites.

None of the sheep/goat could be sexed since horn cores were few and where they were present they were too fragmented. Some authors (Maltby 1990) have used os coxae (pelvic bone) for sexual differentiation but these were also absent from the assemblage.

There were very few sheep/goat bones exhibiting signs of butchery. One or more butchery marks were present on 12% of the total number of sheep/goat bones (counts exclude lost teeth) (Appendix 6). The highest percentage of butchered bone was within the small Phase 1 sample, dropping to Phase 3 and rising again in Phase 4 (Table 6.4). Butchery marks consisted of cut and chop marks and were in most cases associated with the disarticulation of the element from the rest of the skeleton. Examples of this were seen on the humerus, the radius, pelvis, femur and astragalus. Some of the shafts of the long bones (humerus, femur and metapodial) had shaving marks which were in all probability the result of boning. Boning could also have resulted in chop marks on the diaphysis without chopping the bone right through as seen on one femur though another explanation for this could be that there was a division of meat into portions. This latter would fit with the cut through a humerus and chop marks on a pelvis which indicate that the pelvis was severed in half. Knife cuts on some of the shafts (femur, radius, tibia and metapodial) provided evidence for filleting. There was one instance where a metapodial had been cut through longitudinally, possibly for marrow extraction (Maltby 1979; 1990).

Pig

There was a very real difficulty with producing meaningful information from the assemblage. Only five elements could be aged using dental wear and eruption (all from Phases 3 and 4) and information from epiphysial fusion was even more sporadic. In terms of the former, four were sub-adult or adult and one (from Phase 4) juvenile. In terms of the latter, only four bones could be aged. Three were from metapodials, but as only their proximal ends survived, and these fuse before birth, they provided little information. A scapula from layer G19 (C2110) in Phase 3 was from an animal of around 12 months old. As there is little use to keeping pigs into old age except for breeding, then it would be expected that most animals would be slaughtered fairly young. Given the above difficulties then the discernible morphological difference between male

Table 6.04. Occurrence of sheep/goat butchery marks

Phase	Number of sheep/goat bones	Percentage showing butchery marks
1	7	33%
2	95	10%
3	53	6%
4	112	16%
Total	267	12%

Table 6.05. Sex of pigs by phase

Phase	Sex		
	F	M	Subtotal
1		2	2
2	1	1	2
3	1	1	2
4	1	3	4
Subtotal	3	7	10

and female canines allowed for eight of these and two alveoli (from Phase 3) to be sexed (Table 6.05).

The assemblage is probably too small to draw any definitive conclusions but there does seem to be a bias towards males. One or more butchery marks were present on 20% of the total number of pig bones. The highest percentage of butchered material was 67% in Phase 2 dropping to 7% in Phase 3 and rising back to 18% in Phase 4.

The assemblage of butchered bone material yielded fragments of one humerus, two pelves, three femurs, one astragalus and one fifth metacarpal. Most of the butchery marks present on the elements were in all probability the result of disarticulation with the exception of shaving marks on two pelves and a femur which are considered to result from boning. Another exception is the cut mark on the shaft of one of the femurs which could have been the result of filleting (Johnstone and Albarella 2002; Maltby 1989). It is not possible to draw any comparisons from such a small assemblage.

Horse

According to Johnstone and Albarella (2002) a survey within central England of 190 sites showed that horses on average represent 5% of the total. Rural sites showed a higher ratio between cattle and equids (10:1) than towns (25:1). Military sites usually fell between these (20:1).

Based on minimum number of individuals (Table 6.02), the ratio at the present site is 15:1, placing the assemblage closer to rural in nature. Table 6.06 provides the breakdown of ages of horses within the site.

A very general statement regarding the horse bones recovered is that it would appear that they are mainly adult individuals (fused epiphyses). Dental wear seems to support this statement, since all the permanent teeth were in wear. The only exception to the fused epiphyses was the distal end of a Phase 3 femur which was unfused. However, this epiphysis has a late fusing stage and the individual could therefore be considered as sub-adult/young adult.

If the above can be viewed as representative of the population as a whole then it would imply that horses were not bred in the catchment of the assemblage, but used as working animals in the prime of their lives. During the Roman period horses were mainly used for transport or as pack animals (Johnstone and Albarella 2002; Maltby 1979).

One or more butchery marks were present on 23% of the assemblage. The proportion fell over time (Phase 1, 75%; Phase 2, 25%; Phase 3, 14%; Phase 4, 7%). In most of these the butchery relates to disarticulation although exceptions to this were chop marks on a radius and femur and shaving marks on a femur and metapodials which point towards boning (Appendix 6). One of the metapodials showed signs of having been cut through longitudinally for marrow extraction. A mandible had evidence for cheek meat removal, and there was evidence for filleting one of the femurs. From the above it might be concluded that the marks point towards butchery for meat. However, if this were the case then this was probably for consumption by dogs instead of humans. If horses were eaten by humans this served as only a rare supplement to the diet (Maltby 1979). An alternative explanation is that the marks were the result of skinning and dismemberment to dispose of the carcasses (Luff 1982).

Table 6.06. Ages of elements of horse by phase and context

Phase	Group	Feature Type	Feature	Context	Element	Fused?	Age range in months
1	2	Ditch	2351	2352	Femur, proximal	Y	36–42
1	2	Ditch	2351	2352	Femur, distal	Y	>42
2	98	Post-hole	2047	2048	Humerus, distal	Y	15–18
2	121	Pit	2096	2095	Tibia, proximal	Y	>42
3	18	Surface	2108	2108	Femur, distal	Y	>42
3	19	Layer	2110	2110	Femur, distal	Y	>42
3	42	Surface	2107	2107	Femur, distal	N	<42
3	202	Surface	2115	2115	Radius, proximal	Y	18–21
4	95	Pit	2009	2008	Humerus, distal	Y	15–18
4	124	Ditch	1183	1184	Tibia, distal	Y	>24
4	800	Pit/post-hole	2300	2299	Metapodium, distal	Y	12–15

Table 6.07. Distribution of dog body parts within the assemblage

Phase	Group	Feature Type	Feature	Context	Element (only one unless otherwise stated)
2	2	Ditch	1133	1134	2 x mandibular teeth (RP4 and indeterminate) metapodial
2	53	Post-hole	2072	2068	Left scapula Left humerus
2	121	Pit	2141	2140	Tooth = LP2
2	130	Ditch	1302	1311	Right tibia
2	802	Dog burial?	2073	2069	Left and right radius Left and right femur Left and right humerus Left and right ulna Left and right pelvis Right calcaneous Right 5th metatarsal and 5th metacarpal Left 3rd metatarsal and 4th metacarpal
2	901	Ditch	1486	1487	left mandible Right humerus Tooth = LP3
4	134	Pit	1044	1407	Skull; frontal, parietal, left temporal and part left occipital
4	144	Layer	2259	2259	Left maxilla
4?	152	Post-hole	1402	1099	Right ulna
4	800	Pit	2150	2148	Left tibia

Dog

Bones from dogs were only recovered from Phases 2 and 4, including what appears to be a truncated dog burial in G802, Phase 2 (Table 6.07).

In terms of their ages the long bones with proximal or distal ends that survived were all fused and the one skull had all sutures fused except the coronal, which was still fusing. This would indicate that these were adult specimens. None of the bones showed signs of butchery.

Deer

Deer seem to be present in all phases of the site except Phase 1. The only evidence for aging was one fused proximal tibia (26–42 months) and two fused distal tibia (20–23 months). Only one astragalus from G11 (C2066) in Phase 2 showed signs of butchery. Apart from the presence of deer, and the evidence of butchery implying that it may have in a small way formed part of the diet, little else can be deduced from the assemblage.

Birds

Phases 2, 3 and 4 yielded 22 fragments from 11 different bones. Due to the poor levels of preservation on the site and some of the individuals being immature (therefore having unfused bone ends), only two bones could be identified. One of these was from domestic fowl, the proximal end of a coracoid. The other was the left humerus of a raven. These latter were kept in the Roman period as pets.

Other

The only other animal find from the site was a badger bone. There were no fish bones in the assemblage, the only marine finds being oyster shell.

Discussion of the animal bone

Deposits from all phases of the site along with MNI percentages indicate that cattle were the most predominant taxon on the site, often followed by sheep/goat. Animal management in the Roman period mainly focused on cattle management (Grant 1989). Skeletal element analysis demonstrated that all parts of the skeleton were present in both cattle and sheep/goat, particularly in Phases 3 and 4. The low level of pig bone in the assemblage makes it difficult to establish a pattern regarding this. According to Grant (ibid.) this pattern is characteristic of rural assemblages, and ratio of horse to cattle seems to support this assertion.

If there was to be a distinction between the phases then on the basis of the ages of the main taxa it would appear that food in the form of meat was being produced locally during Phases 1 and 2 as most animals were killed before they reached adulthood, whilst in Phases 3 and 4 the indications are more of a consumer society. Here the animals were being used for traction and secondary products such as milk and wool. Though these results should be regarded with a note of caution since the poor preservation of some of the bone could have biased the assemblage towards older and more robust specimens.

Butchery marks were found on the elements of the most common domesticated mammals and horses. Although the total number of bones with butchery marks was not high (again emphasising the more varied use for the animals than simply as a source of meat) a pattern begins to emerge, particularly in the case of cattle. Here the butchery marks were compared with rural and urban assemblages. The overall picture was that of a prevalence to chop marks rather than cut marks, indicative of urban butchery. For the sheep/goat bones these were predominantly cut marks, which was in any case the preferred means of preparing these smaller mammals. Butchery marks were present on both meat bearing and non-meat bearing bones alike. This could indicate that animals were processed from start to finish on the site. By comparison with sites at Exeter (Maltby 1989) and Lincoln (Dobney et al 1995) this assemblage seems to sit fairly comfortably with these urban assemblages, despite a few idiosyncrasies.

6.2. Charred plant remains

Based upon assessment report completed in 2004 by Elizabeth Pearson

The aims of the environmental work were to determine, the state of preservation, type, and quantity of environmental remains recovered from the samples and consider whether these were likely to contribute further to the understanding of the site. The botanical assemblage was taken to assessment stage only due to the generally poor levels of preservation.

Methods

Samples were taken by the excavator from a range of deposits, mostly from well-sealed and securely dated contexts. However, undated contexts were also considered to be of importance where they might be of late Roman or post-Roman date as there is little information about features of this period in Worcester. In this case, sampling may provide material for radiocarbon dating or help characterise the deposit. A total of 140 samples were taken for bulk wet-sieving and flotation from a range of features including spreads, ovens, pits, gullies and ditches; 63 flots were assessed for charred plant remains, the remaining samples were taken for finds retrieval or specialist soil analysis which are not reported on here.

The samples were processed by flotation using a Siraf tank by Archaeological Investigations. The flots were collected on a 300mm sieve and the residues retained on a 1mm mesh. The residues were fully sorted by eye and the abundance of each category of environmental remains estimated. The flots were scanned using a low power EMT stereo light microscope and remains identified using modern reference collections. Iron working residues were also noted (see Chapter 5.9 Ironworking residues) where they were recovered during the processing of the samples, in order maximise information on the industrial nature of this site.

Results

Discussion of the plant remains

Environmental remains were poorly preserved on this site. Charred cereal crop remains were sparsely scattered in a variety of features through Phases 1 to 4. This mostly consisted of cereal grains, some of which were identifiable as barley (*Hordeum vulgare*) and glume wheat (emmer or spelt wheat; *Triticum dicoccum/spelta*). Of the glume

Table 6.08. Results of sample processing

Phase	Group	Feature Type	Feature	Context	Plant remains
1	G89	Charcoal spread	1575	1575	Occasional charred cereal grains including barley and glume wheat grains
1	G7	Pit	1437	1609	Charred barley (*Hordeum vulgare*) grain, glume wheat (*Triticum dicoccum/spelta*) grains, and sedge (Carex sp) seeds
2	G80	Pit	1377	1383	Occasional charred cereal grains including barley and glume wheat grains
2	G65	Pit/gully	1067	1068	Occasional charred cereal grains
2	G65	Pit/gully	1067	1072	Occasional charred cereal grains
4	G123	Ditch	1204	1205	Small quantities of charred cereal crop debris
4	G124	Gully	1095	1083	Spelt wheat grains (*Triticum spelta*), small quantities of charred cereal crop debris
4	G130	Post-hole	1062	1061	Small quantities of charred cereal crop debris
4	G134	Pit	1044	1280	Occasional charred cereal grains including barley and glume wheat grains
4	G137	Oven spread	1157	1157	Low levels of spelt wheat chaff
4	G137	Oven spread	1166	1166	Small quantities of charred cereal crop debris
4	G137	Post-hole	1179	1171	Low levels of spelt wheat chaff
4	G140	Hearth	1117	1118	Small quantities of charred cereal crop debris including spelt wheat chaff
4	G141	Pit	1073	1076	Occasional charred cereal grains
4	G152	Pit	1119	1123	Occasional charred cereal grains

wheat, some grains and chaff were identified as spelt wheat (*Triticum spelta*). Spelt largely replaced emmer as the main wheat cereal in cultivation towards the end of the Iron Age or in the early Romano-British period. Locally, spelt wheat is the most commonly identified glume wheat on Romano-British sites in Worcestershire. Emmer wheat does however, seem to have remained in cultivation on a smaller scale, and has been identified on Romano-British sites from Deansway (Moffett 2004) and Perdiswell, Worcester (Griffin et al 2001).

The low level of environmental remains may partly result from poor preservation in well drained, slightly acidic soils on the gravel terrace. However, as there seems to be intensive industrial activity (metalworking or production) on this site, this may also reflect the non-domestic nature of the settlement, resulting in a low level of domestic and agricultural waste such as stored grain, crop waste and cess deposits.

The small quantity of crop waste present is likely to derive from material brought onto the site as fuel and tinder for ovens. This would have been burnt along with wood and charcoal, which seems to have been the dominant fuel, as samples from these features were very charcoal rich. However, the charcoal was mostly finely fragmented and not suitable for identification.

Only a low level of environmental remains was noted in these samples which are of low significance for the interpretation of activities on the site. In terms of developing a wider understanding across the city it was originally viewed as being useful to confirm identifications of the glume wheat remains to distinguish between emmer and spelt wheat. Although spelt wheat is generally considered to be the main wheat crop in Roman Britain nationally, there are variations in the time at which this dominated over emmer wheat across the country. In Worcestershire, emmer wheat is recognised as still being present on some sites in the Romano-British period.

The assessment had already established that due to the low level of charred cereal crop waste distributed across the site this was unlikely to contribute to further understanding features or deposits within the site itself. Regarding the wider context, and specifically the further identification of the difference between emmer and spelt the large number of samples studied from sites in Worcester City of a similar nature and date such as Conder Buildings (Pearson 2000), The Butts (Smith 2011) and particularly Bath Road (Pearson 2007) provide a much more robust and firmly dated set of information than could be established from this site.

6.3. Sediments

David Jordan

The following is based on an interim report produced on the sediments from the site (Jordan 1998), with further observations made at two points during the excavation.

Natural sands

Consideration of the natural sands and marl on the site indicated that the sand fraction comprised well-sorted rounded quartz grains with the polished surfaces that typically indicate water borne transport, and is consistent with their deposition from Late Devensian outwash. The Marl was not observed.

Buried soil beneath cobbles in eastern area

Samples were also taken to establish whether a buried soil survived beneath the Roman cobble layer that extended over much of the eastern portion of the site, or whether this had been truncated? The rounded water-worn cobbles were set within a fine humic sandy loam matrix. The structure of this fine material was blocky and occasionally granular. The granular material was formed from earthworm casts, many of which were relatively fresh. Immediately beneath the cobbles was a thin (*c* 10–20mm) layer of humic sandy clay loam material, the upper surface of which followed the line of the cobble base very closely. This material was granular in nature with a few visible earthworm casts and few fine roots. Beneath this humic layer there was a deep mixed zone of clean sand and brown loamy material. The amount of humic material declined with depth as the proportion of 'clean' sand increased. Worm channels and fine roots penetrate through this material, and it is the humic infilling of the worm channels that gives the unit its patchy appearance.

There appears to be no logical horizontal relationship between the unit of mixed sands and the overlying humic strata. This implies that the humic material within and immediately beneath the cobbles is probably not a soil A horizon. The most likely explanation is that worm and root penetration around the cobbles has been responsible for the formation of the layer. Before the deposition of the cobble layer, the original soil profile appears to have been heavily truncated down to the level of the 'natural'. This has been contaminated by humic material washing into worm channels and by the decomposition in-situ of plant remains.

Beneath the south-western portion of the surviving cobble layer, a layer of greyish-yellow clay was present. This massive silty clay layer has a mottled appearance and thin iron pans run discontinuously along its top and base indicating post-depositional waterlogging and gleying of this unit. Beneath the clay is what appears to be a truncated soil profile that has formed on the outwash sands. The surviving depth of the greyish-brown humic material is thin (30–40mm) and grades gradually down into the natural sands. Truncation of this profile is likely and must have involved the stripping of the upper topsoil before deposition of the relatively clean clay layer. However, the profile does not seem to have been truncated as severely as that examined to the east of the site directly beneath the cobble layer and some of the topsoil remains. The possible buried soil and underlying sand are slightly grey in colour suggesting that the drainage locally is impeded and some waterlogging and gleying of the deposits has occurred.

'Dark earth' layer exposed in the southern section

This layer was exposed in the southern boundary section of the site and formed a depth of 250–300mm. A possible second exposure had been discovered at the northern end. This unit overlies a mixed unit of outwash sands and humic material. It is itself overlain by a dark humic material interpreted by the excavator as a medieval plough soil (C1001). The deposit is a dark and apparently unstratified unit rich in humified amorphous organic matter, and with a formerly granular structure that has been compressed into blocky and prismatic aggregates following burial. Included within this material is slag and occasional charcoal; the deposit is moderately stony with rounded gravel clasts that have a tendency to occur in sub-horizontal bands. The boundary with the possible plough soil is abrupt and moderately distinct, whilst that with the sands is gradual.

The deposit has been very heavily mixed by earthworms following deposition and no evidence of surviving depositional structures was identified. No variation in soil texture, inclusions or composition was found down through the deposit. This homogeneous appearance is typical of a 'dark earth' type material; Macphail (1983) defines dark earth as an '…urban anthropogenic deposit of the late Roman to early medieval periods. The deposit is dark grey in colour and composed of a variety of occupation debris mixed with soil.' However, in some cases micromorphological analysis has revealed otherwise unseen stratification and has added greatly to our understanding of the parent materials and formation of these deposits.

It is likely that worming has destroyed stratigraphic sequences within this deposit and the presence of small particles of slag prevent a study using magnetic susceptibility which would usually be employed to establish the nature of parent material. Unfortunately, on this occasion further analysis was not deemed likely to be productive.

The possible medieval plough soil above, has a granular structure and possible bands of gravel were identified. If this is a plough soil, the strongly granular structure may suggest a phase of stability and increased earthworm activity following agriculture and before burial.

Discussion of the sediments

Buried soils appear to have been truncated across the site. Beneath the cobbles truncation appears to have removed the topsoil entirely, cutting the profile at the level of the 'natural' (outwash sands). However, beneath the Roman clay layer in the south-west corner of the site there is evidence here to suggest that only the uppermost organic horizons have been lost.

The human bone

Jacqueline I McKinley, Dr P Nystrom, O Craig and S Isaksson

7.1. Cremated bone and aspects of the mortuary rite

Jacqueline I. McKinley (report submitted 2001)

A complete, undisturbed storage jar, functioning as a container for cremated remains, was found in a Phase 2 pit (G126, C2253) (see Illus 3.17, 3.31 and 7.01). The vessel was undamaged save for about three-quarters of the rim having been fractured during machine stripping. No lid had been recovered with the vessel, but the contents clearly demonstrated that a lid had been in situ up until the time of machining and it is probable that one of the various fragments of sandstone noted on the site had acted as a lid.

The vessel was excavated by the writer in a series of 2cm spits, with each spit divided into quadrants which were maintained throughout the subsequent recording and analysis. Very little soil had entered the vessel due to the presence of the inorganic lid, consequently, it was not

necessary to wet sieve the contents as is normally required with cremation burials.

Osteological analysis followed the writer's standard procedure for the examination of cremated bone (McKinley 1994a, 5–21; 2000a). Age was assessed from the stage of skeletal and tooth development (Beek 1983; McMinn and Hutchings 1985; Iscan et al 1985) and the general degree of age-related changes to the bone (Bass 1987). Sex was ascertained from the sexually dimorphic traits of the skeleton (Buikstra and Ubelaker 1994).

Disturbance and condition

The only disturbance to the remains of the burial had clearly occurred at the time of machine stripping, and although the rim of the vessel was slightly damaged, the contents were totally undisturbed and intact. The presence of an inorganic lid was clearly demonstrated by the

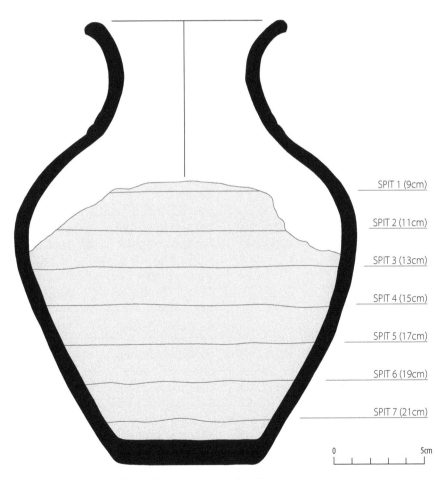

SPIT 1 (9cm)

SPIT 2 (11cm)

SPIT 3 (13cm)

SPIT 4 (15cm)

SPIT 5 (17cm)

SPIT 6 (19cm)

SPIT 7 (21cm)

0   5cm

Illus 7.01. Section through cremation vessel showing the excavated spits

complete absence of soil from the upper 15cm of the 22cm deep vessel. Fine, loose soil particles were present in the lower 3cm of the vessel, with sparse soil particles in one half of the subsequent 4cm. This suggests that, although lidded, the fit was not 'snug' against the rim, particularly on one side, allowing the slight infiltration of fine particles of soil probably during water percolation.

In consequence of the lid having survived the bone was in excellent condition, having maintained its stability and appearing as it would have at the time of deposition. Trabecular and compact bone were equally well represented.

The dead

The bone from the burial represents remains from an adult female of *c* 35–45 years. A cremated fish vertebra was also recovered, together with small fragments of charred soft tissue, fuel ash slag and a fragment of glassy slag.

The woman had been relatively small and of gracile build, but the pathological lesions observed suggested she had been engaged in strenuous physical activity involving lifting and carrying heavy items. Schmorl's nodes (resulting from a rupture in the intervertebral discs) were observed in four of the eight thoracic vertebrae recovered, three in the lower five vertebrae, and three of a minimum of four lumbar vertebrae. Lesions indicative of osteoarthritis (Rogers and Waldron 1995) were observed in two of the lower costo-vertebral joints with osteophytes (bony lipping) in a further two. Exostoses (new bone formation at tendon insertions) along the lateral margins of both iliac crests (abdominal muscle attachments) support the other indications of heavy lifting. Exostoses were also observed unilaterally in the medial epicondyle of the right humerus, at the common insertion for muscles used in flexion of the hand and fingers, which may be indicative of repetitive strain on the right hand linked to occupation.

There were no indications of dental lesions in the 16 mandibular or four maxillary tooth sockets available for examination. Two wormian bones were observed in the left lambdoid suture, whilst it has been suggested that these may be developmental abnormalities (Brothwell 1972, 95–8) they are commonly seen as a 'normal' morphological variation.

Cremation

Although the majority of the cremated bone was white, indicative of a high degree of oxidation (Holden et al 1995a; 1995b), a large minority of the bone showed colour variations indicative of incomplete oxidation and a few small fragments of charred soft tissue residue were also recovered. Both fifth metatarsals were almost unburnt (brown-blue). Patchy blue, or blue-grey bone was recovered from the hip and thigh region, the ankle and foot, and the left frontal, with slightly grey bone from the shoulder areas, chest and spine.

This general distribution of poorly oxidised bone across the skeleton, particularly the almost lack of burning to parts of the feet, suggests the pyre may have been too small for the individual – the feet being on the periphery, possibly extending beyond the edge of the structure. If insufficient fuel was used to construct the pyre it may not have burnt long enough to fully oxidise those bones with a substantial coverage of soft tissues, which would need to burn off before the bone itself could burn, such as the shoulder region, hip and thigh (McKinley 1994a, 72–81; 2000a). However, it should not be assumed that full oxidation of the remains was a requisite of the rite; there are certainly many instances from the Romano-British period to suggest this was not the case (e.g. McKinley 2000b).

Bone weight

The 965g of bone recovered from the burial represents a maximum of 96% of the total weight of bone expected from an adult cremation (McKinley 1993); an assessment of the skeletal elements recovered suggesting more in the region of *c* 80%. The weight falls within the upper reaches of the wide range noted from Romano-British urned burials where, for example, high averages of 900g and 845g were observed in the undisturbed adult burials from St Stephens, St Albans (McKinley 1992) and East London (McKinley 2000c) respectively.

Throughout the history of the rite of cremation it seems that at no time was it ever considered necessary to include the entire cremated remains within the burial (McKinley 2000a). It is unclear, however, why bone weights varied so widely. It has been suggested that this may be a reflection of 'status' or it may be partially indicative of the mode of recovery of bone for burial after cremation (McKinley 1997).

Fragmentation

The vast majority of bone fragments (*c* 90%) were recovered from the 10mm sieve fraction, with a maximum fragment size of 128mm. The size of these fragments are fully commensurate with those observed at modern crematoria following cremation and raking out of the remains, but prior to deliberate pulverisation (McKinley 1993). The role of the urn in providing protection to the cremated bone has been discussed elsewhere (McKinley 1993; 1994b), as has the amount of undetectable fragmentation which may occur due to disturbance and during excavation. The absence of soil from the burial environment is of crucial importance, much fragmentation occurring after burial along dehydration fissures formed during cremation (ibid). The size of the bone fragments clearly demonstrate that they have maintained the size they held at the time of deposition.

The urn, in this case, had a narrow neck, only 6.5cm diameter, and it would have been necessary to 'feed' the bone fragments into the vessel. There is no evidence to support the long-held assumption that bone was deliberately fragmented to fit into narrow-mouthed burial vessels, though a certain amount of incidental breakage may have resulted from tending of the pyre and during recovery of bone for burial.

Skeletal elements

About 74% of the bone was identified to the skeletal element, compared with the more usual 40–50% specifically as a result of the large size of the bone fragments. Bone fragments from all skeletal areas were represented, with no apparent suggestion of preferential selection from any specific area, ease of identification of certain elements having been taken into account (McKinley 1994a, 6). There was, however, a complete absence of carpal bones (wrist), with few tarsals, finger or foot phalanges. These bones survive cremation well, often complete, certainly easily recognised and the total absence of carpals from such a large and representative collection of bone, seems extraordinary.

The absence of small bones may be indicative of the mode of recovery of bone from the pyre site for burial; hand collection of individual bones or raking together of fragments for bulk recovery could both provide a bias towards the recovery of larger fragments, but the absence of any carpal bones still appears out of the ordinary. It has been observed that it is a characteristic of the rite of cremation that all the bone remaining was not collected for burial (McKinley 2000a). Bone fragments not included in the burial have also been recovered from amongst redeposited or in situ pyre debris. However, where it has been possible to link two types of deposit from the same cremation (e.g. burial and redeposited pyre debris), it has been observed that some bone still appears to be 'missing' (McKinley 1997). It has been suggested that bone fragments may have been distributed to relatives and friends (ibid.), if so, recognisable bones from the hand, a tactile and responsive area of the body, may have been favoured?

Pyre goods and debris

The only pyre good recovered was a small (c 5mm diameter) fish vertebra. Although the inclusion of animal remains on the pyre was not uncommon in the Romano-British period, fish remains are rare, possibly for taphonomic reasons, being generally small and particularly fragile, rather than a genuine cultural absence. Cremated fish remains were recovered from two of the burials in East London cemeteries (Reilly 2000, table 25).

Fragments of fuel ash slag are indicative of the cremation being conducted over a sandy soil and represent the accidental inclusion of pyre debris. Pyre debris in the form of fuel ash is largely absent from the burial (six tiny flecks in spit 5), and none was observed in the grave fill.

Burial formation process

The bone fill extended highest in the centre of the vessel, commencing *c* 9cm below the rim and dropping to 12cm around the edges. The 'cone' form of the fill indicates the vessel was upright whilst the bone was being inserted, probably a handful at a time being added, the narrow neck necessitating the latter. It is likely that the bone was placed in a different receptacle during recovery from the pyre site, being transferred into the burial urn later.

The upper 4cm (9–13cm below the rim) of the fill comprised large bone fragments with intervening voids. The central 6cm (13–15cm below the rim) contained progressively more medium-sized fragments amongst the large, with sparse small bone infill. In spit 6 (19–21cm) the small bone infill became dense, with few large bones and dense small fragments in the lowest 1cm. The percentage of bone within the 10mm sieve fraction lessened perceptively between the upper two spits (99% and 96%) and those below (77% in spit 7, 89% in spit 4); this does not so much reflect a variation in the inclusion of large bone fragments within the different levels or the point at which small fragments were added, as the filtering down between the voids of the small bone fragments which were probably added progressively together with the larger ones.

Fragments from different spits and quadrants were found to join. Some fragments may have broken apart and filtered down through the vessel after deposition, such as the fragments of distal humerus in spits 3b and 4b, or the temporal vault in 3c and 4c. However, the deposition of other fragments clearly indicates they were so placed in deposition; a large fragment of mandible from spit 6b joined a smaller fragment from 4cm higher in spit 3b; fragments of scapula from spits 1c and 3b joined; a fragment of occipital vault against the edge of the vessel in spit 6b joined a fragment against the opposite side of the vessel in 5d, and similarly fragments of metatarsal in spit 3a and 3d, and proximal humerus in 2b and 2c. Bone fragments from all skeletal areas and both sides of the skeleton were recovered from all parts of the vessel. There was a lower than average proportion of lower limb fragments in the lower 5cm, and lower than average axial skeletal fragments in spit 6, with higher than average proportions of skull in spits 5–7 (lower 5 cm). The overall impression is for no apparent order of deposition within the burial, which may reflect the previous suggestion that bone was transferred to this burial receptacle from one used during collection from the pyre. However, the disproportional amounts of skull and lower limb in the lower fill of the vessel may be indicative of collection of bone from the pyre being as individual fragments by hand, commencing at one or other end of the pyre, with some subsequent degree of mixing of the bone during transfer between receptacles.

Conclusion

The great importance of a burial such as this is to demonstrate the true condition of cremated bone at the time of burial, both in terms of the quantity of bone, and the size and deposition of the fragments. What may be deduced about the formation processes of both cremation and subsequent burial, based on reliable and intact evidence, assists in furthering our comprehension of the mortuary rite as a whole.

7.2. Analysis of residues in the cremation vessel

O Craig and S Isaksson (report submitted 2012)

A sample of the cremation urn was analysed for residues to establish if there was any evidence for the vessel's primary use, that is before its use as a cremation urn. The complete report is given below as Appendix 7. Traces of both plant and animal fats were found. Plants evidence is in the form of oleic acid, plant sterols and long-chain alcohols. The nature of the plant material suggests it derives from the use of the pot rather than from the depositional soil matrix. The animal fats are more ambiguous. The proportions of palmatic and strearic acid present suggest pig fat, though similar values would be found in human fat and may therefore relate to the cremated remains, particularly since there is evidence (see above) that some parts of the body were poorly fired. Cholesterol present might derive from human remains but the oxidised cremated remains would not have any cholesterol in them and the absence of any heat-degraded lipids suggests remains do not derive from the cremated remains. On balance it seem likely that the vessel was in domestic use before it was used as a cremation urn, though specific details of how and for what it was used, are unclear from this analysis.

7.3. Other human bone

Dr P. Nystrom (report submitted 2001)

Three other residual human bones were recovered from the site. One was found in a Phase 2 ditch (G901, C1486), a right neonate tibia, aged 0–1 month at death, therefore possibly stillborn. The remaining two were found in the same Phase 4 pit (G134, C1044). One was a right adult femur shaft that appears to be from a healthy individual. It was quite robust and so possibly male. The other was the back of a cranium. The piece was the left and right parietal and occipital and, from suture closure, appears to be an adult though it was not possible to determine the age more precisely. The pronounced external occipital protuberance suggests the sex to be male. The external occipital protuberance demonstrates some new bone growth (ossified ligament) possibly from trauma or industrial activity (i.e. manual work). A series of fracture lines could relate to trauma. The sutures show a non-metric trait referred to as the 'inca' bone, although it is not possible to say more. The preservation of the skull is very good. The fact that both bones from this pit belonged to adult males raises the possibility that they belonged to the same individual, though too little remains to confirm this or ascertain how these remains were deposited.

8

Archaeomagnetic dating

Paul Linford (report submitted 2002)

Samples were collected from four features. Two of these could not be dated as the direction of their thermo-remnant magnetism (TRM) appeared to be scattered randomly. The demagnetisation profiles from the samples of these features indicated that they had been exposed to similar levels of heating as the samples from the two features that dated. It is therefore assumed that the clay had been disturbed since firing.

Two features could be dated, although the precision of the dates was initially viewed as being disappointing. Two reasons were proposed for this (Linford 2002). First, the demagnetisation profiles of pilot samples from the features suggest they had not acquired stable magnetisations in their higher coercivity domains, probably because they had not been exposed to intense enough heat during the use of the feature and as a result the mean TRM direction could not be estimated to a high precision. Second, the virtual geomagnetic pole position moved slowly from the 4th century AD onwards adversely affecting the precision of dates that can be obtained for this era.

The two features from which dates were obtained are significant in that they came from two different phases of the site. Both dates have been quoted at the 63% and 95% confidence level where applicable. The sample from (C1304) rendered two date ranges due to its proximity to two sections of the calibration curve. That from (C1265) only provided a single date range at the 95% confidence level.

In both cases the original report on the dates recommends that some caution is applied to using the dates as only seven or six samples (respectively) were used, falling below the minimum of eight required for an estimate of the Fisher precision parameter k. Also, an unusually large proportion of the initial sample set was rejected from the mean calculation owing to the anomalous dispersion of TRM directions. However, despite this, the magnetic dates correlate well with other dating evidence from the site and deficiencies in the samples may simply be due to the apparent low temperatures to which the samples were exposed.

Table 8.01. Results of archaeomagnetic dating

Phase	Group	Feature Type	Feature	Context	63%	95%
2	G17	Oven	1308	1304	275 to 335 AD	265 to 419 AD
2	G17	Oven	1308	1304	170 to 210 AD	130 to 220 AD
4	G137	Oven	1309	1265		260 to 320 AD

9

Interpretation of the archaeology within the site

Andy Boucher

9.1. Date of occupation and activity

The chapters above have referred in various ways to the dates of occupation that occurred within the site. However, a clearer consideration of all the evidence contributing to this and also to the distinction in date between various phases of activity still needs to be undertaken. To provide a picture of the overall length of occupation on the site it is possible to combine all the information from artefacts and the two scientific dates with a view to identifying any potential contradiction or consolidation of these (Illus 9.01).

For the most part the diagram in Illus 9.01 provides a reasonably consistent picture for the dates of the phases. The only outlier is the coin from Phase 2, although this comes from the upper fill of the well and merely indicates that this feature was out of use by the end of Phase 4, possibly having quite a long period of use. Otherwise Phase 1 runs up to AD 175, Phase 2 from AD 125 to 225 and Phases 3 and 4 from AD 250 up to 320. In Phases 3 and 4 there is material that covers the gap between AD 225 and 250 but activity on the site seems to be somewhat reduced during that time. It is also quite clear that Phases 3 and 4 are contemporary.

9.2. Nature of occupation

Phase 1

Occupation on the site starts with the northern ditches (G1, G3) of a multi-phased enclosure, a large proportion of

which was excavated on the adjacent site to the west (see Illus 3.01). It appears that the enclosure had a 5m wide entrance or gap leading into the northern part of the site, with a possible gate structure (G125) and rectangular post-built structure/shelter (G148) immediately to the west (Illus 9.02). Several hearths or ovens (G8, G7), one of which was clearly associated with small-scale ironworking, are likely to be contemporary with this. There was no evidence for occupation in the area to the north, although plough marks were recorded in the sub-strata about 10m north of this entrance and it may be that the area north of the enclosure was being cultivated at this time.

Later the ditch was recut, blocking the entrance (G2), although to the west of the site the former line of the ditch may have been replaced by a fence (G81) (Illus 9.03). Inside the enclosure, in front of this back-filled section, a small 5m diameter circular structure (G31) was erected. Further features that may be hearths or oven bases were identified to the east of this structure.

Throughout Phase 1 the ceramic and animal bone evidence is suggestive of domestic occupation. However, it is also clear from the ironworking waste, both in the ditch fills and from a hearth base and associated features within the enclosure, that small-scale ironworking activity was taking place here. On the basis of the residues this appears to just be smithing. Post-holes and a small slot aligned with the ditch (G148) could relate to a shelter associated with the ironworking. In Phase 1b the small circular structure was probably a workers hut, although it is a bit small for a permanent dwelling. The use of circular structures

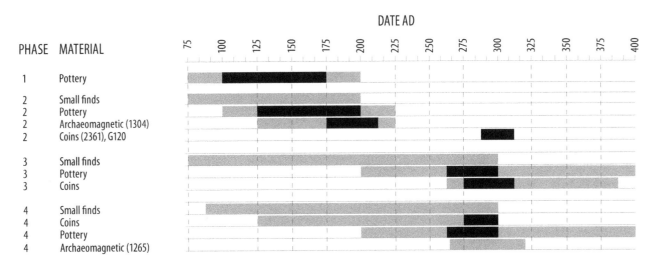

Illus 9.01. Seriation diagram of the elements contributing to the dating of the site and its phases (Potential date range in grey, closely dated material in black)

Illus 9.02. Phase 1a plan

indicates continuing native architectural traditions and the enclosure might indicate the presence of a small domestic unit associated with agricultural activity, on the fringes of the wider nucleated settlement. Certainly in the Roman period farmsteads were often associated with industrial activity such as smithing (Smith 2017, 186). Towards the end of this phase of activity another possible circular structure (G52) was noted in the area of the site to the north of the enclosure. No other features could be definitively associated with this, and its interpretation remains tentative.

The ceramic material from both sub-phases is indicative of a more rural, or at least a low status urban, assemblage. Similarly, the animal bone assemblage demonstrated quite high levels of butchery during this phase and in the case of cattle was more in line with rural butchering traditions, favouring cutting over chopping to remove the meat, particularly from around the mandibles. The assemblage is, however, predominantly domestic in nature. Some evidence exists from early glazed wares for a military presence nearby early in the site's history.

Phase 2

This phase of activity cannot be firmly differentiated chronologically from Phase 1, though continues into the early 3rd century, and also appears to be predominantly domestic in nature from the artefactual and structural evidence, though a possible kiln bar may be linked to 2nd century pottery production in the vicinity (see pottery report, Chapter 4, and Chapter 10). Key elements from this phase are rectilinear post-built structures (G49, G10/G54, G145, G53/G11/G98, G118, G88), exhibiting evidence for timber framing and also demonstrating a change in land ownership and land division. These are the defining features of the change from Phase 1 to Phase 2. The enclosure ditch had been backfilled and the manner in which features were now laid out on the site favours a much more north-east to south-west orientation. Building G10, which lies towards the north-east corner of the site, demonstrates this quite clearly. It is a large three bay hall-type structure with a smaller annex (G54) projecting north-east from the centre of the northern two bays. Although apparently later in date, Building G88 in the south-west corner of the site matched

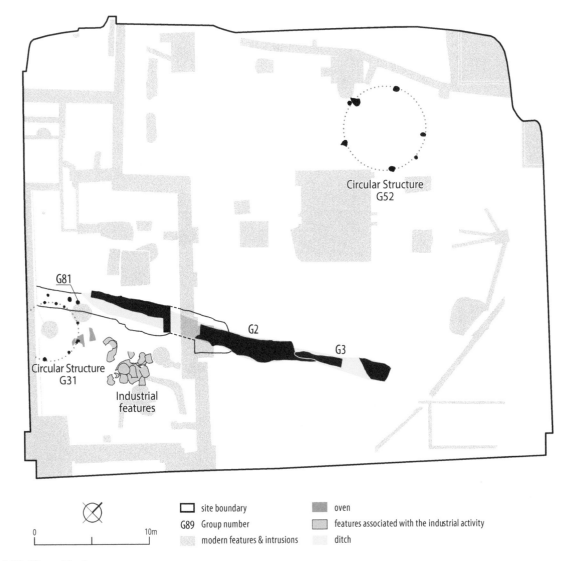

Illus 9.03. Phase 1b plan

the location and alignment of this building very well. The later structure lies over the site of the former Phase 1 ditch and does not appear to have had a floor. To the south of it a small group of features were, again, associated with ironworking on quite a moderate scale. A line of post-holes possibly formed a wind break or fence in front of these or were part of a lean-to shelter against building G88.

Several structures do not match this new alignment and were probably quite short-lived, or due to a lack of evidence to the contrary have been assigned to the wrong phase. The latter could be the case for G145 and G118 as both of these might sit more comfortably alongside Phase 4 features. Structure G53 on the other hand could have been a short-lived building that occupied an area of the site to the south-east of G10 before G11 was built. This latter structure was of some significance as it appears to have been taken down at the point the laying of the Phase 3 surfaces and terracing took place, and reassembled following that (as G98). It is also likely that during this period two other features were created. The first was the construction of a stone-lined well in the south-east corner of the site, possibly surrounded by

a timber structure, notable due to a lack of other features in this area; the second a cremation burial between this and the later rectilinear structure G88.

The animal bone assemblage still appears to be domestic in nature with a third of the cattle showing signs of butchery. The pottery also retains a degree of domesticity, still low in status.

Phase 3

This phase is characterised as a relatively short event or sequence of events, which is followed by the substantial period of activity in Phase 4. It is at this juncture that two important elements of the site's layout are identified. The first is that the 45° orientation seen in earlier buildings was respected, probably to the extent that G10 was still functioning following the laying of surfaces. The edge of the gravel surfaces matches the orientation of G10 and G88 and imply that the part of the site running diagonally between these constitutes a land division. However, G88 was buried beneath a soil layer between Phases 2 and

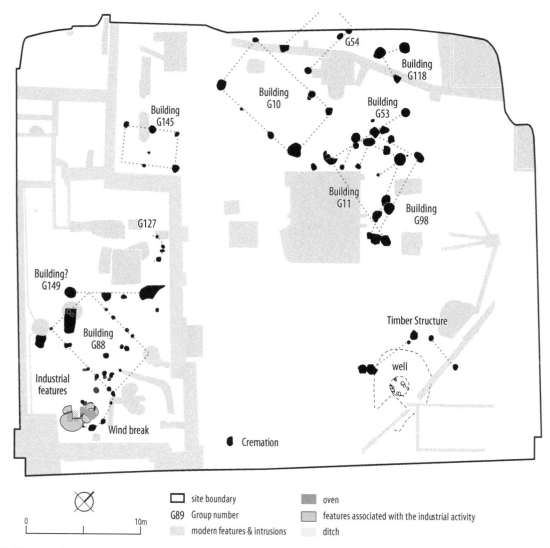

Illus 9.04. Phase 2 plan

4 and some consideration as to how this came about is justified. From the sedimentology assessment of the site it was clear that terracing took place during this phase. The gravels in the north-east part of the site have been laid on a surface that has had not only its topsoil removed but also the upper part of the sub-soil profile. In the south-west part of the site a soil layer was recorded overlying G88 (C1034/C1359). This contained a mix of earlier material which could derive from occupation layers beneath but might equally be redeposited material from the north-east part of the site as an exercise in levelling the whole area.

The second element is the dismantling and reassembly of G11 to make G98. In terms of occupation this tends to suggest that at least initially the north-east part of the site continued to be occupied whilst the south-west area was left unoccupied for a while.

Regarding evidence for metalworking associated with the Phase 3 features then this discussion is best left for Phase 4, as is any evidence for other structures on the surfaces. The

key aspect relating to Phase 3 is the terracing of deposits and laying of surfaces, the evidence for occupation or any other evidence relating to the surfaces belongs with Phase 4 (Illus 9.05).

Phase 4

During the earlier part of this phase it would appear that Building G10 may well still survive at the north end of the site. There is evidence for trample and wear around its margins and the gravel deposits do not extend into the building. To the south-east of this it would also appear that Building G98 survives, possibly having to be realigned so as to enable the surfaces to be laid on the adjacent plot. In the south-west part of the site a rectilinear structure (G45) was recorded with a beaten earth floor (G43). This is the precursor to a larger workshop thought to be associated with metalworking and had two associated ovens (G129, G15) and a clay-lined pit (G134) immediately the west, and what may have been timber troughs (G124) and a possible shelter (G142) to the north (Illus 9.06). These all seem to have served functions related to metalworking.

gravel surface / floor
cobbled surface
site boundary   footprints of buildings
modern features & intrusions   possible structure associated with industrial activity

0   10m

Illus 9.05. Phase 3 surfaces

At a later date the beaten earth floor and workshop (G45) on the south edge of the site were replaced by an iron slag surface (G25) using post-pads rather than post-holes (Illus 9.07). On the basis of metalworking residues throughout this part of the site it appears that a sandstone rubble footing (G131) and associated post-pads to the west were also part of this phase of activity. It is suggested as the remains of a dwelling associated with the workshop.

North and east of this it appears as though a number of other structures were being established on a north-south orientation. In these cases, there is little evidence other than impressions in the gravel surface. It seems that a number of pathways were laid out across the gravel to the north of the site, and that some of the blanks in the gravel may have been associated with the presence of sill-built structures.

The structures in the south-west corner of the site occupy two sides of a courtyard and almost all the cut features

and surfaces provide evidence for ironworking in the form of varying quantities of hammerscale. As discussed above this now appears to be a site using much higher temperatures than before (Chapter 5.9). The discovery of what was interpreted as a billet and two iron bars from these contexts add credence to the fact that there was a likely smithy complex measuring at least 18m by 17m; its extents to the west and south were not fully established as they lay outside the excavation area. The organisation of this complex appears to be a workshop floor made with imported iron slag, post-pads made from iron slag replacing the post-holes that were there before, a sandstone footing and some other cobble post-pads on the west side of a small courtyard. To the north the sequence of rectangular cuts that possibly housed wooden troughs were probably still in use, while south of these there was a large clay-lined pit that must have held water and acted as a quenching pit. The courtyard measured 6m in width by at least 8.5m in length. Within it was a series of hearth bases, one of which (G139) reused what appears to have

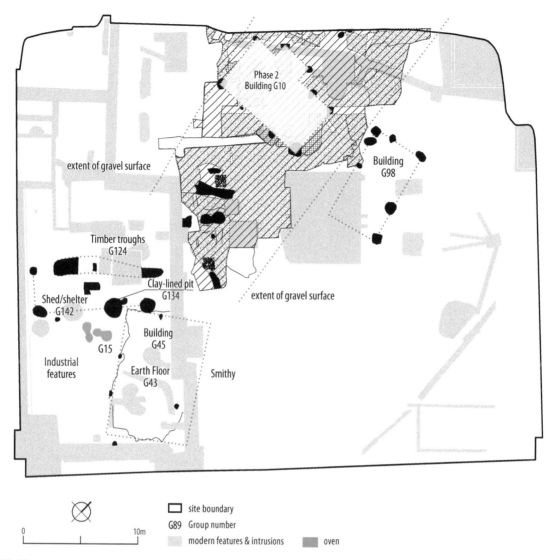

Illus 9.06. Phase 4a structures and surfaces

been a structural trench (although the form and location of the rest of this structure was not in evidence within the extents of the excavation). From the assessment of the slag there was no discernible smithing slag in the assemblage collected from the surface of the workshop floor and the slag post-pads. Also, it is noticeable that whilst this workshop replaced another, there is no evidence for smithing associated with the earlier structure or any of its contemporary features. However, the configuration of features is exactly the same as for the second sub-phase of use for the complex. It seems unlikely (particularly given the troughs etc. to the north) that such a similar layout would be used for a different purpose. One possibility is that the complex was never put into use during this earlier stage and was fully rebuilt before smithing activities took place. There is no evidence to suggest that the previous structure burnt down so some alternative reason would need to be considered for this.

To the north the cobble and gravel surfaces remain in use. There is evidence for this in the spread of hammerscale across the southernmost surfaces directly to the north of the probable smithy. There is no evidence that this continued

further north but what this does imply is that the surfaces and workshop fall within the same land ownership, the hammerscale probably being trampled from one to the other.

Within these areas to the north it is assumed that building G10 must have eventually fallen out of use. There is evidence in impressions in the gravel surfaces for the construction of a timber sill building perhaps replacing the earlier earth-fast one. If this was the case then the new building was built to one side of the old and re-aligned east to west. Given that the orientation of the plot was north-east to south-west originally this re-alignment of what must have been quite a sizeable structure implies that other elements of the settlement landscape (outside the site) were being reorganised around this time. Some raised gravel to the south of the larger building might also have been to construct a small building. There is evidence that pathways with drains to either side were created to link the new building with the old so G10 may well have continued in use following the completion of the new structure.

In terms of the nature of occupation of the site during this later phase then the area to the south-west was clearly

Illus 9.07. Phase 4b structures and surfaces

utilitarian rather than domestic. Given what appears to be common land ownership of the plot running north-eastwards from here then it may be assumed that the associated domestic dwelling comprised G10 and possibly a timber-framed building adjacent to it (G98). The new raised timber sill structure could be a replacement dwelling for this building which appears to have lasted for over a century. If this were the case there is little evidence as there was in the case of G11/G98 that it was dismantled and rebuilt when the site was levelled. Nevertheless, the variation in the gravel surfaces where the building stood cannot be disputed and the most likely explanation for this is that the structure remained in situ, perhaps with a raised floor.

This leaves the sheer volume of domestic waste that was found on the site. The simplest theory would be that there was little pressure on land in this peripheral part of the town and therefore plenty of room for middens to build up within the site around the main plot. On the one hand this is supported by the date of the assemblage reasonably closely matching that of the period of occupation. While the pottery could date throughout the 4th century AD, this would have been at a much lower level by comparison to the material that must have accumulated during the occupation and use of the site. If on the other hand this was waste from the wider settlement that was being brought into the site then it appears that such an activity would have been contemporaneous with the occupation of the site, a scenario that doesn't fit with modern ideals. The fact that the pottery assemblage is noted as changing away from a purely domestic one to a more artisan use with evidence for ceramic tankards lends support to the material being generated within the site itself. The animal bones which indicate a shift towards a more 'urban' style of butchery in these phases as well as a greater level of producer economy rather than just consumer also support the fact that most of this material was accumulating within the site. Given the volume of material it might then be expected that quite a large community was working here. However, the excavation does appear to have defined the extents of the occupation as relatively few archaeological features were found to the west or east of where this activity was taking place. So whatever the make-up of this community it is likely that they all lived and worked pretty much within the confines of the identified features from the site.

10

The site, Roman Worcester and smithing

Andy Boucher and Alex Smith

The earliest archaeological evidence from the site dates back to *c* AD 70, broadly contemporary with the earliest period of settlement seen across many excavated sites in Worcester (see Chapter 2.2). However, it is unlikely that any of the actual features excavated at the Magistrates Court are this early. Instead, it seems that the site lay on the periphery of the settlement at this time, probably being used as agricultural land as was the case with the earliest activity, dating to the 1st/early 2nd century AD, at the Hive to the south-west (Bradley et al 2018). Nevertheless, there are elements of the early Roman pottery assemblage from Magistrates Court, including glazed Roman imported wares, that hint at the proximity of high status, perhaps military, occupation nearby. Certainly, as indicated in Chapter 2.1, there is evidence for a reasonable military presence in the region at this time, which might suggest a degree of continued instability.

The earliest activity on the site probably dates to the first quarter of the 2nd century AD, the period of major expansion at Worcester and, in terms of the number of settlements, in the surrounding countryside. Features of this date comprise what is likely to be a small-scale smithy, along with a small circular structure similar to those observed during the early phases of Deansway (Dalwood and Edwards 2004). In this case the structure clearly lay within an enclosure that had been dug out on many occasions. This enclosure was replaced at least in part by a fence line in its later stages of use, as indicated by the results of excavations on the adjacent site to the west, prior to the construction of the new police station there (Edwards et al 2002; see Illus 3.01). Another early circular structure was observed to the north of the enclosure although no activity was clearly associated with it. Unlike Deansway, if there was a subsequent hiatus of activity then it was short-lived with probably only enough time for the ditch to be backfilled; otherwise occupation on the site appears to continue through the 2nd century AD with the establishment of at least five timber-framed structures. These commence towards the north edge of the site and are rectilinear in plan. By the end of the 2nd century there is some evidence for a change in the way land division was organised across the site. The early boundary and orientation of the enclosure was abandoned and a new alignment of structures at 45° to north became established. Two of the largest structures appear to line up with one another during this phase potentially indicating regularity in the way the site was organised. It is possible that this was part of a more widespread re-organisation of the settlement, with a number of industrial, commercial,

domestic and agricultural 'zones' linked by a system of roads and lanes; indeed it has been suggested that there may have been a degree of civic planning and organisation within the settlement at this time (Bradley et al 2018, 416). At the Magistrates Court this new orientation of features matches the postulated angle of a Roman road that was recorded to the south-west of the site (see Illus 2.02); however, no evidence was found for this road within the site or to its west and the earlier enclosure does not line up with it.

The buildings from Phase 2 join a now substantial body of evidence for structures within the Roman settlement, including a small number of circular buildings as noted above, small 'strip' buildings, aisled buildings and more substantial masonry structures with evidence for high status features such as tessellated floors, tiled roofs and hypocausts. The latter buildings appeared fairly widely dispersed in the settlement with examples *c* 700m to the south of the Magistrates Court at City Arcades (Griffin et al 2004) and also *c* 300 m to the north at Britannia Square (Napthan 2012). Circumstantial evidence for other high-status buildings closer to the current site derive from dumps of building material and plaster from a late Roman well at the Butts (Butler and Cuttler 2011, 37) and smaller quantities of similar material very close by at the Police Station site (Edwards et al 2002, 128) and the nearby Conder Building (Pikes and Sherlock 2003). One of the more unusual finds indicating higher status occupation from the current site was the sandstone furniture fragment (a 'side-table'), an object more typically carved from limestone and found in West Country villas.

The Phase 2 buildings from Magistrates Court are more typical of the timber buildings found across most of Roman Worcester. Nevertheless, one of the structures shows evidence for timber framing and this is worth some further consideration. Unfortunately, the whole structure did not survive, with its south-west end being lost to a brick-lined structure of 19th–20th-century date. However, what did survive was a series of post impressions that were later replicated on nearly the same footprint but a slightly different angle. For this to be achieved it is proposed that the sides and ends of the structure must have remained relatively intact and some form of framing was needed for this to happen.

The overall nature of the activity at Magistrates Court appears to have changed over the course of the Roman period, perhaps at least in part reflecting wider developments within the settlement. During the first two phases of activity on the site, spanning most of the 2nd century AD, it would appear that the occupation was predominantly domestic with some limited metalworking (smithing) taking place to the south-west of the excavation area during Phase 1. Small finds, animal bone and pottery all attest to this. There were a number of ovens and/or hearth bases associated with this period of settlement. A few may have been used in small-scale metalworking, but most were probably domestic in nature. Some could have been associated with the fragments of 'portable ceramic oven material' found at the site and increasingly recognised across Roman Worcester and beyond, thought to have been used primarily for baking bread (Jane Evans 2018). Overall, the nature of the material associated with this phase of occupation is viewed to be low status or at least 'rural' in nature. The site appears to lie to the north of the primary areas of iron smelting at this time and was probably part of an increasing spread of mostly low status, dispersed domestic occupation around the periphery of the nucleated settlement.

Major internal changes occurred on site during the 3rd century, although this does not appear to have initially resulted in any change to the orientation and layout of features. A large area was levelled in a diagonal 15m wide band across the centre of the site and a series of gravel and cobble surfaces were laid across this. The edges of this surface match the extent of the two buildings that were observed in Phase 2 to possibly demarcate a new property boundary. The northernmost of these seems to survive this re-landscaping of the site, as an impression of the building is roughly visible in the newly laid surface. The southernmost structure appears to be buried beneath a layer of soil, the east side of which saw the construction of a post-built rectangular structure with an earth floor, while to the west of this was a hearth base. A series of structures were then built in this area. The earth-floored building was replaced on the same footprint by a workshop with a slag floor and slag post-pad construction. To the north of this is what appears to have been an open structure containing linear impressions, perhaps for timber troughs, similar to those identified from Sidbury (Darlington and Evans 1992). A clay-lined pit was also recorded within this shelter. On the west side of the small courtyard defined by these structures was a sandstone foundation and within the courtyard more hearths. Unlike the earlier phase all these features and surfaces contained hammerscale indicating what would appear to be a substantial workshop likely to have been associated with smithing. Impressions of other structures were seen in the gravel surface to the north and these were also realigned east-west. Alongside this structure there was a change in the nature of the pottery assemblage with more fragments of the large ceramic 'portable ovens' being found, though as noted above these are generally thought more to be associated with baking bread than specific craftworking activity.

This more 'industrial' phase of activity is broadly contemporary with a decline in iron production and corresponding increase in agricultural activity seen elsewhere in Worcester during the late Roman period (see Chapter 2.2). The construction of a large smithy, if such it was, at this time may therefore be just as much or perhaps even more related to the production and maintenance of agricultural tools for the surrounding community than for the iron production industry. Worcester also lay on key road and river transport networks for industrial and agricultural products, and possibly for long-distance cattle droving (as indicated by recent isotope analysis; Gan et al 2018), all which would have required substantial smithing facilities.

Elsewhere in Worcester, evidence for iron smithing is fairly limited, with most of the huge quantities of diagnostic slag being related to smelting. Some hammerscale and a possible iron billet was found in excavations at the Hive, but this was suggested as the opportunistic working of small items taking place as and when required, rather than any sustained smithing activity (Bradley et al 2018, 402). Possible smithing was also noted near to the Magistrates Court site at Conder Building, mainly on the basis of hearths and standing pots to hold water (Pikes and Sherlock 2003). However, although a possible rural smithy has been identified within a farmstead at Bath Road on the southern edge of Worcester (Rogers 2014), the Magistrates Court smithies remain the only ones identified, even if tentatively, within the Roman settlement. Such facilities are, nevertheless, more often found within such nucleated settlements, with other examples at places such as Alcester, Bath and Godmanchester. Excavations at Birch Abbey, Alcester, revealed a rectangular post-built timber building of early to mid-4th-century date that contained two possible smithing hearths; it was later expanded with the addition of a third hearth and had an associated water tank/trough and pits containing smithing debris (Mahany 1994, 61-2). At Bellot's hospital, Bath, a late Roman smithy was recorded within the cellar of a masonry building. A *c* 0.35m layer of slag was present in the room and a rectangular block of Bath stone was identified as an anvil support block (Davenport 2007).

Evidence for smithing in general, in the form of dedicated tools or at least dumps of smithing waste, has been found at *c* 80% of defended 'small towns' and at 68% of other nucleated roadside settlements, compared with less than 40% of farmsteads (Smith 2017, 86-7; see also Dungworth 2015). Throughout most rural sites in particular, such smithing is likely to have been on a small-scale ad-hoc basis, mostly for the repair of iron agricultural tools and cart fittings, and is unlikely to have involved more specialist production (Scott 2016). It was probably an activity integrated with farming practices and such may have been the situation at Magistrates Court during the earlier phases of activity.

At the other end of the scale, many of the larger nucleated settlements are likely to have supported full-time smithing operations, some perhaps even developing more specialist skills. Scott, for example, noted the presence of ironwork with makers' stamps implying smiths who specialised in the manufacture of knives, razors, various tools and styli (Scott 2016). These 'full-time' smiths would have catered for the needs of the local populace and more transient populations utilising the road network. In many instances such smithies may occupy the same areas as other craftworking facilities to create 'light industrial zones' in parts of the settlement (Smith 2017, 235). This may have been the case for the area around Magistrates Court, as there were a number of wastered sherds and a possible kiln bar to suggest that a greyware pottery kiln existed in the vicinity (see pottery report, Chapter 4), while there is also limited evidence for copper and lead (copper alloy?) working at the nearby Conder Building site.

All industrial activity at Magistrates Court appears to have ceased before the middle of the 4th century AD and it seems likely that the area was abandoned. The lack of later 4th century activity is fairly typical of many excavations in the town, though as noted in Chapter 2.2, there were certainly some buildings of this date. Nevertheless, it is likely that any real civic functionality within the settlement – assuming that this had ever existed – had certainly ceased by this point.

Bibliography

Albarella, U, and Davis, S J M 1994 *The Saxon and Medieval animal bones excavated' 1985-1989 from West Cotton, Northamptonshire*, HBMC Ancient Monuments Laboratory report 17/94, London

Allen, M, Blick, N, Brindle, T, Evans, T, Fulford, M, Holbrook, N, Richards, J D and Smith, A 2015 *The Rural Settlement of Roman Britain: An online resource*, Archaeology Data Service, York; doi:10.5284/1030449

Allen, M, Lodwick, L, Brindle, T, Fulford, M and Smith, A 2017 *The Rural Economy of Roman Britain. Vol. 2*, Britannia Monograph Series 30, London

Arthur, P 1978 'The lead glazed wares of Roman Britain', in P Arthur and G Marsh, *Early fine wares in Roman Britain*, BAR British Series 57, Oxford, 293–356

Arthur, P 1986 'Roman amphorae from Canterbury', *Britannia* XVII, 239–58

Barfield, L H and Roe, F E S 2006 'Worked stone', in D Hurst (ed), *Roman Droitwich: Dodderhill fort, Bays Meadow villa, and roadside settlement*, CBA Research Report 146, York, 184–89

Barker, P A 1969 'The origins of Worcester', *Transactions of the Worcestershire Archaeological* Society (3rd series) 2, 1–116

Barrett, A A 1997 *Lunt Roman Fort interim report on excavations western defences*, unpublished excavation report

Bass, W M 1987 *Human osteology*, Missouri

Beek, G van 1983 *Dental Morphology: an illustrated guide*, Bristol

Bell, A and Evans, J 2002 'Pottery from the CfA excavations' in P R Wilson, *Cataractonium; Roman Catterick and its hinterland; excavations and research 1957–1997*, CBA Research Report 128, York, 352–496

Bidwell, P and Speak, S 1994 *Excavations at South Shields Roman fort; volume 1*, Newcastle-upon-Tyne

Bird, J 1986 'Samian wares' in L Miller, J Schofield and M Rhodes *The Roman Quay at St Magnus House, London*, London and Middlesex Archaeological Society Special Paper No 8, London, 139–98

Blakelock, E S 2011 'Metalworking remains', in Butler and Cuttler 2011, 75–83

Booth, P 1991 'Inter-site comparisons between pottery assemblages in Roman Warwickshire: ceramic indicators of site status', *Journal of Roman Pottery Studies* 4, 1–10

Booth, P 1994 'Mortaria', in S Cracknell and C Mahany (eds) *Roman Alcester: Southern extramural area 1964–1966 excavations, Part 2*, CBA Research Report 97, York, 132–43

Booth, P 1996 'Warwickshire in the Roman period: a review of recent work', *Transactions of Birmingham and Warwickshire Archaeological Society* 100, 25–57

Booth, P 2006 'Pottery and other ceramic finds', in J Magilton (ed) 'A Romano-Celtic temple and settlement at Grimstock Hill, Coleshill, Warwickshire', *Transactions of the Birmingham and Warwickshire Archaeological Society* 110, 103–65

Booth, P and Evans, J 2001 *Roman Alcester volume 3: northern extramural area 1969–1988 excavations*, CBA Research Report Series RR127, 2002, *passim*

Booth, P M and Green, S 1989 'The nature and distribution of certain pink, grog-tempered vessels', *Journal of Roman Pottery Studies* 2, 77–84

Boucher, A 1999 *Proposed Magistrates Courts, Castle Street, Worcester, Worcestershire: Archaeological Project Design for excavation and recording*, Unpublished report, Archaeological Investigations Ltd, MS

Brennan, D 2003 'Amphorae' in H James, *Roman Carmarthen; excavations 1978–1993*, Britannia Monograph 20, London, 280–83

Brodbribb, G 1987 *Roman Brick and Tile*, Stroud

Brothwell, D R 1972 *Digging up bones*, London

Brown, D L 1998 'The Roman Small Town of Leintwardine: Excavations and other Fieldwork 1971–1989', *Transactions of the Woolhope Naturalists' Field Club* 48, 1996, 510–72

Bradley, R, Evans J, Pearson, E, Richer, S and Sworn, S 2018 *Archaeological excavation at the site of The Hive, The Butts, Worcester*, Worcestershire Archaeology Research Report no 10, Worcester

Bray, D 2016 *Roman and Medieval Occupation at the Former Worcester City Football Club, St George's Lane, Worcester*, Thames Valley Archaeological Services Occasional Paper 8, Reading

Bryant, V and Evans, Jane 2004 'Iron Age and Romano-British pottery' in Dalwood and Edwards 2004, 240–80

Buckley, D G and Major, H 1983 'Quernstones' in N Crummy, *Colchester Archaeological Report 2: The Roman Small Finds from Excavations in Colchester*

1971–9, Colchester Archaeological Trust Ltd and Department of the Environment, 73–6

Buikstra, J E and Ubelaker, D H 1994 *Standards for data collection from human skeletal remains* Arkansas Archaeological Survey Research Series 44

Burnham, B and Wacher, J 1990 *The Small Towns of Roman Britain*, Oxford

Bushe Fox, J P 1932 *Third report on the excavations of the Roman fort at Richborough, Kent*, Report of the Research Committee of the Society of Antiquaries of London no 10, Oxford

Buteaux, V A 1994 'The pottery' in C H Dalwood, V A Buteaux, and J Darlington, 'Excavations at Farrier Street and other sites north of the City Wall, Worcester 1988–1992', *Transactions of Worcestershire Archaeological Society*, 3rd series, 14, 89–98

Butler, S and Cuttler, R 2011 *Life and Industry in the Suburbs of Roman Worcester*, BAR British Series, Oxford

Casey, P J, Davies, J L and Evans, J 1993 *Excavations at Segontium (Caernarfon) Roman fort, 1975–1979*, CBA Research Report 90, York

Cool, H E M 1990 'Roman Metal Hairpins from Southern Britain', *Archaeological Journal* 147, 148–82

Cool, H E M 2002 *Assessment of Small Finds from Worcester Magistrates Court*, unpublished Assessment Report for Archaeological Investigations, Hereford

Craddock-Bennett, L 2008 *Bleachfield Street, Alcester. Archaeological Assessment*, unpublished report, Archaeological Investigations Ltd

Creighton, J 2006 *Britannia: The Creation of a Roman Province*, London

Croom, A T 2003 'The illustrated vessels' in N Hodgson, *The Roman Fort at Wallsend (Segedunum): Excavations in 1997–8*, Tyne and Wear Museums Archaeological Monograph 3, Newcastle, 241–4

Crummy, N 1983 *Colchester Archaeological Report 2: The Roman Small Finds from Excavations in Colchester 1971–9*, Colchester Archaeological Trust Ltd and Department of the Environment, Colchester

Crummy, N 1995 The Roman small finds from excavations in Colchester 1971–1979. Colchester Archaeological Trust Ltd, Colchester

Crummy, N 2001 'Nail Cleaners: Regionality at the Edge of the Empire. Lucerna', *The Roman Finds Group Newsletter* XXII, 2–6

Cunliffe, B 2005 *Iron Age Communities in Britain: An Account of England, Scotland and Wales* (4th edn) London

Cunliffe, B W and Fulford, M G 1982 *Bath and the Rest of Wessex*, CSIR Great Britain 1.2, Oxford

Curwen, E C 1937 'Querns', *Antiquity* 11, 133–51

Curwen, E C 1941 'More About Querns', *Antiquity* 15, 15–32

Cutler, R, and Evans, J 1998 'A section through the Fosse Way and the excavation of Romano-British features at Princethorpe, Warwickshire, 1994', *Transactions of the Birmingham and Warwickshire Archaeological Society* 102, 57–72

Daffern, N 2016 'Two palaeochannels, the lime decline and the identification of Worcester's first stratified Neolithic deposits: Worcester Arena, Hylton Road, Worcester', *Transactions of Worcestershire Archaeological Society* (Third Series) 25, 101–21

Dalwood, H, Buteaux, V A, and Pearson, E 1998 'Archaeology on the Astley to Worcester Aqueduct', *Transactions of Worcestershire Archaeological Society* (Third series) 16, 1–35

Dalwood, H, and Edwards, R 2004 *Excavations at Deansway Worcester, 1988–89; Romano-British small town to late medieval city*, CBA Research Report 139, York

Darling, M 2004 'The Period 1 pottery', in P Ellis (ed) *The Roman baths and Macellum at Wroxeter; excavations by Graham Webster 1955–85*, English Heritage Archaeological Report 9, London, 258–63

Darlington, J, and Evans, Jane 1992 'Roman Sidbury, Worcester: excavations 1959–1989', *Transactions of the Worcestershire Archaeological Society* (Third Series) 13, 5–104

Davenport, P 2007 *Archaeology in Bath : excavations at the New Royal Baths (the Spa) and Bellott's Hospital 1998-1999*, Oxford Archaeology Monograph, Oxford

Davenport, P 2015 *Excavations at Newport Street, Worcester, 2005: Roman Roadside Activity and Medieval to Post-Medieval Urban Development on the Severn Floodplain*, Cotswold Archaeology/Worcestershire Archive and Archaeology Service, Cirencester

Davis, S J M 1992 *A rapid method for recording information about mammal bones from archaeological sites*, HBMC Ancient Monuments Laboratory report, 19/92, London

Dickinson, B M 1984 'The Samian Ware' in S Frere, *Verulamium Excavations Vol.III*, Oxford University Committee for Archaeology Monograph No 1, Oxford, 175–97

Dickinson, B M 1988 'The stamped and decorated samian' in G D Thomas, 'Excavations at the Roman civil settlement at Inveresk 1976–77', *Proceedings of the Society of Antiquaries of Scotland* 118, Fiche 1: A7–14, B1–14

Dickinson, B M 1991 'Samian pottery' in P S Austen, *Bewcastle and Old Penrith, a Roman outpost fort and a frontier vicus*, Cumberland and Westmorland Antiquarian and Archaeology Society Research Series, vol 6, 112–35

Dickinson, B M 1996 'Samian potters' stamps' in R P J Jackson and T W Potter *Excavations at Stonea, Cambridgeshire 1980–85*, London, 421–27

Dickinson, B, M 2004 'Samian, fabric 43' in Dalwood and Edwards 2004, 274–6

Dickinson, B and Hartley, B 2000 'The Samian' in C Philo and S Wrathmell (eds) *Roman Castleford excavations 1974–85. Volume III, the pottery*, West Yorkshire Archaeology 6, 5–88

Dobney, K, Jaques, D and Irving, B 1995 *Of butchers and breeds: Report on vertebrate remains from various sites in the city of Lincoln*, Lincoln Archaeological Studies 5, Lincoln, City of Lincoln Archaeology Unit

Down, A 1989 *Chichester Excavations 6,* Chichester

Driesch, A von den 1976 *A guide to the measurement of animal bones from archaeological sites,* Peabody Museum Bulletin 1, Harvard

Dudd, S N and Evershed, R P 1999 'Unusual triterpenoid fatty acyl ester components of archaeological birch bark tars' *Tetrahedron Lett* 40, 359–62

Dudd, S N, Regert, M and Evershed, R P 1998 'Assessing microbial lipid contributions during laboratory degradations of fats oils and pure triacylglycerols absorbed in ceramic potsherds', *Organic Geochemistry* 29, 1345–54

Dungworth, D B 2015 'Metals and metalworking', in M Millett, L Revell and A Moore (eds), *The Oxford Handbook of Roman Britain,* DOI: 10.1093/oxfordhb/9780199697713.013.030

Dungworth, D and Wilks, R 2007 *An investigation if Hammerscale* Technology Report Research Department Report Series 26/2007, English Heritage, London

Durand-Lefebvre, M 1963 *Marques de Potiers gallo-romains trouvées à Paris*, Paris

Edwards, R, Griffin, L and Dalwood, H 2002 'Excavations on the site of the new Police Station, Castle St, Worcester', *Transactions of the Worcestershire Archaeological Society* 18, 103–32

Evans, C J, Jones, L and Ellis, P 2000 *Severn Valley ware production at Newland Hopfields: excavation of a Romano-British kiln site at North End Farm, Malvern, Worcestershire in 1992 and 1994*, BUFAU Monograph Series 2, BAR British Series 313, Oxford

Evans, Jane 2018 'Roman oven material: pre-formed ceramic ovens and plates' in Bradley et al 2018, 227–43

Evans, J, 1985 *Aspects of later Roman pottery assemblages in northern England*, unpublished PhD thesis, University of Bradford

Evans, J 1987 'Graffiti and the evidence of literacy and pottery use in Roman Britain', *Archaeological Journal* 144, 191–204

Evans, J 1991 'Not more pot', *Journal of Roman Pottery Studies* 4, 69–78

Evans, J 1993 'Function and finewares in the Roman north', *Journal of Roman Pottery Studies* 6, 95–118

Evans, J 1994 'Discussion of the pottery in the context of Roman Alcester' in S Cracknell and C Mahany, *Roman Alcester: southern extramural area, 1964–1966, Part 2: finds and discussion,* CBA Research Report 97, York, 144–9

Evans, J 1995 'Reflections on later Iron Age and "native" Romano-British pottery in north-eastern England', in B Vyner (ed) *Moorland monuments*, CBA Research Report 101, York, 46–68

Evans, J 1996 'The Gas House Lane (AL23) Roman pottery' in S Cracknell, *Roman Alcester; Vol 2; defences and defended area*, CBA Research Report 106, 58–97

Evans, J 1999 'The Salford Priors Roman pottery' in S Palmer, 'Excavations in the Arrow Valley, Warwickshire', *Transactions of the Birmingham and Warwickshire Archaeological Society* 103, 101–26

Evans, J 2001 'Material approaches to the identification of different Romano-British site types' in S James and M Millett, *Britons and Romans: advancing an archaeological agenda*, CBA Research Report 125, York, 26–35

Evans, J 2002 *The Roman pottery from Middlewich; an assessment,* unpublished report

Evans, J 2003 'The later Iron Age and Roman pottery from Haddon' in M Hinman (ed) *A late Iron Age farmstead and Romano-British Site at Haddon, Peterborough*, BAR British Series 358, Oxford, 68–107

Evans, J 2004 'The pottery vessels' in H E M Cool, *The Roman cemetery at Brougham, Cumbria,* Britannia Monograph No 21, London, 333–63

Evans, J 2005 'Pottery in urban Romano-British life' in A MacMahon and J Price (eds) *Roman working lives and urban living*, Oxford, 145–66

Evans, J 2006 'The Roman pottery' in M Millett (ed) *Shiptonthorpe, East Yorkshire: archaeological studies of a Romano-British roadside settlement*, Yorkshire Archaeological Report 5, Leeds, 126–201

Evans, J 2009a 'The pottery' in T Wilmott, H E M Cool and J Evans 'Excavations at the Hadrian's Wall fort of Birdoswald (Banna), Cumbria: 1996–2000', in T Wilmott, *Hadrian's Wall: archaeological research by English Heritage 1976–2000*, Swindon, 294–349

Evans, J 2009b 'Iron Age, Romano-British and Anglo-Saxon pottery' in S C Palmer, 'Neolithic, Bronze Age, Iron Age, Romano-British and Anglo-Saxon sites excavated on the Transco Churchover to Newbold Pacey gas pipeline in 1999' *Transactions of the Birmingham and Warwickshire Archaeological Society* 113, 107–35

Evans, J 2012 'Iron Age and Roman pottery' in S C Palmer, J Elders and C Jones, Ancient Bubenhall; excavations at Glebe Farm Quarry and Waverley Wood Quarry, Bubbenhall, Warwickshire, 1992–2009, Warwickshire Museum Report No 1127, July 2011, unpublished, 28–45

Evans, J forthcoming 'King Street, the Roman frontier in the North-West and Roman military supply', *Journal of Roman Pottery Studies*

Evans, J in prep 'The Roman pottery from Adel' in P R Wilson 'Report on excavations at Adel, West Yorkshire'

Evans, J, Macaulay, S, and Mills, P 2017 *The Horningsea Roman Pottery Industry in context: An area study of ceramic supply in the Cambridgeshire region*, East Anglian Archaeology Report 162, Cambridge

Evans, J and Rátkai, S forthcoming a 'The Roman pottery from the Oxford North excavations at Walton-le-Dale', in *Excavations at Walton-le-Dale, Lancashire*, Oxford North Monograph

Evans, J and Rátkai, S forthcoming b 'Roman pottery from Mitchell's Brewery 1999 and 2000 (L99/072 and L99/109)', in *Excavations at Mitchell's Brewery, Lancaster*, Oxford North monograph

Evershed, R P 1993 'Biomolecular archaeology and lipids', *World Archaeology* 25:1, 74–93, DOI: 10.1080/00438243.1993.9980229

Evershed, R P, Arnot, K I, Collister, J, Eglington, G, and Charters, S 1994 'Application of isotope ratio monitoring gas chromatography mass-spectrometry to the analysis of organic residues of archaeological origin', *Analyst* 119(5), 909–14

Evershed, R P and Stott, A W 1995 'Formation of Long-chain Ketones in ancient pottery vessels by pyrolysis of acyl lipids' *Tetrahedron Letters* 36(48), 8875–8

Fitzpatrick A P 2016 'Amphorae' in D J Breeze, *Bearsden: a Roman fort on the Antonine Wall*, Society of Antiquaries of Scotland, 171–6 https://doi.org/10.9750/9781908332189

Fulford, M G and Allen, J R 1996 'The distribution of south-east Dorset Black Burnished Category 1 pottery in South-West Britain', *Britannia* XXVII, 223–82

Gan, Y M, Towers, J, Bradley, R A, Pearson, E, Nowell, G, Peterkin, J, and Montgomery, J 2018 'Multi-isotope evidence for cattle droving at Roman Worcester', *Journal of Archaeological Science* 20, 6–17

Gardner, A and Guest, P 2009 'Exploring Roman Caerleon: new excavations at the legionary fortress of Isca', *Archaeology International*, 12, 47–51. DOI: http://doi.org/10.5334/ai.1211

Gillam, J P 1970 *Types of coarse pottery vessels in northern Britain*, Newcastle

Gillam, J P 1976 'Coarse fumed ware in North Britain and beyond', *Glasgow Archaeological Journal* 4, 57–80

Grant, A 1982 'The use of tooth wear as a guide to the age of domestic ungulate' in B Wilson, C Grigson and S Payne (eds) *Aging and sexing animal bones from archaeological sites* BAR British Series 109, Oxford, 91–108

Grant, A 1989 'Animals in Roman Britain', in M Todd (ed.), *Research on Roman Britain: 1960–1989* Britannia Monograph 11, London, 135–46

Green, M J 1976 *The Religions of Civilian Roman Britain*, BAR British Series 24, Oxford

Greene, K T 1978 'Imported fine wares in Britain to AD 250: A guide to identification' in G D Marsh and P R Arthur (eds) *Early fine wares in Roman Britain*, BAR British Series 57, Oxford, 15–30

Greenfield, H J and Arnold, E R 2008 'Absolute age and tooth eruption and wear sequences in sheep and goat: determining age at death in zooarchaeology using a modern control sample', *Journal of Archaeological Science* 35 (4), 836–49

Griffin, S, Hurst, D, and Pearson, E 2001 *Evaluation at Perdiswell Park and Ride, Droitwich Road, Worcester*, Worcestershire CC Archaeological Service internal rep, 894

Griffin, S, Jackson, R, Atkin, S, Dinn, J, Griffin, L, Hughes, P, Hurst, D, Pearson, E, and Vince, A 2004 'Excavation at City Arcade, High Street, Worcester', *Transactions of the Worcestershire Archaeological Society* (3rd series) 19, 45–109

Halstead, P 1985 'A study of mandibular teeth from Romano-British contexts at Maxey' in Pryor, F and French, C (eds) *The Fenland Project Number 1: Archaeology and Environment of the lower Welland Valley, Volume 1*, East Anglian Archaeology Report No. 27

Hambleton, E 1999 *Animal Husbandry Regimes in Iron Age Britain. A Comparative Study of Faunal Assemblages from British Iron Age sites*, BAR British Series 282, Oxford

Hammond, A 2001 'The Animal Bones', in D Vyce, *Worcester Magistrates Court: An archaeological Assessment*, Archaeological Investigations Ltd HAS 475

Hartley, B R 1972a 'The samian ware' in S Frere, *Verulamium Excavations, Vol. I*, Reports of the Research Committee of the Society of Antiquaries of London XXVII, Leeds, 216–62

Hartley, B R 1972b 'The Roman occupation of Scotland: the evidence of the samian ware', *Britannia* 3, 1–55

Hartley, B R 1977 'Two major potteries producing mortaria in the first century AD', in J Dore and K Greene (eds) *Roman pottery studies in Britain and beyond. Papers presented to John Gillam, July 1977*, BAR British Suppl Series 30, 5–17

Hartley, B R and Dickinson, B 1981 'The samian stamps', in Partridge, C *Skeleton Green. A late Iron Age and Romano-British site*, Britannia Monograph Series No 2, London

Hartley, B R and Dickinson, B M 2008–2012. *Names on Terra Sigillata: An Index of Makers' Stamps and Signatures on Gallo-Roman Terra Sigillata (Samian Ware)*, Bulletin of the Institute of Classical Studies Supplement, 9 vols, London

Hartley, B R, and Dickinson, B M 2009 *Names on terra sigillata. An index of makers' stamps and signatures on Gallo-Roman terra sigillata (samian ware), volume 4 (F to Klumi)*, Bull Inst Classical Stud Suppl, 102–04

Hartley, B R, Pengelly, H and Dickinson, B M 1994 'Samian ware' in S Cracknell and C Mahany (eds) *Roman Alcester: Southern Extramural Area 1964–1966 Excavations part 2: Finds and Discussion*, CBA Research Report 97, York, 93–119

Hassall, M and Rhodes, J 1975 'Excavation at New Market Hall, Gloucester, 1966–7', *Transactions of the Bristol and Gloucestershire Archaeological Society* 93, 15–100

Hattatt, R 2000 *A Visual Catalogue of Richard Hattatt's Ancient Brooches*, Oxford

Henig, M 1993 *Corpus Signorum Imperii Romani. Great Britain I fascicule 7. Roman Sculpture from the Cotswold Region British Academy*, Oxford

Heron, C, Evershed, R P and Goad, L J 1991 'Effects of migration of soil lipids on organic residues associated with buried potsherds', *Journal of Archaeological Science* 18, 641–59

Hita, C, Parlanti, E, Jambu, P, Joffre, J and Amblès, A 1996 "Triglyceride degradation in soil, *Organic Chemistry 25, 19–28*

Hobley, B 1969 'A Neronian-Vespasianic military site at 'The Lunt', Baginton, Warwickshire', *Trans Proc Birmingham Archaeol Soc* 83, 65–129

Hodder, I R 1974 'Some marketing models for Romano-British coarse pottery', *Britannia* 5, 340–59

Hodgson, N 2012 'The contribution of commercial archaeology to the study of Roman Warwickshire, 1990–2004' *Transactions of Birmingham and Warwickshire Archaeological Society* 115, 17–30

Holbrook, N and Bidwell, PT 1991 *Roman Finds from Exeter*, Dorchester

Holden, J L, Phakley, P and Clement, J G 1995a 'Scanning electron microscope observations of incinerated human femoral bone: a case study', *Forensic Science International* 74, 17–28

Holden, J L, Phakley, P P and Clement, J G 1995b 'Scanning electron microscope observations of heat-treated human bone' *Forensic Science International* 74, 29–45

Howe, M D, Perrin, R and Mackreth, D 1980 *Roman pottery from the Nene Valley: a guide*, Peterborough City Museum Occasional Paper No 2, Peterborough City Museum and Art Gallery

Hurst, D, 2006 *Roman Droitwich. Dodderhill fort, Bays Meadow villa, and roadside settlement*, York

Hurst, H, 1988 'Gloucester (Glevum)', in G Webster (ed.), *Fortress into city*, London, 48–73

Hurst, H, 1999 'Topography and Identity in Glevum Colonia', in H Hurst (ed.), *The Coloniae of Roman Britain*, Journal of Roman Archaeology Supplementary Series 36, 113–35

Isaksson, S 2000 *Food and rank in early medieval times*, PhD thesis, Archaeological Research Laboratory, Stockholm

Iscan, M Y, Loth, S R and Wright, R K 1985 'Age estimation from the ribs by phase analysis: White females', *Journal of Forensic Science* 30, 853–63

Jackson, R 2012 *Ariconium, Herefordshire: an Iron Age settlement and Romano-British 'small town'*, Oxford

Jenkins, F 1959 'The Cult of the "Pseudo-Venus" in Kent', *Archaeologica Cantiana* 72, 60–76

Johns, C 1963 'Black samian ware from South Wales', *Monmouthshire Antiquaries* 1, iii, 11–19

Johnstone, C and Albarella, U 2002 *The Late Iron Age and Romano-British Mammal and Bird Bone Assemblage from Elms Farm, Heybridge, Essex*. Portsmouth: Centre for Archaeology Report 45/2002

Jones, A 2011 *Roman Birmingham 3: Excavations at Metchley Roman Fort 1999–2001 and 2004–2005. Western settlement, the livestock complex and the western defences*, BAR British Series 534, Oxford

Jones, A 2012 *Roman Birmingham 4: Excavations at Metchley Roman Fort 2004–2005 The western fort interior, defences and post-Roman activity*, BAR British Series 552, Oxford

Jordan, D 1998 Castle Street, Worcester: the soils. Unpublished report, MS

Jurica, J 2008 'Roman Dymock: archaeological investigations 1995–2002', *Transactions of the Bristol & Gloucestershire Archaeological Society* 125, 1–239

Knorr, R 1907 *Die verzierten Terra-sigillata Gefässe von Rottweil*, Stuttgart

Knorr, R 1910 *Die verzierten Terra-sigillata-gefässe von Rottenburg-Sumelocenna*, Stuttgart

Lauwerier, R C G M 1988 *Animals in Roman times in the Dutch eastern river area* Amersfoort, Rijksdienst voor het Oudheidkundig Bodemonderzoek

Lentowicz, I J 1997 'Pottery', in J D Hurst (ed) *A multi-period salt production site at Droitwich: excavations at Upwich*, CBA Research Report 107, 68–74

Linford, P 2002 *Worcester Magistrates Court, Worcester, Worcestershire: Archaeomagnetic Dating Report 2001,* Centre for Archaeology Report 32/2002, English Heritage, Portsmouth

Longley, D, Johnstone, N and Evans, J 1998 'Excavations on two farms of the Romano-British period at Bryn Eryr and Bush Farm, Gwynedd', *Britannia* 29, 185–246

Luff, R 1982 *A zooarchaeological study of the Roman north-western provinces*, BAR British Series 137, Oxford

McDonnell, G and Swiss, A 2004 'Ironworking residues' in Dalwood and Edwards 2004, 368–78

McKinley, J I 1992 *Cremation and inhumation burials from St. Stephen's cemetery, St. Albans*, unpublished report for R Niblett, Verulamium Museum

McKinley, J I 1993 'Bone fragment size and weights of bone from modern British cremations and its implications for the interpretation of archaeological cremations', *International Journal of Osteoarchaeology* 3, 283–87

McKinley, J I 1994a *The Anglo-Saxon cemetery at Spong Hill, North Elmham Part VIII: The Cremations*, East Anglian Archaeology report no. 69

McKinley, J I 1994b 'Bone fragment size in British cremation burials and its implications for pyre technology and ritual', *Journal of Archaeological Science* 21, 339–42.

McKinley, J I 1997 'Bronze Age "Barrows" and the Funerary Rites and Rituals of Cremation', *Proceedings of the Prehistoric Society* 63, 129–45

McKinley, J I 2000a 'The Analysis of Cremated Bone', in M Cox and S Mays (eds) *Human Osteology* Greenwich Medical Media, London, 403–21

McKinley, J I 2000b 'Phoenix rising; aspects of cremation in Roman Britain' in J Pearce, M Millett and M Struck (eds) *Burial, Society and Context in the Roman World,* Oxford, 38–44

McKinley, J I 2000c 'Cremated human remains', 'Cremation burials' and 'Cremated Remains' in B Barber and D Bowsher, *The Eastern Cemetery of Roman London*, MoLAS monograph 5, 61–67, 264–277, 360–265

McMinn, R M H and Hutchings, R T 1985 *A colour atlas of human anatomy,* London

Macphail, R I 1983 'The micromorphology of dark earth from Gloucester, London and Norwich: an analysis of urban anthropogenic deposits from the late Roman to early Medieval periods in England' in P Bullock and C P Murphy (eds) *Soil micromorphology 2: soil genesis,* AB academic publishers, Berkhamstead, 245–52

Macphail, R 2004 'Soil micromorphology', in Dalwood and Edwards 2004, 229–54

McWhirr, A (ed) 1979 *Roman Brick and Tile*, BAR International Series 68, Oxford

Mahany, C (ed) 1994 *Roman Alcester: Southern Extramural Area, 1964-1966 Excavations Part 1: Stratigraphy and Structures*, CBA Res Rep 96, York

Maltby, J M 1979 *The animal bones from Exeter 1971–1975 Vol 2,* Sheffield

Maltby, M 1989 'Urban rural variations in the butchering of cattle in Romano-British Hampshire' in Serjeantson, D and Waldron, T *Diet and crafts in towns*, BAR British Series 199, Oxford

Maltby, M 1990 *The animal bones from the Romano-British deposits at the Greyhound Yard and Methodist Chapel sites in Dorchester*, Dorset, Ancient Monuments Laboratory Report 9/90, English Heritage, MS, London

Manning, W H 1981 *Report on the excavations at Usk, 1965–1976: The Fortress excavations 1968–1971,* Cardiff

Manning, W H 1985 *Catalogue of the Romano-British Iron Tools, Fittings and Weapons in the British Museum,* London

Marsh, G 1981 'London's samian supply and its relationship to the Gallic samian industry' in A C Anderson and A S Anderson (eds) *Roman pottery research in Britain and north-west Europe,* BAR International Series 123, Oxford, 173–238

Martin, T S 2002 'The Late Iron Age and Roman pottery' in S Foreman and D Maynard, 'A Late Iron Age and Roman-British farmstead at Ship Lane, Aveley. Excavations on the line of the A13 Wennington to Mar Dyke road improvement, 1994–5', *Essex Archaeology and History* 33, 138–47

Martin, T S 2003 'Roman Pottery' in M Germany, *Excavations at Great Holts Farm, Boreham, Essex, 1992–94,* East Anglian Archaeology 105, 96–155

Mason, D J P 1980 *Excavations at Chester; 11–15 Castle Street and neighbouring sites, 1974–8; a possible Roman posting house (Mansio)*, Grosvenor Museum, Chester City Council, Chester

Masser, P and Evans, J 2005 'Excavations within the vicus settlement at Burgh by Sands, 2002', *Transactions of the Cumberland and Westmorland Antiquarian and Archaeological Society*, 3rd series, 5, 31–65

Mills, J S and White, R 1994 *The organic chemistry of museum objects*, 2nd edition, Butterworth-Heinemann, London

Mills, P J E 2012 'The coarse pottery', in P Arrowsmith and D Power, *Roman Nantwich: A Salt-Making Settlement Excavations at Kingsley Fields 2002*, BAR British Series 557, Oxford

Miller, D, Griffin, L, Pearson, E 2004 *Archaeological Investigations at Stonebridge Cross, Westwood, Worcestershire: Final Report*. Worcester: Worcestershire Archaeology. Report 797 https://doi.org/10.5284/1026827

Moffett, L M 2004 'Botanical remains', in Dalwood and Edwards 2004, 206–28

Morris, L 1974 'The site of Worcester: its geology and geomorphology' in B H Adlam (ed) *Worcester and its region: field studies in the former county of Worcestershire*, Worcester Branch of the Geographical Association Worcester, 25–34

Napthan, M 2004 *Archaeological Works at 1 The Butts, Worcester*, unpublished report, Mike Napthan Archaeology

Napthan, M 2012 *Archaeological Watching Brief during Alterations to Entrance Gates at Springfield Lodge, Britannia Square, Worcester*, unpublished report, Mike Napthan Archaeology

Napthan, M 2014 'Worcester Castle site: an update on the origins of Worcester', *Transactions of the Worcestershire Archaeological Society* (3rd series) 24, 1–48

Nash-Williams, V E 1930 'The samian potters' stamps found at Caerwent (Venta Silurum) in Monmouthshire', *Bulletin of the Board of Celtic Studies* 5, 166–85

Nicholson, R A and Scott, S A 2004 'Animal remains' Dalwood and Edwards 2004, 506–35

Noddle, B A 1974 'Ages of epiphyseal closure in in feral and domestic goats and ages of dental eruption', *Journal of Archaeological Science 1 (2)*, 195–204

O'Connor, T P 1988 *Bones from the General Accident Site, Tanner Row*, The Archaeology of York 15/2, London

O'Connor, T 2003 *The analysis of urban animal bone assemblages*, The Archaeology of York 19/2, York

Orton, C R 1975 'Quantitative pottery studies; some progress, problems and prospects', *Science and Archaeology* 16, 3–35

Orton, C, Tyers, A and Vince, A 1993 *Pottery in Archaeology*, Cambridge

Oswald, F 1936 *Index of figure types on terra sigillata ('samian ware')*, Supplement to the Annals of Archaeology and Anthropology, University of Liverpool, 1936–7

Oswald, F and Pryce, T D 1920 *An introduction to the study of terra sigillata*, London

Peacock, D P S 1965–7 'Romano-British pottery production in the Malvern district of Worcestershire', *Transactions of Worcestershire Archaeological Society*, 3rd ser, 1, 15–28

Peacock, D P S 1968 'Romano-British Pottery Production in the Malvern District of Worcestershire', *Worcestershire Archaeological Society* 1, 15–28

Peacock, D 1977b 'Ceramics in Roman and medieval archaeology' in D Peacock, *Pottery and Early Commerce: Characterisation and Trade in Roman and Later Ceramics*, London

Pearson, E 2000 *Environmental remains from an evaluation at Conder Buildings, Worcester*, Worcestershire County Council Archaeological Service, unpublished internal report

Pearson, E 2007 'Environmental analysis', in T Rogers, *Updated Project Design for former petrol storage facility, Bath Road, Worcester*, Worcestershire Historic Environment and Archaeology Service internal report 1504

Pikes, P J, and Sherlock, H 2003 *The Conder Building, Worcester: archaeological excavation*, Archenfield Archaeology Ltd unpublished report (project ref AA06)

Purdue, J R 1983 'Epiphyseal closure in white-tailed deer', *Journal of Wildlife Management 47 (4)*, 1207–13

Ray, K 2002 *The Romano-British Period in Herefordshire*. West Midlands Regional Research Framework: Birmingham

Reitz, E J and Wing, E S 2007 *Zooarchaeology*, Cambridge

Rielly, K 2000 'Pyre goods: animal bone and cremation burial' in B Barber and D Bowsher, *The Eastern Cemetery of Roman London*, MoLAS monograph, 571–6

Rigby, V 1977 'The Gallo-Belgic pottery from Cirencester' in J Dore and K Greene, *Roman pottery studies in Britain and beyond*, BAR International Series 30, Oxford 37–46

Rivet, A F 1958 *Town and Country in Roman Britain*, London

Rogers, G B 1974 *Poteries sigillées de la Gaule centrale, I: les motifs non figurés*, Gallia suppl 28, Paris

Rogers, G B 1999 *Poteries sigillées de la Gaule centrale, II. Les potiers, II* Lezoux

Rogers, J and Waldron, T 1995 *A field guide to Joint Disease in Archaeology*, Chichester

Rogers, T 2014 'From the Mesolithic to the Second World War; Archaeological Investigations at the former petrol storage facility, Bath Road, Worcester', *Transactions of the Worcestershire Archaeological Society* 24 , 95–106

Romeuf, A-M 2001 *Le quartier artisanal gallo-romain des Martres-de-Veyre (Puy-de-Dôme)* (2 vols), Les Cahiers du Centre Archéologique de Lezoux 2

Schmid, E 1972 *Atlas of animal bones*, Amsterdam

Schoeninger, M J and DeNiro, M J 1984 'Nitrogen and carbon isotopic composition of bone collagen from marine and terrestrial animals', *Geochemica et Cosmochimica Acta* 48, 625–39

Scott, I R 2016 'Ironwork and its production', in Bird (ed.) *Agriculture and Industry in South-Eastern Roman Britain*, Oxford 301–29

Seager-Smith, R and Davies, S M 1993 'Roman pottery' in P J Woodward, S M Davies and A H Graham, *Excavations at Greyhound Yard, Dorchester, 1981–4*, Dorset Natural History and Archaeological Society Monograph No 12, Dorchester, 202–89

Serjeantson, D 1996 'The animal bones' in F R E Ham and A Spence (eds) *Refuse and disposal at Area 16 east Runnymede,* Runnymede Bridge Research Excavations, Volume 2, British Museum Press, London, 194–223

Silver, I A 1970 'The aging of domestic animals' in D R Brothwell and E S Higgs (eds) *Science in archaeology: a survey of progress and research 2nd edition*, New York, 283–302

Simpson, G 1957 'Metallic black slip vases from Central Gaul with applied and moulded decoration', *Antiquaries Journal* 37, 29–42

Simpson, G 1973 'More black slip vases from Central Gaul with applied and moulded decoration in Britain', *Antiquaries Journal* 53, part i, 42–50

Simpson, G and Rogers, G 1969 'Cinnamus de Lezoux et quelques potiers contemporains', *Gallia* 27, 3–14

Smith, A. 2017 'Rural crafts and industry', in Allen et al 2017, 178–236

Smith, A, Allen, M, Brindle, T and Fulford, M 2016 *The Rural Settlement of Roman Britain, New Visions of the Countryside of Roman Britain. Vol. 1*, Britannia Monograph 29, London

Smith, A, Allen, M, Brindle, T, Fulford, M, Lodwick, L and Rohnbogner, A 2018 *Life and Death in the Countryside of Roman Britain, New Visions of the Countryside of Roman Britain Vol. 3*, Britannia Monograph Series 31, London

Smith, A and Fulford, M 2016 'Conclusions: the rural settlement of Roman Britain', in Smith et al 2016, 385–420

Smith, A and Fulford, M 2019 'The Defended Vici of Roman Britain: Recent Research and New Agendas' *Britannia* 50, 109–47, doi:10.1017/S0068113X19000151

Smith, W 2011 'Roman charred plant remains', in Butler and Cuttler 2011, 27–42

Stanfield, J A and Simpson, G 1958 *Central Gaulish Potters*, Oxford

Stanfield, J A and Simpson, G 1990 *Les potiers de la Gaule centrale* (French edition), Revue Archéologique Sites 37

Swan, V G 1977 'Relief-decorated imitation samian cups from Wanborough, Wilts', in J Dore and K Greene (eds) *Roman pottery studies in Britain and beyond*, BAR Supplementary Series 30, Oxford, 263–68

Sworn, S, Dalwood, H, Evans, C J and Pearson, E 2014 *Archaeological excavation at the City Campus, University of Worcester*, Worcestershire Archaeology Research Report no 2, Worcester http://www.worcestershire.gov.uk/downloads/file/6061/worcestershire_archaeology_research_report_no_2

Taylor, J 1990 'The pottery' in M McCarthy, *A Roman Anglian and medieval site at Blackfriars Street*, Cumberland and Westmorland Antiquarian and Archaeological Society Research Series No 4, Kendal, 197–300

Taylor, J 1991 *Fasicule 4: The Roman pottery from Castle Street, Carlisle; excavations 1981–2*, Cumberland and Westmorland antiquarian and Archaeological Society Research Series No 5, Kendal

Timby, J 1986 'Roman pottery', in H R Hurst, *Gloucester; the Roman and later defences*, Gloucester Archaeological Publications, Gloucester, 54–71

Timby, J R 1999 'Pottery supply to Gloucester *colonia'*, in H Hurst (ed.) *The Coloniae of Roman Britain*, Journal of Roman Archaeology Supplementary Series 36, 33–44

Tomber, R and Dore, J 1998 *The National Roman Fabric Reference Collection: A Handbook*, MoLAS Monograph 2, London

Tomlin, R S O 2001 'Instrumentum domesticum' in R S O Tomlin and M W C Hassall, 'Roman Britain in 2001: II Inscriptions', *Britannia* 32, 393–7

Vernhet, A 1981 'Un four de la Graufesenque (Aveyron). La cuisson des vases sigillées', *Gallia* XXXIX, 25–43

Vink, C 2008 *The animal bone assemblage from Worcester* Unpublished report, University of Southampton, MS

Wainwright, J 2014 *Archaeological Investigations in St John's, Worcester*, Worcestershire Archaeology Research Report 4

Ward, M 1989 'The samian ware' in K Blockley, *Prestatyn 1984–5, an Iron Age farmstead and Romano-British industrial settlement in north Wales*, BAR British Series 210, 139–54

Ward, M 1996 'Samian ware' in S Cracknell (ed) *Roman Alcester series volume 2. Defences and defended area. Gateway Supermarket and Gas House Lane*, CBA Research Report 106, 74–7

Ward, M 1998 'Some finds from the Roman works-depôt at Holt', *Studia Celtica* 32, 4–84

Ward, M 2001 'The samian ware' in P Booth and J Evans, *Roman Alcester volume 3: northern extramural area 1969–1988 excavations*, CBA Research Report Series RR127, *passim*

Ward, M 2008a 'The samian ware', in H E M Cool and D J P Mason (eds), *Roman Piercebridge: Excavations by D W Harding and Peter Scott 1969–1981*, Architectural & Archaeological Society of Durham and Northumberland

Research Report 7, Durham, 169–296. Catalogue and summaries: http://archaeologydataservice.ac.uk/archives/view/piercebridge_eh_2008/downloads.cfm (accessed 18/07/2020)

Ward, M 2008b. 'Samian ware', in M Williams and M Reid, *Salt: Life and Industry. Excavations at King Street, Middlewich, Cheshire 2001–2002,* BAR British Ser. 456, Oxford, 117–58

Ward, M 2011. 'Samian ware from northern Britain: models of supply, demand and occupation' in T Saunders (ed), *Roman North West England: Hinterland or 'Indian Country'?,* Archaeology North West NS 2, Council for British Archaeology North West, 74–104

Ward, M 2012 'A northern odyssey: the first 26,000 samian vessels, and still counting' in D Bird (ed), *Dating and Interpreting the Past in the Western Roman Empire, Essays in Honour of Brenda Dickinson*, Oxford, 19–27

Ward, M 2015 'A gazetteer of the incidence of less common samian ware fabrics and products in northern and western Britain. Part I: Introduction and South Gaulish fabrics', *Journal of Roman Pottery Studies* 16, 131–55

Ward, M 2016 'The samian ware', in J Zant, 'Excavations on a Roman salt-working site at Jersey Way, Middlewich, Cheshire', *Archaeological Journal*, 173:1, 56–153

Ward, M 2018. 'The samian ware', in T Wilmott and D Garner, *The Roman Amphitheatre of Chester. Volume 1: The Prehistoric and Roman Archaeology,* Chester Archaeological Excavation and Survey Report 16, Oxford, 221–76, 446–48 (appendices 1–2)

Ward, M forthcoming a 'A gazetteer of the incidence of less common samian ware fabrics and products in northern and western Britain. Part 2: "early Lezoux" and "black samian" products from Central Gaul', *Journal of Roman Pottery Studies*

Ward, M. forthcoming b 'The samian ware', in C Howard-Davis, I Miller, N Hair, and R M Newman, *Excavations at Mitchells Brewery and 39 Church Street, Lancaster,* Oxford Archaeology North, Lancaster Imprint

Ward, M. forthcoming c 'The samian ware from three locations at Brougham', in J. Zant, *The Roman Extramural Settlement at Brougham: the Excavations of 2007–08,* Oxford Archaeology North, Lancaster Imprint

Waters, P L 1976 'Romano-British Pottery Site at Great Buckhams Farm', *Worcestershire Archaeological Society* 5, 63–72

Waugh, H and Goodburn, R 1972 'The Non-Ferrous Objects', in S Frere *Verulamium Excavations, Vol. I,* Reports of the Research Committee of the Society of Antiquaries of London XXVII, Leeds, 115–62

Webster, P V 1976 'Severn Valley ware; a preliminary study', *Transactions of the Bristol and Gloucestershire Archaeological Society* 94 (1977) 19–45

Webster, P V 1993 'Coarse pottery' in P J Casey, J L Davies and J Evans, *Excavations at Segontium (Caernarfon) Roman fort, 1975–1979,* CBA Research Report 90, 250–309

Webster, P V 1996 *Roman samian pottery in Britain,* CBA Practical Handbook in Archaeology 13, York

Wild, F 2013 'A samian repair and recycling workshop at Kempston Church End, Beds,' *Britannia* 44, 271–75

Wild, J 1970 'Button and Loop Fasteners in the Roman Provinces', *Britannia* 1, 137–55

Williams, D F 1977 'The Romano-British black-burnished industry: an essay in characterization by heavy mineral analysis' in D Peacock, *Pottery and Early Commerce: Characterisation and Trade in Roman and Later Ceramics*, London, 163–220

Williams, D F 1990 'Amphorae from York' in J R Perrin, *The Roman pottery from the colonia:2,* The Archaeology of York 16/4, CBA, London, 342–62

Williams, D F 1997, 'The Amphorae' in J Monaghan, *Roman pottery from York,* The Archaeology of York 16/8, CBA, York, 967–75

Williams, D F 2004, 'Amphorae', in Dalwood and Edwards 2004, 274

Willis, S H 1998 'Samian pottery in Britain; exploring its distribution and archaeological potential', *Archaeological Journal* 155, 82–133

Willis, S 2005 *Samian pottery, a resource for the study of Roman Britain and beyond: the results of the English Heritage funded Samian Project.* E-monograph, Internet Archaeology 17. https://doi.org/10.11141/ia.17.1

Willis, S H 2012 'The Iron Age and Roman pottery' in R Jackson (ed) *Ariconium, Herefordshire; an Iron Age settlement and Romano-British 'small town'*, Oxford, 41–109

Woodiwiss, S 1992 *Iron Age and Roman Salt Production and the Medieval Town of Droitwich,* CBA Research Report 81 York

Worcester City Council 2007 *An Outline Resource Assessment and Research Framework for the Archaeology of Worcester, Worcester*

Wright, M E 2002 'Querns and Millstones' in P R Wilson, *Cateractonium: Roman Catterick and its hinterland: excavations and research 1957–1997,* Part II, CBA Research Report 129, York, 267–85

Young, C J 1977 *The Roman pottery industry of the Oxford region,* BAR British Series 43, Oxford

APPENDICES

Appendix 1

Pottery fabric descriptions

Jeremy Evans and Phil Mills

Class	Name	%Nosh	%Wt
A	amphorae	0.6%	2.7%
B	black burnished wares	3.2%	2.4%
F	colour-coated wares	0.4%	0.2%
G	gritted wares	6.6%	9.1%
M	mortaria	1.2%	2.7%
O	oxidised wares	76.0%	71.2%
Q	white-slipped flagon fabrics	0.4%	0.3%
R	reduced wares	6.4%	7.9%
S	samian wares	4.8%	3.1%
W	whitewares	0.4%	0.3%

Worcester = Worcestershire Fabric Type Series (http://www.worcestershireceramics.org/).

Code	Name/Source	Equivalents/References	Description
A21	Baetican Dressel 20 amphora	Worcester fabric 42.1	common limestone/chalk sand and silver mica, exterior sometimes white-slipped
A22	Pelichet 47/Gauloise amphorae	Worcester fabric 42.3	buff-orange core, margins and surfaces, with some fine rounded calcareous inclusions *c* 0.2mm and occasional sand *c* 0.3mm, and occasional (and rarely common) fine silver mica
B11	Black Burnished 1, Poole Harbour, Dorset	Worcester fabric 22; Williams 1977	
F12	Glazed ware		oxidised fabric with an orange core and margins and green/brown glazed surfaces, with some fine sand *c* 0.2mm
F32	Central Gaulish 'Rhenish ware'	Worcester fabric 44	oxidised fabric with buff-orange core and margins and black slipped surfaces, 'clean' with common very fine chalk sand >0.05mm
F42	Roughcast colour-coated wares, probably fairly local	Worcester fabric 45?; similar tradition to that at Wilderspool	oxidised roughcast fabric with orange-brown core, margins and surfaces, with some sand *c* 0.2-0.3mm
F43		Worcester fabric 31?	brown-slipped oxidised fabric with buff-grey core and orange-brown margins, with some sand *c* 0.2-0.3mm, similar to F42 but not roughcast
F51	Oxfordshire red colour-coated ware	Worcester fabric 29; Young 1977	
F52	Nene Valley colour-coated ware	Worcester fabric 28; Howe et al 1980	parchment ware fabric
F53	Nene Valley colour-coated ware	Worcester fabric 28; Howe et al 1980	oxidised ware fabric
F91	Terra Nigra		
G11	Pink grogged ware, Milton Keynes area	Worcester fabric 17; Cirencester fabric 140; Booth and Green 1989	hand-made fabric with grey core, buff-brown margins and common angular grog temper *c* 0.5–3mm
G15		Worcester fabric 16/16.2?	handmade reduced fabric with black core, margins and surfaces, with abundant angular grey grog *c* 0.1-0.7mm and occasional organic voids up to 0.5mm in length

Code	Name/Source	Equivalents/References	Description
G16		Worcester fabric 16/16.2?	handmade reduced fabric with a black core and dark grey margins and surfaces, with common-abundant red-brown grog *c* 0.1–1mm
G37	Malvernian		handmade reduced fabric with a blue-grey core and mid-grey margins and surfaces, with common black grog(?) inclusions *c* 0.1-0.3mm and occasional translucent quartz *c* 0.5–1mm and occasional white Malvernian stone inclusions *c* 0.2–2mm
G44	Malvernian metamorphic-tempered ware, Malvern Link, Worcestershire	Worcester fabric 3	hand-made fabric with common angular white-pink inclusions *c* 1–6mm and some black igneous inclusions, *c* 0.5–5mm, sometimes with gold mica inclusions
G45	Severn Valley?		handmade, oxidised, Severn Valley type fabric with a light grey core and orange margins and surfaces, with common angular grey grog inclusions *c* 0.3–1mm, and some organic temper voids *c* 0.1–2mm in length, and very occasional moderate sand *c* 0.3mm
G46	Malvernian metamorphic-tempered ware	Worcester fabric 19	wheel-made with a black core, margins and surfaces, with occasional black Malvernian stone inclusions up to *c* 3mm and some fine gold mica.
G47	Malvernian metamorphic-tempered ware	Worcester fabric 3	variant on G44 with a black core, orange-brown margins and grey-brown surfaces, often used for storage jars and portable ovens, inclusions as G44.
G71	Probably a very odd variant on Malvernian metamorphic-tempered ware		handmade reduced fabric with a dark grey-brown core, margins and surfaces, fairly 'clean', with occasional rounded black stone inclusions *c* 0.4mm and occasional angular white quartz-like inclusions *c* 0.7mm and some fine gold mica
G72			handmade(?) reduced fabric with mid-grey core, margins and surfaces, with some angular grey grog *c* 0.5mm and some vegetable temper voids up to 2mm long, (possibly briquetage)
M12	North Gallic mortaria	Worcester fabric 36; Hartley (1977) class I and II	buff mortarium fabric with common fine ironstone *c* 0.1-0.2mm, trituration grits; fine grey flint *c* 1–2mm
M21	Verulamium region mortaria	Worcester fabric 35	abundant sub-angular translucent sand temper *c* 0.3mm, very occasional red-brown ironstone *c* 0.2mm and very occasional white clay inclusions up to 4mm
M22	Mancetter-Hartshill mortaria	Worcester fabric 32	white fabric with red and brown grog trituration grits
M23	Oxfordshire whiteware mortaria	Worcester fabric 33; Young 1977	white fabric with translucent, white, and pink quartz trituration grits
M37	?Wroxeter area mortaria	Worcester fabric 34	whiteware mortarium with a pale orange core and cream-buff margins and surfaces, with abundant angular translucent sand *c* 0.2-0.3mm, trituration grits; common white quartz *c* 2–3mm and common brown ironstone *c* 1–3mm
M44	Worcestershire? / Warwickshire? mortaria		oxidised white-slipped fabric with an orange core and margins, with common moderate sand temper *c* 0.3mm, trituration grits; sub-rounded brown stone, some white quartz and some sub-angular grey stone
M45	Severn Valley mortaria	Worcester fabric 37	oxidised white-slipped fabric with an orange core and margins, a 'clean', 'soapy' fabric, trituration grits; mixed translucent quartz and rounded brown stone, *c* 1–3mm
M71	Oxfordshire oxidised red colour-coated mortaria	Worcester fabric 29; Young 1977	
O20	Severn Valley wares	Worcester fabric 12	
O21	Severn Valley wares	Worcester fabric 12.2	often with grey core and orange-brown margins, with abundant organic temper voids *c* 0.3–3mm
O23	Severn Valley wares	Worcester fabric 12; Cirencester fabric 108	abundant very fine sand temper *c* 0.1mm. Visually similar to O23
O231	Severn Valley wares	Worcester fabric 12	similar to O23, generally pale yellow-orange in colour, sometimes with a pale grey core, with a 'soapy' texture, and with surfaces which have a finely micaceous appearance. There are occasional brown ironstone inclusions *c* 0.5–1mm and sometimes some rounded siltstone *c* 0.5–2mm

Code	Name/Source	Equivalents/References	Description
O24	Severn Valley wares	Worcester fabric 12	some moderate sand temper *c* 0.3mm and brown siltstone *c* 0.2-0.4mm and some ironstone *c* 0.3–2mm
O27	Severn Valley wares	Worcester fabric 12.6; visually very similar to products of the Great Buckman's Farm and Newlands kilns in the Malvern Link complex.	common fairly fine white inclusions *c* 0.1-0.3mm
O29	Severn Valley wares	Worcester fabric 12.5?	common-abundant moderate sand temper *c* 0.3mm
O291	Severn Valley wares	Worcester fabric 12.5?	some moderate sand temper *c* 0.3mm, much less sand than O29.
O35	Severn Valley wares	Worcester fabric 12	fairly 'clean', slightly 'soapy', with occasional fine white inclusions up to 0.2mm, occasional sand *c* 0.2mm, and common very fine silver and gold mica
O36	Severn Valley wares	Worcester fabric 12.2	similar to fabric O21, but with less organic tempering; some-common organic temper voids *c* 0.3mm and sometimes some white ?calcareous inclusions or grog inclusions
O53	Severn Valley wares		hard with common sand *c* 0.3mm and some white stone inclusions *c* 0.3mm
O55	Severn Valley wares		grey core and orange-brown margins soft and with a laminar texture, occasional brown ironstone and occasional limestone/chalk sand inclusions, surfaces appear micaceous
O57			buff fabric with a buff core, margins and surfaces, with common angular black stone inclusions *c* 0.2 and occasional white inclusions *c* 0.2mm
O81	Whitehall Farm, Wiltshire?	Cirencester fabric 96/98	oxidised ware with common fine sand temper *c* 0.1-0.2mm and some moderate red ironstone inclusions.
O91	Severn Valley wares		handmade with an orange-brown core, margins and surfaces, with common clay pellet/grog angular inclusions *c* 0.5-0.7mm and some organic temper voids
Q12			white-slipped oxidised fabric with buff-orange core and orange margins, with common sand temper *c* 0.3mm
Q13			white-slipped oxidised fabric with a black core and orange margins; hard-fired, 'clean', with very occasional ironstone *c* 0.2mm
Q14	South-western white-slipped ware	Cirencester fabric 88	white slipped oxidised fabric with grey core, with common-abundant moderate-coarse sand and some moderate red ironstone
Q151	Severn Valley white-slipped ware	Worcester fabric 20	white-slipped oxidised flagon fabric with orange core, margins and surfaces, 'clean' with occasional black ironstone inclusions *c* 0.1-0.2mm
Q27			white-slipped oxidised fabric with a mid-grey core and brown margins, with some translucent and white quartz sand *c* 0.3-0.4mm in a clean matrix
R01/ R11	?North Warwickshire reduced ware	Worcester fabric 15	reduced fabric with common fairly coarse sand temper *c* 0.4mm
R18	?North Warwickshire / ?Severn Valley reduced ware		reduced fabric with brown core, grey margins and black surfaces, with occasional vegetable temper voids and some fine limestone/chalk sand
R31	Severn Valley reduced ware		hand-made reduced ware with common vegetable voids *c* 0.5–2mm
R32	?Worcestershire reduced ware	Worcester fabric 12.3	reduced fabric with common small vegetable voids *c* 0.3-0.5mm
R341			reduced fabric with a mid-grey core and dark grey surfaces, with abundant sand temper *c* 0.3mm
R41			reduced fabric with some moderate sand temper *c* 0.3mm and occasional brown moderate ironstone
R46			reduced fabric with a mid-grey core and margins and dark grey surfaces, hard, with occasional black ironstone *c* 0.2mm and occasional sand *c* 0.2mm in a 'clean' matrix

Code	Name/Source	Equivalents/References	Description
R52			reduced fabric with some moderate sand temper, occasional black ironstone inclusions and some grey grog inclusions c 1–3mm
R55			reduced fabric with a dark grey core, margins and surfaces, with common sand c 0.3mm, occasional rounded white inclusions c 0.2mm and some fine organic temper voids up to 1–5mm long
R59			hard reduced fabric with grey core, grey or brown margins and grey surfaces with some rounded white calcareous(?) inclusions c 0.2-0.4mm and occasional rounded black ironstone up to 1mm
R813		Worcester fabric 12.1	smooth reduced fabric with a mid-grey core, margins and surfaces, with common-abundant very fine sand temper less than c 0.05mm, occasional black ironstone up to 0.2mm, and some very fine silver mica
S10	South Gaulish samian ware	Worcester fabric 43	
S20	Central Gaulish (Lezoux) samian ware	Worcester fabric 43	
S21	Les Martres-de-Veyre samian ware	Worcester fabric 43	
S30	East Gaulish samian wares	Worcester fabric 43	
W11	Verulamium region whiteware		whiteware with abundant translucent sand temper c 0.3mm
W21	?Mancetter whiteware		whiteware with a white core, margins and surfaces, very hard, 'clean' and 'soapy'
W22			whiteware with a white core, margins and surfaces, hard, fairly 'clean' with some fine sand <0.1mm
W24			whiteware with a buff core, margins and surfaces, with common sand c 0.1-0.3mm in a 'clean' matrix
W25			whiteware with a buff-white core, margins and surfaces, with some very fine sand up to 0.1mm and very occasional ironstone up to 0.5mm
W28			whiteware with a pink core and white margins and surfaces, 'clean', 'soapy', and rather laminar with very occasional rounded white inclusions c 0.2-0.3mm
W29			whiteware with a white core, margins and surfaces, with some moderate sand c 0.3mm in a 'clean' matrix
W37			whiteware with a buff-white core, margins and surfaces, with common translucent sand c 0.3-0.5mm

Appendix 2

Fabric occurrence by phase

Jeremy Evans and Phil Mills

Fabric Code	Phase	% Nosh	% Wt	% MNV	% RE	% BE
A00	3	0.01%	0.01%	0.00%	0.00%	0.00%
A21	0	0.45%	3.64%	0.00%	0.00%	0.00%
A21	1	0.29%	2.20%	0.00%	0.00%	0.00%
A21	2	1.64%	5.05%	0.00%	0.00%	0.00%
A21	3	0.42%	2.29%	0.11%	0.84%	0.00%
A21	4	0.27%	1.60%	0.00%	0.00%	0.00%
A21	6	0.21%	2.08%	0.72%	3.81%	0.00%
A22	3	0.03%	0.09%	0.00%	0.00%	0.26%
B11	0	4.55%	3.68%	10.26%	10.82%	0.00%
B11	1	4.39%	2.71%	5.13%	4.48%	2.82%
B11	2	6.42%	3.82%	9.89%	7.78%	8.90%
B11	3	1.73%	1.33%	4.66%	3.79%	2.40%
B11	4	6.33%	3.86%	12.22%	11.48%	7.99%
B11	6	2.68%	1.50%	6.47%	4.80%	0.00%
F12	1	0.10%	0.03%	0.00%	0.00%	0.00%
F12	2	0.13%	0.03%	0.19%	0.08%	0.00%
F12	4	0.03%	0.01%	0.25%	0.22%	0.00%
F32	2	0.03%	0.00%	0.00%	0.00%	0.00%
F32	3	0.01%	0.00%	0.06%	0.09%	0.00%
F42	0	2.27%	1.16%	10.26%	11.06%	0.00%
F42	1	0.54%	0.22%	0.73%	0.67%	0.61%
F42	2	0.22%	0.05%	0.19%	0.25%	0.00%
F42	3	0.09%	0.06%	0.28%	0.21%	0.74%
F42	4	0.33%	0.20%	0.25%	0.25%	3.19%
F43	2	0.05%	0.01%	0.00%	0.00%	0.00%
F43	4	0.03%	0.11%	0.00%	0.00%	0.00%
F51	0	0.45%	0.39%	2.56%	2.12%	0.00%
F51	3	0.02%	0.03%	0.11%	0.09%	0.16%
F51	4	0.43%	0.31%	1.00%	0.64%	4.57%
F51	6	0.31%	0.36%	0.72%	0.46%	1.31%
F52	0	0.45%	0.06%	2.56%	1.41%	0.00%
F52	2	0.03%	0.00%	0.00%	0.00%	0.00%
F52	3	0.06%	0.03%	0.06%	0.03%	0.00%
F52	4	0.10%	0.02%	0.25%	0.14%	0.00%
F52	6	0.10%	0.13%	0.00%	0.00%	0.00%
F53	4	0.07%	0.02%	0.00%	0.00%	0.00%
F91	2	0.03%	0.02%	0.19%	0.11%	0.00%
G00	3	0.01%	0.00%	0.00%	0.00%	0.00%

Fabric Code	Phase	% Nosh	% Wt	% MNV	% RE	% BE
G15	1	0.05%	0.02%	0.00%	0.00%	0.00%
G16	3	0.01%	0.01%	0.00%	0.00%	0.00%
G44	0	4.09%	1.86%	0.00%	0.00%	0.00%
G44	1	5.70%	5.05%	6.96%	5.23%	2.78%
G44	2	4.61%	3.69%	5.41%	3.77%	1.56%
G44	3	1.07%	1.20%	1.33%	1.15%	0.39%
G44	4	1.40%	1.47%	1.50%	1.51%	1.19%
G44	6	1.44%	0.93%	0.72%	0.61%	1.97%
G45	3	0.01%	0.01%	0.00%	0.00%	0.00%
G46	0	0.45%	0.30%	0.00%	0.00%	3.62%
G46	1	0.05%	0.02%	0.00%	0.00%	0.00%
G46	2	0.62%	0.52%	0.37%	0.24%	0.58%
G46	3	0.71%	0.69%	1.39%	1.49%	1.70%
G46	4	2.63%	3.24%	2.74%	3.35%	9.77%
G46	6	3.40%	3.51%	3.60%	2.59%	2.23%
G47	0	3.18%	1.61%	0.00%	0.00%	0.00%
G47	1	0.98%	1.29%	0.37%	0.25%	0.00%
G47	2	4.39%	4.22%	1.31%	1.24%	2.36%
G47	3	3.18%	5.51%	3.83%	3.46%	3.67%
G47	4	4.50%	12.45%	2.49%	2.18%	2.26%
G47	6	11.23%	14.35%	9.35%	8.23%	10.89%
G48	1	0.05%	0.00%	0.00%	0.00%	0.00%
G48	3	0.13%	0.09%	0.00%	0.00%	0.70%
G57	6	0.31%	0.22%	0.00%	0.00%	0.00%
G71	1	0.05%	0.02%	0.00%	0.00%	0.00%
G71	4	0.03%	0.04%	0.00%	0.00%	0.00%
G72	2	0.05%	0.03%	0.00%	0.00%	0.00%
G72	3	0.01%	0.00%	0.00%	0.00%	0.00%
M00	2	0.03%	0.01%	0.19%	0.05%	0.00%
M00	3	0.02%	0.01%	0.00%	0.00%	0.00%
M12	1	0.05%	0.20%	0.37%	0.32%	0.00%
M21	1	0.15%	0.52%	0.73%	1.02%	0.00%
M21	2	0.05%	0.08%	0.37%	0.16%	0.00%
M21	3	0.01%	0.01%	0.06%	0.03%	0.00%
M21	4	0.03%	0.04%	0.00%	0.00%	0.32%
M22	0	0.45%	0.54%	0.00%	0.00%	0.00%
M22	1	0.05%	0.05%	0.00%	0.00%	0.00%
M22	2	0.22%	0.92%	0.75%	0.74%	0.91%
M22	3	0.74%	2.35%	2.77%	3.44%	1.29%
M22	4	0.47%	1.20%	1.75%	1.59%	1.12%
M22	6	4.53%	10.73%	15.11%	13.19%	3.81%
M23	2	0.08%	0.13%	0.19%	0.08%	0.27%
M23	3	0.13%	0.18%	0.33%	0.47%	0.00%
M23	4	0.10%	0.10%	0.25%	0.00%	0.00%
M23	6	1.13%	1.99%	4.32%	3.43%	4.33%

Fabric Code	Phase	% Nosh	% Wt	% MNV	% RE	% BE
M37	0	0.45%	0.71%	0.00%	0.00%	0.00%
M37	1	0.05%	0.04%	0.00%	0.00%	0.00%
M37	2	0.11%	0.12%	0.00%	0.00%	0.00%
M37	3	0.13%	0.23%	0.50%	0.34%	0.00%
M37	4	0.10%	0.26%	0.00%	0.00%	0.77%
M37	6	0.10%	0.13%	0.72%	0.08%	0.00%
M44	2	0.11%	0.22%	0.00%	0.00%	0.63%
M44	3	0.02%	0.06%	0.06%	0.04%	0.22%
M44	4	0.07%	0.11%	0.00%	0.00%	0.00%
M45	0	0.45%	0.28%	0.00%	0.00%	0.00%
M45	2	0.11%	0.44%	0.75%	0.40%	0.00%
M45	3	0.10%	0.13%	0.17%	0.11%	0.13%
M45	4	0.07%	0.03%	0.25%	0.14%	0.00%
M71	3	0.01%	0.01%	0.00%	0.00%	0.00%
M71	4	0.03%	0.02%	0.00%	0.00%	0.00%
O00	3	0.08%	0.07%	0.00%	0.00%	0.00%
O133	4	0.07%	0.01%	0.00%	0.00%	0.00%
O20	1000	87.18%	79.02%	0.00%	0.00%	
O20	2	0.49%	0.28%	0.00%	0.00%	0.00%
O20	3	65.35%	52.90%	0.00%	0.02%	0.00%
O20	4	8.90%	3.98%	0.00%	0.00%	0.00%
O20	6	53.86%	36.45%	0.00%	0.00%	0.00%
O201	3	0.02%	0.03%	0.00%	0.00%	0.00%
O21	0	0.45%	1.61%	0.00%	0.00%	0.00%
O21	1	1.07%	4.70%	0.73%	0.79%	1.91%
O21	2	0.97%	2.52%	0.37%	0.22%	1.21%
O21	3	0.10%	0.14%	0.11%	0.16%	0.41%
O21	4	0.57%	1.01%	0.25%	0.08%	3.21%
O23	0	0.91%	0.79%	2.56%	0.71%	0.00%
O23	1	0.49%	0.35%	1.47%	0.87%	0.00%
O23	2	0.30%	0.12%	0.00%	0.00%	0.20%
O23	3	0.10%	0.11%	0.39%	0.25%	0.96%
O23	4	0.57%	0.45%	0.25%	0.20%	0.56%
O231	0	11.82%	7.69%	10.26%	4.47%	0.00%
O231	1	6.92%	6.24%	10.26%	13.70%	10.45%
O231	1000	2.56%	10.49%	25.00%	17.65%	
O231	2	10.92%	8.96%	10.07%	8.87%	12.65%
O231	3	5.14%	7.49%	21.25%	22.98%	22.68%
O231	4	24.30%	25.36%	22.19%	26.58%	21.56%
O231	6	3.81%	6.76%	17.99%	22.10%	18.37%
O24	0	0.45%	0.06%	0.00%	0.00%	0.00%
O24	1	0.29%	0.15%	0.37%	0.12%	0.18%
O24	2	0.51%	0.45%	0.37%	0.29%	0.23%
O24	3	0.12%	0.13%	0.17%	0.16%	0.00%
O24	4	1.03%	1.21%	0.75%	0.53%	0.48%

Fabric Code	Phase	% Nosh	% Wt	% MNV	% RE	% BE
O27	0	12.73%	8.68%	10.26%	11.76%	22.62%
O27	1	8.34%	9.11%	8.79%	8.05%	3.02%
O27	1000	5.13%	4.90%	50.00%	82.35%	
O27	2	9.25%	7.54%	7.28%	6.08%	4.37%
O27	3	5.43%	7.97%	22.48%	24.09%	21.26%
O27	4	17.63%	17.96%	14.71%	14.77%	14.34%
O27	6	3.71%	7.90%	15.11%	14.56%	25.72%
O29	1	0.44%	0.31%	0.37%	0.20%	0.00%
O29	2	1.05%	1.05%	1.12%	0.73%	1.05%
O29	3	0.17%	0.21%	0.33%	0.29%	1.13%
O29	4	1.23%	0.89%	1.25%	1.31%	0.00%
O29	6	0.41%	0.30%	2.88%	1.52%	0.00%
O291	0	1.82%	0.58%	0.00%	0.00%	0.00%
O291	1	0.10%	0.08%	0.37%	0.22%	0.29%
O291	2	0.51%	0.80%	0.56%	0.51%	0.73%
O291	3	0.25%	0.37%	0.83%	0.63%	1.52%
O291	4	0.37%	0.44%	1.25%	1.37%	0.00%
O291	6	0.51%	0.69%	0.72%	0.38%	4.46%
O35	1	0.59%	0.62%	1.47%	0.99%	2.69%
O35	2	0.16%	0.22%	0.00%	0.00%	0.45%
O35	3	0.01%	0.01%	0.00%	0.00%	0.07%
O36	0	37.73%	49.85%	23.08%	30.59%	57.01%
O36	1	26.38%	35.59%	21.98%	25.89%	26.19%
O36	2	28.58%	35.33%	20.34%	25.75%	20.72%
O36	3	6.52%	9.84%	23.42%	22.05%	19.84%
O36	4	14.67%	14.56%	13.22%	13.01%	14.10%
O36	6	2.68%	4.90%	9.35%	8.00%	18.24%
O53	6	0.10%	0.15%	0.72%	7.62%	0.00%
O55	1	21.16%	6.79%	4.40%	2.68%	4.18%
O55	2	1.19%	0.73%	0.56%	0.54%	0.33%
O55	3	0.12%	0.15%	0.44%	0.34%	0.53%
O55	4	0.50%	0.67%	0.25%	0.50%	0.56%
O57	6	0.10%	0.03%	0.00%	0.00%	0.00%
O81	3	0.01%	0.01%	0.06%	0.24%	0.00%
O81	4	0.03%	0.01%	0.00%	0.00%	0.00%
O91	2	0.03%	0.07%	0.00%	0.00%	0.00%
Q00	3	0.04%	0.03%	0.00%	0.00%	0.00%
Q12	2	0.03%	0.00%	0.00%	0.00%	0.00%
Q13	2	0.05%	0.08%	0.00%	0.00%	0.00%
Q14	1	0.05%	0.01%	0.00%	0.00%	0.00%
Q14	2	0.16%	0.05%	0.19%	0.17%	0.00%
Q14	4	0.03%	0.00%	0.00%	0.00%	0.00%
Q151	0	0.91%	0.26%	0.00%	0.00%	0.00%
Q151	1	0.49%	0.42%	0.00%	0.00%	0.00%
Q151	2	0.92%	0.69%	0.00%	0.00%	0.75%

Fabric Code	Phase	% Nosh	% Wt	% MNV	% RE	% BE
Q151	3	0.21%	0.17%	0.22%	1.08%	0.68%
Q151	4	0.33%	0.21%	0.25%	2.79%	0.40%
Q151	6	0.10%	0.08%	0.00%	0.00%	0.00%
Q27	4	0.03%	0.01%	0.00%	0.00%	0.00%
R00	3	0.62%	0.51%	0.00%	0.00%	0.00%
R00	4	0.03%	0.01%	0.00%	0.00%	0.00%
R01	1	0.05%	0.01%	0.00%	0.00%	0.00%
R01	2	0.16%	0.13%	0.19%	0.51%	0.00%
R01	3	0.06%	0.16%	0.17%	0.15%	1.00%
R01	4	0.13%	0.06%	0.00%	0.00%	0.00%
R01	6	0.31%	0.52%	0.72%	0.61%	0.79%
R11	2	0.03%	0.01%	0.00%	0.00%	0.00%
R18	0	0.45%	0.17%	2.56%	1.65%	0.00%
R18	1	6.97%	5.70%	12.45%	12.43%	7.36%
R18	2	5.28%	5.19%	7.46%	9.27%	14.21%
R18	3	0.16%	0.18%	0.11%	0.08%	1.03%
R18	4	0.53%	0.34%	1.00%	0.87%	0.00%
R18	6	0.10%	0.06%	0.72%	0.53%	0.00%
R31	1	0.15%	0.08%	0.00%	0.00%	0.00%
R31	2	0.03%	0.04%	0.00%	0.00%	0.00%
R31	4	0.03%	0.12%	0.00%	0.00%	0.00%
R32	0	0.45%	0.19%	0.00%	0.00%	0.00%
R32	1	2.15%	2.68%	1.47%	2.01%	8.54%
R32	2	2.99%	2.02%	4.66%	5.21%	1.06%
R32	3	0.25%	0.29%	0.83%	0.81%	0.84%
R32	4	0.33%	0.25%	0.50%	0.34%	0.53%
R32	6	0.62%	0.35%	0.72%	0.76%	0.00%
R341	4	0.07%	0.06%	0.50%	0.34%	0.00%
R41	0	0.45%	0.43%	2.56%	2.82%	0.00%
R41	2	0.19%	0.07%	0.00%	0.00%	0.00%
R41	3	0.02%	0.01%	0.00%	0.00%	0.00%
R41	4	0.13%	0.07%	0.75%	0.81%	0.00%
R46	3	0.02%	0.01%	0.00%	0.00%	0.00%
R52	1	0.05%	0.03%	0.00%	0.00%	0.00%
R52	4	0.07%	0.05%	0.00%	0.00%	0.00%
R55	3	0.01%	0.00%	0.00%	0.00%	0.00%
R59	1	0.20%	0.08%	0.00%	0.00%	0.00%
R65	3	0.01%	0.00%	0.00%	0.00%	0.00%
R813	0	12.73%	14.85%	20.51%	22.59%	16.74%
R813	1	8.82%	12.18%	13.19%	12.93%	19.36%
R813	2	12.75%	11.30%	19.03%	22.06%	18.06%
R813	3	1.11%	1.06%	2.94%	3.29%	4.55%
R813	4	4.70%	2.97%	6.98%	7.34%	3.53%
R813	6	0.93%	1.23%	1.44%	0.91%	0.00%
S00	4	0.03%	0.01%	0.00%	0.00%	0.00%

Fabric Code	Phase	% Nosh	% Wt	% MNV	% RE	% BE
S10	1	0.39%	0.11%	1.47%	0.32%	0.83%
S10	2	0.40%	0.34%	0.93%	0.62%	2.08%
S10	3	0.04%	0.02%	0.06%	0.09%	0.07%
S10	4	0.17%	0.04%	0.25%	0.14%	0.00%
S11	2	0.03%	0.00%	0.00%	0.00%	0.00%
S20	0	0.45%	0.13%	0.00%	0.00%	0.00%
S20	1	1.41%	1.71%	4.03%	2.95%	6.33%
S20	1000	2.56%	2.80%	25.00%	0.00%	
S20	2	2.67%	1.97%	5.41%	3.09%	6.54%
S20	3	4.87%	3.26%	9.71%	6.82%	10.51%
S20	4	5.43%	2.85%	11.97%	6.98%	7.36%
S20	6	5.56%	3.46%	6.47%	5.03%	7.87%
S21	0	0.45%	0.06%	0.00%	0.00%	0.00%
S21	1	0.39%	0.28%	1.47%	0.42%	0.63%
S21	2	0.32%	0.24%	1.12%	0.78%	0.00%
S21	3	0.09%	0.08%	0.28%	0.23%	0.38%
S21	4	0.13%	0.28%	0.25%	0.22%	1.46%
S21	6	0.41%	0.12%	0.72%	0.46%	0.00%
S30	2	0.03%	0.01%	0.00%	0.00%	0.00%
S30	3	0.08%	0.05%	0.11%	0.03%	0.18%
S30	4	0.13%	0.07%	0.00%	0.00%	0.00%
W00	3	0.08%	0.05%	0.00%	0.00%	0.00%
W00	4	0.03%	0.01%	0.00%	0.00%	0.00%
W00	6	0.10%	0.02%	0.00%	0.00%	0.00%
W11	1	0.05%	0.05%	0.00%	0.00%	0.00%
W11	2	0.11%	0.07%	0.00%	0.00%	0.00%
W11	3	0.01%	0.02%	0.06%	0.15%	0.00%
W11	4	0.03%	0.02%	0.00%	0.00%	0.00%
W21	1	0.10%	0.03%	0.73%	0.52%	1.84%
W21	3	0.01%	0.00%	0.00%	0.00%	0.20%
W22	3	0.04%	0.03%	0.06%	0.04%	0.18%
W22	6	0.10%	0.05%	0.72%	0.30%	0.00%
W24	3	0.01%	0.00%	0.00%	0.00%	0.00%
W25	2	0.08%	0.02%	0.00%	0.00%	0.00%
W25	3	0.01%	0.01%	0.00%	0.00%	0.00%
W28	1	0.34%	0.22%	0.73%	2.95%	0.00%
W28	2	0.13%	0.05%	0.00%	0.00%	0.00%
W28	3	0.03%	0.01%	0.00%	0.00%	0.00%
W28	4	0.07%	0.03%	0.00%	0.00%	0.00%
W29	0	0.45%	0.11%	0.00%	0.00%	0.00%
W29	1	0.05%	0.00%	0.00%	0.00%	0.00%
W29	2	0.49%	0.20%	0.19%	0.19%	0.00%
W29	3	0.04%	0.02%	0.11%	0.39%	0.00%
W29	4	0.07%	0.04%	0.00%	0.00%	0.00%
W37	1	0.10%	0.08%	0.00%	0.00%	0.00%

Fabric Code	Phase	% Nosh	% Wt	% MNV	% RE	% BE
W37	2	0.03%	0.00%	0.00%	0.00%	0.00%
W37	3	0.04%	0.13%	0.00%	0.00%	0.33%
Z20	0	0.45%	0.32%	2.56%	0.00%	0.00%
Z20	3	0.02%	0.02%	0.00%	0.00%	0.00%
Z20	4	0.20%	0.07%	0.00%	0.00%	0.00%
Z20	6	0.10%	0.21%	0.00%	0.00%	0.00%
Z30	1000	2.56%	2.80%	0.00%	0.00%	
Z30	2	0.24%	0.10%	0.37%	0.22%	0.17%
Z30	3	0.09%	0.09%	0.17%	0.04%	0.00%
Z30	4	0.37%	0.79%	0.50%	0.31%	0.74%
Z30	6	1.03%	0.80%	0.00%	0.00%	0.00%

Appendix 3

Catalogue of pottery

Jeremy Evans and Phil Mills
with contributions by Margaret Ward and Brenda Dickinson

The pottery is catalogued by form. The majority of these are illustrated with the illustrations reference given at the end of each entry. The occurrence of these vessels by Phase is given in Appendix 4. The samian ware is catalogued differently, details below (See Fabric S). Form abbreviations are as follows: A = Amphora; BK = Beaker;

BOT = Bottle; B = Bowl; CJ = Constricted-necked jar; C = Cup; D = Dish; DCU = Dish (Curle form); F = Flagon; J = Jar; JUG = Jug; LAG = Lagena; L = Lid; M = Mortarium; O = Other; SJ = Storage Jar; TA = Tankard; WMJ = Wide-mouthed jar

Fabric A21, Baetican Dressel 20, Worcester fabric 42.1

A21.1	A1.1, K22	Dressel 20 amphora rim.	Illus 4.10

Fabric B11, Black Burnished 1, Worcester fabric 22

B11.1	J1.1	Globular BB1 jar with a stubby everted rim, cf Gillam (1976) nos 30–32, Hadrianic-Antonine.	Illus 4.12
B11.2	J1.2	Globular BB1 jar with a stubby, necked rim, cf Gillam (1976) nos 30–32, Hadrianic-Antonine.	Illus 4.12
B11.3	J1.3	Globular BB1 jar with a short, straight, everted rim, cf Gillam (1976) nos 30–32, Hadrianic-Antonine.	Illus 4.12
B11.4	J2.1	BB1 jar with an everted, fairly vertical rim, cf Gillam (1970) type 116, *c* AD 120–50.	Illus 4.12
B11.5	J2.2	BB1 jar with an everted rim and acute lattice decoration, cf Gillam (1976) nos 4–6, later 2nd century.	Illus 4.12
B11.6	J2.3	Necked BB1 jar with a beaded rim, cf Gillam (1976) nos 2–3, early-mid-2nd century.	Illus 4.12
B11.7	J2.4	BB1 jar with a short, everted rim, Hadrianic-Antonine.	Illus 4.12
B11.8	J2.5	BB1 jar of unusually large size with everted, beaded rim, Hadrianic-Antonine.	Illus 4.12
B11.9	J3.1	BB1 jar with a strongly everted rim and obtuse lattice decoration, maximum girth greater than maximum rim diameter, cf Gillam (1976) nos 7–9, *c* AD 200/20–270.	Illus 4.12
B11.10	J3.2	BB1 jar rim with a strongly everted rim, probably later 3rd-mid-4th century.	Illus 4.12
B11.11	J3.3	BB1 jar of very large diameter with an everted rim similar to J2.1, cf Gillam (1976) nos 7–9, early-mid-3rd century.	Illus 4.12
B11.12	B1.1	Flange rimmed bowl, exterior decorated with intersecting arcs, *c* AD 160/80–200.	Illus 4.12
B11.13	B1.2	As B1.1 but with vertical burnished lines on the wall, Hadrianic-Antonine.	Illus 4.12
B11.14	B1.3	Flange rimmed bowl with acute lattice decoration on the wall (and chamfered base), Hadrianic-mid-Antonine.	Illus 4.12
B11.15	B2.1	Developed beaded and flanged bowl, *c* AD 270–350/90.	Illus 4.12
B11.16	B3.1	Incipient beaded and flanged bowl with intersecting arcs on the wall, *c* AD 200–70. Example b unusually has obtuse lattice decoration on the wall.	Illus 4.12
B11.17	D1.1	Simple rimmed dish with oblique lines on the exterior, probably 3rd–4th century.	Illus 4.12
B11.18	D2.1	Simple rimmed dish with intersecting arc decoration, *c* AD 160/80–350	Illus 4.12
B11.19	D2.2	Simple rimmed dish, exterior undecorated, perhaps 3rd–4th century	Illus 4.12
B11.20	D3.1	Groove rimmed dish, the drawn example has intersecting arc decoration, Hadrianic-Antonine, the drawn example is perhaps later 2nd century.	Illus 4.12
B11.21	D4.1	Flange rimmed dish with acute lattice on the exterior, Hadrianic-mid-Antonine.	Illus 4.12
B11.22	D4.2	Flange rimmed dish with intersecting arc decoration, *c* AD 160–200.	Illus 4.12
B11.23	D4.3	Flange rimmed dish with pointed intersecting arc decoration, mid-2nd century.	Illus 4.12
B11.24	D4.4	Flange rimmed dish with undecorated exterior, Hadrianic-Antonine.	Illus 4.12

Fabric F12, glazed ware

F12.1a-b	BK1.1	Bead rimmed bowl with a mid-brown glaze, possibly derived from a Dr 37, Flavian-Trajanic.	Illus 4.15
F12.2		Glazed body sherd from a carinated cup or bowl with rouletted straight wall, Flavian-Trajanic.	Illus 4.15

Fabric F42, roughcast colour-coated wares, Worcester fabric 45?

F42.1	BK1.1	Beaker with a sub-cornice rim and roughcast decoration, later 1st–2nd century.	Illus 4.16
F42.2	BK2.1	Beaker with a bifid rim, later 1st–2nd century.	Illus 4.16
F42.3	BK2.2	Sub-cornice rimmed beaker with a prominent upper bead, later 1st–2nd century.	Illus 4.16

Fabric F51, Oxfordshire colour-coated ware, Worcester fabric 29

F51.1	BK1.1	Bead rimmed beaker, perhaps cf Young (1977) type C22.1, AD 240–400+	Illus 4.18
F51.2	BK1.2	Funnel necked, beaded beaker rim, cf Young (1977) types C23–30, AD 270–400+	Illus 4.18
F51.3	B1.1	Dr 31 bowl copy, Young (1977) type C45, AD 240–400+	Illus 4.18
F51.4	B2.1	Dr 38 copy bowl, Young (1977) type C51, AD 240–400+	Illus 4.18
F51.5		Eroded illiterate Oxfordshire ware stamp, probably from a Dr 31 copy bowl, AD 240–400+	Illus 4.18
F51.6		Fragment from an Oxfordshire ware stamp, probably from a Dr 31 copy bowl, AD 240–400+	Illus 4.18

Fabric F52, Nene Valley colour-coated ware, Worcester fabric 28

F52.1	J1.1	Necked jar, probably later 2nd-mid-3rd century.	Illus 4.17
F52.2	BK1.1	Funnel necked beaker, later 3rd–4th century.	Illus 4.17
F52.3	B1.1	'Castor box' rim fragment, AD 160–400	Not illus

Fabric F91, Terra Nigra

F91.1	D1.1	Cam type 16 Terra Nigra dish rim, *c* AD 40–70(+)	Illus 4.14

Fabric G44, Malvernian metamorphic-tempered ware, Worcester fabric 3

G44.1	SJ1.1	Large storage jar with a straight, everted, rising rim.	Illus 4.19
G44.2	J1.1	Globular jar with a beaded rim and vertical burnished lines down the body.	Illus 4.19
G44.3	J1.2	Simple rimmed barrel jar, 1st–2nd century.	Illus 4.19
G44.4	J2.1	Bucket jar with a beaded rim, 1st–2nd century.	Illus 4.19
G44.5	D2.1	Slightly beaded dish rim.	Illus 4.19
G44.6	J3.1	Everted rimmed jar.	Illus 4.19
G44.7	J4.1	Slightly lid-seated jar(?) rim (or dish?).	Illus 4.19
G44.8	J5.1	Jar with a straight, everted rim.	Illus 4.19
G44.9	J6.1	Jar with a hooked rim.	Illus 4.19
G44.10	D1.1	Dish with a slightly flanged rim, interior and exterior decorated with acute lattice, perhaps 2nd century.	Illus 4.19
G44.11	L1.1	Simple rimmed lid.	Illus 4.19
G44.12	L1.2	Simple rimmed lid with a slightly outcurved rim.	Illus 4.19
G44.13		Unusual simple dish(?) base with radial burnished lines on the interior and acute lattice on the base.	Illus 4.19
G44.14		Most unusual pedestal base.	Illus 4.19

Fabric G46, Malvernian metamorphic-tempered ware, Worcester fabric 19

G46.1	SJ1.1	Storage jar with a straight, everted rim.	Illus 4.21
G46.2	J1.1	Jar with a fairly straight, everted rim.	Illus 4.21
G46.3	J1.2	Jar with an outcurving, everted rim, some might possibly be copies of 2nd century BB jars.	Illus 4.21

G46.4	J2.1	Everted rimmed jar, possibly a BB copy, if so then perhaps early-mid-3rd century.	Illus 4.21
G46.5	B1.1	Incipient flange rimmed bowl, the BB original has a date range of *c* AD 200–70, so this also probably falls in that range.	Illus 4.21
G46.6	B2.1	Flange rimmed bowl, possibly derived from a 2nd century BB form, perhaps 2nd century or later.	Illus 4.21
G46.7	L1.1	Simple rimmed lid.	Illus 4.21
G46.8	BASE 148	Lid knob.	Illus 4.21

Fabric G47, Malvernian metamorphic-tempered ware, Worcester fabric 3

G47.1	J1.1	Jar with an everted, rising rim.	Illus 4.20
G47.2	J2.1	Jar with an everted, lid-seated rim.	Illus 4.20
G47.3	SJ1.1	Storage jar with a straight, everted rim.	Illus 4.20
G47.4	SJ1.2	Storage jar with a long, everted rim.	Not illus
G47.5	O4.1	Portable oven chimney, see Jane Evans (2018) fig 3.	Illus 4.20
G47.6	D1.1	Flange rimmed dish (or bowl), perhaps Hadrianic-Antonine (or later).	Illus 4.20
G47.7	L1.1	Simple rimmed lid.	Illus 4.20
G47.8a-c	O1.1	Fragments from the circumference of the base of portable ovens, see Jane Evans (2018) fig 3.	Illus 4.20
G47.9a-b	O1.2	Fragment probably from the surround of a portable oven mouth, see Jane Evans (2018) fig 3.	Illus 4.20
G47.10a-b	O2.1	Probably also fragments from the surround of a portable oven mouth, see Jane Evans (2018) fig 3.	Illus 4.20
G47.11	O3.1	'Chappati disc', diam *c* 20cms. A flat disc, burnt slightly orange on the concave rough side and with a smooth grey surface on the upper side (cf similar in Evans 2009b and Jane Evans 2018 fig 4).	Illus 4.20
G47.12		Oven wall fragment with two impressed indentations, perhaps an alternate mechanism to the internal ledge with perforations for suspending skewers or a temporary metal grill inside the oven, cf Jane Evans (2018) fig 3.	Illus 4.20
G47.13		Counter, largely complete, cut from a storage jar wall, diameter *c* 55mm. Wt 53g	Illus 4.20
G47.14		Complete counter cut from the wall of a jar or storage jar, *c* 49 x 55mm. Wt 41g	Illus 4.20

Fabric M12, North Gallic mortarium, Worcester fabric 36

M12.1	M1.1	Mortarium of Bushe-Fox type 26–30, a continental import, *c* AD 60–100.	Illus 4.23

Fabric M21, Verulamium region mortarium, Worcester fabric 35.

M21.1	M1.1	Beaded and flanged mortarium with evenly downcurving flange which rises above the bead. AD 60–100.	Not illus

Fabric M22, Mancetter-Hartshill mortaria, Worcester fabric 32.

M22.1a-c	M1.1	Beaded and flanged mortarium of class B with bead rising above flange, with evenly outcurving flange, *c* AD 130–60. a) Stamped 'MAR' retrograde; c) Stamped 'MARCIIL'.	Illus 4.25
M22.2a-b	M1.2	Mortarium of class B with a bead rising above the flange with a downsloping flange, perhaps *c* AD 140–70. Stamped.	Illus 4.25
M22.3a-b	M1.3	Beaded and flanged mortarium, class M, with a straight, downsloping flange, *c* AD 170–200.	Illus 4.25
M22.4	M1.4	Beaded and flanged mortarium, class B, with bead above evenly outcurving flange and a bead at the distal end of the flange, otherwise similar to M22.1, perhaps *c* AD 130–60.	Illus 4.25
M22.5	M1.5	Beaded and flanged mortarium of class B with a downsloping, grooved flange, perhaps *c* AD 160–200.	Illus 4.25
M22.6	M2.1	Hammerhead mortarium (class E) with a bead at the base of the flange, *c* AD 200–240(?).	Illus 4.25
M22.7	M2.2	Hammerhead mortarium (class C) with a bead at the top and bottom of the flange, *c* AD 200–220.	Illus 4.25
M22.8	M2.3	Proto-hammerhead mortarium with a bead and a groove at the base of the flange, perhaps *c* AD 190–230.	Illus 4.25
M22.9	M3.1	Class A beaded and flanged mortarium with the flange rising well above the bead, perhaps *c* AD 100–130. Stamped ' IVNI'.	Illus 4.25
M22.10	M3.2	Class A mortarium with flange about level with bead with fairly horizontal flange with downsloping tip, perhaps *c* AD 120–50.	Illus 4.25
M22.11	M4.1	Reeded hammerhead mortarium (class E), *c* AD 220–350(+).	Illus 4.25
M22.12		Stamped mortarium flange.	Illus 4.25

M22.13		Stamped mortarium flange.	Illus 4.25

Fabric M23, Oxfordshire whiteware mortaria, Worcester fabric 33

M23.1	M1.1	Oxfordshire mortarium with a high bead and folded back hooked flange, Young (1977) type M17, AD 240–300.	Illus 4.26
M23.2	M2.1	Mortarium with a high bead and a short stubby flange, Young (1977) type M23, AD 240–400+	Illus 4.26

Fabric M37, ?Wroxeter area mortaria, Worcester fabric 34

M37.1	M1.1	Beaded and flanged mortarium with the evenly curved and downpointing flange rising above the bead, perhaps later 1st–2nd century.	Illus 4.27
M37.2	M2.1	Beaded and flanged mortarium with an outcurving fairly straight flange, 2nd century.	Illus 4.27
M37.3		Stamped class B mortarium rim fragment, 'ME['	Illus 4.27

Fabric M45, Severn Valley mortaria, Worcester fabric 37

M45.1a-b	M1.1	Beaded and flanged mortarium with flange rising above bead, perhaps later 1st-early 2nd century. b) Stamped 'Aih'	Illus 4.24
M45.2	M1.2	Beaded and flanged mortarium with flange rising above bead and then fairly straight and downsloping, perhaps later 1st-early 2nd century.	Illus 4.24

Fabric O21, Severn Valley wares, Worcester fabric 12.2

O21.1	J1.1	Jar with a beaded undercut rim, perhaps cf Webster (1976) no 22, 2nd-early 3rd century. Cf Evans et al (2000) fig 23, type 4.	Illus 4.29
O21.2	WMJ1.1	Wide-mouthed jar with a triangularly-sectioned, horizontal, everted rim, cf Webster (1976) no 22, 2nd-early 3rd century.	Illus 4.29
O21.3	WMJ1.2	Wide-mouthed jar with a triangularly-sectioned, slightly-undercut rim, cf Webster (1976) no 23, mid-2nd-mid-3rd century.	Illus 4.29
O21.4	TA1.1	Tankard with a beaded rim and fairly vertical, straight wall, cf Webster (1976) nos 38–40, 1st–2nd century.	Illus 4.29

Fabric O23, Severn Valley wares, Worcester fabric 12

O23.1	CJ1.1	Constricted-necked jar with a thickened rim with a slight cordon under the rim.	Illus 4.34
O23.2	J1.1	Small jar with an everted, outcurving rim, perhaps cf Webster (1976) no 15, perhaps cf Evans et al (2000) fig 24, type 7.	Illus 4.34
O23.3	WMJ1.1	Wide-mouthed jar with a thickened rim with a cordon beneath.	Illus 4.34
O23.4	TA1.1	Tankard with a beaded rim and slightly splaying wall, cf Webster (1976) nos 42–3, 2nd–3rd century.	Illus 4.34
O23.5	TA2.1	Tankard with a beaded rim and widely splaying wall, cf Webster (1976) no 44, later 3rd–4th century.	Illus 4.34
O23.6	B1.1	Bead rimmed bowl, a Dr 37 copy, probably 2nd century.	Illus 4.34
O23.7	B2.1	Segmental bowl, cf Webster (1976) no 67, Webster suggests a possible mid-later 3rd century date.	Illus 4.34
O23.8	B3.1	bowl with an everted, rising, outcurving rim, perhaps cf Webster (1976) no 36.	Illus 4.34
O23.9	D1.1	Segmental bowl rim, cf Webster (1976) no 66.	Illus 4.34
O23.10		Body sherd with a handle scar and moustache style cordons from the base of the handle, cf Evans C J et al (2000) fig 19, F16.	Illus 4.34

Fabric O231, Severn Valley wares, Worcester fabric 12

O231.1	F1.1	Flagon rim with a stubby, everted, rising rim.	Illus 4.35
O231.2	F2.1	Cup-mouthed flagon with a beaded rim.	Illus 4.35
O231.3	F3.1	Flagon with a bifid rim, 3rd–4th century.	Illus 4.35
O231.4	JUG1.1	Jug rim with an everted, rising rim, cf Evans C J et al (2000) fig 19, type 2.	Illus 4.35

O231.5	JUG 2.1	Bead rimmed, vertical necked jug rim, cf Evans C J et al (2000) fig 19, type 2.	Illus 4.35
O231.6	JUG 3.1	Bead rimmed cup-mouthed jug, cf Evans C J et al (2000) fig 19, type 4.	Illus 4.35
O231.7	CJ1.1	Constricted-necked jar with a straight, everted, rising rim, cf Webster (1976) type 1, 1st–4th century.	Illus 4.35
O231.8	CJ1.2	Constricted-necked jar with an everted, thickened rim, cf Webster (1976) no 3, 1st - mid-3rd century.	Illus 4.35
O231.9	CJ1.3	Constricted-necked jar with an everted, outcurving, thickened rim, perhaps cf Webster (1976) no 2.	Illus 4.35
O231.10	CJ2.1	Constricted-necked jar with a bifid rim, cf Webster (1976) nos 9–11, 3rd–4th century.	Illus 4.35
O231.11	CJ2.2	Constricted-necked jar with an everted, flanged rim. No close parallel in Webster (1976) or Evans C J et al (2000) but probably 3rd–4th century.	Illus 4.35
O231.12	CJ2.3	Frilled bifid rimmed constricted-necked jar, cf Webster (1976) no 13, 3rd–4th century.	Illus 4.35
O231.13a-b	CJ 3.1	Constricted-necked jar with a triangularly-sectioned, undercut rim, perhaps cf Webster (1976) nos 4 and 6 for which a 2nd–4th century date range is offered. Cf Evans C J et al (2000) fig 21, JNM10.	Illus 4.35
O231.14	CJ3.2	Constricted-necked jar with a broad open hooked rim, cf Webster (1976) no 5, for which a 2nd–3rd century date is proposed.	Illus 4.35
O231.15	CJ3.3	Constricted-necked jar with a wedge-shaped, thickened rim, hooked at the tip. Perhaps cf Evans C J et al (2000) fig 21, JNM7, type 2.	Illus 4.35
O231.16	CJ3.4	Constricted-necked jar with a hooked rim, perhaps cf Webster (1976) no 6, 2nd–3rd century and Evans C J et al (2000) fig 21, type 3.	Illus 4.35
O123.17	J1.1	Jar with an everted, outcurving, rising, slightly thickened rim, cf Evans C J et al (2000) fig 22, type 2.2.	Illus 4.35
O231.18	J2.1	Jar with a slightly splaying, fairly vertical, straight, simple rim.	Illus 4.35
O231.19	J3.1	Fairly small globular jar with a necked, everted rim.	Illus 4.35
O231.20	J3.2	Small globular jar with an everted, short, lid-seated rim, perhaps 1st-early 2nd century.	Illus 4.35
O231.21	J3.3	Jar with an everted, outcurving, rising rim.	Illus 4.35
O231.22a-b	J4.1	Small bead rimmed jar.	Illus 4.35
O231.23	J4.2	Small globular jar, deeply grooved on the girth, with a short, stubby, near vertical, rim.	Illus 4.35
O231.24	J5.1	Carinated jar with an everted, outcurving, rising rim.	Illus 4.35
O231.25	SJ1.1	Storage jar with a heavy, triangular, undercut rim, cf Webster (1976) no 8, 3rd century, and Evans C J et al (2000) fig 25, type 2.	Illus 4.35
O231.26a-b	WMJ 1.1	Wide-mouthed jar with a slightly undercut, widely hooked rim, cf Webster (1976) nos 23–25, 2nd-later 3rd century.	Illus 4.36
O231.27	WMJ 1.2	Wide-mouthed jar with a fairly open hooked rim, cf Webster (1976) nos 24–25, later 2nd–3rd century, and Evans C J et al (2000) fig 23, type 3.	Illus 4.36
O231.28	WMJ1.3	Wide-mouthed jar with a closely hooked rim, cf Webster (1976) nos 27–33, later 3rd–4th century.	Illus 4.36
O231.29	WMJ2.1	Wide-mouthed jar with a thickened, everted rim, slightly cordoned under the rim.	Illus 4.36
O231.30	WMJ3.1	Wide-mouthed jar with an everted, rising, thickened rim, perhaps cf Webster (1976) nos 20–21, 1st–2nd century, and Evans C J et al (2000) fig 23, JWM5 and JWM8.	Illus 4.36
O231.31	B9.1	Beaded and flanged bowl probably later 3rd to 4th century.	Illus 4.36
O231.32	BK1.1	Beaker with a stubby, everted rim.	Illus 4.36
O231.33	TA1.1	Tankard with a beaded rim and slightly splaying wall, cf Webster (1976) nos 41–43, 2nd–3rd century, and Evans C J et al (2000) type 2.	Illus 4.36
O231.34	TA1.2	Tankard with a slightly outsloping wall and tapering simple rim, perhaps 2nd–3rd century.	Illus 4.36
O231.35	TA2.1	Tankard with a beaded rim and widely splaying wall, cf Webster (1976) no 44, later 3rd–4th century.	Illus 4.36
O231.36	TA2.2	Tankard with a simple rim and widely splaying wall, perhaps later 3rd–4th century.	Illus 4.36
O231.37	B1.1	Curving walled bowl with a stubby rim, cf Webster (1976) nos 34–6, 2nd–4th century.	Illus 4.36
O231.38	B1.2	Curving walled bowl with a beaded rim, probably cf Webster (1976) nos 34–6, 2nd–4th century.	Not illus
O231.39	B2.1	Dr31 copy bowl, perhaps mid-2nd century or later.	Illus 4.36
O231.40	B3.1	Flanged reeded rimmed bowl with tapering rim, cf Webster (1976) nos 54–6, 2nd–3rd century.	Illus 4.36

O231.41a-b	B3.2	Flange rimmed bowl with a horizontal, reeded rim, cf Webster (1976) nos 54–6, 2nd–3rd century.	Illus 4.36
O231.42	B3.3	Flange rimmed bowl with a horizontal rim and slight bead, perhaps a hybrid of the reeded rim and segmental bowl types, perhaps 2nd–3rd century.	Illus 4.36
O231.43	B3.4	Flanged reeded rimmed bowl, perhaps cf Webster (1976) no 53, later 3rd–4th century.	Illus 4.36
O231.44	B3.5	Reeded flange rimmed bowl with a prominent central bead, cf Webster (1976) no 53, later 3rd–4th century.	Illus 4.36
O231.45a-b	B4.1	Segmental bowl, beaded and flanged, cf Webster (1976) no 65, 2nd century, and Evans C J et al (2000) fig 28, BT43.	Illus 4.37
O231.46	B4.2	Segmental bowl with a low bead, cf Webster (1976) no 66, 2nd century.	Illus 4.37
O231.47	B4.3	Flange rimmed bowl with downsloping rim, divided into two cordons by a deep groove, perhaps cf Webster (1976) no 57, 3rd century.	Illus 4.37
O231.48a-b	B4.4	Bead rimmed Dr38 copy bowl, cf Webster (1976) nos 62–3, mid-2nd–4th century. A type probably absent from Newlands Hopfields (Evans C J et al 2000).	Illus 4.37
O231.49	B4.5	Bowl with a small beaded rim divided into two cordons by a groove.	Illus 4.37
O231.50	B4.6	Flange rimmed bowl with a grooved, curving, undercut flange, cf Webster (1976) no 51, 3rd century.	Illus 4.37
O231.51	B5.1	Flange rimmed bowl, slightly internally beaded, probably cf Webster (1976) type 50, later 2nd-later 3rd century.	Illus 4.37
O231.52	B5.2	Flange rimmed bowl with a triangularly-sectioned rim, slightly carinated.	Illus 4.37
O231.53	B5.3	Flange rimmed bowl with horizontal flange, slightly internally beaded, cf Webster (1976) nos 45–6, 1st–3rd century.	Illus 4.37
O231.54	B6.1	Bead rimmed Dr 37 copy bowl, cf Webster (1976) no 61, 2nd–4th century.	Illus 4.37
O231.55	B7.1	Simple rimmed bowl with curving wall, cf Evans C J et al (2000) fig 30, BT70, type 6.3.	Illus 4.37
O231.56	B8.1	Flange rimmed bowl with a thin, horizontal rim, slightly undercut.	Illus 4.37
O231.57	D1.1	Grooved rim dish with grooved base and thickened lower wall, a Cam 16 Gallo-Belgic copy, cf Webster (1976) no 70, 1st-early 2nd century.	Illus 4.37
O231.58	D1.2	Simple rimmed dish with a basal chamfer, possibly a Gallo-Belgic copy, 1st–2nd century.	Illus 4.37
O231.59a-b	D2.1	Grooved rimmed dish, cf Webster (1976) no 72, undated.	Illus 4.37
O231.60	L1.1	Grooved rimmed lid, cf Evans C J et al (2000) fig 31, L5.	Illus 4.37
O231.61	L2.1	Simple rimmed lid with a deep lid-seating groove on the interior of the rim.	Illus 4.37
O231.62	O1.1	Bowl with a frilled flange below the beaded rim, probably a tazza.	Illus 4.37
O231.63		Bowl body sherd with a handle stub with 'moustache' cordons running from the base of the handle.	Illus 4.37
O231.64		Colander bowl base with a radial pattern of holes.	Illus 4.37
O231.65		Complete counter cut from a jar or bowl wall, 63 x 55mm. WT 34g	Illus 4.37
O231.66		Thick base sherd, probably trimmed as a large counter, Diam *c*55mm. Wt 63g	Illus 4.37
O231.67		Complete counter (broken into two), Diam *c*45mm. Wt 20g	Illus 4.37
O231.68		Circular-sectioned tankard handle with two horizontal grooves cut across it, probably an illiterate mark of ownership.	Illus 4.37

Fabric O24, Severn Valley wares, Worcester fabric 12

O24.1	JUG1.1	Jug with an everted, rising rim. The illustrated example is very overfired. Cf Evans C J et al (2000) fig 19, type 2, 2nd century onwards.	Illus 4.39
O24.2	WMJ1.1	Wide-mouthed jar with a triangularly-sectioned rim, slightly undercut, cf Webster (1976) no 23, mid-2nd-later 3rd century.	Illus 4.39
O24.3	WMJ1.2	Wide-mouthed jar with a tall neck and straight, everted, rising rim.	Illus 4.39
O24.4a-b	TA1.1	Bead rimmed tankard with a slightly splaying wall, cf Webster (1976) nos 40–43, 2nd–3rd century.	Illus 4.39
O24.5	B1.1	Bowl with a grooved, flange rim, cf Webster (1976) no 56. Webster suggests a 3rd century date for this type.	Illus 4.39
O24.6	B2.1	Bowl with a flange rim, cf Webster (1976) no 50, for which a later 2nd-later 3rd century date is suggested.	Illus 4.39

Fabric O27, Severn Valley wares, Worcester fabric 12.6

O27.1	JUG1.1	Jug with an everted, rising rim, cf Evans C J et al (2000) fig 19, type 2.	Illus 4.40
O27.2	JUG 1.2	Jug with a beaded rim, cf Evans C J et al (2000) fig 19, type 2.	Illus 4.40
O27.3	LAG1.1	Lagena with a double cordoned rim. Type not in Webster (1976). Cf Evans C J et al (2000) fig 19, type 1.	Illus 4.40
O27.4	CJ1.1	Constricted-necked jar with an everted, rising rim, cf Webster (1976) type 1, 1st–4th century.	Illus 4.40
O27.5	CJ1.2	Constricted-necked jar with a triangularly-sectioned, slightly undercut, rim, perhaps cf Webster (1976) nos 3 and 5, 2nd–3rd century.	Illus 4.40
O27.6	CJ1.3	Constricted-necked jar with a triangularly-sectioned rim, cf Evans C J et al (2000) fig 21, JNM10.	Illus 4.40
O27.7	CJ2.1	Constricted-necked jar with an everted, outcurving, rising rim, cf Webster (1976) type 1, 1st–4th century.	Illus 4.40
O27.8	CJ3.1	Constricted-necked jar with a reeded, triangularly-sectioned rim.	Illus 4.40
O27.9	CJ4.1	Constricted-necked jar with a flanged rim.	Illus 4.40
O27.10	CJ4.2	Constricted-necked jar with a bifid rim, cf Webster (1976) nos 10–11, 3rd–4th century.	Illus 4.40
O27.11	SJ1.1	Storage jar with an everted, horizontal, slightly undercut rim, cf Webster (1976) no 7, perhaps 2nd–3rd century.	Not illus
O27.12	SJ2.1	Storage jar with a strongly hooked rim, perhaps cf Webster (1976) no 8, 3rd century.	Illus 4.40
O27.13	J1.1	Jar with a straight, everted, rising rim, cf Evans C J et al (2000) fig 22, type 2.1.	Illus 4.40
O27.14	J1.2	Jar with an everted, fairly straight rim, tapering at the tip.	Illus 4.40
O27.15	J1.3	Jar with an everted, rising, outcurving rim.	Illus 4.40
O27.16	J1.4	Jar with an everted, outcurving rim with beaded tip.	Illus 4.40
O27.17	J2.1	Corrugated jar with a stubby rim.	Illus 4.40
O27.18	J3.1	Small bead rimmed jar.	Illus 4.40
O27.19	WMJ1.1	Wide-mouthed jar with an everted, slightly hooked rim, cf Webster (1976) no 22, 2nd-early 3rd century.	Illus 4.40
O27.20	WMJ1.2	Wide-mouthed jar with an undercut rim, cf Webster (1976) type 25, 2nd–3rd century.	Illus 4.40
O27.21a-b	WMJ1.3	Wide-mouthed jar with a tightly hooked rim, cf Webster (1976) types 27–33, later 3rd–4th century.	Illus 4.40
O27.22	WMJ1.4	Wide-mouthed jar with an everted outcurving, rising, thickened rim, cf Webster (1976) no 22, 2nd-early 3rd century.	Illus 4.40
O27.23	WMJ1.5	Wide-mouthed jar with a rising, wedge-shaped rim, perhaps cf Evans C J et al (2000) fig 23, type 1, perhaps 1st–2nd century.	Illus 4.40
O27.24	WMJ2.1	Wide-mouthed jar with an everted, outcurving, rising rim, perhaps cf Webster (1976) nos 19–20, 1st–2nd century, also cf Evans C J et al (2000) fig 22, type 2.1.	Illus 4.40
O27.25a-b	TA1.1	Tankard with a beaded rim and slightly splaying wall, cf Webster (1976) nos 41–3, 2nd–3rd century, and Evans C J et al (2000) fig 20, type 2.	Illus 4.41
O27.26	TA1.2	Bead rimmed tankard with a fairly vertical wall, cf Webster (1976) nos 38–40, 1st–2nd century, and Evans C J et al (2000) fig 20, type 1.	Illus 4.41
O27.27	TA1.3	Tankard with a beaded rim and strongly splaying wall, cf Webster (1976) no 44, later 3rd–4th century.	Illus 4.41
O27.28	TA1.4	Tankard with a strongly splaying wall and simple rim, cf Webster (1976) no 44, later 3rd–4th century.	Illus 4.41
O27.29	B1.1	Bowl with a stubby, everted rim, cf Webster (1976) nos 34–5, for which he suggests a 2nd–4th century date.	Illus 4.41
O27.30	B1.2	Bowl with a stubby, vertical rim, perhaps cf Webster (1976) nos 34–5, for which he suggests a 2nd–4th century date range.	Illus 4.41
O27.31	B1.3	Bowl with an everted, outcurving, rising rim, cf Webster (1976) no 36, for which he offers a 2nd–3rd century date range.	Illus 4.41
O27.32	B2.1	Segmental bowl with a prominent bead, cf Webster (1976) no 65, for which he offers a mid-2nd-early 3rd century date.	Illus 4.41
O27.33	B2.2	Segmental bowl, grooved on the flange, cf Webster (1976) no 66, for which he suggests a 2nd century date.	Illus 4.41
O27.34	B3.1	Flanged bowl with a deep groove separating the flange into two, cf Webster (1976) no 57, for which he offers a 3rd century date.	Illus 4.41

O27.35a-b	B3.2	Flange rimmed bowl with a rising flange, grooved, possibly cf Webster (1976) type 57, for which he offers a 3rd century date.	Illus 4.41
O27.36	B4.1	Flange rimmed bowl with a reeded rim, perhaps cf Webster (1976) nos 55–6, for which he suggests a 2nd–3rd century date, and Evans C J et al (2000) fig 27, type 3.	Illus 4.41
O27.37	B4.2	Flange rimmed bowl with a reeded, undercut rim, cf Webster (1976) no 53, for which he suggests a later 3rd–4th century date, and Evans C J et al (2000) fig 27, BT21.	Illus 4.41
O27.38	B4.3	Flange rimmed bowl with a fairly horizontal reeded rim, cf Webster (1976) nos 54–5, 2nd century, and Evans C J et al (2000) fig 27, type 3.	Illus 4.41
O27.39	B4.4	Flange rimmed bowl with a pronounced triangular cordon on the rim. Not noted by Webster (1976) or at Newlands Hopfield (Evans C J et al 2000).	Illus 4.41
O27.40	B5.1	Flange rimmed bowl, internally beaded, cf Webster (1976) nos 45–48, 1st–3rd century, and Evans C J et al (2000) fig 26, type 2.	Illus 4.41
O27.41	B5.2	Flange rimmed bowl with a strongly downsloping flange, perhaps cf Evans C J et al (2000) fig 26, type 2.	Illus 4.41
O27.42	B5.3	Bowl with a triangularly-sectioned beaded rim. No parallel in Webster (1976), possibly cf Evans C J et al (2000) fig 26, BT11, type 2.	Illus 4.41
O27.43	B5.4	Flange rimmed bowl, cf Webster (1976) no 46, which he dates to the 2nd–3rd centuries.	Illus 4.41
O27.44	O1.1	Flange rimmed tazza(?) with finger tipped decoration.	Illus 4.41
O27.45	O1.2	Beaded and flanged segmental bowl with a frilled rim, perhaps cf Webster (1976) no 65, mid-2nd-early 3rd century.	Illus 4.41
O27.46	O2.1	Flange rimmed bowl with triangular-sectioned pronounced cordon and finger-tipped rim. The basic form is as B4.4, probably a decorated bowl rather than a tazza.	Illus 4.41

Fabric O29, Severn Valley wares, Worcester fabric 12.5?

O29.1	CJ1.1	Constricted-necked jar with an everted, rising, outcurving rim, cf Webster (1976) no 1, 1st–4th century.	Illus 4.43
O29.2	CJ2.1	Constricted-necked jar with an everted, hooked rim, cf Webster (1976) no 5, 2nd–3rd century.	Illus 4.43
O29.3	CJ2.2	Constricted-necked jar with an everted, undercut rim, cf Webster (1976) no 3, 1st–2nd century.	Illus 4.43
O29.4	CJ3.1	Constricted-necked jar or flagon with a bifid rim, cf perhaps Webster (1976) no 9, 3rd–4th century, and Evans C J et al (2000) fig 21, type 4.	Illus 4.43
O29.5	J1.1	Jar with a straight, everted, rising rim, cf Evans C J et al (2000) fig 22, type 2.1.	Illus 4.43
O29.6	WMJ1.1	Wide-mouthed jar with an open hooked rim, cf Webster (1976) no 25, 2nd–3rd century.	Illus 4.43
O29.7	TA1.1	Beaded tankard rim with a slightly splaying wall, cf Webster (1976) nos 41–3, 2nd–3rd century.	Illus 4.43

Fabric O291, Severn Valley wares, Worcester fabric 12.5?

O291.1	CJ1.1	Constricted-necked jar with an everted, thickened, rising rim, cf Webster (1976) no 2, 1st–2nd century.	Illus 4.44
O291.2	WMJ1.1	Wide-mouthed jar with a tightly hooked rim, cf Webster (1976) nos 27–33, later 3rd–4th century.	Illus 4.44
O291.3	WMJ1.2	Wide-mouthed jar with a slightly hooked rim.	Not illus
O291.4	TA1.1	Tankard with a beaded rim and slightly splaying wall, cf Webster (1976) nos 41–3, 2nd–3rd century.	Illus 4.44
O291.5	TA2.1	Bead rimmed tankard with strongly splaying wall, cf Webster (1976) no 44, later 3rd–4th century.	Not illus
O291.6	B1.1	Flange rimmed bowl with a grooved rim, cf Webster (1976) no 56, 3rd century.	Illus 4.44

Fabric O35, Severn Valley wares, Worcester fabric 12

O35.1	TA1.1	Tankard with a beaded rim and a slightly splaying wall, cf Webster (1976) nos 40–43, 2nd–3rd century.	Illus 4.45

Fabric O36, Severn Valley wares, Worcester fabric 12.2

O36.1	F1.1	Flagon or jug with a vertical neck and beaded rim, cf Evans C J et al (2000) fig 19, type 2.	Illus 4.30
O36.2	F2.1	Cup-mouthed bead rimmed flagon, cf Evans C J et al (2000) fig 19, type 4.	Illus 4.30
O36.3	LAG1.1	Lagena rim with a cordoned neck, cf Evans C J et al (2000) fig 19, type 1.	Illus 4.30
O36.4	JUG1.1	Jug with an outsloping neck and beaded rim, cf Evans C J et al (2000) fig 19, F12, type 2.	Illus 4.30

O36.5	CJ1.1	Constricted-necked jar with a broadly hooked, everted rim, cf Webster (1976) nos 3 and 5, 1st–3rd century.	Illus 4.30
O36.6	CJ1.2	Constricted-necked jar with an everted, slightly hooked rim, cf Webster (1976) no 3, 1st–2nd century.	Illus 4.30
O36.7	CJ1.3	Constricted-necked jar with an everted, rising, thickened rim, cf Webster (1976) no 2, later 1st-mid-2nd century.	Illus 4.30
O36.8a-b	CJ1.4	Constricted-necked jar with an everted, rising, outcurving, thickened rim, cf Webster (1976) no 2, later 1st–2nd century. Vessel b is the complete vessel from the cremation burial C2246. See Illus 3.17, 3.31, 7.01.	Illus 4.30
O36.9	CJ1.5	Constricted-necked jar with a strongly hooked, undercut, triangularly-sectioned rim, perhaps cf Webster (1976) no 6, 2nd–3rd century.	Illus 4.30
O36.10	CJ2.1	Constricted-necked jar with an everted, beaded, faceted rim.	Illus 4.30
O36.11	CJ4.1	Bifid rimmed constricted-necked jar, cf Webster (1976) nos 9–11, 3rd–4th century.	Illus 4.30
O36.12	CJ4.2	Constricted-necked jar with a triangularly-sectioned rim, grooved into two cordons, cf Webster (1976) nos 9–11, 3rd–4th century.	Illus 4.30
O36.13	SJ1.1	Storage jar with a triangularly-sectioned, undercut grooved rim, perhaps cf Webster (1976) no 8, probably 3rd (or 4th century).	Illus 4.30
O36.14	SJ2.1	Storage jar with a triangularly-sectioned, undercut rim, cf Webster (1976) no 8, 3rd century.	Illus 4.30
O36.15	SJ2.2	Storage jar with an everted, rising, thickened rim, cf Evans et al (2000) fig 25, JLS1.	Illus 4.30
O36.16	SJ3.1	Storage jar with an everted, rising, squared rim, possibly cf Evans C J et al (2000) fig 25, type 1.	Illus 4.30
O36.17	J1.1	Small bead rimmed jar (or bowl), cf Evans C J et al (2000) fig 22, type 1.	Illus 4.30
O36.18	J2.1	Necked jar with an everted, rising, outcurving rim, cf Evans C J et al (2000) fig 22, type 2.1/2.3.	Illus 4.30
O36.19	J3.1	Jar with an everted, beaded, undercut rim, with two cordons below the rim. No parallel in Webster (1976) or Evans C J et al (2000).	Illus 4.30
O36.20	J4.1	Jar with an everted, rising, straight grooved rim.	Illus 4.30
O36.21	J5.1	Jar with an everted, rising, outcurving rim, cf Evans C J et al (2000) fig 22, type 2.1.	Illus 4.30
O36.22	J6.1	Jar or large beaker with a stubby, everted rim.	Illus 4.30
O36.23	J7.1	Jar with an everted, outcurving rim, lid-seated. No parallel in Webster (1976), cf R01 J1.1 and R813 J1.4, perhaps 1st-early 2nd century on greyware parallels.	Illus 4.30
O36.24	WMJ1.1	Wide-mouthed jar with a broadly hooked, undercut rim, cf Webster (1976) nos 23–25, 2nd–3rd century.	Illus 4.30
O36.25	WMJ1.2	Wide-mouthed jar with an everted, thickened, tapering rim, cf Webster (1976) no 22, 2nd-early 3rd century.	Illus 4.31
O36.26	WMJ1.3	Wide-mouthed jar with a triangularly-sectioned, faceted rim, cf Webster (1976) no 22, 2nd–3rd century.	Illus 4.31
O36.27	WMJ1.4	Wide-mouthed jar with an everted, thickened, slightly beaded rim, cf Webster (1976) no 21, mid-later 2nd century.	Illus 4.31
O36.28	WMJ1.5	Wide-mouthed jar with a horizontal, slightly undercut rim, cf Evans C J et al (2000) fig 23, JWM6; Webster (1976) no 22–25, 2nd–3rd century.	Illus 4.31
O36.29	WMJ1.6	Wide-mouthed jar with an everted, rising, outcurving rim, cf Webster (1976) no 20, 1st–2nd century; Evans C J et al (2000) fig 23, JWM4.	Illus 4.31
O36.30	WMJ1.8	Wide-mouthed jar with a cordoned shoulder and everted, tapering, triangularly-sectioned rim, cf Webster (1976) nos 22–3, 2nd–3rd century.	Illus 4.31
O36.31	WMJ2.1	Wide-mouthed jar with a tightly hooked rim, cf Webster (1976) nos 27–33, later 3rd–4th century.	Illus 4.31
O36.32	WMJ3.1	Wide-mouthed jar with an everted, thickened, triangularly-sectioned rim with a cordon beneath, perhaps cf Webster (1976) no 22, 2nd-early 3rd century; Evans C J et al (2000) fig 22, JM8.	Illus 4.31
O36.33	WMJ4.1	Wide-mouthed jar with a triangularly-sectioned, broadly hooked, grooved rim, perhaps cf Webster (1976) nos 23–25, mid-2nd-later 3rd century.	Illus 4.31
O36.34	TA1.1	Bead rimmed tankard with a fairly vertical wall, cf Webster (1976) nos 40–41, 2nd–3rd century.	Illus 4.31
O36.35a-b	TA1.2	Tankard with a beaded rim and slightly splaying wall, cf Webster (1976) nos 42–3, 2nd–3rd century.	Illus 4.31
O36.36	TA2.1	Bead rimmed tankard with a splaying wall, cf Webster (1976) no 44, later 3rd–4th century.	Illus 4.31
O36.37	TA2.3	Tankard with a simple rim and splaying walls, cf Webster (1976) no 44, later 3rd–4th century.	Illus 4.31

O36.38	TA3.1	Carinated cup with a beaded rim and cordon on the carination, perhaps cf Evans C J et al (2000) fig 26, type 1.	Illus 4.31
O36.39	B1.1	Reeded flange rimmed bowl with a downsloping rim, cf Webster (1976) no 54, early-mid-2nd century.	Illus 4.31
O36.40	B1.2	Flange rimmed bowl with a horizontal flange and groove near the edge of the flange, perhaps cf Webster (1976) no 56, 3rd century.	Illus 4.31
O36.41	B1.3	Reeded flange rimmed bowl with a rising rim, perhaps cf Webster (1976) no 55, 2nd-early 3rd century.	Illus 4.32
O36.42	B1.4	Reeded, horizontal, flange rimmed bowl, perhaps cf Webster (1976) no 56, 3rd century.	Not illus
O36.43	B1.5	Reeded flange rimmed bowl with downsloping flange with prominent central bead, cf Webster (1976) no 53, later 3rd–4th century.	Illus 4.32
O36.44	B1.6	Reeded flange rimmed bowl with slightly undercut rim and cordon on shoulder, cf Webster (1976) no 56, 3rd century.	Illus 4.32
O36.45	B2.1	Bowl with a horizontal flange rim, cf Webster (1976) nos 46–8 and 50, later 2nd-later 3rd century.	Illus 4.32
O36.46	B2.2	Bowl with a flange rim, slightly downsloping, perhaps cf Webster (1976) no 46, 2nd–3rd century.	Illus 4.32
O36.47	B2.3	Bowl with a flange rim, internally beaded, cf Webster (1976) no 45, 1st–2nd century; Evans C J et al (2000) fig 26, BT5.	Illus 4.32
O36.48	B2.4	Flange rimmed bowl with a horizontal rim, beaded on the interior and exterior, cf Webster (1976) no 45, 1st–2nd century.	Illus 4.32
O36.49	B2.5	Flange rimmed bowl with rounded, horizontal rim, cf Webster (1976) no 50, later 2nd-later 3rd century.	Illus 4.32
O36.50	B3.1	Rounded bowl with a stubby everted rim, cf Webster (1976) nos 34–5, 2nd–4th century.	Illus 4.32
O36.51	B3.2	Bead rimmed bowl with a curving wall, cf Webster (1976) nos 34–5, 2nd–4th century.	Illus 4.32
O36.52	B4.1	Bowl with a downsloping triangularly-sectioned rim, slightly beaded. Not illustrated.	Not illus
O36.53	B5.1	Bowl with a thin, horizontal, flanged rim with a cordon beneath, possibly cf Webster (1976) no 46, 2nd–3rd century.	Illus 4.32
O36.54a-b	B6.1	Bowl with a flange rim divided into two cordons, cf Webster (1976) no 57, 3rd century.	Illus 4.32
O36.55	B6.2	Flange rimmed bowl with a rising rim, divided into two cordons by a deep groove, cf Webster (1976) no 57, 3rd century.	Illus 4.32
O36.56	B7.1	A Dr31 copy bead rimmed bowl, later 2nd century or later.	Illus 4.32
O36.57	B8.1	Bowl with an outcurving wall and double beaded rim, perhaps a campanulate bowl, probably later 1st-early 2nd century.	Illus 4.32
O36.58	B9.1	Segmental bowl, cf Webster (1976) no 66, 2nd century.	Illus 4.32
O36.59	B10.1	Bowl with a grooved simple rim, with a deep lid-seating groove on the top of the rim, perhaps cf Evans et al (2000) fig 26, BT11.	Illus 4.32
O36.60a-b	D1.1	Groove rimmed dish with grooved base, perhaps cf Webster (1976) no 74.	Illus 4.32
O36.61	D1.2	Groove rimmed dish with chamfered base, perhaps 1st–2nd century.	Illus 4.32
O36.62	D2.1	Simple rimmed dish with a grooved base and an internal quarter-round moulding, perhaps a Cam 16 Gallo-Belgic dish copy, 1st-early 2nd century.	Illus 4.32
O36.63	D3.1	Simple rimmed curving-walled dish, perhaps cf Webster (1976) no 71, perhaps 1st–2nd century.	Illus 4.32
O36.64	O1.1	Segmental bowl with frilled rim, possibly a tazza, cf Webster (1976) no 66, 2nd century and Evans C J et al (2000) fig 28, BT40.	Illus 4.32

Fabric O53, Severn Valley wares

O53.1	F1.1	Globular flagon with a flanged rim.	Illus 4.46

Fabric O55, Severn Valley wares

O55.1	SJ1.1	Storage jar with an everted, horizontal rim.	Illus 4.47
O55.2	WMJ1.1	Wide-mouthed jar with a tightly hooked rim, cf Webster (1976) nos 27–33, later 3rd–4th century.	Illus 4.47
O55.3	WMJ1.2	Wide-mouthed jar with an undercut rim, cf Webster (1976) no 25, 2nd–3rd century.	Illus 4.47
O55.4	WMJ1.3	Wide-mouthed jar with a triangularly beaded rim, cf Webster (1976) no 22, 2nd century.	Illus 4.47

O55.5	WMJ1.4	Wide-mouthed jar with an everted, rising rim, perhaps cf Webster (1976) nos 20–21, 1st–2nd century.	Illus 4.47
O55.6	TA1.1	Straight, slightly splaying walled, bead rimmed, tankard, Cf Webster (1976) nos 41–43, 2nd–3rd century.	Illus 4.47
O55.7	B1.1	Flange rimmed bowl rim, grooved on top, cf Webster (1976) no 56, which he dates to the 3rd century.	Illus 4.47
O55.8	B1.2	Flange rimmed bowl with bead and flange, perhaps cf Evans C J et al (2000) fig 28, BT41.	Illus 4.47
O55.9	B1.3	Reeded flange rimmed bowl, perhaps cf Webster (1976) no 54, dated by him to the 1st-early 2nd century.	Illus 4.47
O55.10	D1.1	Groove rimmed dish, cf Webster (1976) nos 72 and 74.	Illus 4.47

Fabric O57, Severn Valley wares

O57.1		Body sherd from the top of a lamp(?).	Not illus

Fabric O81 Severn Valley wares

O81.1	F1.1	Flagon with an everted rim and a cordon beneath probably 1st-early 2nd century.	Illus 4.48

Fabric Q14, South-western white-slipped ware

Q14.1	F1.1	Ring-necked flagon with a prominent upper bead, later 1st-early 2nd century.	Illus 4.49

Fabric Q151, ?Severn Valley white-slipped ware, Worcester fabric 20

Q151.1	F1.1	Flagon with a bifid, beaded rim.	Illus 4.50
Q151.2	F1.2	Lid-seated flagon with a beaded and flanged rim, cf Bryant and Evans (2004) fig 155, no 22.	Illus 4.50
Q151.3	F2.1	Ring-necked flagon with a slightly flaring rim, perhaps later 1st-early 2nd century.	Illus 4.50
Q151.4	B1.1	Bifid rimmed bowl, possibly a tazza.	Illus 4.50

Fabric R01, ?North Warwickshire reduced ware, Worcester fabric 15

R01.1	J1.1	Jar with a stubby, everted, tapering rim.	Illus 4.51
R01.2	J2.1	Jar with an everted, rising rim, perhaps a later 2nd-early 3rd century BB copy.	Illus 4.51
R01.3	B1.1	Incipient beaded and flanged bowl, a BB copy, probably early-mid-3rd century.	Illus 4.51

Fabric R18, ?North Warwickshire / ?Severn Valley reduced ware

R18.1	CJ1.1	Constricted-necked jar with an everted rim and cordon on the neck.	Illus 4.52
R18.2	J1.1	Globular rusticated jar with an everted, lid-seated rim, Flavian-early Hadrianic, cf Bryant and Evans (2004) fig 158, no 2.	Illus 4.52
R18.3a-b	J1.2	Jar with a straight, slightly tapering, everted rim, often with rusticated decoration, Flavian-early Hadrianic.	Illus 4.52
R18.4	J1.3	Jar with a straight, everted rim. Not illustrated.	Not Illus
R18.5	J1.4	Necked jar with an everted rim, perhaps a BB copy, perhaps Hadrianic-Antonine.	Illus 4.52
R18.6	J1.5	Jar with an everted, swelling rim, perhaps cf Bryant and Evans (2004) fig 158, no 1, perhaps later 1st-early 2nd century.	Illus 4.52
R18.7	J1.6	Globular jar with a straight, everted rim with two lid-seating grooves, cf Bryant and Evans (2004) fig 158, no 2, probably later 1st century-early Hadrianic.	Illus 4.52
R18.8	CUP1.1	Carinated cup with a beaded rim and cordon on the carination, probably 1st-mid-2nd century.	Illus 4.52
R18.9a-b	B1.1	Carinated bowl with an everted, outcurving rim and carinated body, deeply grooved at the carination, later 1st–2nd century, cf Bryant and Evans (2004) fig 158, no 12.	Illus 4.52
R18.10	B1.2	Carinated jar with a beaded rim and a cordon at the base of the neck and a groove on the carination, mid-1st–2nd century.	Illus 4.52

R18.11	B1.4	Carinated bowl with a double grooved rim and carination, the wall of the drawn sherd is decorated with wavy line combing, possibly a Dr29 copy, later 1st-early 2nd century.	Illus 4.52
R18.12	B2.1	Carinated bowl with a vertical wall and beaded rim, later 1st–2nd century.	Illus 4.52
R18.13	B2.2	Bowl with a vertical wall, beaded rim and grooved shoulder, probably a Dr37 copy, 2nd century.	Not Illus
R18.14	B3.1	Flange rimmed bowl, later 1st–2nd century.	Illus 4.52
R18.15	D1.1	Wastered simple rimmed dish with a groove under the base, perhaps a Gallo-Belgic copy, later 1st-early 2nd century(?).	Illus 4.52
R18.16	D2.1	Grooved rimmed dish, perhaps 1st–2nd century.	Illus 4.52
R18.17	L1.1	Lid with a slightly beaded rim.	Illus 4.52
R18.18	L1.2	Lid with a beaded rim, grooved inside.	Illus 4.52

Fabric R32, ?Worcestershire reduced ware

R32.1	JUG1.1	Simple rimmed jug.	Illus 4.53
R32.2	CJ1.1	Hooked rimmed constricted-necked jar.	Illus 4.53
R32.3	J1.1	Bead rimmed jar with vertical burnished lines on the body, probably a Malvernian 'tubby cooking pot' copy, perhaps Antonine.	Illus 4.53
R32.4	J2.1	Jar with a straight, everted rim with lid-seating groove, probably rustic ware, cf Bryant and Evans (2004) fig 158, no 2, Flavian-early Hadrianic.	Illus 4.53
R32.5	J2.2	Necked jar with an everted rim, probably a BB copy, Hadrianic-Antonine.	Illus 4.53
R32.6	J2.3	Jar with a straight, everted, slightly wedge-shaped rim.	Illus 4.53
R32.7	J2.4	Jar with an everted, wedge-shaped rim.	Illus 4.53
R32.8	J2.5	Fragment of a rim from a bell-mouthed(?) jar(?).	Illus 4.53
R32.9	J3.1	Bead rimmed jar, possibly a BB copy, perhaps 2nd century, cf Bryant and Evans (2004) fig 158, no 5.	Illus 4.53
R32.10	WMJ1.1	Wide-mouthed jar with a hooked, everted rim, perhaps cf Bryant and Evans (2004) fig 158, no 7.	Illus 4.53
R32.11	B1.1	Carinated bowl with an everted, grooved rim.	Illus 4.53
R32.12	B2.1	Dr37 copy bowl with a beaded rim, perhaps 2nd century.	Illus 4.53
R32.13	B3.1	Carinated bowl with a straight, everted rim.	Illus 4.53
R32.14	D1.1	Gallo-Belgic copy dish, interior rouletted, perhaps later 1st-early 2nd century.	Illus 4.53
R32.15	D2.1	Simple rimmed dish.	Illus 4.53
R32.16	D3.1	Segmental bowl with a grooved flange, perhaps later 1st-mid-2nd century.	Illus 4.53

Fabric R341

R341.1	B1.1	Developed beaded and flanged bowl, *c* AD 270–400.	Not illus
R341.2	L1.1	Lid rim with a squared tip.	Illus 4.54

Fabric R41

R41.1	J1.1	Everted rimmed jar, perhaps a BB copy, perhaps Hadrianic-Antonine.	Illus 4.55
R41.2	B1.1	Flange rimmed bowl, exterior decorated with burnished acute lattice, Hadrianic-Antonine.	Illus 4.55

Fabric R813, Worcester fabric 12.1

R813.1	JUG1.1	Bead rimmed jug.	Illus 4.56
R813.2	LAG1.1	Lagena with a hooked, undercut rim with two large handles and cordoned neck.	Illus 4.56
R813.3a-b	CJ1.1	Constricted-necked jar with a hooked rim.	Illus 4.56
R813.4	CJ2.1	Constricted-necked jar with a beaded rim.	Illus 4.56
R813.5	J1.1	Necked jar with an everted, thickened rim, some examples at least are BB copies and Hadrianic-Antonine.	Illus 4.56
R813.6	J1.2	Jar with an everted, outcurving rim.	Illus 4.56

R813.7	J1.3	Jar with a straight, everted rim, often with rusticated decoration, later 1st century to Hadrianic, perhaps cf Bryant and Evans (2004) fig 158, no 2.	Illus 4.56
R813.8a-b	J1.4	Jar with a straight, everted rim with lid-seating groove, cf Bryant and Evans (2004) fig 158, no 2, later 1st century-Hadrianic.	Illus 4.56
R813.9	J1.5	Jar with an everted, outcurving rim, later 1st-early 2nd century.	Illus 4.56
R813.10	J1.6	Jar with a straight, everted, slightly wedge-shaped rim, probably later 1st-early 2nd century.	Illus 4.56
R813.11	J1.7	BB copy jar with acute burnished lattice decoration, Hadrianic-Antonine.	Illus 4.56
R813.12	J1.8	Jar rim with a thick, everted rim with a deep lid-seating groove.	Illus 4.56
R813.13	B7.1	Bead rimmed bowl, cf Bryant and Evans (2004) fig 158, no 5.	Illus 4.56
R813.14	J3.1	Jar or bowl with a tall neck and everted, rising rim.	Illus 4.56
R813.15	J3.2	Necked jar with a triangularly-sectioned rim.	Illus 4.56
R813.16	J3.3	Jar with a wedge-shaped rim.	Illus 4.56
R813.17	J4.1	Jar with a stubby, everted rim, with acute burnished lattice decoration, probably a BB copy, Hadrianic-Antonine.	Illus 4.56
R813.18	WMJ1.1	Wide-mouthed jar with an everted, hooked rim, cf Bryant and Evans (2004) fig 158, no 7.	Illus 4.56
R813.19a-b	TA1.1	Bead rimmed tankard, 2nd century.	Illus 4.56
R813.20	BK1.1	Bead rimmed beaker.	Illus 4.57
R813.21	BK2.1	Beaker with a tall, vertical, simple rim.	Illus 4.57
R813.22	C1.1	Carinated cup with a simple, everted rim.	Illus 4.57
R813.23a-b	B1.1	Dr37 copy bowl, 2nd century.	Illus 4.57
R813.24a-b	B1.2	Straight-walled carinated bowl with a beaded rim, probably a Dr 30 copy, later 1st-early 2nd century.	Illus 4.57
R813.25	B1.3	Bowl with a straight wall and double cordoned rim, perhaps 2nd century.	Illus 4.57
R813.26	B1.4	Bowl with a slightly outsloping wall and a grooved beaded rim.	Illus 4.57
R813.27	B1.5	Bead rimmed carinated bowl, perhaps later 1st–2nd century.	Not illus
R813.28	B1.6	Bead rimmed carinated, straight-walled bowl with acute burnished lattice decoration on the wall, perhaps later 1st–2nd century.	Illus 4.57
R813.29	B2.1	Carinated bowl with a beaded rim, perhaps a campanulate bowl, perhaps later 1st-early 2nd century.	Illus 4.57
R813.30	B3.1	Curving walled bowl with a straight, everted rim.	Illus 4.57
R813.31a-b	B4.1	Carinated bowl with an outcurving rim and groove on the girth, probably later 1st-early 2nd century.	Illus 4.57
R813.32	B4.2	Necked bowl (or jar) with an everted, outcurving rim. Not illustrated	Not illus
R813.33	B5.1	Reeded rimmed, carinated(?) bowl, perhaps Flavian-Trajanic.	Illus 4.57
R813.34	B5.2	Flange rimmed bowl, grooved, probably a reeded rimmed derived form, perhaps Flavian-early 2nd century.	Illus 4.57
R813.35	B6.1	Flange rimmed bowl, internally beaded.	Illus 4.57
R813.36	D1.1	Groove rimmed dish, perhaps 1st–2nd century.	Illus 4.57
R813.37	D2.1	Beaded segmental dish, later 1st–2nd century.	Illus 4.57
R813.38	L1.1	Simple rimmed lid.	Illus 4.57

Fabric S, Samian Ware

Margaret Ward with contribution by Brenda Dickinson

In contrast to the rest of the pottery catalogue, the samian ware is presented in five separate catalogues, detailing different aspects of their form, decoration and use. Some vessels appear in more than one of these catalogues and here details are given in each entry to allow cross-referencing. To avoid confusion in numbering, each catalogue entry is prefixed by a two letter code as follows: Forms and decoration – SD; Stamps and signatures – SS; Graffiti – SG; Repaired vessels – SR; Re-working and re-use – SW. Fabric abbreviations: CG = Central Gaulish (Fabrics S20 and S21); EG = Eastern Gaulish (Fabric S30); SG = Southern Gaulish (Fabric S10).

Forms and decoration

SD1	CG	Dr 30R	Glossy, rouletted wall sherd. Possibly not the same vessel as fragments found in C1137, Phase 3. Probably Hadrianic to early-Antonine. C1431, G85, Phase 1.	Not illus
SD2	CG	Dr 37	Glossy rim sherd with a fragment only of a blurred ovolo (Rogers 1974, type B14 or B15) above a horizontal wavy line (Rogers A24?). Probably from Les Martres-de-Veyre, and if so, produced in the period *c* AD 100-125. C1488, G902, Phase 1.	Not illus
SD3	CG	Dr 37	Red ware, from Les Martres-de-Veyre. Above a basal beadrow the decoration included a swag, Rogers F21, rosettes (C280), rings (C294?) and acanthus motifs Rogers K13 (but more complete) and K25. Style of Drusus i (X-3); see S and S pl 11.139 from Colchester. *c* AD 100-120/125. C1489, G902, Phase 1.	Illus 4.58
SD4	CG	Dr 37	A rim sherd in a hard red ware with some mica, presumably from Lezoux, but burnt or overfired. A fragment survives (cut off at the top by the bowl-maker's addition of the plain band) of a very small, blurred ovolo (Rogers B41) with no horizontal border above an unidentifiable fragment of decoration. Probably from a bowl in the early style of Pugnus (cf S and S pl 153.1 etc): early in the range AD 135-165. C1591, G1, Phase 1.	Not illus
SD5	CG	Dr 37	Badly blurred fragment of ovolo and horizontal beadrow (Rogers A3?) from a bowl produced in the Antonine period and perhaps *c* AD 160-200. C2196, G145, Phase 1.	Not illus
SD6	CG	Dr 37	Fragment from the bottom of the decoration, displaying sea-creatures. Produced in the Hadrianic-early Antonine period. C2307, G2, Phase 1.	Illus 4.58
SD7	CG	Dr 37	Rim sherd with a fragment only of a repetitive motif used in place of an ovolo. Probably produced at Les Martres-de-Veyre in the period *c* AD 100-125. C2333, G81, Phase 1.	Not illus
SD8	CG	Dr 37	Below a fragment of a horizontal wavy line, a winding scroll terminates in two leaves (Rogers H96 and J89). These were used in the work of Potter X-9 and X-11 at Les Martres-de-Veyre, where this bowl, in a highly-fired red ware, originated. Probably produced in the range *c* AD 100-130; see also Rogers 1999, 326. C1174, G2, Phase 1-2.	Illus 4.58
SD9	CG	Dr 37	This sherd bears the same scroll with leaves (Rogers H96 and J89) as that in C1174. Its ware is more orange, although also from Les Martres-de-Veyre. This bowl was probably produced in the range *c* AD 100-130. C1343, G155, Phase 2.	Illus 4.58
SD10	CG	Dr 37	Orange-red ware. Ovolo with central core and corded tongue ending in a blurred rosette (a variation of Rogers B231; cf S and S pl 159.23). Below an indistinct border (probably A9), a winding scroll included a leaf (H13) used by Cinnamus. The ovolo appears on small bowls of Cinnamus, sometimes with scroll compositions (cf Rogers 1999, pl 33.65). A bowl from Castleford (Dickinson and Hartley 2000, 55.527) was found there in a context later than its 'pottery shop' (burnt probably in *c* AD 140/145); Dickinson and Hartley felt that none of the pottery associated with that bowl was necessarily produced later than AD 160. The bowl represented here originated at some point in the range *c* AD 140-175/180 and perhaps before *c* 160. C1369, G111, Phase 2.	Illus 4.58
SD11	CG	Dr 37	Three small sherds showing fragments only of small stags (Oswald 1777) running left above small leaves (Rogers H186) as used in the early style of Pugnus (cf S and S pl 153.10-12). The piece found in C1379 is badly burnt, but all three sherds appear to be from the same bowl. Early in the range AD 135-165. C1382, 1379, 1435, G908, 134, Phase 2, 4.	Not illus
SD12	CG	Dr 37	Four sherds showing a poorly moulded, badly blurred winding scroll with fragments only of small animals running left. *c* AD 120/125-150. C1487, 1379, 1435, G901, 134, Phase 2, 4.	Not illus
SD13	CG	Dr 37	Overfired and also burnt sherd presumed to be from Les Martres-de-Veyre. Compartments separated by wavy lines and a neatly beaded column (Rogers P10?), flanked on the left by a scroll above a fragment of panther (probably Oswald 1518) which is not shown on the illustration. On the right, a small double medallion contains a motif formed by trifid leaves (G172) as on S and S pl 31.368. A Trajanic-Hadrianic product, probably in the style of Potter X-9, for whom Rogers (1999, 326) suggested a date *c* AD 115-135. C1487, G901, Phase 2.	Illus 4.58
SD14	CG	Dr 37	Rim sherd of a shallow bowl with an indistinct ovolo (B14 or 15?) above panelling with wavy-line borders and indistinct rosette terminals (C280): an arcade with columns (P85?) surmounted by an astragalus contains a cupid (Oswald 420). The panel to the right included a stylised, palmate plant or leaf-and-bud. Probably from Lezoux, rather than Les Martres-de-Veyre, and if so *c* AD 125-145. C1487, G901, Phase 2.	Illus 4.58

SD15	Uncertain origin	Dr 37	Rather orange ware with a large quartzitic inclusion and occasional platelets probably of mica. Two horses confront each other above a basal line (Oswald 1896 and, badly blurred, 1902?). Oswald's incomplete figure-types occur at Rottenburg on a bowl (Knorr 1910, Taf 2.4) which was said to be South Gaulish. The Worcester bowl was more Central Gaulish and earlier 2nd-century. C1487, G901, Phase 2.	Illus 4.58
SD16	CG	Dr 37	Rim sherd of a small bowl with ovolo B144, border A9 and animals set in a freestyle composition interspersed with tufts derived from Rogers type J178. A lion devours a boar (Oswald 1491); cf S and S pl 164.1 signed by Cerialis ii. The Worcester piece represents a bowl typical of the Cerialis ii-Cinnamus ii partnership (cf Dickinson and Hartley 2000, nos 340 and 389 from Castleford); see also SD30 below. *c* AD 135-150/160. C1602, G63, Phase 1-2.	Illus 4.58
SD17	CG	Dr 37	The panelled decoration has very indistinct vertical borders (beaded or astragaloid?) which include a plain festoon immediately above a large animal, probably a panther or dog. This figure-type does not appear in Oswald's catalogue, and no other examples have been found by the writer. To the right, a team of horses probably belonged to Apollo's chariot (Oswald type 102 rather than 101?). The superimposed and partially impressed leaves represent Rogers type J149. This use of J149 and the single-bordered festoon occurs at Canterbury on an unpublished bowl stamped by Belsa and dated in the range *c* AD 170-200. The Worcester bowl may be presumed to represent his style. Burnt piece with a battered footring. There may be evidence of an attempt to cut a hole for cleat-type repair (SR3). C2095, G121, Phase 2-4.	Illus 4.58
SD18	CG	Dr 37	Thirteen sherds, spread between five contexts beginning in Phase 3 in. A small bowl whose decoration includes Cinnamus's common ovolo, Rogers B143, above panelling bordered by beadrows (A2) and a basal line. A double medallion contains a composite ornament made up of motifs K20, T3, U247 and U248. In a panel to the right was a fragment of a dolphin-handled basket (Q58) below the obscured remains of a decorative motif rather than a horizontal plainware stamp (which would be deeper than this). The identifiable motifs are common on bowls with ovolo B143 in the standard style of Cinnamus of the period *c* AD 150-170. Small bowls like this one frequently display a hotch-potch of decorative motifs and it is speculated that they were the work of apprentices of masters such as Cinnamus. A fragment of footring shows much wear from use. Three round rivet-holes through the decoration; a lead rivet has survived in one hole (SR8). C1034, C2139, C1030, C1229, C1002, G41, G19, G24, G25, G1001, Phase 3, 4, 6.	Illus 4.58
SD19	CG	Dr 37	Five sherds adjoin to form two large pieces including the rim. The two sets of sherds have broken at four round rivet-holes, three drilled through the decoration and one through the plain band (SR9). Both sets of sherds may be presumed to represent the same bowl: the ovolo is Rogers B223 with no core, set above a horizontal border (A9). Below, a large winding scroll included a leaf (H99) and a badly blurred, probably naked, figure, possibly of Venus. Standard style of Cinnamus, *c* AD 155-175/180. SF162, C1034, G41, Phase 3-4.	Illus 4.58
SD20	CG	Dr 37	Fragment only of a panel with a neater, astragaloid border horizontally (Rogers A9) and, vertically, large beads (A3); inside a double medallion, a marine monster kicks its forelegs up (smaller than the sea-bull Oswald 52A) and outside it a small, indistinct ring (E51 or E58). The bowl was most probably produced in the period *c* AD 160-200. C1034, G41, Phase 3-4.	Illus 4.58
SD21	CG	Dr 37	Below the rim on the plain band above the ovolo was a small stamp F·ALBINIOF by Flo- Albinus, a potter known to have stamped bowls that were produced at Lezoux from moulds in the style of Laxtucissa and Paternus v (Rogers 1999, 38 f). This stamp represents die 4b, *c* AD 150-180 (SS8). C2106, G42, Phase 3.	Not illus
SD22	CG	Dr 37	Eleven sherds, some adjoining, spread through five contexts, concentrated in Phase 3, Groups 42 and 200, with redeposited sherds in Phase 6. The ovolo is Rogers B223 above a guideline; the panelling has vertical borders (A2) with rosette terminals (C145). Other motifs, not all illustrated here, included a stag (Oswald 1720), an eagle (Oswald 2167), a badly smudged caryatid (Oswald 1206?) and a fragment of a hare (probably Oswald 2119A) in a blurred festoon. A leaf-and-bud ornament appears to be Rogers type G7 rather than G8, which is smaller (see both Rogers 1999, 479 G7 and S and S pl 155.25). The style is that of Pugnus which is closely related to Secundus v (*c* AD 150-180); see S and S pl 155.20 stamped PVGNIM by a potter who was active AD 135-165. However, the general appearance of this bowl with its brownish slip and poor relief suggests a date late in that range. A small fragment of ovolo had broken at a rivet-hole drilled through the plain band (SR17). C2106, C2111, C2116, C2162, C1002, G42, G200, G1001, G1001, Phase 3, 6.	Illus 4.59

SD23	CG	Dr 37	Two adjoining sherds including rim. A blurred ovolo lies above the fragmentary remains of panelled decoration. The plain band below the rim bears a small stamp impressed by the bowl-maker, which reads REGIN[I·MA] Reginus iv was a potter known to have stamped bowls which were produced from moulds in the styles of such potters as Advocisus and Clemens iii at Lezoux (active AD 160-200 and 170-200, respectively). Brenda Dickinson notes that one such stamped bowl in the style of Clemens iii has been recorded previously at Worcester. The activity of Reginus iv is dated *c* AD 150-175 (SS15). C2110, G19, Phase 3.	Illus 4.59
SD24	CG	Dr 37	Battered fragment of ovolo (Rogers B105) above an indistinct horizontal border. Below, a large advertisement stamp reads [PΛTERN]FE retrograde. This represents die 7a of Paternus v whose activity is now dated AD 150-185. (SS12). C2113, G200, Phase 3.	Illus 4.59
SD25	CG	Dr 37	Below the (now missing) decoration on this bowl there remains a fragment of a signature which had been inscribed in the mould, reading most probably CR[retrograde. Brenda Dickinson notes that this is almost certainly a mould-signature of Criciro v (SS35). *c* AD 135-165. The slightly burnt footring is battered, but shows evidence of wear from use. C2114, G19, Phase 3.	Not illus
SD26	CG	Dr 37	Four adjoining fragments showing a large winding scroll of which only the tendrils have survived, above the basal line. The bowl was produced most probably in the period *c* AD 120-160. The base has broken, showing a round hole drilled through the centre (SR18), drilling which may have served some function other than repair. C2117, G16, Phase 3.	Illus 4.59
SD27	CG	Dr 37	Two adjoining fragments of panelling bordered vertically by a beadrow (Rogers A2). One panel included a small double medallion containing a badly battered block-like motif below a bird (Oswald 2251?). None of the motifs are diagnostic of a specific potter, but Docilis was one who favoured such compositions. The vessel was produced at some point in the range *c* AD 130-160. The sherds have broken through the decoration at a repair-hole, apparently of the round variety (SR19). A small fragment showing the same border and medallion was found in C2107, G42, Phase 3 and is likely to represent the same bowl. C2119, G200, Phase 3.	Not illus
SD28	CG	Dr 37	Fragment of the decoration, showing a wing tip to the left of Minerva (Oswald 126B), a type which was used by Cettus at Les Martres-de-Veyre. This fragment may represent his work, *c* AD 130-160. The sherd has broken at a round rivet-hole drilled through the decoration (SR20). C2123, G16, Phase 3.	Illus 4.59
SD29	CG	Dr 37	Poor ware, with a brownish slip, presumed to be Lezoux ware. Two adjoining, battered fragments show an indistinct ovolo, Rogers B156, above blurred decoration: the horizontal border, if ever present, was smeared beyond recognition. Fragment below represents the dancer Oswald 353. Iullinus used both the ovolo and the dancer in the period *c* AD 160-200 at Lezoux, but possibly a late product if not just very poor work. C2123, G16, Phase 3.	Illus 4.59
SD30	CG	Dr 37	The orange-red slip of this bowl is dull in places. Fourteen sherds, several of them adjoining and all small, from the rim and wall, together with part of the very worn footring, all of which can be presumed to represent the same bowl. Ovolo Rogers B144 lies above a beadrow (A2). Interspersed with tufts derived from type J178 is a freestyle animal scene: lions and a boar set upside-down, but all are too fragmentary for illustration. This is the style of the Cerialis ii-Cinnamus ii association, *c* AD 135-150/160. Similar decoration found on another sherd, SD16, does not represent the same vessel although this too may be a small bowl. C2127, G19, Phase 3.	Not illus
SD31	CG	Dr 37	Two adjoining pieces of footring within which a leaf has been stamped, below the centre of the base (SS37). Brenda Dickinson notes that the leaf stamp may represent the same leaf as on a bowl in the style of Secundinus ii at Verulamium. Secundinus ii worked at Lezoux, but is known to have stamped at least one vessel at Les Martres-de-Veyre. As with many other of Secundinus's bowls, it is unclear from the fabric alone whether the Worcester vessel was produced at Les Martres-de-Veyre or at Lezoux. At any rate, it will have been produced at some point in the range *c* AD 110-145. The footring shows evidence of considerable wear from use, and has broken at two rivet-holes drilled below the decoration (SR23). C2156, G200, Phase 3.	Illus 4.59
SD32	CG	Dr 37	Wall sherd with blurred decoration: an indistinct ovolo, probably Rogers B105, lies above a beadrow (A2). A peacock (Oswald 2365) looked left over its shoulder towards a winding scroll. See a bowl from London (S and S pl 107.26), stamped by Paternus v (II) who was active AD 150-185. The sherd appears to have been roughly reworked as a counter or disc (SW3*)*. C1033, G24, Phase 4.	Illus 4.59

SD33	SG	Dr 37	Large rim sherd in a chalky pink ware which shows signs of staining or burning. Ovolo with indistinct trifid-tipped tongue above panelling with wavy-line borders including a fragment from a saltire: the bowl was probably produced in the range *c* AD 80-110. The sherd has broken at three rivet-holes, probably all of the round variety (SR24). C1407, G134, Phase 4.	Not illus
SD34	CG	Dr 37	Two adjoining sherds in a buff fabric with a dull slip, possibly stained. Panels with blurred borders, recorded as probably astragaloid (Rogers A9) include a caryatid (Oswald 1199) and three incomplete groups of figures. The group to the left was badly blurred, but may have represented a figure with hanging drapery, playing a double flute. A double medallion contains a tree (Rogers N4) left of an erotic group (Oswald type H). In the panel to the right was another erotic group (Oswald type B), obscured by an additional detail. The small diamonds (U36) acting as corner-fillers were used in the style of Cinnamus, but all the decorative elements and all but one of the figure-types feature on a bowl in the style of Potter P-15 from Grenoble (Rogers 1999, pl 128.7). The addition of a detail to type B on both vessels suggests that the Worcester bowl was produced from the same mould as that found at Grenoble. Products of this potter are also found in Scotland and a production-date in the range *c* AD 140-160 is suggested. C1407, G134, Phase 4.	Illus 4.59
SD35	CG	Dr 37	Two adjoining sherds showing an indistinct ovolo (probably Rogers B18) above beadrow A2 and the blurred head of a figure in a panel. Probably the style of Sacer i or Attianus ii or an associate, *c* AD 125-150. The plain band has broken at a repair-hole (SR35). C1002, G1001, Phase 6.	Not illus
SD36	CG	Dr 37	Six rim and wall sherds, three of them adjoining and illustrated here, in a heavily micaceous ware with some staining. Ovolo Rogers B144 (rather indistinct) lies above panelling bordered by astragali (A9). The figure-types here include part of a draped female (Victory or similar) flanked by tufts derived from Rogers J178. This bowl's boar (Oswald 1666) and Jupiter (Oswald 13) both appear on a mould stamped by Cinnamus at Lezoux (Simpson and Rogers 1969, pl 2.9). The style is that of the early Cerialis ii-Cinnamus ii partnership, *c* AD 135-150/160. One sherd has broken at a round rivet-hole drilled through the decoration (SR39). C2157, G1000, Phase 6.	Illus 4.59
SD37	SG	Dr 37	Wall sherd from a small, messy bowl with a dull slip and blurred decoration. The split-tongued ovolo above a horizontal wavy line also occurs on bowls produced at Montans bearing mould-stamps of Felicio (London: Museum of London 5450G) and Malcio (Richborough: Bushe-Fox 1932, pl 29.1) (Brenda Dickinson pers com). It also appears on bowls stamped after moulding by Chresimus (York) and Malcio (Montans) and on an unstamped bowl from Inveresk (Dickinson 1988, Fiche 1:B8, 2.58). Below, a recurring acanthus appears to be a *surmoulage* of that on the London bowl of Felicio and on the Inveresk bowl. The larger version also occurs on bowls with internal stamps of Malcio (Lectoure and Wroxeter). At the bottom, a series of large leaves has no exact parallels, but the Wroxeter bowl shows a very similar one. *c* AD 110-145 or 125-150. C1003, G1002, Phase 0.	Illus 4.59
SD38	CG	Dr 30	Three adjoining sherds bearing a stamp of the mould-maker. The panelled decoration in high relief, includes ovolo B102, Mars (Oswald 159A), a draped woman (Oswald 931) and an erotic scene in a version not illustrated by Oswald. The two rosettes in the field are C237 and a finely detailed version of C168. For all these elements of the decoration on a bowl which may indeed have come from the same mould, see S and S pl 113.17 from Corbridge. The Worcester bowl was stamped intra-decoratively with an advertisement stamp reading [ADV]OCISI which represents die 8a of Advocisus (SS1), *c* AD 160-200. C2106, 2108, G42, 18, Phase 3.	Illus 4.59
SD39	CG	Dr 30	Thirteen sherds, some adjoining, found in four contexts, concentrated in G19, Phase 3. Another poor quality product. A slightly blurred ovolo (Rogers B102) was partially obliterated by the bowl-maker when adding the rim. The panelled decoration is bordered by bead rows (A2), faintly reduplicated. The panels appeared to have been set out in pairs and the surviving sherds include a caryatid (distorted), a candelabrum (apparently Q26), a blurred bow (U106), a fragment only of Apollo (Oswald 83) and a blurred mask (probably Oswald 1330). On another sherd, a gladiator (Oswald 1059 or similar) and a very indistinctly seated Bacchus, trailing a cup (see Oswald 571; Rogers 1999, pl 1.7). The advertisement stamp reading ADVOCISI again represents die8a of Advocisus of Lezoux, *c* AD 160-200 (SS2). C2110, 2112, 2084, 2157, G19, 42, U/S, 1000, Phase 3, 5, 6.	Illus 4.60
SD40	CG	Dr 30	Eight sherds including the rim of a bowl with a dull brownish slip. The ovolo is badly blurred. The panelling below was bordered by large beads (A3) and included fragments of a Victory (Oswald 809). The presence of beadrow A3 and this Victory on a bowl of form 30 suggests the work of Doeccus i , *c* AD 170-200 or later (see Samian summary, Chapter 4). C2110, G19, Phase 3.	Illus 4.60

SD41	CG	Dr 45	Rim sherd showing the wall and a little of the gritted base of the mortarium. The small, lion-headed *appliqué* spout on the wall is slightly smaller than that of SD42. It is probably a *surmoulage* of a common Lezoux type (cf Ward 2008a, 180, fig 9.9). The conventional British dating for this form is in the range *c* AD 170-200, but there are suggestions of later production (see Bird 1986, 178-181; Ward 2008a, 172, 178, 189). The interior of this vessel shows signs of wear from use; the wall shows scratching near the spout similar to that inside SD42. The interior of the spout itself shows no evidence of wear from cleaning, etc. C1002, G1001, Phase 6.	Illus 4.60
SD42	CG	Dr 45	Small rim sherd showing a shallow wall and a little of the gritted base of the mortarium. The wall displays a lion-headed *appliqué* spout which is rather battered but was slightly larger than SD41 and may represent a *surmoulage* of the common Lezoux type. The conventional British dating for this form is in the range *c* AD 170-200, but later production is suggested and some British finds may have been later products (cf Bird 1986, 178-181; Ward 2008a, D9: 18, 74, 79; Ward forthcoming c). The interior of this vessel shows signs of wear from use, with similar scratches inside the wall to SD41. The inside of the spout itself shows no evidence of wear from cleaning, etc. C2157, G1000, Phase 6.	Illus 4.60
SD43	CG	Déchelette 74	'Black samian ware' (see Ward forthcoming a). One rim sherd from a handled jar in black-surfaced orangey buff fabric may be presumed to represent the same vessel as part of an *appliqué* mask of Pan (cf Déchelette 1904, vol 2, 225, masque 109?). A mask similar to but not identical with Déchelette type 109 was recorded in 2nd-century imitation samian ware at Wanborough, Wiltshire (Swan 1977, 265). However, 'a black samian goblet,' *c* 140mm high, decorated with a very similar appliqué mask of Pan and a satyr, was found at Chichester Cattlemarket (Down 1989, 101-2, no 218). For other specimens from Silchester, Alchester and York (some including Déchelette's mask 109), see Simpson 1957, pl 14. An example from Caerleon, Simpson 1973, pl 11.23, was dated to the latter half of the 2nd century by Catherine Johns (1963, 15). Another jar with a different mask, Déchelette's type 116, was found at Verulamium (Hartley 1972a, 253f, D112), in a room destroyed by fire in the early Antonine period. At Alcester, two such black jars included one almost complete example, recovered from Pit B 13 in a group for whose filling a date *c* AD 145-155 has been proposed (Hartley et al 1994, 96, no 68; 106, no 270). The Worcester vessel was, unfortunately, not available for physical comparison with the black 'beaker' published from the adjoining excavation, which may well represent the same vessel (Edwards et al 2002, 126). The Magistrates Court vessel could have been produced by a Lezoux potter such as Paternus v (who produced black samian and was active largely in the mid-Antonine period) or one of his followers. SF397, C2107, G42, Phase 3.	Illus 4.60

Stamps and signatures

Brenda Dickinson

Each entry gives: potter (i, ii etc., where homonyms are involved), die, form, reading, published example (if any), date. The dates given in brackets here are those suggested by the form and general appearance of the vessel represented at Worcester. Superscript a, b and *c* indicate: a Stamp attested at the pottery in question; b Not attested at the pottery, but other stamps of the same potter used there; c Assigned to the pottery on the evidence of fabric, distribution, etc. Ligatured letters are underlined.

SS1	CG	Dr 30	Advocisus 8a, [ADV]OCISI (Stanfield and Simpson 1958, pl. 169) Lezoux[b] (SD38), *c* AD 160–190200. C2106, G42, Phase 3.	Illus 4.59
SS2	CG	Dr 30	Advocisus 8a, ADVOCISI (Stanfield and Simpson 1958, pl. 169) Lezoux[b] (SD39), *c* AD 160–200. C2157, G1000, Phase 6.	Illus 4.60
SS3	CG	unidentified form, possibly 38	Aestivus 1a, [AESTI]VIM[A] Lezoux[b], *c* AD 155–195. C2107, G42, Phase 3.	Not illus
SS4	CG	Dr 18/31	Anaillus i 2a, ΛΝΛ[ILL·F] (Durand-Lefebvre 1963, 11, 34) Lezoux[a], *c* AD 125–150. C1002, G1001, Phase 6.	Not illus
SS5	CG	Dr 33	Antiquus 2a, [ANTI]CVI (Dickinson 1996, Illus 142, 10) Lezoux[b], *c* AD 160–195. C2110, G19, Phase 3.	Not illus
SS6	CG	Dr 31	Dester 1a, DE[STER·F] Lezoux[a], *c* AD 155–195. C2082, Phase 2.	Not illus

SS7	CG	Dr 18/31R or 31R	Ericus 1b, ERI[CI·M] (Knorr 1907, Taf. XXX, 126) Lezoux[a], *c* AD 135–160/165. C1602, G63, Phase 1-2.	Not illus
SS8	CG	Dr 37	Flo— Albinus 4b, F·ALBINIOF Lezoux[b] (SD21), *c* AD 150–180. C2106, G42, Phase 3.	Not illus
SS9	CG	Dr 18/31	Gnatius ii 1a, GNATI·M (Romeuf 2001, pl. 35, 86–7) Les Martres–de–Veyre[a], Lezoux[b], *c* AD 140-155 if Lezoux. C2289, G82, Phase 1.	Not illus
SS10	CG	Dr 31	Meddignus 1a, MEDDIGN[VS] Lezoux[c], Antonine. C1002, G1001, Phase 6.	Not illus
SS11	CG	Dr 18/31	Nicephor i 3a, NIC[EPHOR·F] (Romeuf 2001, pl. 35, 119) Les Martres–de–Veyre[a], *c* AD 100–120. C1123, G152, Phase 4.	Not illus
SS12	CG	Dr 37	Paternus v 7a, [PΛTERN]FE retr. (Stanfield and Simpson 1958, pl. 169) (SD24), *c* AD 150–185. C2113, G200, Phase 3.	Not illus
SS13	CG	Dr 31 or 31R	Paullus v 4a, PAVLIM (Nash-Williams 1930, 178, 76) Lezoux[a], *c* AD 160–200. C1002, G1001, Phase 6.	Not illus
SS14	CG	Dr 18/31	Reginus ii 2a, REGI[NVS·F] (Romeuf 2001, pl. 35, 135–6) Les Martres–de–Veyre[a], Lezoux[b], *c* AD 120-150. C1488, G902, Phase 1.	Not illus
SS15	CG	Dr 37	Reginus iv 1b, REGIN[I·MA] Lezoux[b] (SD23), *c* AD 150–175. C2110, G19, Phase 3.	Illus 4.59
SS16	CG	Dr 33?	Satto v 1a, SΛTO[MΛ] retr. Lezoux[a], *c* AD 150–180. C2186, G19, Phase 3.	Not illus
SS17	CG	Dr 79R	Sextus v 4a, SIIXTIMA (Durand-Lefebvre 1963, 225, 697) Lezoux[a], *c* AD 155–200. C2111, G42, Phase 3.	Not illus
SS18	CG	Dr 18/31	Silvanus iii 3c, SILVANI (Hartley 1972, Illus 82, S125) Lezoux[b], *c* AD 125–150. Graffito inscribed under the base, after firing (SG1). SF158, C1488, G902, Phase 1.	Not illus
SS19	CG	Dr 18/31 or 31	Suobnus 2a, SVOBNI·M (Hartley and Dickinson 1981, 267, S.S 15), Les Martres–de–Veyre[a], *c* AD 135-160. C2145, G154, Phase 4.	Not illus
SS20	SG	Dr 18	L. Ter— Secundus 6a, L·TER·SECV (Vernhet 1981, 34, 16) La Graufesenque[a], *c* AD 75–100. C1134, G2, Phase 1-2.	Not illus
SS21	CG	Dr 33	]ILI? (Antonine). C1002, G1001, Phase 6.	Not illus
SS22	CG	Dr 40(?)	]M? (mid-late Antonine). C1002, G1001, Phase 6.	Not illus
SS23	CG	Dr 33	·MA[? (Antonine). C1090, G141, Phase 4.	Not illus
SS24	CG	Dr 33	]·F (Antonine) (SR29). C2084, U/S, Phase 5.	Not illus
SS25	EG	Dr 18/31R or 31R	]N? (later 2nd-3rd century). C2084, U/S, Phase 5.	Not illus
SS26	CG	Dr 18/31R or 31R	V[(second half of 2nd century). C2084, U/S, Phase 5.	Not illus
SS27	CG	Dr 33	NV[or]ΛN (mid-late Antonine). C2106, G42, Phase 3.	Not illus
SS28	CG	Dr 31R	GEN[? mid-late Antonine. C2107, G42, Phase 3.	Not illus
SS29	CG	Dr 31 or 31R	]M (second half of 2nd century). C2110, G19, Phase 3.	Not illus
SS30	CG	Dr 31	]DVI (second half of 2nd century). C2110, G19, Phase 3.	Not illus
SS31	CG	uncertain form, cup or small bowl	Illegible stamp (Hadrianic-Antonine). C2120, G143, Phase 4.	Not illus
SS32	CG	Dr 31(?)	CC4]ONTI? (Antonine). C2131, G19, Phase 3.	Not illus
SS33	CG	Dr 37	D[? in the decoration and perhaps part of a motif, rather than a stamp, Antonine? C2132, G19, Phase 3.	Not illus
SS34	CG	Dr 18/31R or 31R(?)	]M· (Antonine). C2211, G54, Phase 2.	Not illus
SS35	CG	Dr 37	Cr[? retrograde, under the decoration, almost certainly a mould–signature of Criciro v, reading Cr., retr. (SD25), *c* AD 135–165. C2114, G19, Phase 3.	Not illus
SS36	CG	Dr 37	X, under the base; the graffito was inscribed in the mould, perhaps after firing; (Hadrianic-Antonine). C2385, G120, Phase 2.	Not illus
SS37	CG	Dr 37	Leaf, stamped under the base. This motif is possibly the same as one found in the same position on a bowl from Verulamium (Dickinson 1984, Illus 77, 97), in the style of Secundinus ii (Rogers's Secundinus I), though this is not completely impressed and so appears shorter than the one on the Worcester piece (SD31 and SR23). The potter's fabrics make it difficult to decide whether he worked only at Lezoux, or started his career at Les Martres–de–Veyre. A range *c* AD 110–135/145 should therefore be allowed. C2156, G200, Phase 3.	Illus 4.59

Graffiti

SG1	CG	Dr 18/31	Stamped by Silvanus iii, A large piece of the base and the very worn, but also battered, footring. A graffito has been scratched below the base within the footring. Roger Tomlin (2001, 395) has read this as FLM, presumed to be Fl(avius) M(…). *c* AD 125-150 (SS18). SF158, C1488, G902, Phase 1.	Illus 4.60
SG2	CG	Dr 31	Large piece of the base and worn footring, on whose standing surface three lines have been incised. *c* AD 150-200. C1487, G901, Phase 2.	Not illus
SG3	CG	Dr 31R	Two pieces of the worn footring: one is burnt and has a worn or scratched patch on the internal base next to a repair-hole (SR15). There is a group of five small nicks incised on the standing surface. *c* AD 160-200. C2110, G19, Phase 3.	Not illus
SG4	CG	Dr 40	Only an illegible fragment of the basal stamp has survived, but two adjoining sherds of footring, worn from use, display broad incisions below the base which are presumed to represent a rough graffito. Later 2nd century. C2110, G19, Phase 3.	Illus 4.60
SG5	CG	Dish	Badly burnt sherd with a graffito X scratched across the junction of the wall and base. From Lezoux, produced in the range *c* AD 140-200. C2110, G19, Phase 3.	Not illus
SG6	CG	Dr 31	Fragment of extremely worn footring, with a small X incised on its standing surface. *c* AD 150-200. C2084, U/S, Phase 5.	Not illus

Repaired vessels

SR1	SG	Dr 18R	Basal sherd drilled with a round rivet-hole. *c* AD 70-110. C1182, G2, Phase 1-2.	Not illus
SR2	CG	Dr 31	Five sherds from the rim, wall and worn footring. A round rivet-hole was drilled through the base. *c* AD 150-200. C1207, 1224, G72, 73, Phase 2.	Not illus
SR3	CG	Dr 37	Burnt piece of decoration presumed to be in the style of Belsa (SD17). The battered footring may show signs of a little wear from use and there are indications that the piece may have broken at an early stage of an attempt to cut a repair-hole. The piece appears to have been burnt along this edge at a time when it had not yet broken away from the rest of the vessel. *c* AD 170-200. C2095, G121, Phase 2-4.	Illus 4.58
SR4	CG	Dr 45	Two sherds including the rim of this mortarium. The internal wall was very scratched and the basal gritted interior was completely worn away. The sherds have broken at a repair-hole (possibly unsuccessful) cut through the base. *c* AD 170-200. C2140, G121, Phase 2-4.	Not illus
SR5	CG	Dr 18/31R	Wall sherd, broken at a round rivet-hole which retains traces of lead. *c* AD 120-160. C2140, G121, Phase 2-4.	Not illus
SR6	CG	Dr 37	Rim sherd, broken at a possible repair-hole through the plain band below the rim. From Lezoux, *c* AD 120-160. C2275, G2, Phase 1.	Not illus
SR7	CG	Dr 18/31R or 31R	Rim sherd, broken at a round rivet-hole, which retains possible traces of lead. *c* AD 140-180. C1034, G41, Phase 3-4.	Not illus
SR8	CG	Dr 37	Ten sherds from same bowl, some adjoining, spread through five contexts, concentrated in G24, Phase 4. Footring shows much wear from use. Sherds display three round rivet-holes drilled through the decoration, at which they have broken; one retains a lead rivet and at least one other retains traces of lead. The decoration suggests the work of an apprentice of Cinnamus, *c* AD 150-170 (SD18). C1034, C2139, C1030, C1229, C1002, G41, G19, G24, G25, G1001, Phase 3, 4, 6.	Illus 4.58
SR9	CG	Dr 37	Five sherds adjoin to form two large pieces including the rim. The two sets of sherds have broken at four round rivet-holes: three were drilled through the decoration; that through the plain band is one of two holes which retain a lead rivet, while traces of lead survive in a third. Both sets of sherds may be presumed to represent the same bowl. Decorated in the style of Cinnamus, *c* AD 155-175/180 (SD19). SF162, C1034, G41, Phase 3-4.	Illus 4.58
SR10	CG	Dr 37	Rim sherd, broken at a round rivet-hole. *c* AD 150-200. C2106, G42, Phase 3.	Not illus
SR11	CG	Dr 31	Basal fragment, broken at a repair-hole apparently of the cut (dove-tailed) variety which shows possible traces of lead. *c* AD 150-200. C2107, G42, Phase 3.	Not illus
SR12	CG	Dr 37	Fragment, broken at two repair-holes: one cut below the basal line of the decoration may be dove-tailed; that above the line may be of the round (drilled) variety. *c* AD 120-200. C2107, G42, Phase 3.	Not illus
SR13	CG	Dr 31R	Two sherds, the cutting of a hole for repair of the cleat-type was attempted, probably unsuccessfully, below the junction of the wall and base. *c* AD 160-200. C2107, G42, Phase 3.	Not illus
SR14	CG	Dr 18/31R or 31R	Rim sherd, broken at a round rivet-hole which shows possible traces of lead. *c* AD 140-180. C2107, G42, Phase 3.	Not illus

SR15	CG	Dr 31R	One of the two pieces of worn footring is burnt and nicked (SG3). Next to the worn or scratched patch on the basal interior, the piece has broken at a repair-hole, probably of the cut, dove-tailed variety. *c* AD 160-200. C2110, G19, Phase 3.	Not illus
SR16	CG	Indeterminate form	Fragment, broken at a (cut) repair-hole. *c* AD 120/140-200. C2115, G202, Phase 3.	Not illus
SR17	CG	Dr 37	From the same bowl in the style of Pugnus, as sherds found in several other contexts in Phases 3, 6 and 0. A small fragment of ovolo here had broken at a battered, but apparently round, rivet-hole drilled through the plain band (SD22). *c* AD 135-165, but probably late in that range. C2116, G200, Phase 3.	Illus 4.59
SR18	CG	Dr 37	Four adjoining fragments of a decorated bowl (SD26). The base has broken, showing a round hole that had been drilled at the centre: some secondary function rather than repair-work may have been intended. *c* AD 120-160. C2117, G16, Phase 3.	Illus 4.59
SR19	CG	Dr 37	Two adjoining fragments of panelling possibly in the style of Docilis (SD27), which have broken at a rivet-hole apparently of the round variety. *c* AD 130-160. C2119, G200, Phase 3.	Not illus
SR20	CG	Dr 37	Fragment of decoration perhaps by Cettus (SD28), broken at a round rivet-hole drilled through the decoration. *c* AD 130-160. C2123, G16, Phase 3.	Illus 4.59
SR21	CG	Dr 18/31 or 18/31R	Adjoining rim and wall sherd broken at a repair-hole (probably dove-tailed). *c* AD 120-160. C2128, G19, Phase 3.	Not illus
SR22	CG	31R?	Wall sherd, broken apparently in an attempt to drill a rivet-hole *c* AD 160-200. C2134, G19, Phase 3.	Not illus
SR23	CG	Dr 37	Two adjoining pieces with an external basal leaf-stamp (SS37 and SD31). The footring shows evidence of considerable wear from use, and it has broken at two rivet-holes, apparently drilled, below the decoration. *c* AD 110-135. C2156, G200, Phase 3.	Not illus
SR24	SG	Dr 37	Decorated sherd (SD33), broken at three rivet-holes, probably all of the round variety which retain traces of the lead rivets. *c* AD 80-110. C1407, G134, Phase 4.	Not illus
SR25	CG	Dr 31R	Two slightly burnt sherds, broken at a dove-tailed repair-hole which retains traces of lead. *c* AD 160-200. C1124, G139, Phase 4.	Not illus
SR26	CG	Dr 33	Thick sherd showing evidence possibly of wear inside the lower wall and perhaps a failed attempt at cutting a repair-hole. *c* AD 160-200. C2145, G154, Phase 4.	Not illus
SR27	CG	Dr 18/31?	Two adjoining fragments of base and worn footring. The base within the footring has been neatly but incompletely drilled, presumably representing an unfinished attempt at repair-work. *c* AD 120-150. C2172, G800, Phase 4.	Not illus
SR28	CG	Dr 31	Two sherds adjoin to form an almost complete profile of the vessel. The footring is extremely worn from use and the dish has broken at two round rivet-holes drilled through the wall. *c* AD 150-200. C2240, G800, Phase 4.	Not illus
SR29	CG	Dr 33	A small fragment of basal stamp (SS24). The upper surface at the centre is extremely worn and an angular-hole has been cut through it for some purpose other than repair. Antonine. C2084, U/S, Phase 5.	Not illus
SR30	CG	Dr 31 or 31R	Fragment of rim, broken at two repair-holes of the cut variety which retain slight traces of lead. *c* AD 150-200. C2084, U/S, Phase 5.	Not illus
SR31	CG	Dr 18/31R or 31R	Fragment from the junction of wall and base, broken at a round rivet-hole with a possible trace of lead. *c* AD 150/160-200. C2084, U/S, Phase 5.	Not illus
SR32	CG	Dr 31R	Sherd from the junction of wall and base, broken at a dove-tailed repair-hole which retains traces of the lead rivet. *c* AD 160-200. C2084, U/S, Phase 5.	Not illus
SR33	CG	Dr 31R	Fragment from the junction of wall and base, broken at a repair-hole of uncertain variety (probably cut). *c* AD 160-200. C2084, U/S, Phase 5.	Not illus
SR34	CG	Dr 18/31 or 31	Sherd broken at a round rivet-hole drilled above the junction of wall and base. The interior of the junction displays worn bands. *c* AD 120-160/180. C2084, U/S, Phase 5.	Not illus
SR35	CG	Dr 37	Decorated vessel suggesting the work of the Sacer-Attianus group of potters (SD35). The vessel has broken at a repair-hole through the plain band, retaining traces of lead; its variety is unclear. *c* AD 125-150. C1002, G1001, Phase 6.	Not illus
SR36	CG	Dr 38	This sherd has broken at a rivet-hole of the round variety drilled through the upper wall. *c* AD 130/140-200. C1002, G1001, Phase 6.	Not illus
SR37	CG	Indeterminate form	Fragment broken at a rivet-hole of the cut variety. Probably produced *c* AD 160-200. C1002, G1001, Phase 6.	Not illus
SR38	CG	Dr 18/31R	Four slightly burnt, adjoining rim and wall sherds with a lead rivet which remains in the (round) hole. *c* AD 120-150. C2157, G1000, Phase 6.	Not illus

SR39	CG	Dr 37	Six rim and wall sherds, three adjoining, in the style of Cerialis ii-Cinnamus ii (SD36). One sherd has broken at a round rivet-hole drilled through the decoration. *c* AD 135-160. C2157, G1000, Phase 6.	Illus 4.59
SR40	CG	Dr 31R	Two slightly burnt, adjoining rim and wall sherds, now broken at a round rivet-hole which displays a possible trace of lead. *c* AD 160-200. C2157, G1000, Phase 6.	Not illus
SR41	CG	Dr 31R	Two adjoining rim sherds showing an abraded band; one sherd has broken at a round rivet-hole. *c* AD 160-200. C2225, G1001, Phase 6.	Not illus
SR42	CG	Dr 18/31	The almost complete profile of this dish lacks only the centre of the base; its footring is worn. The piece has broken at two possibly unsuccessful attempts at repair-holes. *c* AD 120-145. C2285, G1000, Phase 0.	Not illus

Re-working and re-use

SW1	SG	Dr 18R	A rim sherd which has been re-worked as a perforated disc or counter with a central hole. Diameter *c* 35 mm. Now in two halves, broken across the round hole. *c* AD 80-110. SF165, C1488, G902, Phase 1.	Illus 4.60
SW2	CG	Curle 15	Poorly slipped micaceous ware with burnt spots. There is a worn patch at the centre of the basal interior and the vessel was broken around the very worn footring, within which there is also a worn band below the base. It is possible that, if not merely representing wear from cleaning, this piece was re-used upside-down, perhaps as a mixing palette, after breakage. Produced in the range *c* AD 140/160-200. C2282, G118, Phase 2.	Not illus
SW3	CG	Dr 37	Wall sherd decorated in the style of Paternus v (II) (SD32), which appears to have been reworked roughly as a counter or disc. Diameter varies from 35 to 40 mm. *c* AD 150 -185. C1033, G24, Phase 4.	Illus 4.59
SW4	CG	Cup or bowl	There is a small trace of drilling, sawing or filing (which could, alternatively, represent the edge of a repair-hole). *c* AD 120-200 (if form Dr 27 then before *c* AD 160). C2120, G143, Phase 4.	Not illus
SW5	CG	Indeterminate form	Triangular fragment which shows evidence of sawing or filing. *c* AD 140-200. C2155, G161, Phase 4.	Not illus
SW6	CG	Indeterminate form	Three basal fragments whose internal surface was worn away in use; two sherds show one edge which appears to have been sawn down. Probably produced in the range *c* AD 160-200. C2084, U/S, Phase 5.	Not illus

Fabric W11, *Verulamium region whiteware*

W11.1	A1.1	Verulamium region lagena/amphora rim, later 1st-early 2nd century.	Illus 4.64

Fabric W21, *?Mancetter whiteware*

W21.1	B1.1	Segmental bowl with red painted arcading on the flange, perhaps a Mancetter product, in which case probably 2nd century.	Illus 4.65

Fabric W22

W22.1	B1.1	Flange rimmed bowl, probably 1st–2nd century.	Illus 4.66

Fabric W28

W28.1	F1.1	Ring-necked flagon with prominent upper bead, later 1st-mid-2nd century.	Illus 4.67
W28.2	F2.1	Flagon with an everted rim and broad lid-seating.	Not illus

Fabric W29

W29.1	JUG1.1	Jug(?) with an everted, outcurving rim.	Illus 4.68
W29.2	BOT1.1	Simple bottle rim.	Illus 4.68
W29.3	F1.1	Ring-necked flagon rim, probably later 1st-early 2nd century.	Illus 4.68

Appendix 4

Pottery form occurrence by phase

Jeremy Evans and Phil Mills

This is given in the form :Form x no of rims [Rim Equivalents]

Phase	Function	Fabric Code	Form Details
1	Beaker	F42	BK1.1x1[11], BK2.2x1[16]
1	Bowl	B11	B1.3x1[17]
1	Bowl	O23	B1.1x1[14]
1	Bowl	O231	B1.1x4[10,15,3,20], B3.2x1[16], B3.3x1[5], B4.2x1[26], B4.4x1[53], B6.1x3[11,11,8]
1	Bowl	O27	B1.1x1[11], B1.3x1[2], B2.1x1[15], B3.1x1[14]
1	Bowl	O36	B000x1[15], B1.0x1[12], B2.1x4[16,4,3,8], B4.1x3[10,3,4]
1	Bowl	R18	B1.1x10[14,13,15,14,21,27,19,12,13,13], B1.3x1[10], B1.4x3[17,11,12], B2.0x1[2], B2.1x2[3,10], B2.2x1[6]
1	Bowl	R32	B2.1x1[14], B3.1x2[8,32]
1	Bowl	R813	B1.1x5[7,6,10,16,23], B1.2x1[2], B1.3x2[7,9], B1.5x1[8], B2.1x1[7], B4.1x4[29,8,15,5]
1	Bowl	S10	B37x1[4]
1	Bowl	S20	B30x1[10], B37x1[3], B37x1[8], B37x1[9], B37x1[4]
1	Bowl	S21	B37x3[5,7,4]
1	Bowl	W21	B1.1x2[8,13]
1	Constricted-necked jar	O231	CJ1.1x1[30], CJ1.3x1[11], CJ3.2x1[4]
1	Constricted-necked jar	O27	CJ1.2x3[11,35,28], CJ4.1x1[7]
1	Constricted-necked jar	O36	CJ1.1x2[18,33], CJ1.2x3[40,7,10], CJ1.4x8[6,17,11,15,27,22,15,23], CJ2.1x1[24]
1	Constricted-necked jar	R18	CJ1.1x1[60], CUP1.1x1[11]
1	Cup	S20	C33x1[6], C33x1[8]
1	Dish	B11	D3.1x1[16], D4.0x1[3], D4.3x3[5,13,15]
1	Dish	O36	D1.1x2[32,10], D2.1x1[35]
1	Dish	O55	D1.1x2[6,8]
1	Dish	R18	D1.1x1[10], D2.1x1[1]
1	Dish	R32	D3.1x1[25]
1	Dish	R813	D000x1[5], D1.1x1[15], D2.1x2[5,3]
1	Dish	S10	D18/31x1[5], D18Rx1[3], D18Rx1[1]
1	Dish	S20	D18/31x1[55], D18/31/31x1[1], D18/31x1[4], D18/31x1[11]
1	Dish	S21	D18/31/18/31Rx1[1]
1	Flagon	W28	F1.1x1[100], F2.1x1[19]
1	Jar	B11	J1.1x1[15], J2.1x1[22], J2.2x3[14,12,10], J2.3x2[16,23]
1	Jar	G44	J1.1x15[15,6,6,23,7,7,15,6,10,11,19,10,4,16,10], J2.1x3[3,6,32], D2.1x1[5]
1	Jar	O231	J4.2x1[23]
1	Jar	O27	J000x1[10]
1	Jar	O36	J3.1x1[32], J5.1x1[3]
1	Jar	R18	J1.1x1[22], J1.2x1[11], J1.3x4[15,16,19,14], J1.4x2[15,15], J1.5x2[27,16], J1.6x1[5]

Phase	Function	Fabric Code	Form Details
1	Jar	R813	J000x1[8], J1.1x2[13,61], J1.2x1[14], J1.3x4[12,20,34,22], J1.4x3[12,7,13], J1.7x2[35,30], J3.1x2[11,11]
1	Lid	G47	L1.1x1[10]
1	Lid	R18	L1.1x1[13]
1	Lid	R813	L1.1x3[11,10,11]
1	Mortarium	M12	M1.1x1[13]
1	Mortarium	M21	M1.0x1[9], M1.1x1[32]
1	Storage Jar	O55	SJ1.1x2[16,6]
1	Tankard	O21	TA1.1x2[25,7]
1	Tankard	O23	TA1.1x1[5]
1	Tankard	O231	TA1.1x10[25,64,86,6,8,5,8,11,10,9]
1	Tankard	O24	TA1.1x1[5]
1	Tankard	O27	TA000x2[1,10], TA1.1x9[49,15,17,6,9,5,15,11,5], TA1.2x1[6]
1	Tankard	O29	TA1.1x1[8]
1	Tankard	O291	TA1.1x1[9]
1	Tankard	O35	TA1.1x4[4,10,10,16]
1	Tankard	O36	TA1.1x3[9,14,6], TA1.2x8[9,8,6,82,9,5,3,9], TA3.1x2[6,11]
1	Tankard	O55	TA000x1[1], TA1.1x2[15,15]
1	Wide-mouthed jar	O23	WMJ000x1[11], WMJ1.1x1[5]
1	Wide-mouthed jar	O231	WMJ1.1x1[4], WMJ1.3x1[13], WMJ3.1x1[29]
1	Wide-mouthed jar	O27	WMJ1.2x2[6,7], WMJ2.1x1[30]
1	Wide-mouthed jar	O36	WMJ000x1[2], WMJ1.0x1[7], WMJ1.1x7[8,19,4,7,5,15,10], WMJ1.2x7[34,3,18,13,97,21,4], WMJ3.1x3[30,8,6]
1	Wide-mouthed jar	O55	WMJ000x1[6], WMJ1.0x1[2], WMJ1.1x1[9], WMJ1.2x2[7,17]
2	Beaker	F12	BK1.1x1[5]
2	Beaker	F42	BK1.1x1[16]
2	Beaker	R813	BK1.1x1[16], BK2.1x1[15]
2	Bowl	B11	B1.1x2[7,15], B1.2x1[5], B1.3x1[5], B2.1x1[5], B3.0x1[5]
2	Bowl	O231	B1.1x1[14], B3.3x2[7,7], B4.1x4[10,16,16,3], B5.2x2[9,4], B6.1x3[13,3,3]
2	Bowl	O27	B3.1x2[10,5], B4.2x1[3], B5.1x3[6,3,16], B5.3x1[8]
2	Bowl	O36	B000x1[2], B1.1x1[6], B1.3x2[5,7], B1.4x1[2], B2.1x1[4], B3.1x2[26,14], B3.2x3[10,6,12], B8.1x1[12]
2	Bowl	R18	B000x2[2,6], B1.0x2[6,5], B1.1x2[15,11], B1.2x2[10,17], B1.3x3[16,22,6], B2.1x4[35,1,11,5]
2	Bowl	R32	B1.1x2[11,5], B2.1x2[8,3], B3.1x1[4]
2	Bowl	R813	B000x1[6], B1.1x17[10,4,9,22,15,8,7,7,4,9,8,6,6,13,6,8,4], B1.2x2[32,14], B1.3x4[6,6,8,5], B1.4x1[4], B1.6x1[8], B3.1x1[13], B4.1x19[6,3,52,13,4,7,6,5,8,10,25,3,5,9,10,8,12,15,12], B4.2x2[10,5], B5.1x1[8]
2	Bowl	S10	B37x2[6,8], B37x1[7]
2	Bowl	S20	B31x2[18,6], B31x1[2], B37x1[3], B37x1[2], B37x1[4], B37x1[6], B38x1[6]
2	Bowl	S21	B37x1[4], B37x2[1,5], B37x1[5]
2	Constricted-necked jar	O231	CJ1.1x2[23,20], CJ1.3x2[15,5], CJ3.1x1[45]
2	Constricted-necked jar	O27	CJ000x3[5,7,3], CJ1.2x2[16,11], CJ1.3x2[10,6], CJ2.1x2[20,12]
2	Constricted-necked jar	O29	CJ000x1[2], CJ1.1x1[23], CJ2.2x1[8]
2	Constricted-necked jar	O36	CJ000x2[9,6], CJ1.1x5[25,9,16,13,14], CJ1.2x9[52,14,15,11,8,26,7,19,10], CJ1.3x3[10,25,25], CJ1.4x13[12,19,21,30,51,17,12,19,7,29,11,10,100], CJ4.2x1[11]

Phase	Function	Fabric Code	Form Details
2	Constricted-necked jar	R813	CJ1.1x1[11], CJ2.1x1[12]
2	Cup	R813	C1.1x1[9]
2	Cup	S20	C27x1[9], C27x1[5], C33x1[5], C33x1[9], C33x2[7,12]
2	Cup	S21	C33x1[18]
2	Dish	B11	D1.1x1[7], D2.1x6[6,6,17,9,4,7], D3.1x3[5,3,2], D4.0x1[6], D4.1x3[4,9,9], D4.2x1[6], D4.3x1[15]
2	Dish	F91	D1.1x1[7]
2	Dish	G44	D1.1x2[6,14]
2	Dish	O231	D1.1x1[7], D2.1x2[11,6]
2	Dish	O27	D000x1[2]
2	Dish	O36	D1.1x3[25,21,2], D1.2x1[16], D2.1x1[40], D3.1x1[4]
2	Dish	R32	D2.1x1[4]
2	Dish	S10	D18/31/31x1[8], D18Rx1[10]
2	Dish	S20	D000x1[6], D18/31x2[13,3], D18/31/31x1[1], D18/31/31x1[14], D18/31x1[20], D18/31Rx1[5], D18/31R/31x1[6], D18/31R/31Rx2[7,3], D18/31R/31Rx1[4], D18/31Rx1[8], D36x1[2], DCU23x1[6]
2	Dish	S21	D18/31x1[16]
2	Flagon	O231	F3.1x1[28]
2	Flagon	O36	F1.1x1[11]
2	Flagon	Q14	F1.1x1[11]
2	Jar	B11	J1.1x5[9,13,7,6,12], J2.1x2[10,15], J2.2x10[11,7,4,6,11,13,5,3,43,15], J2.3x6[13,13,23,10,10,8], J2.4x1[6], J3.1x5[14,2,2,6,18], J3.2x1[12], J3.3x1[7]
2	Jar	G44	J1.1x16[8,13,15,20,3,2,13,7,6,7,12,5,3,3,7,7], J1.2x2[3,4], J2.1x4[17,3,6,4], D2.1x5[7,11,13,13,6]
2	Jar	G46	J1.2x2[5,10]
2	Jar	O231	J1.0x2[15,7], J1.1x1[7], J2.1x1[9], J3.1x1[9], J3.2x1[10], J3.3x1[7], J5.1x1[20],
2	Jar	O27	J000x2[4,6], J1.3x1[5]
2	Jar	O29	J000x1[3], J1.1x1[5]
2	Jar	O36	J000x1[7], J5.1x1[7], J6.1x1[6]
2	Jar	R01	J2.1x1[32]
2	Jar	R18	J000x5[11,5,5,6,3], J1.1x9[8,13,10,10,33,26,10,11,31], J1.2x8[23,8,11,20,3,12,10,6], J1.3x1[24]
2	Jar	R32	J1.1x1[12], J2.0x1[10], J2.1x5[49,5,7,11,8], J2.2x2[14,25], J2.3x2[12,6], J2.4x1[11], J2.5x2[5,5], J3.1x1[13]
2	Jar	R813	J000x6[7,8,5,7,6,8], J1.1x1[28], J1.2x4[8,9,4,13], J1.3x14[8,14,16,16,9,22,21,27,16,8,31,10,8,8], J1.4x10[7,4,4,10,10,14,13,19,13,11], J1.5x3[9,33,20], J1.6x2[23,23], J3.0x1[12], J3.1x1[7], J3.3x1[6], J4.1x2[16,10]
2	Jug	O231	JUG1.1x1[8]
2	Jug	O24	JUG1.1x1[9]
2	Jug	O27	JUG1.1x1[39]
2	Jug	R32	JUG1.1x1[45]
2	Jug	R813	JUG1.1x1[10]
2	Jug	W29	JUG1.1x1[12]
2	Lagena	O36	LAG1.1x1[23]
2	Lagena	R813	LAG1.1x1[100]
2	Lid	G47	L1.1x1[11]
2	Lid	R18	L1.1x1[10], L1.2x1[8]
2	Mortarium	M00	M000x1[3]

Phase	Function	Fabric Code	Form Details
2	Mortarium	M21	M000x1[4], M1.1x1[6]
2	Mortarium	M22	M1.1x2[17,20], M2.0x1[5], M2.2x1[5]
2	Mortarium	M23	M1.1x1[5]
2	Mortarium	M45	M000x1[6], M1.0x1[3], M1.1x1[8], M1.2x1[8]
2	Other	G47	O1.2x1[6]
2	Other	O27	O1.2x1[5]
2	Storage Jar	G47	SJ000x1[6], SJ1.1x2[31,6], SJ1.2x2[6,12]
2	Storage Jar	O36	SJ2.1x2[74,3]
2	Tankard	O231	TA000x2[1,3], TA1.1x11[6,6,11,10,24,7,20,9,9,8,5], TA1.3x3[4,6,13], TA2.1x1[8]
2	Tankard	O27	TA1.1x5[16,9,46,16,4], TA1.3x2[3,8]
2	Tankard	O29	TA000x1[5]
2	Tankard	O291	TA1.1x2[4,9]
2	Tankard	O36	TA000x4[2,2,7,7], TA1.0x1[5], TA1.1x7[59,7,15,16,6,27,4], TA1.2x10[22,15,10,14,6,6,6,7,10,3], TA2.1x1[3], TA3.1x1[22]
2	Tankard	R813	TA1.1x1[4]
2	Wide-mouthed jar	O21	WMJ1.1x1[9], WMJ1.2x1[5]
2	Wide-mouthed jar	O231	WMJ000x1[4], WMJ1.1x2[25,2], WMJ1.2x1[3], WMJ1.3x2[5,10], WMJ3.1x1[4]
2	Wide-mouthed jar	O24	WMJ1.2x1[9]
2	Wide-mouthed jar	O27	WMJ000x1[5], WMJ1.1x1[27], WMJ1.2x4[2,6,6,7], WMJ1.3x3[4,8,4], WMJ1.4x1[11]
2	Wide-mouthed jar	O291	WMJ1.1x1[19]
2	Wide-mouthed jar	O36	WMJ000x1[2], WMJ1.0x1[7], WMJ1.1x10[7,6,10,7,8,9,98,8,10,10], WMJ1.2x8[10,3,6,7,7,19,13,2], WMJ1.4x1[15], WMJ1.5x2[9,9], WMJ1.6x1[9], WMJ1.8x1[5], WMJ4.1x1[9]
2	Wide-mouthed jar	O55	WMJ1.3x1[7], WMJ1.4x2[5,22]
3	Amphora	A21	A1.1x2[100,16]
3	Amphora	W11	A1.1x1[21]
3	Beaker	F32	BK1.1x1[12]
3	Beaker	F42	BK1.1x1[6], BK2.1x1[10], BK2.2x3[5,6,2]
3	Beaker	F51	BK1.1x1[8]
3	Beaker	O231	BK000x1[4], BK1.1x2[17,8]
3	Beaker	R813	BK000x1[8]
3	Bottle	W29	BOT1.1x1[40]
3	Bowl	B11	B1.0x1[6], B1.1x3[1,2,12], B1.2x1[9], B2.1x9[6,6,7,5,4,6,4,5,11], B3.0x1[3], B3.1x3[6,2,10]
3	Bowl	F51	B2.1x1[4]
3	Bowl	G46	B2.1x3[9,12,7]
3	Bowl	O23	B2.1x2[3,6], B3.1x1[2]
3	Bowl	O231	B000x4[9,7,3,5], B1.1x7[1,9,11,20,7,8,8], B1.2x2[5,5], B2.1x1[6], B3.0x1[13], B3.1x3[2,6,4], B3.2x15[3,6,9,23,13,7,6,14,9,16,7,6,13,7,19], B3.4x6[12,4,4,6,7,8], B3.5x3[10,6,6], B4.0x2[5,6], B4.1x8[4,1,3,5,3,2,12,7], B4.2x2[5,20], B4.3x5[6,10,25,4,5], B4.4x1[10], B4.5x1[8], B4.6x1[5], B5.1x16[9,7,7,11,4,8,2,5,9,5,5,3,3,8,5,2], B5.2x11[9,5,6,18,6,6,6,8,4,2,2], B5.3x1[7], B6.1x2[3,23]
3	Bowl	O24	B1.1x1[8], B2.1x1[11]
3	Bowl	O27	B000x1[1], B1.1x10[5,11,6,14,12,6,8,14,13,7], B1.2x2[2,6], B2.1x1[7], B3.1x8[7,4,5,1,5,4,6,4], B3.2x3[8,10,8], B4.0x4[2,4,3,6], B4.1x6[4,2,6,11,8,4], B4.2x7[5,1,19,6,10,9,7], B4.3x5[12,8,6,11,8], B4.4x5[2,9,3,5,10], B5.0x3[3,7,3], B5.1x19[6,6,3,7,7,6,8,5,6,9,10,4,6,7,4,5,6,7,5], B5.2x5[6,7,19,11,3], B5.4x12[6,6,7,5,3,6,7,13,4,5,6,2]
3	Bowl	O29	B000x1[3]
3	Bowl	O291	B1.1x2[6,1]

Phase	Function	Fabric Code	Form Details
3	Bowl	O36	B000x1[4], B1.0x4[2,8,3,3], B1.1x8[47,2,5,11,5,2,3,3], B1.2x1[5], B1.3x5[4,2,25,2,9], B1.4x4[8,9,4,7], B1.5x2[2,15], B1.6x1[8], B2.0x1[3], B2.1x1[13], B2.2x8[3,2,3,10,3,2,11,11], B2.3x11[4,4,3,6,2,3,6,5,7,2,6], B2.4x11[7,7,3,4,10,5,8,8,6,2,5], B2.5x8[3,15,9,5,4,8,7,4], B3.1x3[7,6,17], B3.2x2[7,25], B4.0x1[3], B4.1x2[6,1], B5.1x5[7,6,5,6,11], B6.1x2[10,2], B6.2x3[1,8,7], B9.1x2[2,8]
3	Bowl	O55	B000x2[9,5], B1.1x3[5,3,12], B1.2x1[5], B1.3x1[4]
3	Bowl	Q151	B1.1x1[15]
3	Bowl	R01	B1.1x1[3]
3	Bowl	R18	B1.1x1[5], B3.1x1[6]
3	Bowl	R32	B000x2[4,6], B2.1x2[3,2], B3.1x1[7]
3	Bowl	R813	B000x1[4], B1.1x13[4,4,10,6,10,9,5,4,8,5,2,2,11], B1.2x1[9], B4.1x15[9,11,6,7,4,13,8,17,7,4,7,3,4,6,11], B5.2x1[9], B6.1x1[6]
3	Bowl	S10	B37x1[12]
3	Bowl	S20	B000x2[2,6], B000x2[5,3], B30x3[9,2,13], B30/37x1[4], B30/37x1[1], B30/37x1[4], B31x13[10,2,4,3,2,5,6,3,3,7,8,5,10], B31/31Rx11[2,6,2,6,3,5,2,2,2,8,4], B31x2[4,6], B31x2[7,2], B31Rx15[2,4,3,1,5,4,8,2,2,5,2,2,7,2,3], B37x7[5,7,3,9,6,5,10], B37/38x1[1], B37x4[8,5,9,6], B37x1[4], B37x2[5,3], B37x1[7], B37x2[6,6], B37x10[4,2,5,4,2,5,4,7,6,3], B37x4[6,2,6,1], B37x1[20], B38x3[5,2,7], B38x1[9], B38x4[5,4,3,5], B81x2[6,6]
3	Bowl	S21	B37x2[12,6], B37x1[5]
3	Bowl	S30	B31Rx1[2]
3	Bowl	W22	B000x1[6]
3	Constricted-necked jar	O23	CJ1.1x1[11]
3	Constricted-necked jar	O231	CJ000x3[6,4,9], CJ1.0x1[10], CJ1.2x2[11,11], CJ1.3x5[14,3,8,12,10], CJ2.1x4[15,14,19,10], CJ2.2x1[28], CJ3.1x15[12,11,12,28,8,11,21,13,10,5,39,11,15,13,17], CJ3.2x6[13,9,6,9,12,14], CJ3.3x2[38,11], CJ3.4x1[6]
3	Constricted-necked jar	O27	CJ000x3[6,6,7], CJ1.1x7[9,2,6,6,4,6,8], CJ1.2x5[23,29,37,4,14], CJ1.3x38[14,13,10,17,10,5,10,13,10,8,13,12,20,17,18,11,10,14,37,30,5,11,20,8,1,9,9,12,6,20,22,9,5,10,8,7,25,10], CJ2.1x2[8,4], CJ4.2x3[8,5,30]
3	Constricted-necked jar	O29	CJ1.1x1[6], CJ2.0x1[6], CJ2.1x1[15]
3	Constricted-necked jar	O291	CJ000x1[17]
3	Constricted-necked jar	O36	CJ000x6[9,6,6,5,11,11], CJ1.1x8[15,11,5,9,7,3,10,19], CJ1.2x11[11,4,15,14,15,6,5,4,6,15,11], CJ1.3x3[12,10,13], CJ1.4x22[15,8,6,22,8,11,5,10,14,11,9,5,27,6,13,8,10,22,7,5,3,3], CJ1.5x15[10,10,6,10,10,15,18,7,7,4,13,10,7,31,6], CJ2.1x3[10,10,20], CJ4.1x1[38]
3	Constricted-necked jar	R32	CJ1.1x1[11]
3	Constricted-necked jar	R813	CJ1.1x1[21]
3	Cup	R813	C1.1x1[15]
3	Cup	S20	C33x3[5,9,6], C33x2[10,9], C33x3[5,5,5], C33x1[11], C33x1[10], C33x2[6,6], C33x9[6,13,4,5,17,20,6,6,4], C33x7[13,1,3,7,7,3,22]
3	Dish	B11	D2.1x8[3,2,7,4,1,5,2,7], D2.2x8[4,5,3,3,2,11,2,3], D3.1x1[5], D4.2x5[7,7,6,4,1], D4.3x2[7,6], D4.4x5[4,8,4,13,7]
3	Dish	G44	D1.1x1[7]
3	Dish	G47	D1.1x2[4,2]
3	Dish	O231	D1.2x2[4,9], D2.1x2[12,29]
3	Dish	O36	D1.1x2[4,4], D1.2x1[5]
3	Dish	O55	D1.1x1[4]
3	Dish	R32	D1.1x1[11]
3	Dish	R813	D1.1x1[4]

Phase	Function	Fabric Code	Form Details
3	Dish	S20	D000x2[2,2], D000ax1[4], D000bx1[5], D18/31x2[4,4], D18/31/18/31Rx4[4,5,2,4], D18/31/18/31Rx1[4], D18/31/31x1[5], D18/31/31x3[3,7,5], D18/31x2[4,15], D18/31Rx6[6,3,5,2,2,6], D18/31R/31Rx2[2,4], D18/31R/31Rx2[6,4], D18/31R/31Rx3[6,10,6], D18/31R/31Rx4[3,1,4,3], D18/31R/31Rx3[4,1,7], D18/31Rx1[3], D18/31Rx2[2,4], D31x1[4], D36x2[4,7], D36x2[3,4], D79x2[5,3], DCU23x2[12,14]
3	Dish	S21	D000x1[1], D18/31x1[5]
3	Dish	S30	D32x1[2]
3	Flagon	O231	F1.1x1[10], F2.1x1[15], F3.1x2[11,38], F3.2x2[16,17]
3	Flagon	O36	F1.1x1[8]
3	Flagon	O81	F1.1x1[33]
3	Flagon	Q151	F1.1x2[28,100], F1.2x1[6]
3	Flagon	W29	F1.1x1[14]
3	Jar	B11	J000x2[7,1], J1.1x1[11], J1.2x1[6], J2.1x2[6,3], J2.2x8[9,7,5,16,6,12,7,14], J2.3x2[6,6], J2.4x2[7,12], J2.5x1[13], J3.0x2[5,6], J3.1x11[7,3,7,14,6,7,3,5,7,13,18], J3.2x3[5,5,4], J3.3x1[4]
3	Jar	F52	J1.1x1[4]
3	Jar	G44	J000x2[6,4], J1.1x6[8,6,11,5,6,4], J1.2x2[6,2], J3.0x1[3], J3.1x1[12], J4.1x1[11], J5.1x1[11], J6.1x1[6]
3	Jar	G46	J000x3[3,6,1], J1.1x5[6,10,7,10,11], J1.2x9[7,19,6,11,8,10,5,4,4], J2.1x3[8,6,13]
3	Jar	G47	J1.1x11[11,6,5,5,3,3,5,10,6,10,7]
3	Jar	O21	J1.1x1[13]
3	Jar	O23	J1.1x1[10]
3	Jar	O231	J000x8[3,3,3,4,2,5,3,3], J1.1x3[12,8,6], J2.1x1[6], J3.0x2[5,5], J3.3x4[6,8,3,5], J4.1x1[12], J5.1x1[10]
3	Jar	O27	J000x9[6,7,2,3,4,8,5,1,1], J1.1x2[15,6], J1.2x2[6,17], J1.4x2[8,11], J2.1x1[16]
3	Jar	O36	J000x7[3,4,5,7,5,2,3], J1.1x2[5,4], J2.1x2[11,5], J4.1x1[12], J5.0x3[6,8,8], J5.1x4[7,6,13,5]
3	Jar	R01	J1.1x1[11], J2.1x1[6]
3	Jar	R32	J000x1[7], J2.1x2[10,15], J2.2x3[12,8,8], J2.4x1[5]
3	Jar	R813	J000x4[2,4,6,4], J1.0x3[5,7,6], J1.1x1[8], J1.2x3[11,12,7], J1.3x1[8], J1.4x2[13,10], J1.5x1[6], J1.8x1[5], B7.1x1[5]
3	Jug	O231	JUG1.1x2[18,17]
3	Jug	O27	JUG1.2x4[10,9,18,7]
3	Jug	O36	JUG1.1x5[7,14,20,19,15]
3	Lid	G44	L1.1x2[6,6], L1.2x2[5,12]
3	Lid	G46	L1.1x1[13]
3	Lid	G47	L1.1x6[16,3,8,4,11,6]
3	Lid	O291	L000x1[5]
3	Mortarium	M21	M000x1[4]
3	Mortarium	M22	M000x3[13,3,7], M1.0x13[7,7,4,6,7,1,1,6,8,1,4,10,5], M1.1x5[16,11,19,11,25], M1.2x7[10,15,32,7,14,1,10], M1.3x3[5,2,12], M1.4x2[4,15], M1.5x1[4], M2.0x1[5], M2.2x7[10,3,9,7,7,9,7], M2.3x1[10], M3.1x2[18,6], M4.0x2[4,6], M4.1x3[4,9,5]
3	Mortarium	M23	M000x3[6,13,19], M1.1x2[7,11], M2.1x1[8]
3	Mortarium	M37	M000x5[6,6,8,3,3], M1.0x1[3], M1.1x2[10,2], M2.1x1[6]
3	Mortarium	M45	M000x3[1,6,8]
3	Mortarium	S20	M43x1[7], M45x1[4]
3	Other	G47	O1.1x6[3,3,3,5,3,3], O1.2x1[10], O2.1x1[8]
3	Other	O231	O1.1x1[9]
3	Other	O36	O1.1x1[5]
3	Storage Jar	G44	SJ1.1x4[5,9,4,3]

Phase	Function	Fabric Code	Form Details
3	Storage Jar	G46	SJ1.1x1[8]
3	Storage Jar	G47	SJ000x2[5,5], SJ1.1x29[6,9,6,1,4,10,16,9,17,5,14,4,9,9,6,5,8,18,8,5,2,5,4,4,3,4,1,6,9], SJ1.2x9[5,20,8,10,8,8,4,3,8], SJ2.1x2[11,7]
3	Storage Jar	O231	SJ1.1x6[49,15,7,12,20,11]
3	Storage Jar	O27	SJ1.1x1[7], SJ2.1x16[15,25,18,6,18,6,18,16,5,6,6,8,9,4,17,9]
3	Storage Jar	O36	SJ2.1x11[33,5,11,22,14,35,16,8,4,10,11], SJ2.2x2[5,6], SJ3.1x1[5], SJ3.2x1[4]
3	Tankard	O21	TA1.1x1[9]
3	Tankard	O23	TA1.0x1[2]
3	Tankard	O231	TA000x6[5,3,3,5,3,4], TA1.1x22[26,8,3,4,6,8,6,2,5,16,6,6,11,5,5,8,8,19,4,13,2,9], TA2.1x 46[7,12,7,9,4,7,6,7,7,3,11,3,5,7,10,6,4,2,12,5,5,6,9,5,6,4,7,7,8,5,6,3,10,7,12,4,3,3,8,3,7,5,5,7, 9,7], TA2.2x3[5,3,13]
3	Tankard	O24	TA000x1[3]
3	Tankard	O27	TA000x5[6,3,4,1,1], TA1.0x1[1], TA1.1x13[5,12,22,5,5,6,11,8,10,6,3,3,5], TA1.2x4[5,15,2,6], TA1.3x54[4,9,6,8,8,4,4,12,10,6,8,6,14,5,7,12,11,5,7,6,2,5,4,6,37,9,8,6,4,3,4,4,16,3,5,8,8,4,8, 4,8,3,6,9,10,5,6,8,6,8,5,16,4,5], TA1.4x3[5,5,3]
3	Tankard	O29	TA1.1x1[7]
3	Tankard	O291	TA1.1x3[6,8,4], TA2.1x1[2]
3	Tankard	O36	TA000x2[9,2], TA1.0x2[5,6], TA1.1x8[4,19,6,7,5,6,3,10], TA1.2x14[11,15,5,5,6,8,3,5,3,11,3,5,14], TA2. 1x25[6,7,3,10,10,9,2,3,8,3,7,2,10,1,7,14,5,3,30,4,4,7,5,5,5], TA2.2x1[10], TA2.3x2[7,8]
3	Wide-mouthed jar	O23	WMJ000x1[1]
3	Wide-mouthed jar	O231	WMJ000x8[3,3,4,8,4,4,2,3], WMJ1.1x46[5,7,4,3,2,7,6,3,9,4,3,7,3,4,6,5,8,5,3,6,10,4,6,4,4,9, 5,6,10,13,11,11,6,10,2,2,4,3,4,3,9,2,2,7,6,3], WMJ1.2x18[15,6,5,6,4,9,5,5,7,6,6,11,4,14,3,3, 7,2], WMJ1.3x51[7,10,5,11,7,3,4,5,6,5,9,13,6,24,6,7,6,3,4,21,7,14,4,13,10,5,8,6,7,4,7,2,4,6, 2,6,9,6,3,5,7,2,5,10,10,12,8,6,2,13,7], WMJ2.1x3[36,5,7], WMJ3.1x3[6,3,2], B9.1x1[7]
3	Wide-mouthed jar	O27	WMJ000x13[3,1,2,1,5,2,4,4,1,7,5,2,2], WMJ1.0x1[1], WMJ1.1x5[18,2,11,7,5], WMJ1. 2x49[15,6,5,6,9,4,5,19,1,17,4,3,4,5,5,15,6,7,10,6,5,13,4,2,2,6,6,6,6,3,9,3,3,3,3,9,6,11,14,5,6,2, 2,5,5,5,4,50,21], WMJ1.3x64[3,6,3,9,10,7,5,6,6,3,4,19,4,6,3,15,6,9,3,3,2,5,10,5,8,6,9,2,9,10, 2,3,16,4,15,9,5,4,4,4,6,4,2,2,6,6,2,7,12,3,4,6,6,5,6,9,4,4,2,6,8,2,9,14], WMJ1.4x3[13,5,2], WMJ1.5x2[15,6]
3	Wide-mouthed jar	O29	WMJ1.1x1[3]
3	Wide-mouthed jar	O291	WMJ000x2[7,2], WMJ1.1x3[7,5,5], WMJ1.2x2[8,3]
3	Wide-mouthed jar	O36	WMJ000x26[3,5,2,5,3,2,2,2,3,3,3,2,5,1,2,2,3,3,2,3,4,3,3,3,2,4], WMJ1.0x2[4,8], WMJ1. 1x54[5,6,6,4,6,8,3,7,4,2,3,7,10,6,11,9,2,3,6,5,2,12,9,3,4,5,6,3,4,3,4,5,5,8,2,17,7,5,5,12,4,9,2 ,2,5,5,6,1,6,6,3,1,3,9], WMJ1.2x18[3,6,4,4,4,2,3,3,3,6,4,6,7,3,7,18,4,4], WMJ1.3x3[9,13,4], WMJ1.4x4[4,5,5,7], WMJ1.5x3[3,5,3], WMJ1.6x4[4,6,7,4], WMJ1.8x1[7], WMJ2. 1x38[22,10,2,11,5,17,7,6,4,3,7,4,7,2,2,4,6,7,4,7,3,1,6,6,1,4,4,4,6,5,5,5,6,9,8,6,38,2], WMJ3.1x2[4,4], WMJ4.1x1[6]
3	Wide-mouthed jar	R32	WMJ1.0x1[2]
4	Beaker	F12	BK1.1x1[8]
4	Beaker	F42	BK1.1x1[9]
4	Beaker	O231	BK000x1[5],
4	Bowl	B11	B1.1x3[11,8,6], B2.1x3[19,3,6], B3.1x2[3,5]
4	Bowl	F51	B1.1x3[2,3,6], B2.1x1[12]
4	Bowl	F52	B1.1x1[5]
4	Bowl	G46	B1.1x1[4]
4	Bowl	O231	B000x2[5,4], B1.1x2[6,15], B2.1x1[5], B3.0x1[3], B3.2x1[3], B4.1x4[18,14,17,5], B4.2x1[26], B4.3x1[13], B5.1x8[11,15,11,14,7,19,12,4], B5.2x1[4], B7.1x2[14,17]
4	Bowl	O24	B000x1[1],
4	Bowl	O27	B000x1[3], B1.1x1[1], B2.1x1[7], B3.1x1[4], B4.1x1[5], B4.2x1[3], B4.3x1[25], B5.2x2[14,4]
4	Bowl	O36	B1.0x1[8], B2.0x1[4], B2.1x1[3], B2.3x4[8,2,10,2], B3.1x1[3], B6.2x1[3], B7.1x1[33]

Phase	Function	Fabric Code	Form Details
4	Bowl	R32	B3.1x1[3]
4	Bowl	R341	B1.1x1[9]
4	Bowl	R813	B1.0x3[5,7,5], B1.1x6[6,5,7,5,8,8], B4.1x6[7,3,12,4,10,17]
4	Bowl	S10	B37x1[5]
4	Bowl	S20	B/D000x1[1], B000x1[1], B30x1[3], B31x6[5,2,3,3,2,5], B31/31Rx2[2,5], B31/31Rx2[4,1], B31x2[5,16], B31Rx2[5,1], B37x2[2,7], B37x1[3], B37x1[7], B37x1[2], B37x1[3], B37x1[10], B37x1[14], B37x1[5], B37x1[5], B38x1[8]
4	Constricted-necked jar	O231	CJ000x1[4], CJ1.1x1[30], CJ1.2x1[15], CJ1.3x3[40,14,13], CJ2.1x1[8], CJ3.1x1[10], CJ3.3x1[12]
4	Constricted-necked jar	O27	CJ000x1[3], CJ1.1x5[11,9,15,7,12], CJ1.2x3[12,10,15], CJ1.3x3[20,8,11]
4	Constricted-necked jar	O29	CJ1.1x2[11,15], CJ2.1x1[13]
4	Constricted-necked jar	O291	CJ000x1[4], CJ1.1x1[17]
4	Constricted-necked jar	O36	CJ1.1x1[16], CJ1.2x2[8,6], CJ1.3x1[6], CJ1.4x1[9], CJ1.5x2[11,15], CJ2.1x1[11], CJ4.1x1[15]
4	Cup	S20	C27x1[6], C33x1[1], C33x3[5,7,13], C33x1[2]
4	Dish	B11	D1.1x1[8], D2.1x7[6,3,3,5,6,7,5], D2.2x3[7,4,11], D3.1x1[3], D4.1x1[6], D4.2x6[6,13,5,4,12,3], D4.3x1[6]
4	Dish	O23	D1.1x1[7]
4	Dish	O231	D1.2x1[5]
4	Dish	O36	D1.1x1[5]
4	Dish	R813	D1.1x2[2,3]
4	Dish	S20	D000x2[5,1], D18/31Rx2[6,3], D18/31R/31Rx3[5,3,5], D18/31R/31Rx2[4,10], D18/31R/31Rx3[5,3,8], D79x2[18,1]
4	Dish	S21	D18/31Rx1[8]
4	Flagon	O36	F1.1x1[6], F2.1x1[10]
4	Flagon	Q151	F2.1x1[100]
4	Jar	B11	J1.3x1[11], J2.1x1[16], J2.2x5[7,19,6,10,10], J2.3x2[6,4], J3.0x2[3,4], J3.1x4[7,23,19,10], J3.2x5[11,7,8,10,10], J3.3x1[26]
4	Jar	G44	J1.1x1[3], J2.1x1[13], J3.1x1[13]
4	Jar	G46	J1.1x2[19,15], J1.2x8[16,6,15,12,8,3,11,11]
4	Jar	G47	J1.1x1[22]
4	Jar	O231	J1.1x2[7,15], J2.1x2[12,8], J3.0x1[8]
4	Jar	O27	J000x1[2]
4	Jar	O36	J2.1x1[16], J5.0x1[6]
4	Jar	R18	J000x2[6,6], J1.1x2[10,9]
4	Jar	R32	J2.2x1[9]
4	Jar	R41	J000x1[5], J1.1x2[9,15]
4	Jar	R813	J000x2[7,11], J1.1x3[6,11,16], J1.4x4[13,13,6,15], J3.2x1[11]
4	Jug	O231	JUG2.1x1[14], JUG3.1x1[48]
4	Lid	G44	L1.1x2[7,12], L1.2x1[6]
4	Lid	R341	L1.1x1[3]
4	Mortarium	M22	M1.1x1[11], M1.2x1[3], M2.0x1[2], M2.1x2[5,5], M2.2x1[20], M4.1x1[11]
4	Mortarium	M45	M000x1[5]
4	Other	G47	O1.1x3[6,4,4]
4	Other	O231	O1.1x2[17,5]
4	Other	O27	O000x2[7,3], O1.1x1[4], O2.1x1[3]

Phase	Function	Fabric Code	Form Details
4	Storage Jar	G47	SJ1.1x3[23,2,8], SJ1.2x1[3], SJ2.1x1[6]
4	Storage Jar	O231	SJ1.1x1[10]
4	Storage Jar	O27	SJ1.1x1[12], SJ2.1x2[14,10]
4	Storage Jar	O36	SJ1.1x1[14], SJ2.1x1[17]
4	Tankard	O231	TA000x1[5], TA1.1x9[11,6,12,50,6,11,8,10,4], TA1.2x2[2,14], TA2.1x12[8,7,9,17,6,11,6,3,2,6,5,9]
4	Tankard	O24	TA1.1x1[5]
4	Tankard	O27	TA000x1[2], TA1.1x4[4,9,7,50], TA1.3x6[7,4,8,5,6,14]
4	Tankard	O29	TA1.1x1[4]
4	Tankard	O291	TA1.1x1[18]
4	Tankard	O36	TA1.1x1[11], TA1.2x3[14,6,4], TA2.1x4[17,7,11,2], TA2.2x1[3], TA2.3x1[27]
4	Wide-mouthed jar	O21	WMJ000x1[3]
4	Wide-mouthed jar	O231	WMJ000x1[3], WMJ1.1x7[7,6,6,10,3,6,22], WMJ1.2x3[7,6,9], WMJ1.3x7[15,3,4,4,6,2,7], WMJ2.1x1[6], WMJ3.1x1[4]
4	Wide-mouthed jar	O24	WMJ1.1x1[13]
4	Wide-mouthed jar	O27	WMJ1.1x3[3,13,3], WMJ1.2x11[6,6,6,5,6,26,7,1,12,19,12], WMJ1.3x5[7,10,8,6,3]
4	Wide-mouthed jar	O29	WMJ000x1[4]
4	Wide-mouthed jar	O291	WMJ1.2x2[5,5]
4	Wide-mouthed jar	O36	WMJ000x2[8,3], WMJ1.0x1[4], WMJ1.1x8[11,5,14,8,6,6,2,10], WMJ1.2x3[8,6,4], WMJ2.1x2[8,9], WMJ3.1x1[5]
4	Wide-mouthed jar	O55	WMJ1.1x1[18]
4	Wide-mouthed jar	R813	WMJ1.1x1[5]

Appendix 5

Occurrence of samian vessels across contexts

Margaret Ward

A list follows of those samian vessels of which sherds were found scattered across different contexts: the sherds belong to the same vessels, but not all are joins. All were of Central Gaulish origin. Numbers are given for those catalogued above.

Vessel	Sherds	Context	Group	Phase
Jar, c150–200	2	2352	2	1
	1	2376	U/S	0
Same jar?	2	2106	42	3
	3	2107	42	3
	4	2111	42	3
	1	2145	154	4
	1	2192	19	3
	3	2084	U/S	5
	23	2110	19	3
	11	2112	42	3
	2	1002	1001	6
Walters 81, c120–160/180	1	2340	2	1
	1	2352	2	1
Dr 18/31 stamped by Gnatius, c140–155 SS9	2	2340	2	1
	1	2285	1000	0
	1	2289	82	1
	1	2352	2	1
Dr 18/31R, c100–125	1	1644	109	1
	2	1635	157	1
Dr 37, c100–125	1	1489	902	1
	1	1487	901	2
Dr 37, c120/125–150 (SD12)	1	1487	901	2
	1	1379	134	4
	1	1435	134	4
Dr 37 style of Pugnus, c130–160 (SD11)	1	1382	908	2
	1	1379	134	4
	1	1435	134	4
Dr 30 c150–200	1	2110	19	3
	1	2084	U/S	5
Dr 30 Advocisus stamp, c160–190 (SD39, SS2)	3	2110	19	3
	2	2084	U/S	5
	1	2112	42	3
	7	2157	1000	6
Dr 30 Advocisus stamp, c160–190 (SD38, SS1)	2	2106	42	3
	1	2108	18	3

Vessel	Sherds	Context	Group	Phase
Dr 37 style of Cinnamus, c150–170 (SD18, SR8)	2	1034	41	3
	1	2139	19	3
	2	1229	24	4
	4	1030	25	4
	1	1002	1001	6
Dr 37 Pugnus/Secundus style, *c* 150–180 (SD22, SR17)	3	2106	42	3
	2	2111	42	3
	2	2116	200	3
	1	1002	1001	6
	3	2162	1001	6

Appendix 6

Bone butchery marks

Callista Vink

The following tables show the frequency of different types of butchery marks based on Lauwerier (1988).

Cattle

Type	Mandible	Scapula	Humerus	Radius	Pelvis	Astragalus	Metapodial
	14%	13%	11%	8%	8%	6%	6%/6%
1					2	1	1
1a						1	
2		1		1	1	2	
3		1		1			
4				1			1
4a				2			1
5					1	1	
5a					1		
6	6	1		2		1	
7						3	2
8			2	1			2
9	2		2	1		2	1
10	3					1	1
11							
12			1	1			
13			1				2
13a							1
14			1			1	2
14a							2
15							1
15b	1		1				
16		2					
16a				1			
17			1		2		
18	1	1	3			1	1
18a							2
19	1	1			1		6
19b							2
20	1		1		2		1
20a			1		2		
21							2
22							
22a					1		
23			1	2			1
24			1				
25	2		1				1

Type	Mandible	Scapula	Humerus	Radius	Pelvis	Astragalus	Metapodial
25a			1		1		
26	8	1					
27	1	1	1				1
27a					1		
28				1			
29			1				
30		1					1
31			1		1		1
32		1	1				1
33					1		
34	1	2	2	1			
35				2	1		
36	1	2	1	1			
37			1		1		
8	1	1					

Sheep/goats

Type	Humerus	Radius	Pelvis	Femur	Tibia	Astragalus	Metapodial
6						1	
7		1					
7b	1						
8		1				1	
10						1	
13							2
15	1						
16					1		
17		1		1			
17a				1			
18					1		
18a							1
19							1
20				1		Gt	
24		1					
25	1			1	1		
27a		1	1				
29		1	1				
30			1				
35		1					

Horses

Type	Mandible	Scapula	Humerus	Radius	Pelvis	Femur	Skull	Metapodial
1		1						
6	1							
13							1	
16a						1		

Type	Mandible	Scapula	Humerus	Radius	Pelvis	Femur	Skull	Metapodial
17						1		
17a						1		
18b						1		
19					1	1		
23				1				
24						1		
25	1					1		
27			1					
30					1			
38	1							

Appendix 7

Lipid analysis of cremation vessel

O Craig and S Isaksson

A sample of the cremation urn was analysed for residues to establish if there was any evidence for the vessel's primary use, that is before its use as a cremation urn. A 3.4g sample of the vessel was extracted from a depth of 15cm below its rim following removal of a 4mm thickness of internal surface to avoid contamination. From this 1g was powdered, freeze dried and solvent extracted with 3ml of a 2:1 mixture of chloroform and methanol, rotary evaporated to 1ml and then dried under nitrogen in a screw top vial (for the purpose of quantification a 20μg of an internal standard [tetratriacontane – C36 n-alkane] was added prior to extraction).

Extracted samples were re-dissolved in hexane and split into two equal aliquots and dried again. Samples for gas chromatography mass spectrometry (GCMS) were treated with 20μl of N,O-bis(tymethylsilyl) terafluroacetamide containing 1% v/v chlorotrimethylsilane at 65°C for 30 minutes to produce trimethylsilyl derivatives which were then dried under nitrogen. Samples for gas chromatography combustion ratio mass spectrometry (GC-IRMS) were first saponified with 2ml methanolic sodium hydroxide (5% w/v) at 70°C for one hour and then neutralised with 6M HCl. The lipids were subsequently extracted by hexane. The saponified extracts were methylated by the addition of 2ml of BF_3-methanol (14% w/v) at 70°C for one hour. The methyl ester derivatives were extracted with hexane and solvent removed under nitrogen. Fatty acid methyl esters (FAMEs) were re-dissolved in hexane prior to analysis.

In total, 33.18μg of lipid were extracted from the sample. The percentage composition of individual lipids in this total extract is given in the table below.

Results of lipid analysis

Compound	% composition	Compound	% composition
Fatty Acids		Sterols	
C9:0	1.35	Cholesterol	0.88
C14:0	0.64	B-sitosterol	2.25
C16:0	20.26		
C17:0	2.07	Monoglycerides	
C18:0	38.98	1-M16	4.61
C20:0	0.87	1-M18	2.67
Alcohols		Diglycerides	
C16	1.59	1,2-D32	1.46
C18	0.99	1,3-D32	2.01
C22	1.07	1,2-D34	5.15
C24	1.65	1,3-D34	6.37
C25	0.73	1,2-D36	0.54
Esters		1,3-D36	0.45
C18 methyl ester	3.40		

The quantity and type of lipids present within the ceramic matrix would suggest that the pot accumulated organic matter prior to deposition. As no associated soil sample was available it was not possible to estimate the exchange of lipids with the surrounding matrix, although as noted in Chapter 7 the vessel contained very little soil so it would only be the cremated remains that might interact here. Also previous research (Heron et al 1991), has shown that the effect of lipid migration between soil and pot is minimal; thus the majority of lipids found in archaeological pottery relate to their original use.

The lipids are dominated by the presence of the palmatic (C16:0) and stearic (C18:0) fatty acids and their respective mono- and diacylglycerides. These are decomposition (hydrolosis) products of triglycerides, the main component of natural fats and oils. Unfortunately, although these compounds survive well, they are present in most plant and animal products. Whilst the relative abundance of these fatty acids can be used to identify modern foodstuffs, alteration of these characteristic abundances in the burial environment prevents specific identification (Evershed 1993). The distribution of saturated fatty acids from experimentally decomposed plant lipids is dominated by C16:0, while the contribution of C18:0 is larger in experimentally decomposed animal adipose lipids (Isaksson 2000). The higher level of C18:0 in the sample is thus more indicative of animal lipids.

The detection of the C9:0 fatty acid may be more significant. As no other short chain acids are found this is likely to be the decomposition product of oleic acid (C18:1(9)), formed by autoxidation decomposition to aldehydes and alcohols and subsequent decomposition to fatty acids. Oleic acid is common in many plant tissues and to a lesser extent in the adipose tissue of herbivores.

The presence of animal (cholesterol) and plant sterols (B-sitosterol) is more informative. These would indicate that the ceramic has come into contact with both animal and plant products. Cholesterol is present in most human tissues (including bone) and may be derived from human material placed in the pot after cremation. However, if that were the case one would also expect to find decomposition products of cholesterol, such as cholestanone and colestane. The presence of plant sterols cannot be explained in this way and is more consistent with non-funerary use of the pot prior to cremation. The long chain alcohols present are also indicative of plant lipids (derived from wax esters) but are not distinctive enough to allow more specific identification. The C16 and C18 alcohols are probably derived from plant waxes. Their restricted distribution and absence of corresponding fatty acids and alkanes typical of soil plant material, suggests that these molecules are from the original use of the pot rather than from the depositional matrix.

The absence of any heat degraded lipids, such as long chain keytones (Evershed and Stott 1995), also suggests that molecules present are not derived from the cremated remains. Only the presence of the C18 fatty acid methyl ester (FAME) is indicative of heat exposure (Mills and White 1994, 65). However, this compound forms at relatively low temperatures, obtained during cooking, and hence often found on domestic cooking pots. Alternatively the C18 FAME may have been produced by microbial degradation of triglycerides (Hita et al 1996). The detection of low amounts of the C14:0, C17:0 and C20:0 fatty acids may indicate bacterial contribution to the lipids (Dudd et al 1998), possibly also supporting the origin of the C16 and C18 alcohols (by enzymatic reduction).

Finally the abundance of palmatic and stearic acid allows us to go one step further and measure the isotopic value of carbon ($\delta^{13}C$) in these molecules. Carbon isotopes may be used to study the diet of organisms (Schoeninger and DeNiro 1984). When lipids are synthesised by the body they derive their carbon from consumed foodstuffs. As different species consume different foodstuffs (e.g. herbivores, omnivores, carnivores) and have different metabolic pathways the isotopic value of the carbon will vary. The absolute values can be measured and compared to known standards based on modern controls. This approach has been taken by Evershed et al (1994) to identify the origin of archaeological residues. Using the same technique the carbon isotopic values for palmatic and stearic acid were measured as –26.53 and –25.97. These were similar to published values for pig fat (Dudd and Evershed 1999) but are equally consistent with any omnivore fat (including human, although no modern reference has been analysed). Therefore the isotopes do not rule out a human source for the fatty acids.

Vegetable and animal fats have been identified from the vessel. Whilst both may derive from the vessel's use prior to cremation, a human origin as the source of animal fats can not be ruled out. The nature of the cremation and the condition of the remains may be used for further interpretation. For example, remains that have been well cremated and exposed to prolonged periods at high temperature will be devoid of substantial amounts of lipids and would suggest that animal lipids found derived from foodstuffs prior to the addition of cremated remains. Alternatively poorly cremated remains may retain substantial amounts of lipid which would suggest a human origin of animal lipids present on the ceramic.

Printed in the USA
CPSIA information can be obtained
at www.ICGtesting.com
CBHW061238071023
1266CB00019B/315